JOHN LOCKE

ESSAYS ON THE
LAW OF NATURE

An lex hæc cognosci potest ratione.
Hominum consensu. 1. Neg

Vox populi, vox Dei, quam inepta quam
fallax sit hæc regula malorum firma-
ment; nec certe infelix magis documento. Dicemus, non ut si huic tandem
conformem ... quod enim si iam
reformavim, quam inepti, tam contra
jus omne fallax, et sui ... aliquando
... insanientis obsequenti,
suis potius comparatio huic spoliata
Deorum templa, cum ... aviaria,
et hospitalium, violabat leges susciga
regna usurpavimus, ad certe si hæc sit
vox Dei, contraria plane est, primo
illi, Fiat, quo oppidum Deum compagem
struxit, et ... ex nihil, nec unquam
sic hominis alloquitur Deus, nisi cum
omnia illorum inferum ... in illos re-
signa ... frustra citatur in formas
rum compages quærentur rationis, sic
leta aut occulta ... Congressus autem
hominum eiusmodi conspicari

Vox populi, vox Dei, quam inepta quam fallax
sit hæc regula et malorum furiis, quando partim
studio quam alioqui certius in vulgus factitatum
sit hoc mali omnis e nutritum, nec certe nisi fui
nimi documento sibi ... certe et si huic vocé
tanquam legi Divinæ præconi usurpari usurnus
vox aliquam tandem universum esse ... Deum

The opening pages of Locke's 66b essay on natural law (ff. 61v and 62r)

JOHN LOCKE

ESSAYS ON THE
LAW OF NATURE

THE LATIN TEXT
WITH A TRANSLATION, INTRODUCTION
AND NOTES, TOGETHER WITH
TRANSCRIPTS OF LOCKE'S SHORTHAND
IN HIS JOURNAL FOR 1676

EDITED BY

W. von LEYDEN

OXFORD
AT THE CLARENDON PRESS

OXFORD
UNIVERSITY PRESS

Great Clarendon Street, Oxford OX2 6DP

Oxford University Press is a department of the University of Oxford.
It furthers the University's objective of excellence in research, scholarship,
and education by publishing worldwide in

Oxford New York

Auckland Bangkok Buenos Aires Cape Town Chennai
Dar es Salaam Delhi Hong Kong Istanbul Karachi Kolkata
Kuala Lumpur Madrid Melbourne Mexico City Mumbai Nairobi
São Paulo Shanghai Singapore Taipei Tokyo Toronto

with an associated company in Berlin

Oxford is a registered trade mark of Oxford University Press
in the UK and in certain other countries

Published in the United States
by Oxford University Press Inc., New York

First published 1954
Reprinted 1958, 1965, 1970
Reissued 1988
First published in paperback 2002

British Library Cataloguing in Publication Data
Data available

Library of Congress Cataloging in Publication Data
Data available

ISBN 0-19-824142-9 (hbk.)
ISBN 0-19-925421-4 (pbk.)

1 3 5 7 9 10 8 6 4 2

Printed in Great Britain
on acid-free paper by
Biddles Ltd., Guildford and King's Lynn

PREFACE

THIS book contains three sets of early writings of John Locke, published here for the first time from manuscripts in the Lovelace Collection now in the Bodleian Library, Oxford.

The first set is a series of eight essays on the law of nature,[1] written by Locke in Latin shortly after 1660. He was then just over thirty, and it was almost another thirty years before he published his chief philosophical work, *An Essay concerning Human Understanding*. Those who criticize adversely Locke's mature doctrine in the *Essay* must think there will be stronger reasons yet for criticizing a work of his youth—a work, in fact, about which he himself may have felt diffident, since he never published it, and which deals with a topic now regarded by many as obsolete. To criticize a work, however, does not necessarily mean to wish that it had never been written or published. And I feel confident that the reader will welcome the recent discovery and appearance in print of a manuscript which contains Locke's detailed views on natural law. In the first place, though this notion is of central importance for several of his doctrines, disappointingly little is said about it in his published writings. Secondly, any views on this subject, especially if held by a foremost and comprehensive thinker such as Locke, should be of general interest: they appeal alike to the moralist, the political theorist, the legal philosopher, and the theologian. The essays have the further significance that they are the starting-point from which Locke's thoughts on human understanding developed up to the point of their publication in the *Essay*: they can indeed claim to be the earliest form of part of that work.

Since Locke wrote his essays in Latin, the language used by most of the exponents of the traditional theory of natural law, I have thought it advisable to publish the Latin text and to give the reader an opportunity of comparing Locke's terminology with that of other Latin writers. A critical apparatus has been provided throughout, and in making this, as well as in editing the text, I have attempted to avoid the distortions which Locke's words and thoughts have sometimes suffered in editions of other of his writings. An English translation of the essays is printed side by side with the Latin text and there is also an analytical summary. In the Introduction I have sought to make clear any points

---

[1] They are published here under this general title; Locke only provided special titles for each essay.

that call for discussion in connexion with Locke's early literary activities and the place of the essays in the history of thought. Throughout the Introduction I have made use of other unpublished manuscripts in the Lovelace Collection, such as Locke's two treatises on the civil magistrate, his correspondence, his journals, and his notebooks. It will be found that a study of this material has led me in several cases to a reinterpretation of some of Locke's known philosophical doctrines.

The second writing included in this volume is a Latin speech composed by Locke in 1664 and possibly delivered by him at the end of that year, when he retired from the Censorship of Moral Philosophy at Christ Church, Oxford. The speech is of interest for its quips and graces and for the biographical information it contains. However, my chief reason for including it in the present volume is that it is closely connected with a course of lectures delivered by Locke (as part, apparently, of his duties as Censor) on the subject of natural law, probably along the lines laid down in his eight essays on that subject; moreover, the speech was originally designed by him to follow the last essay of the series.

Finally, I have printed transcripts of shorthand entries in Locke's Journal for 1676. These entries are all the philosophical shorthand writings of his in the Lovelace Collection. My reasons for including the transcripts in this volume are four: (1) A number of the entries, e.g. those on 'Faith and Reason', take up ideas contained in Locke's essays on natural law. (2) Like the essays, they show Locke's first thoughts on several topics discussed by him in the *Essay concerning Human Understanding* and in part were incorporated by him in that work. (3) They would undoubtedly have been printed in previous editions of Locke's journals, if the editors had been familiar with the shorthand in which they are written. (4) They do not run to more than 10,000 words and by themselves would not fill a volume, and therefore it seemed suitable to relegate them to the end of one, as Professor R. I. Aaron and Mr. J. Gibb did with their selection of Locke's philosophical longhand entries in *An Early Draft of Locke's Essay*.

I wish to end this Preface by acknowledging my obligations to those who have helped me in the preparation of this book. The initial stage of my research was made possible by the help of Mr. K. Sisam, at that time Secretary to the Delegates of the Clarendon Press. I am indebted to the authorities of the Bodleian Library, through whose co-operation, over a period of ten years, I was enabled to examine at

leisure the contents of the Lovelace Collection. I wish to express my particular appreciation of the constant assistance and courtesy of Mr. P. Long, of the Department of Western Manuscripts. I owe much to Mr. P. Laslett, of St. John's College, Cambridge, who has read my manuscript and with whom I have had many stimulating discussions. To the Council of the Durham Colleges in the University of Durham I offer my special thanks for granting me sabbatical leave for one term, during which I was able to start on the writing of this work.

My chief debt, however, is to the Rev. E. G. Pace, D.D., Hon. Canon of Durham, without whose support this book could not have been written. He has helped me in preparing the Latin text and has been at pains to polish and repolish my translation, thereby saving me from many pitfalls. Throughout he has given me advice about language and style. His kind co-operation and unfailing patience have made the work a pleasure. I should like to express my gratitude by dedicating this book to him.

W. v. L.

HATFIELD COLLEGE, DURHAM
August 1952

PREFACE TO THE THIRD IMPRESSION

A few alterations have been made in the Introduction, and a number of corrections and changes in the Latin text, the English translation and the notes. Some references and comments have also been added to the textual apparatus.

I would like to express my gratitude to Gavin Townend, Emeritus Professor of Latin at the University of Durham, and to Dr Robert Dyson of the Politics Department, University of Durham, for their help with certain passages of the translation.

W. v. L.

DURHAM
September 1987

CONTENTS

ESSAYS ON THE LAW OF NATURE

Contents

LOCKE'S VALEDICTORY SPEECH AS CENSOR OF MORAL PHILOSOPHY

PHILOSOPHICAL SHORTHAND WRITINGS

Contents

PLATES

INTRODUCTION

I

The Lovelace Collection

I BEGIN with a general description of the large manuscript collection of which Locke's essays on the law of nature form a part.

When John Locke died in 1704, at the age of seventy-two, he left half his library of over 3,000 books and all his papers and letters to his cousin, the Lord Chancellor, Peter King.[1] The legacy remained in the custody of Lord King's descendants until 1942, when their last owner, the Earl of Lovelace, deposited most of the manuscripts (though only a handful of the printed books) in the Bodleian Library, Oxford. During the next few years the collection was examined by the present writer on behalf of the Clarendon Press, Oxford, with a view to reporting on its contents and importance and preparing the publication of selected papers.[2] The report was submitted to an Oxford University committee in 1946.[3] When, with the financial help of the Pilgrim Trust, the collection was purchased by the Bodleian in 1947, an abundance of new biographical information about Locke and a great variety of his unpublished writings became accessible to the public.[4]

The Locke papers in the Lovelace Collection fall into two groups, viz. (*a*) the correspondence, consisting of nearly 3,000 letters, (*b*) miscellaneous manuscripts, including journals and notebooks, all forming a collection of 1,000-odd items.

(*a*) The major part of the correspondence consists of original letters addressed to Locke, while about 150 are his draft replies. Most letters

[1] Peter King (1670–1734) was the son of Anne King, daughter of Peter Locke, John Locke's uncle.

[2] It should be pointed out that the contents of the Lovelace Collection were reported to the Royal Commission on Historical Documents in 1919 (No. 241) but were never examined in detail.

[3] The committee consisted of Mr. Kenneth Sisam, at that time Secretary to the Delegates of the Clarendon Press, Sir Edmund Craster, at that time Bodley's Librarian, Sir David Ross, at that time Provost of Oriel College, and Sir George Clark, at that time Regius Professor of Modern History in the University of Cambridge.

[4] The following reports about the Lovelace Collection have appeared in print: (*a*) an article by Sir Edmund Craster in *The Times* of 12 Jan. 1948 and a broadcast talk by him in the Third Programme of 19 March 1948, published in the *Listener* of 1 April 1948; (*b*) summary accounts in the *Manchester Guardian* of 21 May 1948 and in the *Seventeenth Annual Report* (1947) of the Pilgrim Trust; (*c*) two articles of mine, i.e. 'John Locke's Unpublished Papers', in *Sophia*, Jan.–Mar. 1949 (summarized in *Revue philosophique*, July–Sept. 1950, and in *Les Études philosophiques*, Oct.–Jan. 1951), and 'Notes concerning Papers of John Locke in the Lovelace Collection', in the *Philosophical Quarterly*, Jan. 1952.

are written in English but several hundred are in Latin or French. Their contents vary from matters of mere day-to-day interest to others that are of more weighty concern, just as among Locke's correspondents some were unimportant people, while others were leading figures of the time. Apart from gossip, family news, and administrative accounts of Locke's property in Somerset, discussion in the correspondence ranges from new publications and scientific pursuits to parliamentary affairs, the coinage, and conditions in the colonies. Many of Locke's correspondents were women, and some particulars of his early life in Oxford can be recovered from a collection of so-called loveletters to him and from him. Of special importance is a series of forty letters written to him by a lady with the fictitious name of *Philoclea*. These, it appears,[1] were written by Lady Masham, daughter of Ralph Cudworth, and in her later life one of Leibniz's correspondents. There are in the collection a few letters and papers by Leibniz himself and several others which have a bearing on Locke's *Essay concerning Human Understanding*. There are letters by contemporary physicians, scientists, scholars, and theologians, some of whom were French or Dutch. On the whole, the information contained in the correspondence is chiefly biographical. Locke's biography could not only be revised and enlarged, but even rewritten on the basis of the new material. Moreover, the collection forms a supplement to existing publications: it contains the replies to most of Locke's letters so far printed and to others from him that are lost.

(*b*) Let us turn now to the miscellaneous manuscripts in the collection. Locke's accounts form the largest part of them; next come his book-lists and library catalogues, papers on theology and medicine; then those concerned with money, economics, colonial and political history; least extensive, but perhaps equally, if not more, important, are his philosophical manuscripts. His journals and notebooks, together thirty-eight in number, cover a period of almost fifty years.[2] They

---

[1] Cf. my 'Notes concerning Papers of John Locke in the Lovelace Collection', *Philosophical Quarterly*, Jan. 1952, pp. 68 f.

[2] One volume of the journals, covering the last year of Locke's residence in France (1679), found its way into the British Museum (Add. MS. 15,642) in 1845. A commonplace book containing entries from 1661 onwards, and among them a manuscript copy of the *Essay concerning Toleration* (1667) and one of the early drafts of the *Essay concerning Human Understanding* (1671), has been in the possession of Lord Lovelace until 1952 when it was sold to America. Locke's Almanac-diary for 1672 is in the hands of Lord Lovelace's sister, Lady de Hosszu; his Almanac-diary for 1684, formerly in the collection, was bought by Sawyers from Sotheby's (Catalogue No. 313 of the sale of 29 May 1934) and subsequently became part of the Pierpont Morgan Library, New York. Another such diary, of 1667, was offered for sale

contain excerpts from books, which are valuable for dating the times of Locke's reading, and information about his practice as a physician and his movements in England and on the Continent. Part of the entries is written in shorthand, the key to which has now been found. Among the biographical documents there are speeches by the young Locke at Westminster School and Christ Church, Oxford, papers relating to his activities as a college tutor and in other official posts occupied by him during his life, inventories, lists of legacies, and agreements between him and his publishers. There is abundant information about the composition and growth of his library, the most complete catalogue of which numbers 3,100 items. Locke bequeathed one portion of his library to Peter King, and this has been preserved intact by King's descendants, the other to Francis Cudworth Masham, but this was dispersed at various dates between 1762 and 1916.[1]

The most important among the theological papers in the collection are early writings by Locke concerning toleration and the competence of the civil power and church respectively. Later writings touch on the doctrine of the immortality of the soul, natural and revealed religion, the controversy about the doctrine of the Trinity, and the rights of Protestant dissenters. On the whole, discussion on these topics in Locke's and other people's papers is prompted by endeavours to defend, or to refute, his theological doctrines.

Locke's medical papers in the collection have never been made use of, probably because many of them are written in shorthand. Those in longhand alone contain important information, especially about his relationship to Thomas Sydenham.

The scientific papers consist mainly of astronomical and geographical memoranda, most of which were the result of Locke's contacts with French scientists in Montpellier and Paris. There is evidence to show that throughout his life Locke was also interested in alchemy and the literary output of the Rosicrucians.

By means of the many early drafts of Locke's writings on money and the recoinage, which are preserved in the collection, the development of his thought on the money question can be traced further backward and in greater detail than has hitherto been possible. The earliest draft dates from 1668, i.e. twenty-four years before the publication

---

by Arthur Rogers, Newcastle-on-Tyne, in autumn 1933 (Catalogue No. 85). The Almanac-diary for 1669 was presented to the British Museum in 1947 (Add. MS. 46,470).

[1] Cf. P. Laslett's letter on 'Lord Masham's library at Oates' in *The Times Literary Supplement*, 15 Aug. 1952, p. 533.

3

of his first book on money (1692), the next from 1674, and the final draft from 1690. The importance of these 'old papers' has been conjectured by Fox Bourne,[1] who thought they were lost. The preparatory work for his second book on money, published at the end of 1695, can likewise be reconstructed from several hitherto unknown papers by him, written in the summer of 1695 in answer to official reports forwarded to him by friends of his in the government. The papers throw light on Locke's contribution to the various measures taken by the government in preparation for the recoinage bill of December 1695.

Papers concerned with economics and colonial history, of which some are written by Locke, some by others, deal with trade at home and abroad, pauperism, Irish linen-manufacture, the administration of Virginia, and the Scottish colony on the Isthmus of Darien. They have in several cases been published or calendared from the originals, which are preserved in the Public Record Office. Several of those not published show that, when Locke served as a Commissioner to the new Board of Trade set up by Sir John Somers in 1696, the part taken by him in preparing instructions was far greater than has hitherto been supposed.

The most important of Locke's unpublished philosophical manuscripts are a set of early essays on the law of nature—those printed in the present volume—and several shorthand essays, transcriptions of which are also included in this volume. Besides these there are amongst the manuscripts criticisms of the *Essay* by William King, Archbishop of Dublin,[2] Locke's 'Answer' to John Norris's *Cursory Reflections*, of 1692, some short papers forming part of Locke's attempt to demonstrate ethics, and several manuscript drafts of his published writings, which in some measure differ from the printed texts.

From this brief survey it can be seen that a considerable part of the newly available material in the Lovelace Collection is concerned with the early period of Locke's life, of which little is known otherwise. Biographical details during this period can now be documented and evidence of Locke's early activity as an author can be substantiated. His views on toleration, the law of nature, the money question, and other topics will thus come to be seen in their chronological sequence. It will also be possible to revise, as well as add to, a number of papers already published, drawn from material in other collections. For often

[1] *The Life of John Locke*, 1876, i. 313.
[2] Cf. Molyneux's letter to Locke of the summer of 1692 (*Works*, 1801, ix. 291).

the worst of the variant versions of Locke's writings have been printed, as also only the drafts of letters from his friends or copies of their letters, and all these imperfectly, whilst better preserved, or more carefully revised, manuscript copies of his writings and the letters actually sent to him have lain in the Lovelace Collection unused.

As will have appeared from previous remarks, some parts of the Lovelace Collection have already been published, and a list of such publications, in chronological order, may conveniently be given here. Mention will be made of authors who have either consulted the collection or obtained transcripts of documents for purposes of publication.

1. Letters and documents relating to the proceedings in 1696 against Thomas Aikenhead for blasphemy were printed in *State Trials* (ed. T. B. Howell), xiii (1812), 917–34. They are there acknowledged to be the property of Lord King and thus were published from the originals in the Lovelace Collection.

2. The seventh Lord King, in *The Life and Letters of John Locke* (1829, 3rd ed., 1858), included or utilized ninety-eight letters and many manuscripts and excerpts from Locke's journals. He doubtless published most of the interesting parts of the collection, but his use of it was far from complete and the information he provided is in many cases inaccurate. Locke's principal biographer, H. R. Fox Bourne (*The Life of John Locke*, 1876), who was unacquainted with the original Lovelace papers, reprinted some of them from Lord King's *Life*.

3. Lord Campbell, *Lives of the Lord Chancellors*, iv (1846), 583 note, and 4th ed., iv (1857), 233 note.

4. J. Edelston, *Correspondence of Sir Isaac Newton and Professor Cotes*, 1850, p. 276 note.

5. J. Brown, *Locke and Sydenham*, 1866, p. 133.

6. W. D. Christie, in *The Life of Anthony Ashley Cooper, First Earl of Shaftesbury* (1871), published a few documents related to his subject-matter (cf. especially Preface, p. ix, and ii. 219).

7. A. C. Fraser, *Locke*, 1890, Preface, p. vii.

8. B. Rand, *The Life, Unpublished Letters etc. of Anthony, Earl of Shaftesbury*, 1900, p. 273, n. 1.

9. B. Rand edited ninety-one letters to Locke from his friend Edward Clarke (*The Correspondence of John Locke and Edward Clarke*, 1927) and one of the two early drafts of Locke's *Essay*, of 1671 (*An Essay concerning the Understanding, Knowledge, Opinion, and Assent*, 1931).

10. R. I. Aaron and J. Gibb published another early draft of

Introduction

Locke's *Essay*, of 1671, and excerpts from his journals (*An Early Draft of Locke's Essay together with Excerpts from his Journals*, 1936). Some of these excerpts had previously been printed by Lord King. Professor Aaron also made use of some new material in his *John Locke*, 1937 (cf. Preface, p. vii, and p. 4, n. 1).

11. J. W. Gough (*John Locke's Political Philosophy*, 1950) published excerpts from some documents in the first and last chapters of his book and some of the final corrections of Locke's *Essay concerning Toleration*, of 1667, in the appendix.

12. Miss C. S. Ware quoted from some new material in 'The Influence of Descartes on John Locke. A Bibliographical Study', *Revue internationale de philosophie*, April 1950, pp. 1–21.

13. G. Bonno published sixteen letters of the Abbé Du Bos to Locke, in *Revue de littérature comparée*, 1950, pp. 481–520. A book by him on Locke's intellectual contacts in France is to be published soon.

14. H. J. McLachlan (*Socinianism in Seventeenth Century England*, 1951, pp. 326 and 330, n. 1) consulted Locke's library catalogues and some other papers.

15. J. A. Passmore utilized some letters in his *Ralph Cudworth*, 1951; see p. ix.

16. J. Lough published a list, drawn up by Locke, of books banned in France in 1679, in *French Studies*, 1951, pp. 217–22.

17. J. Lough re-edited Locke's journals in France and published some of his correspondence and other papers under the general title of *Locke's Travels in France (1675–1679)*, 1953.

In spite of these publications the value of the Lovelace Collection itself remains unimpaired, and it is enhanced by the fact that most of the Locke papers preserved elsewhere are either scattered in many hands or have largely been published. The number of those kept in the library of Christ Church, Oxford, the Bodleian Library, and the British Museum, is relatively small. The contents of the Nynehead Collection (formerly the property of Colonel E. C. A. Sanford, a direct descendant of Locke's friend Edward Clarke) have been partly published, partly dispersed by auction in 1922. The great mass of information about Locke contained in the Shaftesbury Papers (in the Public Record Office, London, and calendared in the 33rd Report of the Deputy Keeper of the Public Records, 1872, Appendix No. 3) has also been largely exploited. A singular value, then, can be attached to the rich and generally unknown material in the Lovelace Collec-

6

tion, which is kept intact owing to the successful effort made by the authorities of the Bodleian Library.

II

Locke's Essays on the Law of Nature

AMONG the many manuscript pieces in the Lovelace Collection is a set of essays on the law of nature. No mention of this set is made in Lord King's *Life* or in the catalogue that accompanied the collection on its way into the Bodleian Library. In my report of 1946 I attempted to elucidate the nature of this document and to describe in some detail its contents and importance. Here I shall collect all the relevant information about it, including any references to it that occur in other parts of the collection.

(*a*) A notebook of Locke's entitled *Lemmata*[1] contains rough drafts, in Latin and in Locke's hand, of six essays on the law of nature. Originally the notebook was used by Locke for comments on books he had read, and, since the latest date of publication of books cited is 1654, the further use he made of the notebook must have been after this date. I shall name this set of essays MS. A and refer to it thus, in order to indicate that it is the earliest draft of Locke's essays on the law of nature.[2]

(*b*) The collection contains a leather-bound notebook in small octavo,[3] bearing the initials of Locke's name on both the front and the back cover. Inside the cover, as was his usual practice, Locke specified the period over which he filled the notebook with entries—in this case the year is 1663. The booklet contains nine essays on the law of nature, written in Latin and in a strange hand, probably that of an amanuensis. While the last six of these essays are more or less identical with those in MS. A, the first three have nothing corresponding to them in that MS. Between the second essay and the third and between the sixth and the seventh there are titles for yet two others which were never written. In a continuous series Locke attached a number to each title, to those he merely contemplated as well as to those which have essays corresponding to them. Thus there are twelve titles in all, and nine

---

[1] Bodl. MS. Locke e. 6. Here and elsewhere I give the shelf-marks of the manuscripts in the Lovelace Collection as they have been assigned by the Bodleian Library.

[2] I choose the phrase MS. A rather than Draft A in order to avoid confusion between the various drafts of Locke's essays on the law of nature and the two drafts he wrote for his *Essay concerning Human Understanding* in 1671, which Professor Aaron has christened Draft A and Draft B (*An Early Draft of Locke's Essay*, 1936, p. xi).

[3] MS. Locke f. 31.

completed essays. Most of the titles and the many corrections and additions that occur throughout the text are written in Locke's hand. At the end of the eighth essay Locke added the remark *Sic Cogitavit J. Locke, 1664*, and at the beginning of the ninth he wrote *Oratio Censoria funebris*, *'64*. I shall refer to this manuscript as MS. B. The 'Notebook on the Law of Nature' which is listed in an inventory,[1] dated December 1680, of Locke's belongings in Christ Church, Oxford, is possibly the one we have just described.

(*c*) A parchment box of octavo size[2] contains a large number of loose leaves, half of which are filled with notes in Locke's hand relating to the New Testament, and half with a neatly written copy of all his essays on the law of nature. This copy is in the handwriting of Sylvester Brownover, who entered Locke's service as his personal servant and amanuensis in France on 14 November 1678[3] and died in London in December 1699.[4] There are many errors of transcription in this copy and many lacunae caused by Brownover's inability to read words or phrases in the original he had to copy. There is no trace whatever that Locke remedied any of these faults or made use of the copy ever after. Obviously this uncorrected manuscript is of no great importance, and it adds nothing to the textual evidence beyond what we learn from MS. B. I shall refer to it as MS. C.

(*d*) Apart from these three manuscript copies of Locke's essays there are some letters in the collection containing further information about this work. During his early years in Oxford Locke had been friendly with Gabriel Towerson, who, in 1660, was elected a Fellow of All Souls and, in 1676, published *An Explication of the Decalogue* together with a lengthy introduction concerning the law of nature.[5] Four letters from Towerson to Locke are preserved,[6] of which three are dated between October 1660 and April 1661. The letter that concerns us here is undated but most probably was written about the same time and certainly not later than in the early sixties. In this letter Towerson writes:

> The papers that have past between us being now growne so voluminous that I conceive it more difficult to informe our selves of the state of the controversie between us, than to refell what either of us hath said; I shall crave

---

[1] MS. Locke c. 25, fols. 30–31.   [2] MS. Locke f. 30.
[3] Cf. a notebook, mainly concerning books and covering the years 1678–81 (MS. Locke f. 28, p. 24).   [4] Cf. a letter to Locke from Mrs. M. Brownover of 5 Jan. 1699/1700.
[5] For frequent references to Towerson see R. B. Schlatter, *The Social Ideas of Religious Leaders, 1660–1688*, 1940. His early connexions with Locke have so far escaped notice.
[6] MS. Locke c. 22, fols. 1 ff.

leave for my owne ease, and because I would willingly be Mr. Ailmer's
Auditor this 5th of November to respite my answer till the next weak in the
which intervall I intend (God willing) to peruse all that hath past between us
upon this head and then on mine owne part to put a period to this contro-
versie, if I find you inclinable therto. Which I no way doubt but you will be,
if you consider but these two things which I have now to propose to you.
1. Whether (it being agreed upon between us that there is such a thing as a
law of nature and one of those arguments which I produc'd for it admitted
without any scruple) it were not much more for our advantage to proceed in
our enquiry touching the law of nature, than to contend any longer about a
2d argument. 2. I would willingly know of you whether you thinke the being
of the law of nature can be evinc'd from the force of conscience in those men
who have no other divine law to square theire actions by. If you doe (as for
my owne part I doe because I thinke it to be St. Pauls owne argument) I shall
then thinke it incumbent upon you, who have engag'd in the same designe
with your servant, to answer in short your owne objections. If not, I shall
despaire of perswading you, if what I have already said and shall in my next
(which will I beleive be all that I can say for it) be not of force so to doe.[1]

In this letter it is clearly stated that Locke and Towerson, over a
period of years, exchanged views on the law of nature and both wrote
on the subject. Further comments on this letter may be postponed
until the summing up.

(*e*) Another friend, James Tyrrell, who in 1692 published *A Brief
Disquisition of the Law of Nature*, wrote sixty-three letters to Locke
between the years 1677 and 1704.[2] On 6 May 1687, at a time when
Locke was still in Holland, Tyrrell wrote to him from London:
'. . . and now you have finished that Discourse' (i.e. the *Essay concerning
Human Understanding*) 'I should be glad to hear whether you have
done what you intended concerning the Law of nature which you so
often promised to reveiw'. And again on 29 August, in the same year,
he wrote: 'I am sorry you will not promise me to finish your Essay of
the Law of nature and doubt there is somewhat of lazynesse more then
the fear of being thought to savour of the short perruke and plain
cravat, since I never thought either good morality or good manners

---

[1] The references to Mr. Ailmer and to 'this 5th of November' provide a minimum amount
of internal evidence on which to base an attempt at dating the letter. I myself have not been
successful in following up the clue. A similar reference to a sermon on 5 Nov. in St. Mary's,
Oxford, occurs in Towerson's letter of 23 Oct. 1660, where mention is also made of his
'argumentations', his 'undigested thoughts', and his 'papers'. This may tempt one to assign
to Towerson's undated letter a date around 1 Nov. 1660, but the connexion between the
references in the two letters is not sufficiently evident to turn conjecture into certainty.

[2] MS. Locke c. 22. Only four of these letters were published by Lord King in extracts.

can be suspected of Quakerisme.' In 1690, after Locke's return from Holland, Tyrrell communicated to his friend various objections raised by people in Oxford against his idea of the law of nature as set forth in his recently published *Essay*. The letters are of 30 June, 27 July, and 30 August, and Locke, in a lengthy reply of 4 August 1690,[1] tried to defend himself against his critics and to make his meaning clearer. This part of the correspondence, to be considered in section VII of the present Introduction, does not concern us here, since it refers to Locke's mature doctrine of natural law in the *Essay*, not to his thoughts on the subject in the early essays. But in his letter of 27 July, after mentioning Locke's *Essay* and the writings on natural law by Richard Cumberland and Samuel Parker, Tyrrell again insisted: 'And I could wish you would publish your owne thoughts upon this excellent and material subject; since I know you have made long since a treatise or lectures upon the Law of nature which I could wish you would revise and make publick, since I know none more able then your self to doe it, and which would likewise make a 2d part to the former worke: and I have heard you say more then once that you intended it.' After finishing in manuscript his own *Disquisition of the Law of Nature*, Tyrrell asked his friend to read and consider it and again encouraged him to publish his own thoughts on the subject.[2]

I have indicated all available evidence about Locke's authorship of the essays on natural law, and have now to turn it into a coherent picture.

The years around the Restoration of 1660 appear as an important period in Locke's literary career. About that time a topic began to occupy his mind, which for centuries had attracted the attention of lawyers, political theorists, theologians, and moralists. His thoughts in this direction, expressed in Latin and in accordance with some of the traditional techniques of academic discussion, were part of a joint effort between him and his friend Towerson, whose share in the combined effort may have been about equal to that of Locke. The time when the two men embarked on their work is uncertain. They may have started in the late fifties and at that time have produced arguments for the existence of a law of nature roughly in the form in which we find them in Locke's first essay in MS. B. However, it is unlikely that Locke completed all or even most of his essays before 1660, since there is evidence to show that in the last essays of the series he was largely

---

[1] This was published by Lord King, *Life*, 1858, pp. 198–201.
[2] Cf. Tyrrell's letters of 22 Oct. 1691, 19 Mar. 1691/2, 9 Aug. 1692.

under the influence of authors whose works he did not study until after 1660 (a point to be argued more fully in section v), and since his fifth essay contains a lengthy reference to a book of travels, most probably to the English edition of it of 1662. It would seem then that the six essays in MS. A were written by Locke sometime in the early sixties, though, as will be explained presently, not later than 1664. After having written the draft version of these essays in his own hand, Locke had it copied by an amanuensis in a notebook bearing the date 1663, and along with it, from papers now lost, the first three essays, which are missing in MS. A. The amanuensis was an illiterate man, obviously not versed in Latin, and Locke had to make a detailed revision of the copy and to fill in lines missed out by the amanuensis in the process of transcription. He also added passages and remoulded others, thereby turning the copy into something slightly different from the original draft. This copy is what I have named MS. B and it is the one edited and printed in the present volume. The explanation why Locke had this copy made can be derived from the last of the essays, and it is thus advisable to see first what this essay is about and then to follow up the clue it provides.

The title of the last essay, in MS. A, consists of the question whether anyone, according to the law of nature, can be happy in this life, to which the answer is in the negative. Though this essay, as can be seen from its title, is connected with the main body of the other essays, Locke did not write it down immediately after the preceding one but separately at the other end of his notebook. It is also noteworthy that some Latin words in the draft version of this essay, i.e. in MS. A, were first written by Locke in shorthand. Since all available evidence makes it more than likely that Locke learned to write in shorthand during the year 1664, this last essay cannot have been composed by him until then. Moreover, in MS. B, the title of the essay, instead of the phrase 'according to the law of nature', has the more general phrase 'according to nature'. In a superscription in MS. B Locke specified that this essay was to be the Censor's 'funeral' speech of 1664 and, by affixing at the end of the preceding essay the remark *Sic Cogitavit J. Locke, 1664,* he indicated that the last essay was to be kept separate from the main body of his essays and to be intended for a special purpose—a Censor's valedictory speech. We know that in 1664 Locke was Censor of Moral Philosophy, and obviously this is the speech written and perhaps delivered by him in Christ Church at the end of 1664 when he retired from the Censorship. The superscription

Introduction

can be explained by the traditional formula of 'burying the Censor.'[1] In a semi-humorous style Locke describes in this oration the unhappiness of life and man's longing for death. He explains that not even the ancient philosophers have found happiness, for *Philosophia Oceano similis, cui salis inest plurimum, quietis nihil* (f. 122). In the second part where this theme is connected with the labours of the Censor's office and the deliverance from it which is 'death', Locke surveys the fortunes of Christ Church during the year and bids farewell to John Fell, the Dean, to Jasper Mayne, the Sub-dean, and to all the other officers and students of the college. At the beginning of each individual speech he inserted the proper name of the person addressed or such collective terms as *Praebendarii, Magistri, Vespillones, Baccalaurei, Scholares,* none of which expressions occurs in MS. A. The speech ends 'Morior'. In this volume it is printed on pp. 220 ff.

What light does Locke's valedictory speech throw on the question we asked before about his essays on natural law and particularly about MS. B? During his term of office and as part of his duties as Censor, Locke delivered lectures, and the number and names of students he had at the time can be gathered from various documents in the Lovelace Collection. From a document preserved elsewhere and hitherto not fully utilized in this connexion, we learn that a certain William Coker, who matriculated at Christ Church in April 1663, sent Locke, after his appointment to the Censorship, a congratulatory letter of 31 January 1663/4, asking to be admitted to the disputations and the group of 'wranglers' (*velites*) in the 'second form'.[2] When addressing the *Baccalaurei* in his Censor's speech,[3] Locke himself refers to the 'wranglings' (*velitationes*) of his students in which he had participated and by which he had greatly benefited during the year, and he expressly mentions the fact that the disputations were about the law of nature. There can be little doubt, therefore, that it was on this subject that Locke was lecturing in 1664[4] and that it was for this purpose that he had his early draft essays copied by an amanuensis in his notebook of 1663 (MS. B) and extensively revised them in his own hand.

[1] For some details about the ceremony of 'burying the Censor' in the eighteenth century see H. L. Thompson, *Christ Church*, 1900, pp. 137 f.

[2] Bodleian, Rawl. MS. D. 286, f. 6. The letter is written in Latin and only the second part of it is printed in C. Bastide, *John Locke, ses théories politiques*, &c., 1906, p. 18. On f. 7 there is another letter, of 14 Dec. 1664, addressed to Locke's friend Benjamin Woodroffe. There are several other letters and entries in this notebook of Coker's, covering the years 1663–9, and his short essays in Latin on various moral questions resemble Locke's essays as far as the formulation of titles is concerned. [3] ff. 132–3.

[4] Note that Tyrrell, in his letter of 27 July 1690, refers to Locke's essays as 'lectures'.

Locke's Essays on the Law of Nature

It may be that after retiring from the Censorship Locke busied himself with the essays for another few months, but from then onwards until later in his life the question of natural law receded from his mind and his writings. At the end of 1665 he was called away from Oxford, and for the next twenty years his interests and pursuits led him in different directions. It is not until the years 1687–92 that Locke's essays were again mentioned in the letters written to him by Tyrrell. From these we learn that Locke had repeatedly expressed to his friend an intention to revise and to complete his early essays and that Tyrrell had encouraged him in this project and desired him to publish his thoughts on natural law. But by this time Locke appears to have lost interest in the design; all he did was to order his amanuensis Brownover to make a neat copy of the essays (MS. C), to which, once it was ready, he paid no further attention. It is unlikely that the fear of being suspected of Quakerism[1] was Locke's real reason for abandoning his plans of publication; Tyrrell himself seemed doubtful about it. There is nothing in the essays, not even Locke's appeal to the 'light of nature' and his sceptical remarks concerning tradition and the general consent of men, that could in the least savour of Quakerism.

On the other hand, we have to consider that Locke's *Essay concerning Human Understanding*, completed in manuscript in the late eighties, contains some passages concerning natural law in Book I and elsewhere and that these, as we learn from Tyrrell's letters of 1690, gave rise to misunderstanding and to a charge of Hobbism by critics in Oxford; all this was disconcerting to Locke and caused ill feeling all round. It was partly because of these difficulties that Tyrrell urged his friend to publish his early thoughts on natural law and to resolve thereby any ambiguities in the *Essay*. A detailed exposition of Locke's meaning, he believed, 'would make a second part to the former work'. It is indeed a strange fact, and many a critic has been puzzled by it,[2] that natural law, a basic idea in Locke's whole system, is not discussed at length in any of his published works, and even the investigation of it expressly declined.[3] This is to be explained perhaps by Locke's original intention to reserve his early thoughts on this topic for special publication. It may be that the controversies following the publication of his writings on philosophy and theology made him change his mind

[1] Cf. Tyrrell's letter of 29 Aug. 1687.
[2] e.g. H. C, Foxcroft, *Life of Halifax*, 1898, ii. 283.
[3] *Two Treatises of Government*, bk. II, ch. ii, par. 12. Cf. also R. I. Aaron, *An Early Draft of Locke's Essay*, 1936, par. 26, p. 39.

and prefer to leave his detailed thoughts on that controversial question unpublished. However, he appears to have had doubts of that kind already before the appearance in print of his other books, and we should therefore seek for some other reason to explain his change of mind.

Five such reasons suggest themselves, and it may be that any one of these is sufficient to account for the fact that Locke's essays remained unpublished.

1. Writers in the second half of the seventeenth century on the whole preferred the vernacular to Latin. Samuel Parker's[1] explanation why he had written his treatise on natural law in English, though his predecessor Richard Cumberland had published his in Latin, was that those who had turned sceptics or atheists and therefore were most in need of moral instruction were unfamiliar with the Latin tongue. Similarly Tyrrell's book on natural law, as he explains in the Epistle Dedicatory, was intended as a generally accessible version in English of Cumberland's *De Legibus Naturae Disquisitio Philosophica* of 1672. It is not unreasonable to suppose that Locke's scruples were caused by the idea of a laborious retranslation of his essays into English.

2. A good deal of what Locke wrote in the essays found its way into the *Essay* of 1690.[2] The passages in question are concerned not so much with natural law as with certain epistemological arguments, and these Locke incorporated chiefly in Book I of his *Essay* as part of his attack against innate ideas. Thus, in a sense, the essays were used by Locke as if they had been a preliminary draft of part of the *Essay*, and before publishing them he would have had to cast out from them all the passages taken over in the *Essay*.

3. It can be seen that Locke's idea of the possibility of a system of demonstrated ethics, so much insisted on in his published works and his letters to William Molyneux, had its roots in his early doctrine of natural law. We may suspect that the reason why he never proved able to produce a detailed or convincing exposition of this idea was that he felt some doubts about the very foundation supporting it. As we shall try to show in section VII of this Introduction, the development of his hedonism and certain other views held by him in his later years made it indeed difficult for him to adhere whole-heartedly to his doctrine of natural law.

[1] Cf. *A Demonstration of the Divine Authority of the Law of Nature and of the Christian Religion*, 1681, Preface, pp. i and ix.

[2] And in part already into the early drafts of the *Essay*, of 1671, especially into Draft B (edited by Rand, 1931).

14

4. Between the Restoration of 1660 and the Revolution of 1688 Locke's outlook, possibly under the influence of the Earl of Shaftesbury, had changed also in that at the outset he defended law and civil authority and in the end he vindicated individual rights and liberty. A change like this must have shaken to some extent his confidence in the tenability of his early views.

5. The essays were, after all, the work of his youth, and though Locke was a man of thirty when he wrote them, it was not until almost thirty years later that he published his first books. The essays certainly lack the maturity of his later thought and may have induced in him a feeling of diffidence.

III

New Information about Locke's Early Life

LOCKE was born in 1632 and spent six years (1646–52) as a King's Scholar at Westminster School. In the summer of 1652 he was elected to a Junior Studentship at Christ Church, Oxford, taking his B.A. in February 1655/6 and his M.A. in June 1658. Six months later he was appointed Senior Student at Christ Church, then, in 1660, Reader in Greek and, in 1662, Reader in Rhetoric. In December 1663 he was appointed Censor of Moral Philosophy for the year 1664.

A number of documents in the Lovelace Collection enlarge our knowledge of this early part of Locke's life. Most of the documents concerned have hitherto been unnoted or unidentified.

When at Westminster, Locke wrote and probably delivered two orations in Latin,[1] in which the persons addressed may be Dr. Busby, the headmaster, and other masters of the school. About the year 1652 he wrote several letters and poems, chiefly also in Latin, to a certain P.A. Allowing for Locke's habit of transposing initials,[2] this person may have been Colonel Alexander Popham, who acted as Locke's patron in his early days at Westminster and Oxford. Popham is extolled by Locke not only as his benefactor but as a defender of the laws and liberties of the nation.

---

[1] One oration is referred to by Locke in a letter to his father of 11 May 1652, printed by R. I. Aaron, *John Locke*, 1937, p. 4, n. 1..

[2] Most of Locke's early correspondents are anonymous or only indicated in his draft letters by initials. It can be found that names of several addressees were marked by him by transposed initials (e.g. U. W. for William Uvedale), presumably for reasons of disguise. Fox Bourne (op. cit. i. 256) was puzzled by this fact in Locke's later correspondence, but he has not correctly interpreted it (cf. also Bastide, op. cit., pp. 52–54).

Introduction

Of special interest for Locke's early history is a booklet[1] containing an almost complete account of money received and spent by him in Westminster School and Oxford from 1649 to 1657, and of the names of his students at Christ Church whose finances he supervised between 1661 and 1666. His money grants in the early period came from his father and were handed out to him by two friends of his father. Between November 1650 and May 1651 he received £14.[2] His expenses were for shoe repair, clothes, toilet things, candles, haircutting, bedmaking, laundry, the butler, his quarterly fees (£1), stationery and postage and, above all, books. He purchased many of the ancient authors from Homer to Epictetus, geography books and Hebrew grammars, as also declarations of Parliament and political pamphlets.

Locke's earliest philosophical manuscript is a booklet filled with notes in Latin written by him either before 1652 or during his first year in Oxford. The notes are on logic and on Greek dialects and etymology. Those on logic are derived from Aristotle and Porphyry and are similar to passages in Robert Sanderson's *Logic*.[3] Two other notebooks, of 1652 and 1659, were filled by Locke with medical observations, those of his own being indicated by his initials. They afford evidence of his early interest in medicine, which for the subsequent years, when he attended Thomas Willis's lectures at Christ Church and met Sydenham (1666), is documented by nine of his medical memoranda-books preserved in the Lovelace Collection.

In the large correspondence between Locke and his relatives, by means of which the connexions between various branches of his family can be reconstructed, are nine letters from him to his father, covering the years 1652–60.[4] They contain references to political events, news from Oxford University, and expressions of Locke's belief in God and a future life. In particular, Locke told his father what he thought of the Quakers, whom he regarded as 'mad' and 'jugglers', 'keeping their heads too hot'. When in London, he had something to say of the examination of James Nayler and his proselytes by the specially appointed Committee of the House of Commons on 15 November

[1] MS. Locke f. 11.
[2] In May 1651 Locke's only brother Thomas joined him at Westminster.
[3] For Sanderson, afterwards Bishop of Lincoln, see below, pp. 30–34.
[4] One of these was published by Lord King (*Life*, p. 2) and another by Aaron (*John Locke*, 1937, p. 4). Three letters to Locke from his father, also in the collection but not hitherto identified as such, are worth mentioning, because biographers have assumed that none of the letters of Locke's father had been preserved.

16

1656. On that day Locke saw Nayler and his women followers in the Painted Chamber, with their white gloves on, humming and exhorting each other. He did not exactly understand what Nayler had to say in his defence, speaking as he did in an uncouth language. At that time, then, Locke disliked the Quakers, though later in his life he became the friend of William Penn and Benjamin Furly. In fact it would seem that in these early years Locke felt little sympathy with non-conformity, despite his Calvinistic family background, his Parliamentary patron Popham, and the well-known influence on him of John Owen, the Independent divine, then Dean of Christ Church. It was not until some time after the Restoration that his manifold defence of nonconformity began. Shortly before the Restoration he appears to have been unable to side with either party in the struggle; his hopes for a settlement were nil, and he was seized with a deep contempt for mankind. As he tells his father,[1] he thought of taking up arms himself except that he did not know on which side to fight. Arms for him were the last and worst refuge, yet 'this is a time when few men enjoy the privilege of being sober'.

This attitude of mind towards the issues of the Puritan Revolution and, particularly, the extravagance of the sects, is worth noticing, for, as we shall find, it was reflected in a writing of his a year later; in fact, traces of it are to be found in writings of his of a much later date.[2] For him, the thinking man, the real issue of the day was the struggle of truth and reason against the powers of fancy and passion, knowledge being but 'opinion moulded up between custom and interest'.[3] In his early writings Locke made the attempt to define his conceptions of truth and reason and to answer Puritanism, at least in its radical forms. In this he probably derived support from such thinkers as Henry More[4] and Richard Hooker. Like Hooker, to whom he refers in his writings of 1660, he endeavoured to vindicate reason and, besides, human laws and institutions, in opposition to the Puritan contention that Scripture was to take the place of human legislation. Both, in

[1] In a letter that is undated, but from internal evidence must have been written in Dec. 1659 (MS. Locke c. 24).

[2] Cf. the early draft of the *Essay*, of 1671, edited by Aaron (par. 42, p. 64), Locke's Journal for 19 and 20 Feb. 1682 (ed. Aaron, pp. 119–23), his notes on Inspiration of Dec. 1687 (MS. Locke c. 27, fols. 73–74), and the chapters on 'Faith and Reason' and 'Enthusiasm' (chs. 18–19) of Bk. IV of his *Essay*.

[3] A philosophical discourse on some such topic is preserved in a letter of Locke's of 20 Oct. 1659, addressed to 'Tom', most probably his brother Thomas (MS. Locke c. 24, fol. 182).

[4] Cf. his *Enthusiasmus Triumphatus*, 1656, sect. xxv, and *passim*; also his *Explanation of the Grand Mystery of Godliness*, 1660, bk. iii, ch. ix, par. 5.

17

their own way, argued that much of man's safety and spiritual dignity depend upon his obedience to natural law.[1]

During his early years at the University Locke was in Oxford during term time, in Somerset during the vacation, and from time to time he paid visits to London. When he was away from any of the many friends he had in these places, he kept in touch with them by letter, and we still possess parts of his correspondence with William Godolphin, William Carr, Samuel Tilly, Gabriel Towerson, and William Uvedale.[2] The last three must have been among Locke's most intimate friends and they and Locke were closely acquainted with a group of young women in Oxford with whom they also corresponded. The collection of so-called love-letters to and from Locke, which is more extensive than has hitherto been supposed, extends from the fifties to the sixties. The letters teem with expressions of affection, couched in a humorous allegorical style that is sometimes heavy and difficult to appreciate. Several details in this love-correspondence are still obscure, chiefly because it is difficult to know how many ladies there were in all, and who was who. There was an Anne Evelegh, writing from Black Hall; since we know that there was a John Eveleigh of Black Hall, St. Giles',[3] who was made Dean of Ross early in 1664, Anne may have been his daughter. There were Elia, Berelisa, and Scribelia, P.E., and 'Madam'.[4] Most probably, all these were sisters or cousins living at Black Hall, Oxford. We hear of intrigues there between three 'goddesses' or 'muses', who during Locke's absence looked dismally at each other, 'sighing in a pitiful tone: Ah, Mr. Lock!'[5]

Black Hall, however, was a centre not only of courtship and correspondence but also of discussion.[6] Frolic was mingled there with 'high

[1] For Hooker see E. T. Davies, *The Political Ideas of Richard Hooker*, 1946, pp. 50–51.

[2] Most of this early correspondence is unpublished and several of the addressees are only indicated by initials or a transposition of initials. However, the anonymity which Locke's correspondents often sought to maintain or in which they were wrapped in his draft answers can in most cases be dispelled.

[3] Cf. A. Wood, *Life and Times*, ed. A. Clark, i. 279. The site of Black Hall, St. Giles', and of Blackhall Rd. is east of the point of divergence of Banbury Rd. and Woodstock Rd.

[4] Letters to 'Madam' are referred to by R. I. Aaron, *John Locke*, 1937, p. 6, n. 1. Locke, in his draft letters to P. E., very often addressed his correspondent as 'Sir'. However, in several cases he spontaneously wrote 'Madam' first, which he then crossed out, obviously for reasons of disguise. A widow in Pensford, mentioned in a letter to him from his father (21 May 1659) as a prospective bride for him, has nothing, obviously, in common with his women friends in Oxford. But one of these may be alluded to in letters from Locke to his father of 20 Dec. 1660 (Lord King, *Life*, p. 2) and to John Parry of Dec. 1666 (ibid. p. 29) as the person he intended to marry.

[5] W. Uvedale to Locke, probably Sept. 1659 (MS. Locke c. 22, fol. 174).

[6] 'I have often heard him say', Lady Masham reported later, 'that he had small satisfaction

language', and 'so divine a tongue' as Locke's used to dwell on subjects that invited serious reflection. It was his 'genius', his 'clear judgement', that made his friends find pleasure in his company and talk. Through Towerson, a frequent visitor at Black Hall, the subjects which Locke was writing about in the early sixties may well have been broached among the genial circle assembling there. For it was with Towerson's co-operation that Locke was then inquiring into the law of nature, and it was by his instigation that in 1660 he wrote a pamphlet against a nonconformist divine with a view to publication. Letters to and from Black Hall indicate that this pamphlet passed freely from hand to hand. Moreover, as we know from a note in Fox Bourne's biography,[1] Locke 'spent a good part of his first years at the University in reading romances, from his aversion to the disputations then in fashion there'. In a letter of 1659, William Godolphin refers to a romance written by Locke himself, comparing him with Sir Thomas More and James Harrington. It might be that about this time Locke wrote the précis of a play called 'Orozes King of Albania', which is still among his papers[2] and which possibly reflects his relationships to the friends, men and women, he had in Oxford about 1660. It was at that time, too, that volumes of La Calprenède's fashionable romance *Cléopâtre* were exchanged between Locke and the young ladies at Black Hall, just as between William Temple and Dorothy Osborne a few years before. Other books read at Black Hall were Francis Osborne's *Remedies of Love*, his *Advice of a Father to his Son*, and Madeleine de Scudéry's *Le Grand Cyrus*.

If we turn to Locke's life in college in the years following the Restoration we find him occupied in various ways. He did chemical experiments with Peter Stahl and collected books on alchemy,[3] while at the same time preparing a speech on the occasion of the visit to Oxford of Prince Christian, later King of Denmark.[4] A good deal of his time must have been taken up by his duties as lecturer and afterwards as Censor. We know the names of his students, of whom,

in his Oxford studies . . . and that in conversation and correspondence much of his time was then spent' (Fox Bourne, op. cit. i. 61–62).

[1] Vol. i, p. 54; Spence, *Anecdotes* (ed. Singer), p. 107.

[2] MS. Locke e. 6; the précis runs to four pages.

[3] Cf. letters from the physician David Thomas, especially his last letter to Locke of 11 Dec. 1693; cf. also MS. Locke f. 27, p. 19.

[4] The speech is preserved in MS. Locke f. 31, fols. 136^v–134^v. It is in Latin and headed *Principi Daniae Oxonium ex Itinere divertente, 62*. The Prince was in Oxford on 26–27 Sept. 1662, and he came to dinner at Christ Church, as is stated by A. Wood, *Life and Times*, ed. A. Clark, i. 457.

Introduction

between 1661 and 1665, he had about two dozen;[1] we also know that he lectured to them on the law of nature, and that they did exercises for him on this theme. The books he made them buy were textbooks on logic and treatises on metaphysics, and he also recommended to them Cicero, Bodin's *Methodus*, Grotius's *De Veritate Christianae Religionis*, and the books by Richard Allestree, then in fashion. So far as his own reading is concerned, we know that he studied Spinoza's *Principia* shortly after its publication in 1663 and that he was curious to know what other writings there were by Spinoza.[2] He also took excerpts from Gassendi's *Life of Peireske* and from a great many books of travel. He followed with interest each new publication of his friend Robert Boyle and skimmed authors for arguments on the existence of God. If we consult a notebook of his containing excerpts of books he read about 1667,[3] a period falling just outside the scope of this survey, it can be seen that little of what was noteworthy in the field of letters escaped his attention.

In 1664, when he was Censor,[4] Locke learned shorthand, a skill that must have stood him in good stead during his stay at Cleves in the winter of 1665–6, when he was secretary to Sir Walter Vane on a mission to the Elector of Brandenburg. A letter from Charles Perrot of 21 August 1666,[5] in which Locke was offered the post of secretary to Sir Thomas Thynne, the King's envoy to Sweden, reveals that this was another choice presenting itself to him after his return from Cleves besides the offer of a secretaryship under the new ambassador to Spain, the Earl of Sandwich. That Locke was then faced with the difficulty of choosing a profession is explained in a draft letter by him of 27 November 1666 on the back of a letter from Strachey, who in 1663 had dissuaded him from becoming a clergyman.[6] However, we need not enter here into Locke's life after 1664, the year when his early days in Oxford, the first part of his literary career, and his initial study of natural law came to an end. He spent the years of middle life, under Shaftesbury's patronage, as a man of the world, and, while travelling in France and Holland, as a writer of broadening outlook.

[1] MS. Locke f. 11, containing accounts of money disbursed by Locke on behalf of his students. Cf. also a group of letters from the fathers of his students concerning his duties as a tutor.   [2] MS. Locke f. 27, p. 5.   [3] MS. Locke f. 14.   [4] His Censor's fee for the year was £22 (MS. Locke f. 11, fol. 50ᵛ).   [5] MS. Locke c. 17, fols. 70–71.
[6] From a letter by Locke to another friend, of 1666, an extract from which is printed in Lord King's *Life* (p. 29), we learn that Locke had refused a clerical office in Dublin. The name of his correspondent, not mentioned by Lord King, cannot be doubtful, since there is a letter in the Lovelace Collection by John Parry (Dublin, 2 Dec. 1666) in which Locke is asked to become chaplain to the Duke of Ormond.

New Information about Locke's Early Life

It appears from his journals that in the four years he spent in England between his return from France (1679) and his departure for Holland (1683) he went to Oxford for as many as twenty-seven visits. In 1684, while in Holland, he was deprived of his Studentship at Christ Church, and after his return to England in 1689, for the remaining fifteen years of his life, he never set foot again in Oxford. During this last period several of the writings composed by Locke during his earlier life appeared in print. Most of these presupposed the idea of a law of nature, and yet the essays he had written on this theme never saw the light. Still earlier treatises by him on the civil magistrate, another outcome of his formative years in Oxford, were equally forgotten and remained unpublished. These treatises, nevertheless, deserve to be examined for a full understanding of what follows, and we shall consider them in the next section.

IV

Locke's Two Early Treatises on the Civil Magistrate

In this section we shall discuss Locke's two writings on the civil magistrate, which throw light on the circumstances under which he embarked on the study of natural law.

We may begin by mentioning briefly an undated lengthy letter by Locke to a certain S. H.,[1] in which he discussed a book recently published by his correspondent on the subject of toleration. Internal evidence puts it beyond doubt that this letter was written in 1659, that Locke's correspondent was Henry Stubbe, and that the book in question was Stubbe's *Essay in Defence of the Good Old Cause; or a Discourse concerning the Rise and Extent of the Power of the Civil Magistrate in Reference to Spiritual Affairs*, &c., of 1659. The letter is important for four reasons. (1) It is the earliest document in our possession containing a reasoned argument by Locke. (2) It shows that Locke's attitude towards toleration was already defined eight years before he wrote his *Essay Concerning Toleration* of 1667. For Locke's chief exception to Stubbe's treatment was precisely the latter's idea of including Roman Catholics in a general indulgence. 'The only scruple I have is how the liberty you grant the Papists can consist with the security of the Nation (the end of government).' (3) From this quotation and the full title of Stubbe's book we learn that Locke's thoughts, shortly before the Restoration, were dwelling on the questions of national

---

[1] MS. Locke c. 27, fol. 12.

security and the power of the civil magistrate. (4) A passage in the letter expresses Locke's complaint that Stubbe had not continued his history of toleration down 'to these times, and given us an account of Holland, France, Poland,[1] etc., since nearest examples have the greatest influence'. Locke thus contended that theory and study, in order to become more effective polemically, should be directed towards contemporary and practical questions. This letter to Stubbe, as we shall see, set the stage for Locke's own activity as a writer in a treatise composed in 1660, the year of the Restoration. In a polemical spirit and in connexion with one of the most controversial issues of the day, he set out to argue against a too general toleration and, for the purpose of preserving the peace, in favour of a wide exercise of influence by the civil power.[2]

From the postscript of Towerson's letter to Locke of 23 October 1660 we learn that Locke was at that time siding with John Pearson and Henry Savage against Cornelius Burges's contention that the doctrine of the Church of England was in need of reformation. Such a contention had been the object of Hooker's criticism in the *Preface* to his *Laws of Ecclesiastical Polity*. As we shall see, Locke had read Hooker's *Preface* when, in the winter of 1660–1, he himself took part in a controversy concerning the magistrate's right of interference in matters of religious worship. He wrote two treatises on this question, one in English amounting to thirty-six pages,[3] another in Latin amounting to eighteen pages.[4] The English treatise is called *Question: whether the Civill Magistrate may lawfully impose and determine the use of indifferent things in reference to Religious Worship?* The Latin treatise has the

---

[1] The mentioning of Poland intimates Locke's early interest in Socinianism, which for the following years can be traced in greater detail in his notebooks and book-lists. Some references, though by no means all, are given by H. J. McLachlan (*Socinianism in Seventeenth-Century England*, 1951, pp. 326 ff.).

[2] I shall not discuss here the *Reflections upon the Roman Commonwealth*, printed by Fox Bourne (op. cit. i. 147 ff.) from the Shaftesbury Papers in the Public Record Office and regarded by him as a work written by Locke about 1660. The Fragment was ascribed to the third Earl of Shaftesbury by P. Ziertmann (*Archiv f. Gesch. d. Philos.* x (1904), 318), but H. F. Russell Smith (*Harrington and his Oceana*, 1914, pp. 139, 143, 217–18) has shown that it is the work of Walter Moyle, in whose collected works (1726, vol. i) it is published as an *Essay on the Constitution of the Roman Government*, together with a second part that is missing in the manuscript printed by Fox Bourne. No notice of this discovery has been taken by L. Fargo Brown (*The First Earl of Shaftesbury*, 1933, p. 156, note) and J. W. Gough (*John Locke's Political Philosophy*, 1950, p. 184).   [3] MS. Locke e. 7.

[4] MS. Locke c. 28, fol. 3. Both treatises are written in Locke's hand. The draft of the Latin treatise is preserved in a notebook entitled *Lemmata* (MS. Locke e. 6), which contains also the drafts of some of his essays on natural law. The beginning of the draft is missing and it differs slightly from the final copy.

Locke's Two Early Treatises on the Civil Magistrate

title *An Magistratus Civilis possit res adiaphoras in divini cultus ritus asciscere, eosque populo imponere? Aff.* The similarity, in point of form, between the latter title and those of Locke's essays on natural law is striking. Since there exist in fact important affinities among all these early writings by Locke, we must now turn our attention to his two treatises on the civil magistrate.[1]

The English, but not the Latin, treatise is directed against a particular adversary. From internal evidence it can be ascertained that this was Edward Bagshaw jun., an extreme nonconformist (and the later adversary of Richard Baxter), who in 1660 had published anonymously a pamphlet called *The Great Question Concerning Things Indifferent in Religious Worship*.[2] Each of Locke's arguments is directed against one by Bagshaw and introduced by a quotation from his pamphlet together with a reference to the page where it occurs. Locke's treatise was ready in manuscript by 11 December 1660, since this is the date of a letter appended to it.[3] In Towerson's letters to Locke of 12 March 1660/1 and 9 April 1661[4], in which mention is made of Bagshaw and a pamphlet by him, Locke is urged to print his answer to it, so as to 'doe God and the Church a peice of seasonable service'. Locke let himself be encouraged and composed a preface to his treatise, addressed to the reader, in which he explained that his discourse 'was written many months since' and was not originally intended for publication; that he wanted to publish it now but, like his opponent, to remain anonymous. A reference in the preface to 'the transactions of the late and the opening of the present Parliament' indicates that the preface was written after 8 May 1661, the day when Charles's Second (the Cavalier) Parliament met.[5] In May 1661 a treatise of Locke's due to be printed was discussed between two friends of his, James Allestry and

[1] The Latin treatise is unpublished. A few passages of the 'Preface' to the English treatise are printed in Lord King's *Life*, 1858, pp. 7–8. J. W. Gough (op. cit., pp. 179–81) has quoted the opening paragraphs of the English treatise (though not, as he thought, in full) and three other passages occurring in it.

[2] For the authorship of Bagshaw see A. Wood, *Athen. Oxon.*, 3rd ed. iii. 947, and Halkett and Laing, *Dictionary of Anonymous and Pseudon. English Literature*, 1926, ii. 409. There were three editions of Bagshaw's pamphlet in 1660; a second and third part followed in 1661 and 1662 respectively. A printed copy of the pamphlet is among the papers in the Lovelace Collection.

[3] The letter was afterwards crossed out by Locke and his own signature made almost illegible.　　　　　　　　　　　　　　[4] MS. Locke c. 22, fols. 5–7.

[5] The Preface was probably written in the early summer of 1661, at any rate not long afterwards, since before 1662 Charles had already broken his promises of a general Indulgence and a scheme of Comprehension with the Presbyterians, which he had made to the two parliaments and which Locke in his preface regards as absolutely reliable.

Samuel Tilly.[1] Tilly himself kept a manuscript copy of it during the winter of 1661-2 and did not return it to Locke until March 1662.[2] Though Locke's treatise remained unpublished, it probably had some effect on Bagshaw's ill-fated career. After his early education at Westminster School Bagshaw had been elected to a Studentship at Christ Church six years before Locke's election and he retained this Studentship until 1661. On 10 January 1661/2 he complained of 'having lately been deprived of my just Right in a Freehold I had at Christ-Church for no Reason at all that I know of unless for the impartial and unbyassed Discovery of my Judgment about indifferent, or rather doubtful Things in religious Worship'.[3]

All we know about Locke's Latin treatise, so far as its history and time of composition are concerned, is that it was not written before the autumn of 1660. It contains a reference to the Bishop of Lincoln, and this must have been Robert Sanderson, Oxford Professor of Divinity, who was consecrated on 28 October 1660.[4] The treatise may have been written in the winter of 1660-1, but since Locke was then putting the finishing touches to his English treatise, it may have been undertaken after he had abandoned the plan of publishing the latter, i.e. during 1661 or 1662.[5] There is no allusion in the Latin treatise to Locke's adversary Bagshaw; and it differs from the English treatise both in tenor and composition, being concerned with fundamentals rather than with a particular issue. There is no evidence to show that Locke intended to publish this treatise either under his own name or anonymously.

Locke's arguments in the two treatises must now be discussed. I shall first deal with the English, then with the Latin treatise.

(a) *The English treatise*. Bagshaw's and Locke's positions in the controversy can be summarized thus: Bagshaw maintained 'that none can Impose, what our Saviour in his Infinite Wisedome did not think

---

[1] Cf. a letter from James Allestry to Samuel Tilly, 14 May 1661 (MS. Locke c. 3, fol. 21).

[2] Cf. Tilly's Letters to Locke, 5 Dec. 1661 and 7 Mar. 1661/2 (MS. Locke c. 20, fols. 179-80 and 173-4).

[3] White Kennett, *Register and Chronicle Ecclesiastical and Civil*, 1728, p. 603 (quoted by A. G. Matthews in *Calamy Revised*, 1934, pp. 21-22, s.v. Edward Bagshaw).

[4] The reference occurs both in the Latin treatise and the preliminary draft of it, but Locke cancelled it in the former. Both in the English treatise and Bagshaw's pamphlet Sanderson is referred to by name (together with Hooker). The importance of Sanderson in connexion with Locke's early writings will be stressed in section v.

[5] In that case the time of composition of Locke's Latin treatise and of his essays on natural law would fall within the same period (between 1661 and 1663), an hypothesis strengthened by the fact that both sets of writings were drafted by him in the same notebook (MS. Locke c. 6).

Necessary, and therefore left Free'.[1] Locke's view was that 'allowing every man by nature as large a liberty as he himself can wish, yet . . . whilst there is Society Government and Order in the world Rulers still must have the power of all things indifferent'.[2] Thus, in opposition to the extreme nonconformist position taken up by Bagshaw, according to which no religious matters whatever are subject to the magistrate's interference, Locke argued for a widening of the extent of the power of civil authority, allowing its influence over all matters indifferent.[3] His reason for this was that the way in which indifferent things are determined has a bearing on the maintenance of peace but is of no consequence to that of religion. In support of his argument (and this is a point of no small importance) Locke made use of a particular conception of natural law.

An appeal to the law of nature in connexion with questions similar to those debated by Locke had been made frequently by contemporaries of his, both Anglican and Puritan.[4] Bagshaw's language, on the other hand, was not that of natural law, at least not in the sense in which Locke was making use of the concept. His appeal was to faith, conscience, and liberty: the fundamental law, for him, was the law revealed in the New Testament and received by faith. Anything in the religious sphere not commanded or prohibited in the Gospel was left for individual conscience to determine. Hence Scripture was to be accepted as a charter of spiritual rights. And just as the function of the state was to guarantee the freedom of individuals, so its origin was to be derived from their will, i.e. it was contractual in character. If a notion of natural law was at all in Bagshaw's mind, it was there only to serve as a fulcrum for his defence of men's rights and liberties.

As against Bagshaw's position, then, Locke's view was, first, that human faculties other than faith, e.g. reason, can attain to the know-

---

[1] Cf. the Preface by the publisher of Bagshaw's pamphlet.

[2] Locke's Preface to the English treatise, p. 5.

[3] By indifferent things both Bagshaw and Locke mean the time and place of meeting for religious worship, bowing at the name of Jesus and towards the altar, the making of the sign of the cross in baptism, the wearing of the surplice in preaching, kneeling at the Lord's Supper, set forms of prayer, &c.

[4] e.g. E. Stillingfleet, *Irenicum*, 1659 (the principles of the law of nature are referred to in the full title of the book, on pp. 14-15, and in ch. ii; a comparison between Stillingfleet's arguments in ch. ii of the *Irenicum* and those advanced by Locke in his English treatise makes it more than probable that Locke had read the *Irenicum* in 1660 and borrowed from it freely in his writing against Bagshaw; in later years, we may remind the reader, Locke became a stern opponent of Stillingfleet); John Owen, *Two Questions concerning the Power of the Supream Magistrate about Religion*, 1659 (most arguments in this pamphlet are derived from the 'Light and Law of nature').

ledge of God's laws; in the second place, that conscience cannot be regarded as a sufficient plea for toleration, 'some being as conscienciously earnest for conformity as others for liberty, and a law for *Toleration* would as much offend their consciences as of *Limitation* others'.[1] Besides, Locke thought it was dangerous to leave people to their own devices and fancies, for 'there hath beene noe designe soe wicked which hath not worne the Vizor of religion, Nor Rebellion which hath not beene soe kinde to its self as to assume the spetious name of Reformation'.[2] Finally, Locke's view was that

mankinde was by the light of Nature and their own conveniencys sufficiently instructed in the necessity of laws and government . . ., the light of reason and nature of government its self makeing evident that in all Societys . . . the supreme power (where ever seated in one or more) must be . . supreme. . . . It was not therefore requisit that we should looke for the Magistrates commision to be renewed in Scripture who was before even by the Law of Nature and the very condition of Government sufficiently invested with a power over all indifferent actions.[3]

It was in this way, then, that natural law served Locke's particular purpose in his controversy with Bagshaw, and the opening paragraphs of his treatise show that he regarded this notion as fundamental.[4] On a foundation like this he felt able to controvert, on Bagshaw's own premises, the conclusions drawn by his opponent from his plea for individual rights and liberties and the consent of the governed. Though Locke's intention at this point was not 'to meddle with that Question whether the Magistrats Crowne drops downe on his head immediately from Heaven or be placed there by the hands of his subjects',[5] none the less, for the sake of argument, he assumed with Bagshaw that government was first derived from the consent of the people.[6] His view then was that, even on the assumption that man, being by nature entirely free, conveyed his liberty to another by compact, after such a resignation he was bound to submission by the law of God enjoining fidelity in contracts. The points stressed by him in connexion with the contract theory were that every particular man must *unavoidably*[7] part with his

[1] English treatise on the magistrate, ff. 10 and 11.   [2] Ibid., f. 33.

[3] Ibid., f. 24.

[4] Cf. the preliminary propositions printed by J. W. Gough, op. cit., p. 179.

[5] Locke's treatise, ff. 2, 3ᵛ, and 35. Several of Locke's arguments in the Preface and the opening part of his treatise are more or less the same as those in the letter appended to it.

[6] Ibid., ff. 5 and 35. The hypothetical character of Locke's arguments here has been overlooked by J. W. Gough, op. cit., p. 181.

[7] i.e. on account of the 'unalterable condicon of Society and Government'. J. W. Gough

original right to liberty and that he must entrust the magistrate with *as full power* over all his actions as he himself has. Thus Locke proved that the civil authority of every nation, even if first derived from the people, must necessarily have an absolute and arbitrary power over all indifferent actions. The ultimate support for his proof he derived from the concept of natural law; it was this concept which helped him to undermine Bagshaw's plea for natural right.[1] It may be that one of the reasons why he refrained from publishing his treatise was that the authoritarian views expressed in it were superseded by his own theory of consent and his advocacy of toleration.[2]

(*b*) *The Latin treatise.* Throughout this tract we find Locke engaged in a full discussion of the concepts of law and obligation, liberty and indifferent things, only briefly defined by him in the opening paragraphs of the English treatise. His analysis of the nature of obligation, carried out with the help of a traditional terminology,[3] is briefly this. Subjects are bound either to active obedience or to passive obedience, according as to whether the power of civil authority is directive or coercive. They are always bound to passive obedience, because a magistrate's command is itself always lawful, i.e. permitted by God, no matter whether or not the thing commanded is lawful. They are bound to both active and passive obedience if the thing commanded is lawful, i.e. according to God's will, and if the command is also issued by a law-giver instituted by God. Thus the rule of obedience that imposes an obligation is the will of the supreme law-giver, i.e. God, and it would follow (though this is a point not discussed by Locke explicitly) that if an action is not commanded by the magistrate but willed by God, a subject has to do it, though forbearance of it on his

has omitted to print a sentence of explanation containing this phrase, which was added by Locke at the beginning of par. 5, on f. 1. The italics in the above passage are mine.

[1] For the way in which Locke, not unlike Hobbes (*Leviathan*, pt. i, ch. 14, p. 99, ed. Pogson Smith) and Pufendorf (*Elementa Jurisprudentiae Universalis*, 1660, lib. i, def. xiii, par. 3), distinguished between natural right and natural law, see his first essay on the law of nature, f. 11.

[2] Another possible reason will be advanced in section v. The reason suggested here would thus lie in Locke's own development, not in that of post-Restoration policy towards authoritarianism, as was suggested by Lord King (*Life*, p. 8) and J. W. Gough (op. cit., p. 177, n. 1).

[3] p. 6. Throughout his Latin treatise Locke employs scholastic terms which he may have derived directly from St. Thomas or Suarez. It is possible, however, that he derived the material of his discussion from various books on conscience such as those written by William Perkins (1608), William Ames (1630), Henry Hammond (1645), Joseph Hall (1649), Jeremy Taylor (1660). His main inspiration, as I wish to suggest later, was Robert Sanderson's lectures on obligation, of 1646 and 1647. Locke's library contained the books of all the authors mentioned in this note.

part would not make him suffer punishment, i.e. the action cannot be enforced on him physically.

In the next place,[1] in order to throw into relief the fundamental point of the question, Locke introduces his definition of law. He explains that for the purpose he has in mind (i.e. an inquiry into the nature of indifferent things) he will disregard certain traditional definitions and choose others that are more suitable. The definitions passed over by him are the division of law into natural and positive, divine and human, civil and ecclesiastical. In their place he distinguishes divine or moral law, political or human law, fraternal or charity law, monastic or private law. Only the first of these distinctions need be considered here. Divine law, for Locke, can be subdivided into natural and positive, according as it is made known to men either by a natural and innate light of reason, or by supernatural revelation. The difference between the two would thus lie only in their clearness and the way in which they are promulgated. Together they constitute the eternal foundation of morality and, by the intervention of inferior laws derived from divine law, introduce moral values even into things indifferent, so that these become either good or bad. It follows[2] that, in respect of their binding force, all laws, no matter whether political, fraternal, or monastic, are divine, for they constrain men in virtue of the divine law on which they are founded and which alone binds by its intrinsic force. Accordingly, the commands of the civil power have a binding force for no other reason than that God wills that every man should be subject to a magistrate's jurisdiction; they must be obeyed not for fear of punishment but for conscience' sake.

By the help of this theory of law Locke provides an answer to the two controversial questions awaiting solution.[3] In the first place, all indifferent things must necessarily fall under the jurisdiction of the civil power. Secondly, no matter which view of the origin of political power is adopted, whether the contract theory or that of divine right,[4] full obedience to the commands of the civil authority is required in either case. For no civil authority can be established unless every single person surrenders to it whatever liberty of action he may have; and since without such an authority there can be no society and no state, God's will that there should be fellowship and order in men's life would otherwise remain unfulfilled.

In order to show that, by an argument such as this, the plea for liberty

---

[1] pp. 7-8.   [2] p. 9.   [3] pp. 11-13.
[4] *Verum de his nihil statuo . . .*, p. 12.

is not altogether abolished, Locke draws a further distinction, explaining that the binding force of human laws can be either material or formal and that, accordingly, the liberty of subjects can be either one of judgement (or conscience), or one of the will.[1] If a magistrate commands a thing which binds of itself and is necessary in virtue of the divine law (*obligatio materialis*), e.g. not to commit theft or adultery, a subject is not at liberty to withhold the assent either of his judgement or of his will, and he is thus bound both materially and formally. The fact that man's liberty of conscience is annulled in such a case, however, cannot be laid to the magistrate's charge: the restriction is imposed not by the magistrate but by God. If, on the other hand, a lawfully instituted magistrate commands a thing otherwise indifferent, which binds only because the magistrate orders it (*obligatio formalis*), a subject is at liberty to withhold the assent of his judgement (i.e. he need not approve of it upon his conscience), though not that of his will (i.e. he must do the thing). Being thus only formally bound, his liberty of conscience is left unrestricted. Neither in this case, then, is there any justification for heaping reproaches on the magistrate. For, *ex hypothesi*, no civil or ecclesiastical law concerning indifferent things affects man's essential liberty, i.e. that of his conscience.

These, in brief, are the leading arguments in Locke's Latin treatise on the magistrate. They display some subtle analysis, but the interest they may have had has now passed. The attention we have paid to this and also to the English treatise appears nevertheless justified for three reasons.

In the first place, it can be seen that Locke's essays on the law of nature to a large extent grew out of his two treatises on the magistrate. The manner in which the rather desultory treatment, in the treatises, of law in general and of natural law in particular paved the way for Locke's detailed doctrine on this subject in the essays seems to be somewhat as follows. At first, in the English treatise, Locke's preoccupation lay in the attempt to controvert the views of a particular nonconformist divine on the question of the competence of the civil power in religious affairs. The chief point of the controversy was whether indifferent matters were to be left undetermined in the interest of toleration and individual rights, or whether they should fall within the sphere of civil law and political obligation. The question of the origin of government, inevitably, arose as part of the discussion, and in support of their arguments both disputants made frequent use of the

[1] pp. 16–17.

Scriptures. It is true that most points in this controversy had been at issue all through the Puritan Revolution. But when Locke and his adversary took them up in the year of the Restoration, they received a new and special significance. Next, in the Latin treatise, Locke sought to reformulate his position more clearly: he preferred to write in Latin and to advance more theoretical arguments concerning the fundamentals of law and obligation. There are no references now to Bagshaw or to Scripture, and the original background and occasion of the controversy is hardly recognizable. Finally, in his essays on natural law, we find Locke engaged in a detailed philosophical inquiry teeming with erudition and academic subtlety. Apart from natural law, scarcely any topic dealt with in his previous writings has survived in the new work. But there is this process of thought linking all his early writings: from the mere appeal to natural law at the outset he passed to the fairly detailed attempt at classifying laws and obligations, and, thence, to a full inquiry into natural law itself. Thus, much in Locke's eight essays on natural law, above all his sixth essay, is best understood if seen in the light of his previous writings on the civil power and the nature of obligation. All his three early writings form one single whole as do the eight books of Hooker's *Laws of Ecclesiastical Polity* and the *Preface* containing his criticism of Puritanism.

In the second place, it is important to realize that throughout the development of his celebrated doctrine of toleration Locke adhered to the recognition of authoritative interference in precisely those matters which he had tried to define in his letter to Henry Stubbe of 1659 and in his two treatises on the magistrate of 1660–1.

In the third place, Locke's two treatises are of value to us in that they provide a clue to what appears to be one of the literary sources of his essays on the law of nature. To this we must now turn.

v

Sources of Locke's Essays on the Law of Nature

BOTH of Locke's treatises on the magistrate contain references to Richard Hooker and Robert Sanderson. In the Latin treatise,[1] the reference is to two definitions of law by Hooker and Sanderson respectively, and it is of interest to note that Hooker's definition occurs almost unchanged in Locke's first essay on the law of nature,[2] though with no indication that it is Hooker's. The reason why Hooker and

---

[1] p. 6; the reference also occurs in the preliminary draft.   [2] f. 18.

Sanderson are quoted at all by Locke in his treatises is this. In Bag-shaw's pamphlet no authors' names appeared except these two.[1] When Locke, in his English treatise,[2] endeavoured to challenge Bagshaw on each of his arguments, he too referred to Hooker and Sanderson, taking their side in a question debated by his adversary. Like Bag-shaw's pamphlet, Locke's English treatise contains the names of only these two authors: no wonder, then, that they survived in his Latin treatise.

When mentioning Hooker and Sanderson in his English treatise Locke says that he is not a person sufficiently qualified to speak in defence of 'two such eminent champions of Truth', especially as he has 'never yet had the opportunity to peruse the writeings of the former beyond his preface, and the lectures of the latter at their first appeare-ance in publique I run over with that haste and inadvertency that I could be able to give but a very slander account of their reasonings'.[3] We need not doubt this statement of Locke's, nor feel sceptical if, in a passage farther on,[4] he is emphatic in asserting that he did not meddle with the literature on the subject discussed by him and Bagshaw. However, though at the time of writing his English treatise Locke may have 'sequestered his thoughts from books', we need not infer that he adopted the same attitude in his Latin treatise and in his essays on natural law. If we compare the views of the two authors mentioned by him with his own, we are led to the conclusion that, before writing his Latin treatise on the magistrate and his essays on the law of nature, he consulted less haphazardly than on his first reading what these two eminent ecclesiastics taught on the subject.

Of the two, Sanderson appears to have exercised the stronger in-fluence on Locke at this early period. He was Bishop of Lincoln from October 1660 until his death in January 1663. In the winter 1660–1 he was chosen moderator at the Savoy conference with the Presby-terian divines, and one of the points debated was the nature of a lawful command,[5] a topic which was then of special interest to Locke. His teaching, which he had derived from a study of Aristotle, Cicero, Thomas Aquinas, and Hooker, and which he combined with a systematic approach to ethics which was his own, had a stimulating effect upon many subsequent generations. It appears that among those

[1] p. 14.   [2] f. 32.   [3] f. 32, lines 13 and ff.
[4] f. 35 (this is the opening paragraph of the letter appended to the English treatise).
[5] Cf. Izaak Walton, *Life of Dr. Sanderson*, 1678 (Jacobson's edition of Sanderson's *Works*, 1854, vi. 335).

who borrowed from the manuscript copies that were in circulation before Sanderson's works themselves were printed was Jeremy Taylor.[1]

In all there are three sets of writings by Sanderson to be considered here, and I will deal with the two more important ones first.

In 1646, when Regius Professor of Divinity at Oxford, Sanderson delivered seven lectures entitled *De Juramenti Promissorii Obligatione*, which were published in 1647[2] and in an English translation by Charles I[3] in 1655. There can be little doubt that Locke derived from these lectures, especially from the first, several of the legal and ethical distinctions in his sixth essay on the law of nature. A few instances may illustrate this. When defining obligation in terms of a traditional formula derived from the *Corpus Juris Civilis*, both he and Sanderson extend this definition from the sphere of civil law to that of divine or natural law, leaving it to the lawyers to deal with the civil sphere.[4] Another and by no means usual distinction of obligation, i.e. that between *debitum officii* (a liability to pay dutiful obedience) and *debitum supplicii* (a liability to punishment) is drawn by Sanderson and Locke in almost the same language.[5] Since these, as also certain other legal phrases and distinctions to be found alike in the writings of Sanderson and Locke, were not in use among ancient and medieval lawyers, they must have been introduced either by Sanderson himself or by a school of commentators in the sixteenth or early seventeenth century. We know[6] that Sanderson's chief legal textbook was Richard Zouch's *Elementa Jurisprudentiae*,[7] but this contains no more than a summary account of the law-books of Justinian and none of the unusual technical terms we meet in Sanderson's and Locke's writings. Unless some relevant information is forthcoming, the question of derivation that we have raised is a matter on which it is impossible to write with any great assurance.

In 1647 Sanderson delivered another set of ten lectures at Oxford, entitled *De Obligatione Conscientiae*. In 1658 Thomas Barlow and

[1] In his *Ductor Dubitantium or Rule of Conscience*, 1660; cf. W. Whewell's edition of Sanderson's *De Obligatione Conscientiae*, 1851, p. iv.

[2] The edition of Sanderson's lectures of 1647 is included in Locke's final library catalogue of *c.* 1697 (MS. Locke e. 3).

[3] Cf. Walton's *Life*, loc. cit., p. 305; also A. Wood, *Athen. Oxon.* 3rd ed., iii. 624, 627.

[4] Locke's sixth essay, f. 83; Sanderson, *De Juramenti*, &c., first lecture, par. 11 (ed. of 1686, pp. 12–14).

[5] Locke's sixth essay, ff. 84–85; Sanderson, *De Juramenti*, &c., first lecture, par. 12 (p. 14). The more usual terms of the distinction in the legal tradition were 'obligation to guilt' (*ad culpam*) and 'obligation to punishment' (*ad poenam*).

[6] Walton's *Life*, loc. cit., p. 342.   [7] Oxford editions of 1629, 1636, 1652.

Robert Boyle asked him to revise these lectures,[1] and they were published in 1660 and reprinted in 1661.[2] An English translation of them by R. Codrington appeared in 1660.[3] Obviously, it was this set of lectures which Locke referred to when mentioning Sanderson at the end of his English treatise on the magistrate. He borrowed from it a number of arguments and further distinctions concerning obligation which appear both in his essays on natural law and in his Latin treatise on the magistrate.[4] In the fourth lecture there are passages on the light of reason, the light of nature, the divine law, the various principles of natural law compelling assent, and on Puritan sectaries, all of which are analogous to passages in Locke's Latin writings.[5] In the seventh lecture we find Sanderson objecting to the view that, because the power of princes is derived from the people, the consent of the people is required in the making of laws;[6] from this objection Locke could draw support in his discussion of the origin of political power in his two treatises on the magistrate.

In this connexion we must mention a third writing by Sanderson which had some bearing on Locke's essays on natural law and undoubtedly influenced his thought in the early sixties.

In 1640 James Usher, Bishop of Armagh, wrote a book entitled *The Power Communicated by God to the Prince, and the Obedience Required of the Subject.* Usher's grandson, James Tyrrell, whom we have already mentioned as Locke's intimate friend, edited the manuscript of this book in 1661, prefixing a dedication to Charles II,[7] while Sanderson, then Bishop of Lincoln, supplied a lengthy preface. Both the preface and the book itself deal with the problems occupying Locke's mind during the years following the Restoration.

Sanderson is concerned with arguments against the Social Contract theory. His two main points are (*a*) that a contract as such, without the help of some other law enforcing it, can operate only on the contractors, not on those who have never given their consent to it; and (*b*) that whatever the terms of the contract may be, they are certainly not the

[1] Cf. Walton's *Life*, loc. cit., pp. 330–1, 357; also *D.N.B.* iii. 225–6, s.v. Thomas Barlow.
[2] Locke's final library catalogue of *c.* 1697 (MS. Locke e. 3) includes the edition of 1661.
[3] The Preface to the work, dated December 1659, is addressed to Robert Boyle.
[4] Locke's sixth essay, ff. 86–88; Latin treatise on the magistrate, pp. 6, 9, and 16–17; Sanderson, *De Obligatione*, &c., fourth lecture, pars. 5 and 6, fifth lecture, par. 5, sixth lecture, pars. 2–4.
[5] The relevant passages in the fourth of Sanderson's lectures are pars. 12, 17–19, 20, 24, 25.
[6] Pars. 14–15.
[7] The dedication opens with a phrase about the law of nature. Usher's treatise had been written by order of Charles I.

dictates of natural law. This second point was obviously directed against those Puritan theorists who regarded the Social Contract as based on, and expressive of, the law of nature. The upshot of Sanderson's discussion is that the duties of subjection and obedience to superiors are perpetually binding, a point argued by Locke at length in his seventh essay.

The pervasive feature of Usher's treatise is the attention paid to natural law as the principle underlying society, government, and obedience. As we may remember, this was one of Locke's fundamental points in both his treatises on the magistrate. Usher also holds that the external government of things belonging to religion was by God committed to the king, and that he owed to natural law (being God's law) as much obedience as the lowest of his subjects.

One reason for paying attention to this book is that by means of it we can reconstruct some of the personal relations that must have existed between Sanderson and Locke. Visiting Tyrrell at his home near Oxford, as he frequently did, Locke might well have seen, if not read, Usher's manuscript, and he must have met Sanderson about the time when the latter was publishing it jointly with Tyrrell. With the publication of Usher's treatise and Sanderson's Preface in 1661, the position defended by Locke in his English treatise on the magistrate received a powerful backing in the eyes of the world.[1] Perhaps it was for this reason that, during the latter part of 1661, he abandoned the idea of publishing his own treatise[2] and began to concentrate on a special study of law and obligation.

Sanderson's influence, we thus conclude, is noticeable throughout Locke's literary activities between 1660 and 1663—a fact which may confirm us in our view of the continuity of thought linking Locke's treatises on the magistrate with his essays on natural law. But it is in these essays themselves and in the treatment of legal technicalities which they contain, that Sanderson's influence upon Locke appears most obvious.

Let us inquire now into the existence of other literary sources of Locke's essays. We know that he himself rarely hinted at the foundations upon which he built. In order to clarify the filiation of his thought, therefore, we must take into account any covert references in his essays as well as his open allusions to previous thinkers, and, in

[1] Usher's treatise and Sanderson's Preface come in for severe criticism towards the end of *A Letter from a Person of Quality to his Friend in the Country*, printed in 1675 in defence of Shaftesbury's policy and included in Locke's *Works* (1801, x. 244–6).
[2] Another possible reason why Locke refrained from publication has been suggested on p. 27.

order not to overlook any of his debts that he left completely un-
acknowledged, we must keep in mind the major stages in the development of the theory of natural law and attempt a brief estimate of the
importance they may have had as antecedents of his thought.

In his first essay Locke quotes two passages from Aristotle's *Nicomachean Ethics* concerning the rational nature of man and the distinction between legal and natural justice.[1] Certain passages in the *Ethics*
and in Aristotle's works on logic probably suggested to him the arguments concerning the principles of reasoning contained in his third
essay.[2] Since information about Locke's early training in Aristotelian
philosophy at Oxford is scanty, the two or three manifest examples of
it in his essays should not be overlooked. They show that it was the
original text,[3] not the Aristotle of the Schoolmen, that interested him;
they also show that his alleged reaction against Aristotelianism is not
an altogether accurate description of his bent of mind at the time when
he wrote the essays.

So far as Cicero is concerned, there is no reference to him in any
of Locke's essays, not even to his famous definition of natural law in
the *De Republica* (iii. 22), persistently quoted by writers on natural
law throughout the ages and in Locke's own time. Here and there,
however, Locke deals at length with concepts forming an integral part
of Cicero's definition, and in essays V and VIII, where he throws
doubt on the general consent of men and the principle of utility as
possible bases of natural law, his arguments are reminiscent of passages
in the *De Legibus* and the *De Officiis*, Book III.[4]

There is no evidence showing that Locke was acquainted with the
original sources of either Roman law or Canon law at the time when
he wrote his essays.[5] Whatever legal terms or definitions occur in his
essays were taken by him from post-Renaissance commentators or
lexicographers, or from the writings of political thinkers, theologians,

[1] f. 13.   [2] ff. 50–51.

[3] There is evidence in Locke's early notebooks showing that he recommended Aristotle's
Nicomachean Ethics to his students. In an account book of his (MS. Locke f. 11) he records
that in October 1655 he lent to a friend his own copy of the *Nicomachean Ethics*.

[4] From MS. Locke f. 11 we know that in the early sixties Locke made his students read
Cicero's works. His final library catalogue of *c*. 1697 (MS. Locke e. 3) includes Cicero's
De Officiis of 1664 and others of Cicero's writings.

[5] His final library catalogue of *c*. 1697 (MS. Locke e. 3) includes an edition of the *Corpus
Juris Civilis* of 1663 and two separate editions of the *Institutes* of 1553 and 1647 respectively,
but it is difficult to say whether any of these formed part of his library in the early years. He
also possessed J. Gothofredus's *Manuale Juris* (1665) and J. Calvinus's *Lexicon Juridicum*
(1622). We know that in later years he recommended Cowell's *Interpreter* as a useful dictionary of law terms (*Some Thoughts concerning Reading and Study*, in *Works*, 1801, iii. 276).

or moralists. Since he generally modified the terminologies he borrowed from his predecessors, it is not easy to ascertain, except in the case of Sanderson, which were the exact sources of his second-hand knowledge of legal theory.

Turning to Locke's only reference to St. Thomas Aquinas, which occurs in his first essay, we find that what he cites there as a statement by St. Thomas concerning the eternal law is a paraphrase by Richard Hooker of passages in the *Summa Theologica*. Yet we are justified, it seems, in assuming that Locke did read St. Thomas in the original, for a number of Thomistic arguments, especially in his seventh essay, can be traced to definite passages in the *Summa Theologica*. Besides, the opening paragraph of the first essay, where Locke discusses man's nature and his relation to God and the universe, and also the way in which he formulates the titles of his essays—all this betrays Thomist influence. Surely we need not be surprised at finding scholastic influences in Locke's essays, which were written early and for the most part in a conventional style: we find such influences even in his mature writings, in which his thought is more independent and novel. Admittedly, however, it is difficult to decide whether for any of his scholastic notions Locke was indebted to St. Thomas rather than to Hooker[1] or Suarez.

As to Hooker's influence on Locke, we observed in an earlier section that, before writing his English treatise on the magistrate, Locke had read the *Preface* of the *Laws of Ecclesiastical Polity* and had followed Hooker in the polemic against Puritanism. Passages in Locke's essays, particularly his first essay, leave no doubt that at the time of writing the essays he was acquainted also with Book I of Hooker's *Laws*, of which he made a detailed study in later years and from which he took lengthy excerpts in his Journal for 1681.[2] A long paragraph in the first essay containing arguments to show that the general consent of men concerning moral principles indicates the existence of a law of nature was unmistakably inspired by Hooker. Since Locke, however, deleted this passage and expressed very different views on the matter in his fifth essay, Hooker's contribution to his thought cannot be regarded as decisive. As regards Suarez, there is reason to believe that Locke was acquainted with his *Tractatus de Legibus ac Deo Legislatore*, which

---

[1] For St. Thomas's influence on the outlines of Hooker's theory see A. P. d'Entrèves, *The Medieval Contribution to Political Thought*, 1939, p. 89.

[2] Gabriel Towerson, with whom Locke exchanged ideas on the law of nature in the early sixties, frequently quoted from Bk. I of Hooker's *Laws* in his *Explication of the Decalogue*, discourse i, which was published in 1676.

provides a comprehensive and at the same time detailed exposition of medieval doctrines of natural law. I have indicated in section VI of this Introduction, and also in footnotes to the present edition of Locke's essays, several doctrines in Suarez's work which may have had an influence upon Locke. To say, however, that any of the scholastic notions in the essays were derived by Locke from Suarez is to minimize the effect that other thinkers who borrowed from the late Scholastics had on him.

We come now to the seventeenth century, the hey-day of natural-law theory. From Locke's library catalogues we know that he possessed all the main works of Hugo Grotius and John Selden, but the editions he possessed are all later than the period in which he composed his essays. Moreover, the interest in natural law on the part of these two thinkers and the method they employed in the study of it had but little in common with Locke's. His interest was chiefly epistemological, theirs was mainly legal or historical. His view of natural law had a metaphysical foundation; theirs was more scientific, more 'secular'. In particular, Locke rejected Grotius's views that the general consent of men could serve as a proof of the existence of natural law, and that this law could be described as the dictate of reason. Whatever resemblance there is among the three writers does not seem to consist in more than that they sometimes discussed the same sort of questions and attempted to answer them with the help of a similar rational approach. In some of his essays, however, Locke quotes Grotius (though, as was his custom, without acknowledgement), and he cites quotations from other authors, contained in the Prolegomena and Book I, chapter i, of Grotius's *De Jure Belli ac Pacis*.

There are in Locke's essays a number of covert references to Hobbes. The impression one receives here, as also from Locke's published works, is that Hobbes interested and fascinated Locke, in spite of, or perhaps because of, their divergent views. Locke's attitude towards him is, in the main, polemical, but it seems fair to say that it was by the suggestive force of Hobbes's radical views that Locke and others with him were driven to explore all possible implications in the theory of natural law and to meet the challenge of any extreme position. The reasons why Locke appears elusive whenever he broaches a subject connected with the name of Hobbes are not far to seek. In cases where he agreed with Hobbes and borrowed his views, as he did no less than Pufendorf did,[1] he could not have easily acknowledged his

---

[1] Cf. the interesting passage on Hobbes towards the end of Pufendorf's Preface to his *Elementa Jurisprudentiae Universalis* (1660).

debt for fear of being decried as a Hobbist. In cases where he argued against him, the questions under discussion had won such a notoriety in connexion with the controversy around Hobbes that to mention his name would have been superfluous. In fact, in several cases where Locke discusses Hobbes's doctrines it is plausible to suggest that he was stimulated not so much by a passage in one or the other of his works as by remarks he found in the contemporary literature against Hobbes. It follows that anyone attempting to study the relation between Locke and Hobbes would have to view it in its proper historical setting, against the background of the seventeenth-century battle against Hobbism. The need to realize the importance of such a procedure in general is the greater because it is only by the employment of the same methods that the relationship between Locke and Descartes can be fully understood.[1]

In 1660, the year when Locke began to think about natural law, two books appeared which must briefly be mentioned. One, written by Robert Sharrock of New College, Oxford,[2] was probably seen, if not read, by Locke, since the author belonged to the circle around Robert Boyle,[3] of which Locke and, as we have seen, Sanderson also were members. The tendency of the book is, on the whole, Thomistic, and it contains,[4] in a convenient arrangement, various traditional definitions of the law of nature. There are certain similarities between Sharrock's treatise and Locke's essays, but these can be sufficiently accounted for by the identical subject-matter with which both authors deal and by their proximity to one another in place and time. Two points which might be mentioned here are that Sharrock is referred to favourably in Richard Cumberland's treatise on natural law of 1672, and that, not unlike Locke in his eighth essay, Sharrock considered the principle of utility to depend on moral goodness, rather than moral goodness to depend on utility.[5]

The other book that appeared in 1660 was Samuel Pufendorf's *Elementa Jurisprudentiae Universalis*. In that year Pufendorf was appointed to a chair of Natural Law, established specially for him in the University of Heidelberg.[6] His name became widely known twelve

[1] Cf. my article 'Locke and Nicole, their proofs of the existence of God and their attitude towards Descartes', in *Sophia*, 1948, pp. 41–55.

[2] Ὑπόθεσις ἠθική: *De Officiis secundum Naturae Jus, seu de Moribus ad Rationis normam conformandis Doctrina.*

[3] Sharrock's book is dedicated to Boyle; Sharrock also wrote the prefaces to three of Boyle's books published in the sixties.　　　　[4] pp. 188 ff.　　　　[5] Cf. p. 62.

[6] Cf. P. Koschaker, *Europa und das Römische Recht*, 1947, p. 250.

years later when he published his *De Jure Naturae et Gentium* and *De Officio Hominis*. Locke possessed two copies of the *Elementa*, i.e. the edition of 1672 which he had bought, together with the *De Jure Naturae*, in 1681,[1] and the edition of 1660 which he may have acquired shortly after it was published. There can be little doubt that he consulted this book when writing his essays, for a number of points raised in it are discussed by him, especially in his seventh essay. His belief in a demonstrative science of ethics may have been stimulated by remarks in Pufendorf's Preface, though of course there had been other thinkers in the seventeenth century who held this belief.[2] He definitely shared Pufendorf's notion of law as the expression of God's will and his view that the law of nature cannot be said to have arisen from the general consent of men.[3] On the other hand, Locke differed from Pufendorf in that he clearly distinguished between the law of nations and the law of nature, and that his theory did not hinge upon the idea of the social nature of man, on which Pufendorf laid great emphasis. Besides, Pufendorf was mainly concerned with an examination of specifically legal points, and these attracted little of Locke's attention. Thus, since the fields of their special inquiries did not coincide, a further comparison of their doctrines could hardly be fruitful.

The upshot of our discussion so far is (*a*) that Locke had studied, sometimes in a rather desultory fashion, the works of several leading theorists of natural law from antiquity onwards; and (*b*) that he was indebted to Sanderson more than to any other of his predecessors hitherto referred to. His debt to Sanderson, however, as we have observed, was limited: he borrowed from him chiefly the legal technicalities employed in his sixth essay. We must inquire now to what sources, if any, the great variety of arguments in his essays and the general drift of his doctrine can be traced.

I have left till the end of this section the mention of the name of Nathanael Culverwel who, as I hope to show, provided an important stimulus for Locke's doctrines in the essays. Culverwel was one of the Cambridge Platonists who had a direct influence on the formation of Locke's mature doctrines, and Culverwel has sometimes been suggested, though rather vaguely, as a likely source of several Lockian ideas.[4]

---

[1] Journal for 1681 (MS. Locke f. 5), pp. 62, 66.

[2] The inspiration in this direction certainly did not come from Sanderson, who maintained that in morals we cannot have mathematical certainty (*De Obligatione Conscientiae*, viii. 16).

[3] Cf. Pufendorf's *Elementa*, lib. I, def. xiii, par. 2.

[4] Cf., for example, John Cairns's critical essay in J. Brown's edition of Culverwel's *Discourse*, of 1857, pp. xxxii, xxxv–xxxvi, liv.

The suggestion can now be substantiated in the case of Locke's essays on natural law by comparison of these with Culverwel's chief work, *An Elegant and Learned Discourse of the Light of Nature.* This book was written in 1646[1] and published in 1652.[2] It was originally projected on a much larger scale, with a view to showing 'that all the moral law is founded in natural and common light—in the light of reason; and that there is nothing in the mysteries of the gospel contrary to the light of reason'.[3] Both these doctrines, of which the *Discourse* itself offers only a preliminary discussion, suggested the general trend of Locke's essays; the latter doctrine increased for him in importance during the later years of his life. I shall discuss now a number of points which to all appearance Locke borrowed from Culverwel for insertion in his essays.

1. Culverwel was as emphatic as Locke in asserting that the formal obligation of laws does not lie in their inherent rationality but must be sought in a supreme will. Both admitted, it is true, that law presupposes an act of the intellect, and also that there is an 'eternal order of things' and certain 'essential features of things' which set the standard that actions require in order to conform to reason and to become dutiful; but they insisted that it is the will of a law-giver, not his understanding or 'the right and reason of the case',[4] which makes a law. Though they both recognized the existence of what Suarez has termed 'natural' obligations, i.e. such as arise from the harmony between human nature and law, and accepted God's wisdom as a sufficient foundation for a law, they stressed the importance of 'moral' obligations arising from the commands of a superior will, which they regarded as the formal cause of obligation. They accordingly believed that the reason why the law of nature as a divine law is actually binding does not lie so much in the equity of its commands as in God's sovereignty. As a result, they argued that God's will cannot be actually and formally binding unless it is made known to men, either positively by divine revelation, or indirectly by the discerning power of man's reason, i.e. the light of nature. Reason, thus, they both maintained, does not make or declare a law; it merely discovers it just as a candle renders an object visible but does not produce it. A corollary of their doctrine was

---

[1] Cf. Dillingham's preface 'To the Reader', p. 6, and Brown's preface to his edition, p. xxv.

[2] Further editions appeared in 1654, 1661, and 1669; after that there was no reprint until Brown's edition of 1857.

[3] Cf. Dillingham's preface, p. 7.

[4] The phrase was used by Whichcote, *Aphorisms* (1703), no. 76, and later by Joseph Butler in his *Analogy of Religion*, pt. i, ch. vi, sect. 16, note (ed. Gladstone, 1896).

that animals can have no obligations, since their lack of reason makes it impossible for them to perceive or understand a law.[1]

2. Both Culverwel and Locke held that there are no innate or connate ideas and hence that the law of nature cannot be imprinted in the minds of men. The knowledge of it by the light of nature, like all other fundamental beliefs or primary notions, enters the mind through the influence of sense-experience upon reason. Such first principles as 'that it is impossible for the same thing to be and not to be' are not present to the mind from birth, but are gradually acquired by the observation and comparison of objects, so that in the end every sane person is compelled to assent to them. When first principles, being either speculative or practical, are combined and give rise to secondary notions, all sorts of conclusions can be drawn, amongst them the dictates of the law of nature. Since such inferences are not unlike mathematical deductions, it is possible to make out a case for a science of demonstrated ethics.[2]

3. Believing that the precepts of natural law are discovered by a combination of sense-perception and reason, both Culverwel and Locke dismissed every attempt to show that the law of nature becomes known to men by tradition. Of the claim that the knowledge of this law can be derived from the general consent of nations Culverwel's view differed in some measure from Locke's. Next to reason, there was for him a secondary way in which natural law can be proclaimed or discovered, i.e. the tacit and spontaneous agreement on the part of all men to observe the most fundamental moral rules. Hugo Grotius[3] had accepted it as a fact that there is such a universal consent of the more civilized nations at least and he had regarded it as part of an *a posteriori* proof of the existence of natural law. Selden, Sharrock, and William Grotius had availed themselves of the same argument, and Culverwel cited in support of it Grotius's list of ancient authorities, including Hesiod, Cicero, Seneca, and Quintilian. We also find him mentioning the proverb *Vox populi vox Dei*, the truth of which, however, he accepted with reservation. His main point was that the knowledge of natural law, though not the binding force of it, is derived from reason in the first place and from the general consent of men in the second. Locke, on the other hand, in his discussion of the argument,

---

[1] The relevant passages in Culverwel's *Discourse* can be found in ch. iv (Brown's ed., p. 45), ch. v (pp. 52, 56), ch. vi (pp. 59–66, 71, 74, 77), ch. ix (pp. 98–99).

[2] Cf. Culverwel's *Discourse*, ch. vii (pp. 81–83), ch. xi (pp. 124–7).

[3] *De Jure Belli ac Pacis*, lib. i, c. 1, sect. 12.

denied that there is any truth in the maxim *Vox populi vox Dei*, and
he rejected the view that the knowledge of natural law, let alone the
binding force of it, can in any way be derived from the general consent
of men. Though there is this difference between their views, there can
be little doubt that the reason why Locke was led to the discussion of
this topic at all was that Culverwel had devoted to it a whole chapter
of his book.[1]

Admittedly, an attentive reader will detect further differences between Locke's treatment of natural law and the matter and manner of
Culverwel's *Discourse*. For instance he will find in Culverwel leanings
to Neoplatonic speculation and to a utilitarian view of morality which
were absent in Locke. While Locke argued from ground to consequent
and passed from proposition to counter-proposition, Culverwel tended
to disrupt most of his arguments by endless quotations. It is chiefly
from such countenance as he could find among traditional schools that
he added weight to his reasonings, and it is chiefly by the cumulative
effect of his eloquence that they carry conviction. Yet whatever points
of difference there are between Culverwel's treatise and Locke's essays
in style and presentation, the parallel between them, on a number of
points, remains surprisingly close. No other thinker, apart from these
two, ever built a theory of natural law upon the basis of all those
assumptions we have specified. It is thus to Culverwel that we must
point as the chief intellectual force behind several of Locke's views on
natural law in the essays.

Before concluding this section, I wish to deal with one more point
of resemblance between Culverwel and Locke—namely, the elusive
character of their allegiance to Calvinism. As for Culverwel, there
does not seem to be any doubt that, despite his connexions with the
Cambridge school of Platonists, he remained constant to the Puritan
Calvinism in which he had been brought up,[2] and yet, as one com-
mentator has observed,[3] there is little sign of it in his *Discourse*. Locke,
too, was brought up a Calvinist, and his debt to his Parliamentary
patron Popham and to John Owen, the ruling power at Oxford during
the Protectorate, was a large one. The lectures on moral philosophy
which he attended in Oxford between 1653 and 1655 were given by
Henry Wilkinson, an eminent Presbyterian, and by Francis Howell,
an eminent Independent.[4] Even before the Restoration, however, he

---

[1] Cf. Culverwel's *Discourse*, ch. viii; ch. ix (p. 102); ch. x (pp. 109–18).
[2] Cf. W. R. Sorley in the *Cambridge History of English Literature*, vol. vii, ch. xii, p. 279.
[3] J. Tulloch, *Rational Theology*, 1872, ii. 414.   [4] H. R. Fox Bourne, op. cit. i. 46.

appears to have detached himself from Calvinism and to have been attracted by the teaching of Anglican churchmen, especially their latitudinarian representatives. The answer to the question as to which side, if any, inspired him in his early writings, is not without difficulty, since Calvinists and Anglicans not infrequently agreed in several points of doctrine, particularly those which Locke adopted in his early writings. For instance, an Anglican such as Sanderson would have found little fault with Calvin's teaching that liberty of conscience concerning indifferent things does not imply that men need not obey the civil laws concerning these, and that obedience to the magistrate's orders is a duty commanded by God and still holds despite Christ's advent.[1] Likewise, the so-called 'voluntarist' notion of law as the expression of God's will, which Locke shared with Culverwel, was part of the teaching of the Reformers; at the same time, it provided the ground for the legislative ethics of the Nominalists, found favour with Suarez, and was adopted by Descartes, Spinoza, Pufendorf, and such Anglicans as Sanderson. Hence, these and other such doctrines expressed by Locke in his treatises on the magistrate and his essays on natural law tell us little about the extent of his adherence to Calvinism. On the other hand, the fact that, as Culverwel stated his 'voluntarist' theory of ethics moderately, so Locke tempered his with 'intellectualist' notions derived from the teaching of Cambridge Platonists, shows that his attachment to Calvinism was not absolute.

VI

The Argument of Locke's Essays and its Relation to the Background in Contemporary Thought: A Critical Analysis

SINCE a summary of each of Locke's essays can be found at the beginning of this edition, there is no need here to follow his arguments in the order they have in the text. There is a particular reason, in fact, why it is advisable to adopt a special method of exposition. Every doctrine of natural law not only is in some degree obscure but also endeavours to establish logical relations between propositions which, as we shall see, are different in kind and themselves doubtful. Without a critical approach, therefore, no account of any such doctrine can be sufficiently clear. I propose in this section to analyse the notion of natural law into its main components and to discuss Locke's own theory under each specific heading.

[1] Cf. Calvin's *Institutes*, bk. iii, ch. 19, and bk. iv, ch. 20.

43

Introduction

We start from the observation that the notion of a law of nature is ambiguous in that it is derived from confused ideas about reason and universality.[1] The types of statement implied in most theories of natural law appear to be four in number: (1) There are factual statements such as that all men are rational, i.e. that they possess reason and use their reason, and from this it is concluded that reason is an essential property of man. (2) There are statements concerning the operations and effects of reason, such as that reason can make discoveries and, if properly employed, will always attain to the knowledge of the same moral truths, i.e. of natural law. (3) There are ethical assertions to the effect that the moral standards revealed by reason are themselves rational, i.e. they are part of the divine reason or of a rational purpose pervading the universe, and that they are laid down in the form of commands and prohibitions that are universally binding. (4) There are statements about the truth or demonstrability of these moral principles, and it is maintained that, like those in mathematics, they are either self-evident or can be proved by logic. Thus reason, it is said in this case, demonstrates the validity of moral rules.

It can be seen that in these different statements the term 'reason', as also the term 'universality', has not always the same meaning. If exponents of the theory of natural law had sorted out the various statements implicit in their doctrines and had noted that it is not always possible to pass from one statement to another, their arguments might well have lost the conviction which they have carried throughout the ages. For instance, to speak of natural law as rational because reason postulates it and leads not only to the knowledge of it but also to the confirmation of its validity is to confuse the distinctions between rational demands, matter-of-fact propositions about reason, and the certainty of rational truth. Likewise, to speak of this law as universal, because all men are rational and without fail discover the same sort of moral rules, which are binding on them all and are necessarily true, is to confuse different meanings of universality.

[1] M. B. Foster (*The Political Philosophies of Plato and Hegel*, 1935, pp. 145–6) has pointed out that the term 'natural law' is ambiguous in that both man's passions and his reason are natural and therefore two meanings can be, and have been, given to the terms 'state of nature' and 'law of nature'. The word 'nature', which is the cause of the equivocation, has given rise to a similar confusion between the notion of natural law referring to human behaviour and that referring to physical phenomena. To maintain (as A. P. d'Entrèves, *Natural Law*, 1951, p. 7, has done) that this latter confusion between different meanings of the word 'nature' 'was the source of *all* [my italics] the ambiguities in the doctrine of natural law' is to give undue preference to one among several sources (in a similar statement on p. 10, Prof. d'Entrèves substitutes 'many of' for 'all').

There arises a further point of criticism, related to the former, namely this: if these theorists had clearly distinguished between the various types of statement implicit in their doctrines, they would not have wished to apply to each the same method of corroboration. They might have found then that most of their statements are in fact doubtful. That men are rational can be accepted as a fact, but that they must be so in order to be truly men is not so much an indisputable fact as a proposition derived from Aristotle's idea of 'fixed natures'.[1] Whether reason can discover moral values is another open question, and so is the statement that moral rules can be proved, and, more than that, can be apprehended as necessary in the same way as a logical proof.

Locke's theory of natural law, as expounded in his early essays, can be conveniently discussed on the basis of the four types of statement which we have distinguished. His main doctrine centres round the second and third types in our list and concerns (*a*) the epistemological question how we know the law of nature and (*b*) the moral question of its binding force. Concerning the first and fourth types Locke's comments are brief and little varied, indicating a dogmatic trend on his part and little thought-out argument. Most of his essays, however, contain detailed definitions of concepts which in the traditional theories of natural law had remained vague. And though several of the arguments discussed by him are probably the same as those disputed in the Oxford schools which he frequented in his youth, there is scarcely one passage in the essays which does not reveal the unmistakable Lockian spirit. The first essay, it may be noted here, serves as a general introduction: arguments to prove the existence of a law of nature are stated haphazardly and in a rather rudimentary fashion before being taken up again and developed in the main body of the work.

1. While accepting the view that men possess reason, Locke is careful to distinguish, on the one hand, between reason as the discursive faculty of the mind, which seeks to discover truth by forming arguments from things known to things unknown, and, on the other hand, 'right reason', i.e. a set of moral principles which can become the object of knowledge and a rule of action. Whereas the discursive faculty, like the organs of sense, is inborn in men, 'right reason' is not. And the moral principles coming before the mind are not made or dictated by human reason, but merely discovered and interpreted by it. Thus, when Locke asserts that man is 'endowed abundantly with mind, intellect, and reason', he merely ascribes to him a faculty of

[1] Cf. M. MacDonald, 'Natural Rights', *Proc. Ar. Soc.*, 1946-7, pp. 234 ff.

arguing and does not maintain that from birth he carries within himself a body of rational truths or rules of conduct or that he is capable of bringing such truths or rules into existence. Nor does he explicitly aver, like so many of the ancient and medieval upholders of natural law, that man is rational in so far as he has a share in the rational nature of the universe or in the divine reason.

Thus far, then, Locke's starting-point is simple: it consists in the factual statement that men can reason. It is of course a fact, too, that there are some men who cannot reason and that some of those who can do not use their reason. This is admitted by Locke and he refers to idiots and children, as being by nature devoid of understanding, and to all those who, because they are either careless or emotional or given to pleasure or to some habit, make no proper use of their reason. One may wonder how from his premiss Locke can proceed to a theory of moral obligation. His next step, however, is to show that men not only can reason but are obliged to use their reason, inasmuch as it, i.e. reason as the discursive faculty, is an essential property of theirs and their special function is to exercise this faculty. In his first essay Locke makes this statement on the authority of Aristotle, but in the sequel we are told that it is reason itself which demonstrates the truth of it. Thus the very question at issue, namely, whether or not reason is an essential quality of humanity, is decided affirmatively by reason itself. Moreover, it is from a merely factual statement concerning man's essential nature that the moral proposition is inferred that he has a duty to live in conformity with this nature. The conformity itself, again, is twofold: it implies an actual exercise of reason and also strict acceptance of the findings of reason, so that there is an implicit inference from man's duty to use reason to his duty to obey it. Since Locke does not disentangle these various meanings and the difficulties to which they give rise, I shall not pursue the matter but shall examine his doctrine in more detail.

2. Since, according to Locke, reason by itself provides no primary notions and thus cannot be regarded as a source of knowledge, some material is needed to serve as a starting-point of its operations. There are, for Locke, three possible sources of knowledge, viz. inscription or knowledge by innate ideas, tradition or knowledge by hearsay, and sensation or knowledge by the senses. (Supernatural and divine revelation is omitted by Locke from this list because his inquiry is to be confined to the natural origins of knowledge.) In his third essay five reasons are given to show that no moral or speculative principles are written in

the minds of men by nature. The reasons are that the theory of innate ideas is an unproved hypothesis; that generally there is no agreement among men about moral rules and, whenever it does exist, it can be explained by the influences of early education; that illiterate and insane people are ignorant of morality; and that scientific axioms, such as the principle of non-contradiction, are not innate but are the result of an empirical generalization. Similar views are expressed in Book I of his *Essay* and there is no need here for further comments. What is essential for Locke's argument is that, though (as appears from some passages in his second essay) he does not want to commit himself to an outright rejection of innate knowledge, he sees no justification for regarding it as a source of moral truths.[1]

Tradition or second-hand knowledge, discussed by Locke in a section of his second essay, finds no more favour with him than innate ideas. For a time he seems to have intended to devote a special essay to knowledge by hearsay and it is to his credit, I think, that he accepts for consideration in a philosophical treatise what since the days of Herodotus has been regarded as one of the sources of historical information. Yet, though Locke recognizes that true knowledge and true morality may be handed on by parents and teachers, he denies that the fact of such transmission is itself a proof of their truth. In his fifth essay he opposes in a similar way the view that truth can be inferred from a *consensus gentium*. While admitting that the coincidence of one man's opinion with that of another may be taken as a suggestion of its truth, he is careful not to make this coincidence identical with the truth of the opinion. It would not be fair to Locke to say that at this point he merely avoids making what is an obvious mistake, for to Adam Smith, for instance, the mistake was not obvious and he appears to have failed to make the distinction.[2] We may note here in passing that if in the course of his argument and, particularly in his essay on general consent, Locke gives tedious accounts of customs found among different nations—among civilized ones such as the Greeks and

---

[1] It should be noted, however, that in two passages of his first essay and in one of his second Locke speaks of the moral law as innate. Furthermore, in a long paragraph in the original form of his first essay, where the influence of Hooker is apparent, he expressed the belief that there are some moral principles which the whole of mankind accepts unanimously and that this general consent of men indicates the existence of a law written in their minds by nature. When, in his third essay, he had severely criticized the doctrine of innate ideas, Locke significantly changed his mind about general consent: his views about it in the fifth essay are the opposite of those in the long paragraph originally in the first and, accordingly, he deleted that paragraph.

[2] Cf. A. N. Prior, *Logic and the Basis of Ethics*, 1949, pp. 66–67.

47

Romans, and among uncivilized ones such as the Hottentots and Indians—his purpose is to show that while a large number of these customs have nothing in common with the standard rule of morality of which he is in quest, others fundamentally conform to it. In either case his illustrations from history can be regarded as a beginning of the comparative study of law. It may be that a passage in Grotius suggested to him this line of historical inquiry.[1] As regards the law of nations, referred to by Locke in a passage of his fifth essay, it is sufficient to point out that for him it comprises all forms of a general agreement between men which are based on contract, either tacit or expressly stated, and that it is based on grounds of common expediency, not imposed by natural law. Unlike Hobbes and Pufendorf, Locke makes a clear distinction between *jus gentium* and *lex naturae*, and he draws the distinction even more sharply than did Suarez and Grotius.

We turn now to the third source of knowledge still remaining to be examined, namely, sense-perception. This is not a matter of belief but an immediate apprehension of fact, and it is from such data as the senses supply that reason, if properly employed, can advance to the knowledge of things otherwise unknown. In his fourth essay Locke shows by what steps it is possible for reason, starting from the basis of a truth perceived by the senses, to lead to the knowledge of a law of nature.

First our senses tell us of bodies, and their conditions and properties, which all originate from certain arrangements of moving particles. We further observe regularity in the motions of stars, in the changes of the seasons, and in the cycles of birth, growth, and decline in the lives of all animate beings. From the contemplation of the order and beauty to be found in the world, reason, then, infers the existence of a most powerful and wise Creator. Besides this argument from nature, Locke makes use also of the argument from man's own existence and imperfection. For since man cannot owe his existence to any of the inanimate things or living beings, which are less perfect than he is, and since he cannot have created himself, because—with the exception of God—nothing is its own cause, and also because he is himself imperfect (e.g. devoid of an everlasting life with which he would certainly have endowed himself had he been his own maker), it necessarily

---

[1] Cf. *De Jure Belli ac Pacis*, proleg., par. 46 : 'History in relation to our subject is useful in two ways : it supplies both illustrations and judgements. The illustrations have greater weight in proportion as they are taken from better times and better peoples; thus we have preferred ancient examples, Greek and Roman, to the rest. And judgements are not to be slighted, especially when they are in agreement with one another. . . .'

follows that there exists some superior power which has created man and to which man is subject.

It may be noted at this point that Locke has singled out the argument from design and the anthropological argument from among the other proofs of God's existence, precisely because these two arguments are derived from sense-experience and, apart from rational inference, require no further support. He allows the cogency of two of the other arguments, namely the one from conscience and the one from the innate idea of God, but he remarks that their authority is not based on reason and sensation alone and, in fact, presupposes *a priori* notions which it is difficult to accept. A very similar attitude is adopted by him in his *Essay* of 1690, Book IV, chapter 10, where he takes his proofs from 'our own existence and the sensible parts of the universe' (par. 7). Whereas his versions of the anthropological argument in the two places are not unlike the one furnished by Descartes, it is clearly in opposition to Descartes that he expresses his doubt about metaphysical proofs and stresses the importance of the argument from design which Descartes had failed to consider on account of his denial of final causes.

Having shown that man can attain to the knowledge of God by the exercise of his natural faculties, i.e. the senses and reason, Locke's next step is to offer a teleological interpretation of human nature. He explains that since God is not only powerful but also wise, He has designed the world for some end and has prescribed to everything a definite rule or pattern of life, appropriate to its nature. Since man alone has been endowed with reason and all the requisites for working, it is obvious that God has made him to fulfil His purpose and that He wishes him to live according to reason. The special functions he is designed to perform, apart from the duties he has towards himself, are to worship God, to contemplate His works, and to live in society with other men. That these functions, among others, are of the nature of a law can be seen from the fact that they imply the two requisites of any and every law previously established by reason and sense-experience, namely (*a*) that there exists a law-maker, i.e. some superior power to which man is rightly subject, and (*b*) that there is some will revealed by the law-maker. It is for the following reasons, it seems, that a law thus known is called by Locke a *natural* law: (*a*) the knowledge of it is acquired by man's natural faculties, i.e. sensation and reason, the joint exercise of which constitutes what Locke calls the light of nature; in other words, it is a law promulgated by God in a natural way, i.e. it is other than a positive law which is known by

revelation; (*b*) it is a law in conformity with the natural constitution of the universe and, particularly, with the nature of man; (*c*) the precepts of this law are the same for all men and, like the laws attaching to natural phenomena but unlike those of different states, they do not vary from place to place and from one time to another. To what extent this law of nature is binding on men is explained by Locke in greater detail in his sixth and seventh essays and his arguments will be discussed under the next heading. The question dealt with so far has been an epistemological one. It has been argued that reason in co-operation with sense-experience reveals the existence of a natural law and at the same time the dictates of this law. In Locke's view it would be indeed absurd to suppose that there existed a law of nature which all men were to observe but whose dictates remained obscure.

3. The best way to understand what Locke means by the binding force of natural law is to keep in mind the relationships which he believes to exist between God, natural law, and human nature. In the first place, natural law, together with divine revelation, is the expression of God's will. In the second place, God has created man and endowed him with a rational faculty. In the third place, natural law is in keeping with human nature, or, in other words, God's will is in conformity with what He has created. Thus, on the one hand, there are moral obligations which are binding because they arise from the commands of a superior will, which, as Locke puts it, is the formal cause of all obligation. On the other hand, there are natural obligations which are binding because they arise from man's nature, which, as we might say, is the material cause of obligation. The two types of obligations, while they differ in the way in which they are derived, are essentially the same and form the law of nature. We shall first examine moral obligations.

Locke starts from the assumption that in so far as we are subject to another we are so far under an obligation. The power which a superior has over us, however, can be twofold, and we can be bound to obey his commands either for moral or for physical reasons. The difference is brought out by Locke by means of an awkward terminology, borrowed from Bishop Sanderson. The distinction Locke draws is this: Man is bound to obey the authority of a superior will if his being and work depend on this will. The obligation here is ultimately founded in God, in the natural right which the Creator has over His creation. It can also be derived from the authority which someone has over another either by the right of donation, as in the case of monarchs

to whom God has delegated part of His power, or by the right of contract. Throughout we are concerned with a moral obligation, which binds conscience because it arises from the recognition that obedience to God's will is right. If a man were to neglect his duty, his own conscience would declare that he deserves punishment. On the other hand, a man is bound to obedience if subjected by force to another's will, a tyrant's or a pirate's. Here coercion, or the fear of punishment, alone imposes the obligation: no one's right would be violated and, in fact, conscience would give its approval, if instead of obeying the oppressor, a man had regard for his own well-being. The authority which someone exercises over another is in this case unjust, and obedience to it can only be enforced physically.

From what Locke has to say in his sixth essay it appears that he regards natural law as a set of commands proceeding from the will of God and that it is on this account that this law is righteous and binding. The position he adopts in that deep-reaching question of scholastic controversy concerning the essence of law[1] is that of the Nominalists, represented by the so-called 'voluntarist' theory, i.e. he adopts a legislative ethics. Yet, as we shall see presently, his position shifts and inclines towards the 'intellectualist' theory of the Realists, according to which law has its foundation in a dictate of Right Reason, in the essential nature of things, and is thus independent of will. There can be little doubt, as I have argued earlier, that in his attempt to reach a position midway between the two theories, Locke was influenced by Culverwel. Both men may have derived their notions from Grotius or, more likely, from Suarez, who had reviewed at length all the scholastic opinions on this question. However, the possibility cannot be ruled out that the case for the voluntarist notion of law as the expression of God's absolute will was derived by them from Protestant sources, for both Culverwel and Locke were brought up Calvinists and the voluntarist theory had passed from the Nominalists to the Reformers and played a prominent part in Calvin's theology.

After having shown that natural law is binding on men because it is the declaration of God's will, Locke explains that man's rational nature not only indicates to him what are his duties but at the same time constitutes the reason why his duties are binding. He maintains, in his seventh essay, that the bonds of natural law are coeval with the human race, and that all men are subject to this law because it is 'so

---

[1] An account of the principles of the controversy can be found in O. Gierke, *Political Theories of the Middle Age* (tr. Maitland), 1938, pp. 172–3, note 256.

Introduction

firmly rooted in the soil of human nature'. Here natural law and man's reason are thought of as interdependent. The 'harmony' (*convenientia*) which is said to exist between the two arises from the fact that man's rational nature is always the same and that reason itself 'pronounces' a fixed and permanent rule of morals. And the way in which Locke now sets out to define the ground of obligation is this: he derives natural law from man's rational nature and this, in its turn, from God's wisdom and the eternal order that prevails in the universe. In the last analysis it is again God who accounts for the binding force of natural law, not in the sense that He wills this law to be the rule of man's life, and that His will is the formal cause of obligation, but in the sense that His infinite wisdom has given birth to 'certain essential features of things', which are immutable and subject to special laws of operation, and that He has made man such that certain duties necessarily follow from his inborn constitution. The theological presupposition of the argument, however, does not seem to be Locke's main preoccupation at this point. By his voluntarist notion of law he has shown that he regards God as the ultimate source of morality. What he is attempting now is to give an *alternative* explanation and to arrive at a purely rational foundation of ethics. He considers moral rules to be valid independently of any command or external cause, not only because man can discover them by the use of his own reason but because they have their origin and justification in his rational nature. By holding that moral values cannot be other than they are on account of their suitableness to the essential nature of man, Locke provides law with a natural foundation and makes human reason a self-dependent source of obligation.

This part of Locke's theory is reminiscent of Hugo Grotius's hypothetical argument that natural law would remain valid even if God did not exist.[1] The argument was advanced by Grotius as a protest against the voluntarist theory of law, not against a theological presupposition in ethics as such; he introduced it as a reminder that for all their divine origin the principles of law have a binding force of their own, because they are intrinsically necessary and are founded in reason.[2]

[1] *De Jure Belli ac Pacis*, proleg., par. 11.

[2] The source of Grotius's statement and also of the term *convenientia* (harmony) which appears in his as well as in Locke's argument is Gabriel Vasquez (*Comment. in Sum. Theol. Thom. Aquin.* i. 2, disp. 150, c. 3). Vasquez's views were summarized and explained by Suarez (*Tractatus de Legibus ac Deo Legislatore*, 1613, lib. ii, c. 5, sects. 1–4, and c. 6, pp. 75 ff.), and it is most probably from him that Grotius derived his argument and terminology. Locke's inspiration, in the passage in question, appears to have come directly from Culverwel, who in some

52

The difficulty in such a rationalist view of moral obligation is obvious. Reason can perhaps declare what type of action is in accordance with man's essential nature and is therefore in some sense neces-' sary. But it does not thereby indicate or prove a moral obligation to perform the action. Both Vasquez and Grotius admitted that natural law, if defined as a dictate of right reason, only *indicates* whether or not an action is morally necessary, and Suarez[1] pointed out that in this capacity it would be of the nature of a directive rule rather than of a law in the strict sense, a law having a compelling force. In Hobbes's theory the difficulty was resolved by reducing the law of nature to 'a means of the conservation of men', i.e. to a body of 'convenient' rules or articles of peace, 'suggested'[2] by reason and 'guiding'[3] men to avoid war. These rules, for him, were lawful and immutable inasmuch as 'it can never be that Warre shall preserve life, and Peace destroy it'.[4] But they were not themselves laws, because 'Law properly is the word of him, that by right hath command over others';[5] only if considered as delivered in the word of God, or as the commands of the commonwealth,[6] are they properly laws.

Hobbes's doctrine of law and his interpretation of human nature were unacceptable to Locke. In the opening paragraph of his sixth essay and throughout the eighth, he advances arguments to show that self-preservation or self-interest cannot be regarded as the basis of natural law. On the other hand, Locke nowhere emphasizes the view, expounded by Grotius, Pufendorf, and the Cambridge Platonists, that the instinct of sociability, as the most essential part of man's rational nature, is the origin of this law.[7] Instead of maintaining that the binding force of natural law is derived from man's social nature or from the common good of rational beings, as Richard Cumberland[8] did, he shows over and again that human society depends on government, jus-

detail, and not without mentioning Vasquez and Suarez, discusses the notion of harmony between human nature and law and the scholastic argument *si Deus non esset*, &c., and in some measure accepts the idea of natural obligations (*Discourse of the Light of Nature*, ed. Brown, 1857, ch. vi, pp. 71–77).

[1] 'Principium enim *movens* ad exercitium actionis, est *voluntas*; nam *intellectus* potius dicitur *dirigere*, quam *movere* . . . intellectus solum potest *ostendere* necessitatem, . . . voluntas autem *confert* necessitatem' (*Tractatus de Legibus ac Deo Legislatore*, 1613, lib. i, c. 5, 15, p. 18).   [2] *Leviathan*, part i, ch. 13 (ed. Pogson Smith, p. 98).
[3] Op. cit., part ii, ch. 31 (p. 274).   [4] Op. cit., part i, ch. 15 (p. 121).
[5] Ibid. (p. 123).   [6] Op. cit., part ii, ch. 26 (p. 205).
[7] Grotius did not regard the social instinct, as Pufendorf did, as the only source of natural law. On this point Robert Sharrock (1660) failed to interpret him correctly, as was pointed out by Samuel Rachel (*De Jure nat. et Gent.*, 1676, diss. i, 28).
[8] *De Legibus Naturae Disquisitio philosophica*, 1672.

tice, and the fulfilment of pacts, and all these, in turn, on the law of nature. An argument to show that this law is binding because, in case it were not, there would be no fellowship among men and no fidelity, is regarded by Locke as a mere argument *a posteriori*.

How, then, does Locke answer the question: What precisely is there in human nature that by itself can give natural law its binding force? His answer, as we shall see presently, is in terms borrowed from the language of mathematics, and we shall therefore discuss it under a separate heading.

4. After he has introduced, in his seventh essay, the notion of 'harmony' between natural law and man's rational nature, Locke goes on to say: 'In fact it seems to me to follow just as necessarily from the nature of man that, if he is a man, he is bound to love and worship God and also to fulfil other things appropriate to the rational nature, i.e. to observe the law of nature, as it follows from the nature of a triangle that, if it is a triangle, its three angles are equal to two right angles.' Farther on, in the same essay, Locke produces another illustration of how man's duties necessarily follow from his very nature, and it might appear there that he regards moral truths as self-evident; for he likens the way in which these are apprehended to the way in which men, so long as they use their eyes and the sun shines, must of necessity come to know the alternations of day and night and the differences between colours and between a curved and a straight line. However, the point he seems anxious to make here as well as in the passage quoted is that so long as men make proper use of their mental faculties, i.e. pay attention to, and reflect upon, what they perceive, they can arrive at certain knowledge, and this knowledge concerns moral as well as mathematical truths. In the case of mathematics, he maintains, reasoning starts from such perceptible and obvious things as the nature and properties of figures and numbers;[1] in the case of morality, it starts from the idea of man as a rational creature. Just as from the ideas of a triangle and a right angle it is possible to demonstrate that the three angles of a triangle are equal to two right ones, so, according to Locke, from the idea of man it can be demonstrated that he has certain duties, namely to revere God, to be just, to have regard for another's property, to live in society with other men, &c. It is thus from self-evident propositions or from definitions that it is possible in either case to draw necessary consequences and hence to arrive at certain truths.

Here, in the setting of his early doctrine of natural law, we meet

---

[1] Cf. Locke's answer to an objection raised at the end of the second essay.

with the first example of Locke's celebrated contention that mathematics and morality are parallel in that they are both capable of
demonstration.[1] At the time of writing his essays, several of Locke's
contemporaries had expressed a belief in a demonstrative science of
ethics, and it is not easy to say whether this belief was suggested to him
by Grotius or Spinoza, Culverwel or Hobbes. The proposition concerning the angles of a triangle was, of course, a stock-example;
Thomas Aquinas made use of it when discussing the universal validity
of natural law[2] and Descartes introduced it in his *Fifth Meditation*[3] to
illustrate his belief that in the ontological argument God's existence
is proved in the same way as a necessary proposition of mathematics.
There is no need here to repeat Kant's objections to Descartes's argument nor Berkeley's criticism of Locke's view of a demonstrative
science of ethics. It is sufficient to point out that moral ideas, like those
of mathematics, might indeed be said to entail one another and that
moral judgement might be regarded as a matter of deduction, such that
the relation between moral ideas or moral judgements could be perceived to follow of necessity. To deny a moral proposition, such as
'gratitude is due to benefactors', would then be as self-contradictory as
to deny a mathematical proposition. But from this it does not follow
that the reason why a moral rule is said to be binding is of the same
sort as the reason why a geometrical demonstration is valid. Even if in
ethics, as in mathematics, the truth of a proposition were formally
demonstrable by reference to basic axioms or definitions so that the
denial of it is *demonstrably* self-contradictory, moral obligation could
still be regarded as a kind of necessity differing from logical necessity
as it does from causal necessity.

[1] The passage under discussion contains the same illustration of Locke's belief in the
demonstrability of ethics that we find in his Journal entry for 26 June 1681 (Lord King, *Life
of John Locke*, ed. 1858, pp. 120–2; R. I. Aaron and J. Gibb, *An Early Draft of Locke's Essay*,
1936, pp. 116–18) and in his *Essay* of 1690, bk. IV, ch. iii, sect. 18. Professor J. A. Passmore
(*Ralph Cudworth*, 1951, pp. 92–93) has argued that in the passage of his Journal for 1681
and in the rationalist doctrines of his mature ethics Locke was probably influenced by Cudworth's conception of eternal and immutable morality so far as that was developed in *The
True Intellectual System of the Universe* (1678). He admits that Richard Cumberland's book
on natural law (1672), rather than Cudworth, may have been Locke's inspiration, or (p. 96)
that both Cudworth and Locke may have derived their doctrines from some common source.
Since the first indication of the peculiar tortuousness in Locke's ethical theory, i.e. the
combination of a Platonic approach to ethics with a commitment to a legislative ethics, can
now be seen to be already contained in Locke's essays on natural law and to be a consequence
of Culverwel's influence upon his early thought, the problems raised by Mr. Passmore might
be said to have found a satisfactory solution.
[2] *Summa Theologica*, Ia IIae, q. 94, art. 4.
[3] *Works*, ed. Haldane and Ross, i. 181.

The reason why Locke, in the passage in question, insists on the analogy between moral and mathematical necessity is his desire to show that from the concept of man's nature, if suitably defined, propositions concerning moral obligation would follow either analytically or by the rules of deductive inference. It seems as though he feared that, unless ethics could be shown to be grounded in God's will or to admit of mathematical demonstration, natural law might appear as a mere *lex indicativa*, i.e. indicating, but not binding men to, moral rules. But how, it will be asked, could Locke entertain such a doubt, seeing that he has accepted the voluntarist theory of law and thereby given a reason why the precepts of natural law are binding? It would appear, then, that for some reason Locke considered the voluntarist theory as not altogether satisfactory: perhaps he felt that it was too one-sided a doctrine and that along with the concept of will it introduced an element of arbitrariness into morality. Hence he formed the view that natural law, besides being the will of God, is a body of rules in conformity with rational nature, and that it is binding on men not only because it is the expression of God's will, but also because to grasp the conformity between the decrees of natural law and rational nature is the same as to intuit the truth of a tautologous proposition or to demonstrate the truth of a geometrical theorem. These two accounts of the nature of law and of its binding force must have seemed to Locke to be compatible. For him to affirm that moral principles are deducible from human nature was not to deny that they are God's commands.[1]

However, by advancing this further reason for the binding force of natural law, Locke impairs the strength of his voluntarist theory. The wording of some of the phrases in the passage in question is significant. Twice Locke affirms that it is 'reason itself' that 'pronounces' natural law, and yet in his first essay, in due appreciation of the 'dignity of the supreme legislator', he objects to calling natural law the dictate of reason rather than the decree of the divine will. The objection, clearly, is directed against Grotius, and in defining natural law in the first essay Locke closely follows Grotius's definition[2] with the view of improving upon it in the light of the voluntarist theory. But even there Locke is so far under Grotius's influence as to state that the decree of the divine will 'indicates what is and what is not in conformity with

---

[1] Benjamin Whichcote, commonly regarded as the originator of the Cambridge school of Platonists but whose works were not published until after his death in 1683, appears to have held a similar view, for in his *Aphorisms* (no. 76) he wrote 'to go against *Reason* is to go against *God*: it is the self same thing, to do that which the Reason of the Case doth require; and that which God Himself doth appoint'. [2] *De Jure Belli ac Pacis*, lib. i, c. i, sect. 10, par. 1.

rational nature and *for this very reason*[1] commands or prohibits'. Thus it appears that the commands proceeding from the will of God are themselves determined by what is in keeping with rational nature, i.e. by what on Locke's as well as Grotius's showing is morally right. Besides, Locke sometimes maintains that God's authority over men is not only powerful but rightful and that the ultimate ground of obedience to any law is not so much the will of a law-maker as a 'rational apprehension of what is right'. It would follow from this that right and wrong are independent of the will of God and that it is not tautologous to say of an action commanded by God that it is right or good. Moreover, throughout the greater part of his essays where Locke expounds his voluntarist theory, he explains that a moral law cannot be regarded as binding unless it is known, and that it is by the light of nature that God's will and hence natural law is discernible. Elsewhere, however, and especially in the passage in his seventh essay, he tells us that what the light of nature discerns is the conformity between natural law and man's rational nature. It would seem, then, that the perception of moral obligation is concerned with a system of natural relations rather than with the will of a superior law-maker. Finally, Locke's notion that the law of nature is immutable implies that the binding force of it does not lapse even at God's own command. For him, this law is so much part of the nature of things that, in order to revoke it, God would have to undo mankind.

These several aspects of Locke's doctrine present difficulties within the framework of any voluntarist theory. But since they occupy no prominent place in the essays and seem successfully assimilated with the main body of his doctrine, the difficulties they raise might not be readily perceived. It is only by reference to the work of British moralists following Locke that we can realize to what extent a voluntarist theory is in real conflict with such of Locke's views as we have examined; in fact that, if these are accepted, it must be abandoned. That there are necessary moral truths independent of God's will and in conformity with the intelligible nature of things was the underlying assumption of Cudworth's doctrine concerning 'eternal and immutable morality' and of Samuel Clarke's belief in 'eternal fitnesses'.[2] Both these philosophers were defenders of ethical rationalism and of the

---

[1] My italics.
[2] Suarez, who in his controversy with Vasquez predicted this development of natural-law theories in the seventeenth century, has an interesting passage in his *Tractatus de Legibus ac Deo Legislatore*, 1613, lib. ii, c. 5, 2 and 4, p. 76.

intellectualist theory of law; and while their arguments were mainly directed against Hobbes's particular form of ethical naturalism, the voluntarist notion of law as the expression of God's will fell just as much within the range of their criticism. Their theories can be summed up in a phrase used by George Rust[1] and then by Cudworth:[2] 'Things are what they are, not by Will but by Nature.' Among those criticized by Cudworth is Descartes, one of whose arguments was that 'it is because God willed the three angles of a triangle to be necessarily equal to two right angles that this is true and cannot be otherwise'.[3] Cudworth's objection to this is 'that if the Natures and Essences of all things, as to their being such or such, do depend upon a Will of God that is essentially Arbitrary, there can be no such thing as Science or Demonstration'.[4] If we turn to Bishop Butler we find that, while his ethical theory in the *Sermons* hinges upon the notion of virtue as acting in accordance with man's true nature, his ethics in the *Analogy* is in part based on the assertion that 'there is, in the nature of things, an original standard of right and wrong in actions, independent upon all will, but which unalterably determines the will of God. . . .'[5] The truth contained in this assertion is compared by Butler with the mathematical truth that the three angles of a triangle are equal to two right ones. We may, then, regard Locke's second thoughts on his voluntarist theory of law as a half-formed new doctrine[6] more fully developed in English ethical writing in the seventeenth and eighteenth centuries. When writing his essays on the law of nature he had in mind, no doubt, Culverwel, who had put forward a voluntarist theory of law tempered with the Platonic approach to ethics. Without Culverwel's influence upon him Locke might have retained in his essays the purely voluntarist theory embedded in his two early treatises on the civil magistrate.

In conclusion I wish to recapitulate points raised in the previous

[1] *Discourse of Truth*, 1682, sect. xviii.

[2] *A Treatise concerning Eternal and Immutable Morality*, 1731, bk. i, ch. ii, par. i, p. 14 (Selby-Bigge, *British Moralists*, par. 813). See also Richard Price, *Review of the Principal Questions in Morals*, ch. i, sect. iii, p. 50 (ed. Raphael, 1948).

[3] *Reply to the sixth set of Objections to the Meditations*, par. 6 (*Works*, ed. Haldane and Ross, ii. 248).

[4] Op. cit., bk. i, ch. iii, par. 6, p. 33 (Selby-Bigge, *British Moralists*, par. 827).

[5] Pt. ii, ch. viii, sect. 25 (Gladstone's ed. of Butler's *Works*, 1896, i. 368). Cf. also pt. i, ch. vi, sect. 16, note (i. 151–2).

[6] This has survived in the *Essay* of 1690 in several passages, particularly in the following: 'God himself *cannot* choose what is not good; the freedom of the Almighty hinders not his being determined by what is best' (ii. xxi. 50; in the first edition this is section 31).

discussion and to add two more observations. We have tried to explain that, despite a number of valuable distinctions which Locke draws in matters of importance, he fails to keep distinct four main aspects of the theory of natural law. He passes from the recognition that man is rational to the assumption that man's reason, on the basis of sense-experience, leads to the discovery of moral truths, nay, if properly employed, to the discovery of one and the same set of moral truths, i.e. natural law. From this he passes to the belief that the truths thus discovered are divine commands binding on all men, and hence to the assertion that the validity of such commands can be proved, and even shown to be necessary in the same way as a geometrical demonstration. The steps in his argument whereby he seeks to explain the existence, the disclosure, the binding force, and the validity of natural law, are thus treated by him on one level, as if they were all concerned with one and the same meaning of rationality, and as if there was no difference in kind between a matter of fact, a way of knowledge, a dogma, and a logical truth.

Locke's chief doctrines in the essays concern two questions—namely, the epistemological question: how we know the law of nature, and the moral question: how and to what extent it is binding. In the first place, then, as to his investigation of how natural law is known, it might be said that, before deciding the issue between empiricism and so-called innate knowledge, he should have shown whether natural law is in fact one of those things of which it makes sense to say that judgements about them can be justified by reference to empirical facts, or to self-evident truths, or to methods of inference. Locke evaded this issue. He made the question whether natural law is a proper object of knowledge dependent on the *proper employment* of men's natural faculties, i.e. on whether men proceed to correct reasonings from data supplied by the senses; yet men's senses and their reason, however efficient, are no criterion by which to decide of what things it makes sense to say that judgements about them are capable of cognitive justification. Such a decision is to be derived from rational argument, not from the fact that men are endowed with sense-organs and a capacity for thought. The reason for Locke's attitude would seem to be that he was more anxious to vindicate the new empirical philosophy[1] than to provide a logical analysis of the concept of natural law.

---

[1] That Locke's debt to Hobbes as 'the first English teacher of the philosophy of experience' must not be underrated has been shown by Fox Bourne (op. cit. ii. 89 ff.). Then there was, of course, Locke's friend, Robert Boyle, who provided a stimulus for him in this direction and,

Introduction

In the second place, as to Locke's investigation of how and to what
extent natural law is binding, it might be said that, even if there are
moral principles which can be taken as proper objects of knowledge
and as capable of validation, it is by no means as obvious as it seems to
Locke that they can be regarded as axiomatic, i.e. as supplying a
general criterion of all moral duties, and besides, in case they can be
so regarded, that they are axiomatic in the same sense as principles in
mathematics. Here again, it would seem, Locke's primary aim was not
so much to study the notion of natural law on its own merits as to
justify a universal application of the geometrical method then in
fashion, or, alternatively, to establish an absolute basis of moral obligation and of political obedience. In fact, his purpose in studying natural
law was to lay the foundation of a moral theory. As such, his attempt
forms a valuable contribution to the tradition of English ethical writing
and differs from the legal and, as viewed from a scientific standpoint,
more critical interpretations of natural law by Continental writers of
the seventeenth and eighteenth centuries. It is certainly of interest to
find that in the further development of his ethical theory he retained
the notion of natural law in the form of a mere premiss, as something
he believed in but barely discussed or investigated, and that he had
difficulties in reconciling this notion with some of his more mature
doctrines. But this is a topic to be dealt with in the next section.

VII

Locke's Essays in Relation to His Later Works

OUR chief interest here lies in a comparison of Locke's essays with his
Essay Concerning Human Understanding of 1690, and particularly with
the two drafts of the *Essay* which he wrote in 1671.[1] In that year five
or six of his friends used to gather in his rooms at the London home of
Anthony Ashley Cooper, who was created first Earl of Shaftesbury in

among the empirically inclined churchmen, John Pearson (cf. *An Exposition of the Creed*, 1659,
p. 32), whose writings Locke esteemed, as we know from the postscript of Towerson's letter
to him of 23 Oct. 1660. Whether Gassendi's influence on Locke, rightly stressed by Prof.
Aaron (*John Locke*, 1937, pp. 33 ff.), can be traced back to the early sixties is doubtful.
Quotations from Gassendi's *Life of Peireske* occur in Locke's notebook of 1664–6 (MS. Locke
f. 27), but from Gassendi's *Physics* for the first time in the notebook of 1667 (MS. Locke f.
14), i.e. after the essays were written.
  [1] The earlier of the two drafts was edited by R. I. Aaron and J. Gibb in 1936 and is known
as Draft A. The later draft was printed by B. Rand in 1931 and is known as Draft B. What
appears to be a still slightly earlier version of Locke's first thoughts on the *Understanding* is a
document among the Shaftesbury Papers in the Public Record Office, to which P. Laslett has
drawn attention (*Mind*, January 1952, pp. 89–92).

1672. Lord Ashley himself probably was one of the group, others perhaps were Thomas Firmin and Nathaniel Hodges, chaplain to Lord Ashley, and we know from reports[1] that David Thomas and James Tyrrell came to the meetings, the latter having recorded his presence in a marginal note in his own copy of the *Essay*, now preserved in the British Museum. Locke informs us[2] that the topic discussed by the group at the outset was 'a subject very remote' from the special inquiries into the understanding which arose out of the discussions at a later stage and of which the *Essay* of 1690 was the final outcome. Tyrrell's comment on this point is more explicit. 'The discourse', he says, 'began about the principles of morality and reveal'd religion'. Now that we have come to know more about Locke's literary activities before 1671, Tyrrell's hint appears significant. I presume that the discussion among Locke's friends was at first about the law of nature as the basis of morality and its relation to natural and revealed religion. Locke's early thoughts on this topic served as a convenient starting-point; and some other member of the group, possibly Lord Ashley himself, may have contributed the short essay, originally among the Shaftesbury Papers,[3] beginning: 'The Light of Nature is reason set up in the soul at first by God in man's Creation, second by Christ.' But then, as Locke tells us, difficulties arose in the course of the discussion, possibly concerning the question how natural law comes to be known. This question had played a prominent part in Locke's essays, but we can understand if his solution of it left room for doubts and puzzles. So it was decided to start afresh and to approach the subject-matter under discussion on a strictly epistemological basis, i.e. to inquire into the origin and extent of human knowledge. The new course was taken up by Locke himself, and after reading out at the next meeting 'some hasty and undigested thoughts' he pursued his inquiries during the summer and autumn of 1671 in the two preliminary drafts of the *Essay* which we know.

Since the original question concerning the principles of morality and revealed religion had been shelved for the time being, we should not expect to find much discussion of it in either draft. However, there is a reference to it in both, which is of great interest in that it shows that Locke continued to bear in mind some of the leading ideas of his early speculations. Speaking of moral ideas or rules of our actions

---

[1] Cf. Fox Bourne, *The Life of John Locke*, 1876, i. 248, n. 2.
[2] *Essay, Epistle to the Reader* (ed. Fraser, i. 9).
[3] Cf. P. Laslett, 'Locke and the First Earl of Shaftesbury', *Mind*, January 1952, pp. 91–92.

which are not of our own making, his words are as follows:[1] 'But because we cannot come to a certain knowledge of those rules of our actions, without first making known a lawgiver with power and will to reward and punish and secondly without showing how he has declared his will and law, I must only at present suppose this rule till a fit place to speak of those, God, the law of nature, and revelation, and only at present mention what is to our present purpose.' We know now that, when writing these lines, Locke did not defer consideration of the questions mentioned because he had nothing explicit to say about them. On the contrary, with his essays on natural law probably lying in the drawer of his desk, his thoughts on the subject were far too detailed to be inserted within the small compass of a purely epistemological treatise. His intention, obviously, was to continue his investigation on a more comprehensive scale so as to be able to introduce into it the relevant material contained in his essays. The 'fit place' for such an insertion would have been in connexion with his discussion of moral ideas. In fact, it would seem that some of the importance he formerly attached to the doctrine of natural law stimulated him to the discussion of morality in the drafts. Moral relations are for him 'the most considerable of all', and in defining them as the conformity or disagreement between the actions of men and some rule or law, he might have had in mind the idea of *convenientia* which, in the essays, he had applied to the relation between natural law and human nature.

These, then, are the first points we have sought to establish—namely, (a) that Locke's early doctrine of natural law formed the starting-point for the discussions that gave rise to the drafts of the *Essay* of 1671, (b) that it is reflected in a paragraph of the drafts themselves, and (c) that it was intended to be made use of in further inquiries into the nature of moral ideas.

However, there is a much closer connexion between Locke's essays and his drafts of the *Essay*, and it seems we are justified in regarding the former as being in some sense the earliest draft of the *Essay*. Let us look at Draft A first. It opens with a detailed analysis of sensation, one of the three ways of knowing distinguished by Locke in the essays and the only one he had found adequate for a knowledge of natural law. The doctrine of innate ideas, which was shown in the essays to be mistaken, is not discussed by him at length in Draft A nor does he think it requires refutation there. Likewise tradition, the third way of

---

[1] Draft A, par. 26, p. 39. Draft B, par. 160, p. 303, has almost the same words. In my quotation I have modernized Locke's spelling and punctuation.

knowing considered by Locke for discussion but then dismissed by him in the context of the essays, drops out of account in Draft A; it only survives in occasional phrases such as 'report of others', 'testimony of historians', particularly in discussions about probability and faith,[1] where similar references to the grounds for believing in the existence of Caesar occur as in the section on tradition in the essays.[2] In this connexion Locke also refers briefly to the question of the general consent of men,[3] about which he has so much to say in the essays; like tradition, this question of a general consent is of no interest to him any more from the strictly epistemological point of view prevalent in Draft A. However, when giving his reasons for the rise of prejudice,[4] Locke takes over from his essays[5] almost *verbatim* a lengthy passage about the force of principles imbibed in childhood through the influence of education and hence accepted as unquestionable—a passage which in its original context was meant to explain how it happens that men believe their pet notions to be innate and to be laws of nature. Likewise, one of the rules distinguished by Locke in the drafts, whereby men arrive at their ideas of virtues and vices[6], was anticipated by him in the essays.[7] Furthermore, Locke's well-known doctrine that our knowledge reaches no further than what the mind can establish by comparing, uniting, enlarging, or refining simple ideas, was already set forth by him in his essays.[8] The same applies to his notion that maxims, identical propositions, moral ideas, and all our reasoning concerning God, spirits, and the like, are ultimately derived from sense-experience. Of special interest in this connexion is that the careful precautions Locke takes in Draft A[9] against a purely sensationalist doctrine have their counterpart in the stress he lays on the deductive powers of reason in the second and fourth essays.[10]

Let us now look at Draft B. Much of what has been said already in relation to Draft A applies to Draft B as well, but there are some

[1] Pars. 33 and 42d; the whole topic is again discussed more fully in the *Essay* of 1690, IV. xv. 4–6, xvi. 7–8, 10–11, xviii. 3–4 and 6, and 15–17.

[2] Second essay, f. 26. [3] Par. 34; also par. 25.

[4] Draft A, par. 42, pp. 63–64. [5] Third essay, ff. 42–45.

[6] Draft A, par. 25; Draft B, par. 157; this becomes the *law of reputation or fashion* in the *Essay* of 1690, II. xxviii. 10–12. [7] Second essay, f. 35.

[8] Second essay, f. 24; fourth essay, ff. 48–52. [9] Par. 43.

[10] There are further parallels between the essays and Draft A, e.g. the cause of ignorance, Draft A, par. 39, to be compared with the second essay, ff. 33–35; the difference between the wise and the foolish, possibly arising from a defect in the body's organs, Draft A, par. 41, to be compared with the third essay, f. 45; the certainty of knowledge when our eyes are open, Draft A, par. 31, p. 54, to be compared with the seventh essay, f. 101 (fin.).

further points of interest. Arguments borrowed from the essays, which are scattered throughout Draft A, are found mainly in the first part of Draft B (pars. 1–16). They are marshalled now for an elaborate attack upon innate knowledge, and it is this part of Draft B that has given rise to Book I of the *Essay*. However, the first part of Draft B differs from Book I of the *Essay* in precisely those aspects in which it agrees with the essays: it deals with practical principles before dealing with speculative principles, and with the latter much more briefly than the *Essay*, though not so briefly as the early essays.

Here are some details in which Draft B resembles the essays. It begins with an emphasis on the pre-eminence of man's understanding and a comparison between it and the eye;[1] this can be seen to correspond with Locke's emphasis on the light of nature and his analogy between it and sunlight in the essays.[2] In another passage[3] the nature of the understanding is illustrated by the simile of the dark room which is lit by the windows of sense; this simile also has its parallel in the essays.[4] Again, in both his writings Locke speaks of the senses providing the groundwork of all those sublime thoughts built up by the intellect and raised as high as heaven.[5] The suspicion that, because of the many different persuasions among men, there either is no truth or no knowledge of truth[6] has its counterpart in the suspicion, often expressed by Locke in the essays,[7] that either there is no natural law or this law cannot be known. The attack on innate ideas, opened in paragraph 4 of Draft B, is carried out with the help of much the same arguments that are familiar to the reader of the essays. Locke's points are (1) that the doctrine of innate ideas is a mere assertion which has so far never been proved, (2) that such a proof cannot be derived from the general consent of men or from the fact that men often agree about principles that appear to them self-evident, (3) that no such general consent does in fact exist, (4) that true notions can be arrived at only by a careful employment of men's faculties, (5) that speculative principles, generally accepted as innate because immediately assented to at first hearing, are not self-evident, and (6) that so-called innate principles least appear among children, idiots, savages, and illiterate people, in whose minds one would expect to discover them most readily.

---

[1] The analogy between the understanding and the eye, a favourite one with Locke, occurs in the *Essay* of 1690 in *The Epistle to the Reader* (ed. Fraser, i. 8), the *Introduction* (par. 1), and bk. iv, ch. xiii, par. 1.   [2] Third essay, f. 37, fourth essay, f. 47.

[3] Draft B, par. 31, p. 84.   [4] Fourth essay, f. 49.

[5] Draft B, par. 21, p. 69, to be compared with the fourth essay, f. 50.

[6] Draft B, par. 2, pp. 17–18.   [7] e.g. in the second essay, ff. 29–30.

The substance of all this teaching in Draft B is taken from the second, third, and fifth of Locke's essays, which general reference must suffice here.

Draft B differs from the essays in that it contains a greater number of arguments and presents these in a new order, and that its scope is wider. For while in the essays Locke confines himself to showing that it is the knowledge of natural law only that is not innate and cannot be derived from the general consent of men, in Draft B he seeks to disprove innate knowledge in general. As regards Locke's illustrations in the two works, it appears that very often they are more abundant and more explicit in the essays, as where it is shown that self-preservation is disregarded in India.[1] On the other hand, a single brief reference in the fifth essay[2] to the beliefs of the inhabitants of Saldanha Bay and of peoples in Brazil is repeated more than once both in Draft B and in the *Essay* of 1690. More important, however, is the relation between Locke's discussion of God's existence in the essays and that in Draft B. In the fourth essay he makes use of two arguments for God's existence, the anthropological argument and the one from design, both of which he bases upon the evidence of the senses; he also refers to the argument from conscience and to Descartes's argument from the idea of God, with neither of which he is altogether satisfied. In Draft B, the less philosophical proofs, i.e. the arguments from design and from conscience, are not at all mentioned. The anthropological argument, however, is again introduced, and it is broadened so as to include the cosmological argument, while Descartes's argument from the idea of God is now fully discussed but definitively rejected.[3]

We may conclude then that to a certain extent Locke's drafts of the *Essay* of 1671 were quarried out of his early essays on the law of nature. It is true that the drafts were meant by him as epistemological inquiries into the extent and limitations of knowledge, containing a wealth of new discussion ranging from the principles of empiricism, the nature and origin of ideas, and the signification of words to inquiries into cause and effect, substance, space, time, number, and infinity. But though the drafts were thus professedly divorced by Locke from his previous interests in the principles of morality and religion, some of the inspiration and material of his speculations on natural law could

---

[1] Fifth essay, ff. 74–76, to be compared with the short passage in Draft B, par. 6.
[2] f. 76.
[3] Par. 94, pp. 203–8; par. 140, pp. 281–3. There are corresponding passages in Draft A (par. 2, pp. 9–10; par. 16, pp. 30–31), but they are not fully worked out.

conveniently be fitted into their scheme. The essays that were exploited by him for his design in 1671, i.e. essays II to V, are precisely
those dealing with epistemological matters; the essays that were of less
interest to him then are those dealing with questions of morality and
theology. Among the themes transferred by him from the essays to
the drafts are the principles of empiricism, arguments against the
theory of innate ideas, and views concerning the general consent of
men, maxims, moral relations, and the existence of God. While the
illustrations used in the drafts are also often the same as those in the
essays, they are not always intended to prove the same points, and thus
there are differences in order as well as in emphasis. I suggest, then,
that the importance of Locke's essays on natural law in relation to his
later writings lies precisely in the fact that much of his epistemological
theory, as stated in the essays, is reproduced by him in the two drafts of
the *Essay* of 1671, which in their turn contain the germ of his final
doctrine concerning human understanding. As to Locke's early doctrine of natural law, on the other hand, we have found that only that
aspect of it which is concerned with the relation between actions and
a rule is elaborated by him in the drafts, whereas most of its metaphysical and theological aspects are lost sight of by him during the year
1671. With the publication of Richard Cumberland's treatise on the
law of nature in 1672 Locke might indeed have given up the thought
of publishing his own essays on the subject.

We turn now to the remaining part of our survey of the development of Locke's theories. His chief interest after 1671 lay in a fuller
presentation of his views on the understanding. The published Journals
for the years he spent in France (1675–1679) show how he sometimes
pursued this interest in connexion with a study of Descartes[1] and the
thinkers of Port-Royal.[2] His entries, however, reveal that on some
occasions his mind returned to reflections about the existence of God
and the nature of law, and that he also made it part of his study to
observe the 'opinions or traditions' among men concerning God, Creation, Revelation, and duty.[3] His Journals for 1681 and 1682 contain
further passages on our knowledge of God by natural reason and a

[1] For details see Charlotte S. Ware, 'The Influence of Descartes on John Locke', *Revue intern. de philos.*, April 1950.
[2] Cf. the entry for 29 July 1676 (ed. Aaron, pp. 81–82), where one of Pierre Nicole's *Essais de Morale* is discussed and where the influence of Pascal (*Pensées*, fr. 451, p. 954, ed. Pléjade) is also noticeable in connexion with Locke's views on atheism.
[3] Cf. Journal of 29 July 1676 (ed. Aaron, pp. 81–82), and 4 Sept. 1677 (pp. 92–93), respectively.

number of references to arguments for His existence advanced by
Cudworth in *The True Intellectual System of the Universe* (1678).[1]
About that time Locke must have carried forward his preparatory
work on the *Essay* to such an extent that it already included the substance of his views concerning God's existence as we find them in the
tenth chapter of Book IV in the final version of 1690. For in January
1683 the Earl of Shaftesbury talked of this chapter on his death-bed
in Holland.[2]

From the unpublished entries in Locke's Journal for 1681[3] we
learn that during June of this year his attention was again drawn to
the idea of the law of nature. He bought the works of Pufendorf and
the 1666 edition of Hooker's *Laws of Ecclesiastical Polity*,[4] and he
took numerous excerpts from the 1676 edition of Hooker's *Works*,
all being from the opening paragraphs of Book I of his *Laws*.[5] The
longest and most interesting excerpt is from paragraph 3,[6] where
Hooker, in preference to a legislative ethics and 'somewhat more
enlarging the sense of law', adopts the Thomistic definition of it as
'any kind of rule or canon whereby actions are framed'. It would
seem that consideration of Hooker's position, at that time, contributed
to a further weakening of Locke's voluntarist theory of law and, in
addition, to the establishment of his view that, while men arrive at
moral ideas by a comparison of their actions to a rule, this rule can be
threefold, i.e. the divine law (of which natural law is a branch), the
civil law, and the law of reputation or fashion.[7] It is of great interest
in this connexion to find that after quoting a passage from Bk. I, par. 9,
of Hooker's *Laws*, where it is said that man's observation of the law
of his own nature is righteousness and his transgression of this law sin,
Locke noted down in his Journal some remarks of his own, which
have not hitherto been printed.[8] He writes: 'The observation of the
laws of one country *officium civile*, the breach of a penal law *crimen* or
delictum; the observation of what in any country is thought enjoined
by the law of nature *virtus*, the contrary *vitium*; the observation or
omission of what is in credit and esteem anywhere *laus* and *vituperium*;

---

[1] Cf. Journal of 3 April 1681 (pp. 114–16), and of 18 Feb. 1681 (p. 118), respectively.
[2] Thomas Cherry to Thomas Hearne, 25 July 1706 (*Letters addressed to Hearne*, ed. Ouvry, 1874), quoted by Fox Bourne, op. cit. i. 469.
[3] MS. Locke f. 5.   [4] pp. 62, 66, 67.   [5] pp. 69, 73–86.
[6] pp. 74–75.   [7] *Essay*, II. xxviii. 7.
[8] The entries on p. 86 of the Journal for 1681, which have been printed by Mr. Gough (*John Locke's Political Philosophy*, 1950, p. 22, n. 2) as views held by Locke on the law of nature, are extracts by Locke from Hooker's *Works*, 1676, pp. 82–83.

licitum is what is not forbidden or commanded by the laws of the society. *Indifferens* what is so by all the other laws.'[1] These remarks in conjunction with the sentence quoted from Hooker form the basis of Locke's distinction in the *Essay* between the three sorts of rules or laws to which men compare their actions and in relation to which they judge whether or not their actions are sins, crimes, or vices, respectively. In the two drafts of the *Essay* of 1671, we must remember, Locke distinguished only between two such rules, i.e. the divine law, and the fashion of the country. On 26 June 1681, when studying Hooker, Locke also noted down in his Journal a belief in the demonstrability of ethics[2] similar to the one which he expressed in his seventh essay on natural law and which he reiterated in his *Essay* of 1690.[3] One of the reasons for Locke's renewed interest in the theory of natural law and the principles of morality during 1681 may well have been the publication in that year of Samuel Parker's treatise on the law of nature,[4] in which the idea of a demonstrated science of ethics was set forth along the lines laid down by Cumberland in his work of 1672. Locke, certainly, must have been surprised at finding striking resemblances between Parker's treatise and his own essays,[5] and the points of difference between the two writings[6] must likewise have roused his interest. Another possible reason why the nature of law attracted Locke's attention in 1681 is this: For most of that year he lived in Oxford at the home of his friend Tyrrell, who was then publishing his *Patriarcha non Monarcha*, a refutation of Filmer's patriarchal theory of Divine Right. Throughout this treatise Tyrrell appeals to the law of nature and refers to Grotius, Selden, and Pufendorf. Since we know that in the years 1681–3 Locke and Tyrrell together

---

[1] Journal of 28 June 1681, pp. 86–87 (the spelling and punctuation in this quotation are my own); cf. similar remarks in Locke's Journal for 4 Sept. 1677 (ed. Aaron, p. 93).

[2] Printed by Aaron, p. 116. There is nothing corresponding to this in the drafts of the *Essay* of 1671.

[3] IV. iii. 18.

[4] *A Demonstration of the Divine Authority of the Law of Nature and of the Christian Religion.*

[5] Parker argues against *inscriptio* or innate notions and for the view that knowledge of the law of nature is derived from reason and sense-experience (pt. i, par. 2, pp. 6–7); he believes that 'all that is requisite to make a law or enact an obligation is (1) the declaration of the will of the lawmaker to all his subjects that are capable of observing it, (2) the engaging their obedience to it by the sanctions of rewards and punishments' (Preface, xix–xx, pt. i, par. 1, p. 4, and par. 4, pp. 23–24).

[6] Unlike Locke, Parker believes that 'the consent of nations is a great proof and confirmation of the laws of nature' (pt. i, par. 3, pp. 11–12), and that man's natural instincts make these laws known to him (pt. i, par. 7, pp. 42 ff.).

wrote a lengthy paper in defence of nonconformity,[1] we may assume that Locke's interest in the nature of law during 1681 was stimulated, if not aroused, by Tyrrell's book and by discussions between the two friends.

Between September 1683 and February 1689, when living in exile in Holland, Locke does not seem to have carried his study of natural law farther than by taking excerpts, in one of his memoranda books,[2] from a review of a book written jointly by Pufendorf and some of his friends. The years in Holland, on the other hand, were most formative years in the career of the author of the *Essay*, and there is one piece of evidence that shows in what particular and decisive manner the direction of his thought during those years affected the scheme of his early doctrine of natural law. Let us therefore examine the document in question.

One of Locke's papers in the Lovelace Collection bears the title *Of Ethick in General*.[3] It is attached to another dealing with a division of the sciences into physics, ethics, and logic.[4] This latter paper bears marks by Locke indicating that it was to become chapter 20 of Book IV of the *Essay*, and in the first edition (1690) chapter 20 of Book IV, the last chapter of the whole work, did in fact treat 'Of the division of the sciences' in the manner previously planned by Locke.[5] From reference marks by Locke in the paper *Of Ethick in General* we learn that he intended it to follow the paper on division and to become chapter 21 of Book IV of the *Essay*. From the manner in which Locke marked both papers[6] it is obvious that they were written during the last years of his visit to Holland, when he formed a habit of regrouping his chapters before finally fixing their order for the first edition of the *Essay*. Having ascertained the purpose, context, and time of composi-

---

[1] MS. Locke c. 34; extracts printed in Lord King's *Life* (1858), pp. 346–58.

[2] MS. Locke c. 33, fols. 29–30. The date of Locke's entry is 22 Jan. 1686/7. The review is printed in the *Bibliothèque universelle et historique* for Sept. 1686, iii. 485–97.

[3] MS. Locke c. 28, fols. 146–52; printed in Lord King's *Life* (1858), pp. 308–13. Mr. Gough (*John Locke's Political Philosophy*, 1950, p. 7, n. 2), in a remark on this paper, has confused it with another in Locke's commonplace book of 1661, printed in Lord King's *Life*, pp. 292–3, and reprinted by Fox Bourne (op. cit. i. 162–4).

[4] MS. Locke c. 28, fols. 155–6ᵛ.

[5] By insertion of the chapter on 'Enthusiasm' (iv. xix) in the fourth (1700) and following editions of the *Essay*, Book IV came to have twenty-one chapters and the one on the division of the sciences became chapter 21.

[6] At first the chapter on division was to be the twenty-third and that on ethics the twenty-fourth, then the former was made successively the twentieth, the twenty-first, and again the twentieth, while the latter suffered corresponding changes and became the twenty-first, then the twenty-second, and again the twenty-first.

tion of the paper on ethics, we can show now what it is that makes it interesting for us here.

The paper is a comprehensive account of Locke's thoughts on morality. Such an account is in fact wanted at the end of the *Essay*, for Locke's statements on ethics, scattered as they are throughout the *Essay*, are for the most part inconsistent. Besides, of the three divisions of the sciences mapped out in chapter 20, only two, i.e. *natural philosophy* and the *doctrine of signs*, are treated thoroughly in Locke's work, while the third, i.e. *ethics*, is only touched on lightly. In section 3 of the paper we are told that morality, being 'the great business and concernment of mankind, deserves our most attentive application and study', and that it is 'the proper province of philosophers, a sort of men different from priests and lawyers: a plain argument to me of some discovery still amongst men of the law of nature'. In section 10 Locke proceeds to speak of the proper and true foundation of the rules of good and evil, and in the following section,[1] where he refers to the will of a lawgiver and the law of nature as prerequisites for the knowledge of these moral rules, he repeats the statement we have quoted earlier from the two drafts of the *Essay* of 1671,[2] and again defers discussion of these questions 'till a fit place'. Whereas in the drafts this discussion is nowhere forthcoming, section 12 of the paper on ethics shows signs of taking it up in this way: 'To establish morality, therefore, upon its proper basis, and such foundations as may carry an obligation with them, we must first prove a law, which always supposes a law-maker: one that has a superiority and right to ordain, and also a power to reward and punish.' After remarking that this sovereign law-maker is God, 'whose existence we have already proved' (i.e. in *Essay*, IV. x), Locke goes on to say: 'The next thing then to show is, that there are certain rules, certain dictates, which it is his will all men should conform their actions to, and that this will of his is sufficiently promulgated and made known to all mankind.' Here the paper ends, contrary to the expectation raised by the last sentence. It would appear then that until shortly before the publication of the first edition of the *Essay* Locke's plan was to deal in his paper on ethics in some detail with the subject treated by him in his essays on natural law and possibly to incorporate some parts of these in what he intended then to be the

[1] Section 11, beginning 'but because we cannot come to the knowledge of those rules', and section 12, beginning 'To establish morality, therefore, upon its proper basis', are not indicated as such in Lord King's edition.
[2] p. 62, above. Draft A, par. 26, p. 39; Draft B, par. 160, p. 303.

concluding chapter of his major work. We are faced now with the question why Locke did not continue this paper on ethics and omitted it from the *Essay*, thereby leaving the latter with such an unsatisfactory conclusion as the chapter on the division of the sciences.

One answer to this question can be derived from the paper on ethics itself, and I shall deal with it before suggesting several others.

Sections 7 and 8 of the paper contain some definitions of morality, stated in hedonistic terms. Moral good or evil, according to Locke, derives its name from a tendency in objects to produce pleasure or pain in a person, by the intervention of his will.[1] This element of hedonism in Locke's doctrine is absent from the two drafts of the *Essay* of 1671 and it first appears, probably as a result of his contact with the Gassendists during his sojourn in France, in some shorthand entries in his Journal for 1676,[2] which anticipate the chapter on pleasure and pain in the *Essay* of 1690.[3] Before the development of his hedonistic theory Locke accepted moral goodness as the name for 'the rectitude of actions, which is nothing but the conformity of the actions of men to some rule'.[4] When his ethics became hedonistic, he attempted to reconcile it with his earlier doctrine by conceiving of moral goodness or badness as the reward or punishment, i.e. the pleasure or pain, following the observation or breach of a law made by God.[5] Locke's emphasis on rewards and punishments as the enforcements of God's will became in fact stronger in proportion to the growth of his hedonistic theory. In his early essays on natural law he noted, but he never stressed, the connexion between God's law and the sanctions engaging men's obedience to it.[6] His view there was that the divine law lays an obligation on the conscience, 'so that men are not bound by fear of punishment but by a rational apprehension of what is right'.[7] For Pufendorf, Cumberland, and Parker, on the other hand, the divine rewards or punishments annexed to the observance or neglect of a moral precept were a necessary condition for its validity. Perhaps under their influence Locke adapted his early assumptions concerning natural law to his hedonistic theory.

However, the two strands in Locke's ethical thought are not easily

[1] Sect. 8. Prof. Aaron (*John Locke*, 1937, p. 261) seems to me to imply that Locke is speaking here of the intervention of God's will, but this can hardly be the case, since Locke throughout sections 7 and 8 means by 'an intelligent free agent' a human person, not God.
[2] These are printed now for the first time in the present volume, pp. 263 ff.
[3] II. xx.   [4] Draft A, par. 4, p. 11.
[5] *Of Ethick in General*, sects. 8–9; *Essay*, II. xxviii. 5.
[6] Fifth essay, f. 76; sixth essay, f. 85.   [7] Sixth essay, ff. 85–86.

assimilated to one another. To hold a belief in an ultimate moral law, or law of nature, and to maintain that 'good and bad, being relative terms, do not denote anything in the nature of the thing, but only the relation it bears to another, in its aptness and tendency to produce in it pleasure or pain',[1] is to express two doctrines which, if not altogether incompatible, are bound to produce vacillation and vagueness in the mind of him who holds them. That they can lead to open conflict is shown by a passage[2] in section 8 of the paper on ethics, in which sympathy with hedonism is expressed in a radical form and which Locke afterwards deleted, obviously at the time when he intended to pursue his discussion on natural law at the end of the paper. The first and larger part of the passage is as follows:

> Why does a man pay another a debt he owes him when he wants the money to supply his own conveniences or necessities? Or why does another forbear his neighbour's wife? It will perhaps be answered because there is moral rectitude and goodness in the one, and moral turpitude or illness in the other. Good words. This moral rectitude, which when considered is but conformity to the natural law of God, would signify nothing and moral goodness be no reason to direct my action, were there not really pleasure that would follow from the doing of it and pain avoided greater than is to be found in the action itself.

The passage, I think, reveals the inherent difficulty in the issue between Locke's hedonism and his belief in an absolute system of moral principles.[3] Since he wished to retain both, he had on the one hand to avoid strong hedonistic expressions in his theory of the nature of the good, and on the other to show reserve in putting his case for natural law and the 'proper basis' of morality. Thus in the paper on ethics he advanced the discussion of this law as little as he did in the *Essay* of 1690. On the other hand, three years after the publication of the *Essay* in a context where he had not to fear the competing force of his belief in natural law, Locke formulated on a commonplace sheet[4] a thought not unlike the one he had previously suppressed in his paper on ethics. This, too, is unpublished, and I will quote it in full.

> Voluntas: That which has very much confounded men about the will and its determination has been the confounding of the notion of moral rectitude and giving it the name of moral good.[5] The pleasure that a man takes in any action

---

[1] *Of Ethick in General*, sect. 7.
[2] The passage was not printed by Lord King. It occurs between the second and third sentence of section 8 (p. 311), following after 'does not bring pain to him'.
[3] For some compromise solution of the difficulty in the *Essay* see Locke's chapter 'Of Power' (II. xxi. 68–72). [4] MS. Locke c. 28, fol. 114ᵛ, dated 1693.
[5] Locke himself did this in Draft A, par. 4, p. 11, quoted above, p. 71.

or expects as a consequence of it is indeed a good in the self able and proper to move the will. But the moral rectitude of it considered barely in itself is not good or evil nor any way moves the will, but as pleasure and pain either accompanies the action itself or is looked on to be a consequence of it. Which is evident from the punishments and rewards which God has annexed to moral rectitude or pravity as proper motives to the will, which would be needless if moral rectitude were in itself good and moral pravity evil. J.L.[1]

With hedonism becoming a definitive part of his ethical teaching, Locke's earlier thoughts on natural law and moral obligation, particularly the line he had taken against utilitarianism in his eighth essay, could not easily be resumed in the writings of his maturity. As we have seen, James Tyrrell, who between 1687 and 1692 frequently urged Locke to publish his essays, obtained no response.

There were other reasons, however, which made it difficult for Locke to pursue his old interest in the law of nature, and these reasons are found in the scheme of the *Essay* itself, to which we must now turn.

Let us begin with Book III, in which Locke deals with the nature of words. Except for the opening sentence,[2] this part of the *Essay* shows no trace of any of the notions expressed by Locke in his essays on natural law, but there can be no doubt that the problems raised by him in Book III forced themselves on him in the course of his prolonged inquiries into morality. Throughout the last three chapters of this Book, where he deals with the 'imperfection' and 'abuse' of words and suggests ways of remedy, he urges the necessity of defining the exact meaning of words especially in the province of morals.[3] 'In the interpretations of laws', he exclaims, 'whether divine or human, there is no end';[4] and thus, 'in discourses of religion, law, and morality, . . . there will be the greatest difficulty'.[5]

The result of Locke's examination is twofold. (*a*) Because, on account of the imperfections of language, the will of God, as revealed in the Scriptures, is liable to doubt and uncertainty, men must turn to the light of reason and the precepts of natural religion, from which

---

[1] A similar line of thought is taken up by Locke in the same manuscript, fol. 113, under the entry 'Ethica'.

[2] To be compared with a passage concerning language as the tie of society in the fourth essay, f. 61.

[3] That the chief purpose of Locke's discussion here is to stress the linguistic difficulties inherent in moral speculations is illustrated by his frequent use of the phrase 'especially in moral matters', and the like. The point seems never to have been noticed, except perhaps by Å. Petzäll ('Ethics and Epistemology in John Locke's Essay', &c., *Göteborgs Högskolas Årsskrift*, xliii, 1937, 2, p. 72). [4] III. ix. 9 (ed. Fraser, ii. 109).

[5] III. ix. 22 (ii. 120); cf. also III. x. 12–13 (ii. 130–1).

they can derive plainly and without fail all that it is necessary for them to know about God and the obedience they owe Him.[1] Their concern is 'to know things as they are, and to do what they ought, and not to spend their lives in talking about them'.[2] Thus, while on the one hand the 'fountains of knowledge, which are in things themselves' can never be corrupted, no matter what ill use is made of language,[3] knowledge itself and the study of things are at all times beset with the difficulties of language and cannot therefore be really advanced. The upshot, then, of Locke's discussion would seem to be that he and others should not take trouble over arguments concerning the nature of law and morality, for 'were the imperfections of language, as the instrument of knowledge, more thoroughly weighed, a great many of the controversies that make such a noise in the world, would of themselves cease'.[4]

(*b*) At the same time, it is Locke's considered opinion that most disputes in the world, being merely verbal, would end of themselves if the terms introduced into them were clearly defined;[5] and since, according to him, there are good reasons for claiming that moral terms can be exactly defined, he is 'bold to think that morality is capable of demonstration, as well as mathematics'.[6] There is no need for us here to enter again into this favourite theme of Locke's ethical theory. It is sufficient to remark that this part of his teaching is left by him as little substantiated as his treatment of the foundations of morality anywhere in the *Essay*. The fact that Locke's reticence shows itself in relation to two lines of ethical thought suggests that for him these are interdependent. In Book III their relationship is this: the necessity of observing the law of nature is the lesson drawn from the *imperfection* of language; the demonstrative certainty of morality is the consequence of remedying its *abuse*. In Book IV, where Locke repeats his vindication of the demonstrability of ethics,[7] he introduces it in connexion with views familiar to the reader of his essays on natural law. There is reason to suppose, then, that Locke's theory of the law of nature lacks detailed treatment in the *Essay* and elsewhere in his mature works in

---

[1] III. ix. 23 (ii. 120–1).
[2] III. x. 13 (ii. 131); cf. also Locke's 'Introduction' to the *Essay*, pars. 5–7.
[3] III. xi. 5 (ii. 149).   [4] III. ix. 21 (ii. 119–20).
[5] III. xi. 7 (II. 151).   [6] III. xi. 15–16 (ii. 156–7).
[7] IV. iii. 18 (ii. 208). This section as well as a third passage in the *Essay*, where Locke maintains that morality is capable of demonstration (I. ii. 1), contains the same illustration, i.e. the proposition concerning the angles of a triangle, as the passage in his seventh essay on natural law, where he maintains that the binding force of the law of nature is universal.

proportion as he found himself at a loss to give full expression to his view of the demonstrative character of morality. Just as he never succeeded in this latter task, despite the frequent encouragements of his friend William Molyneux in the years 1692 and 1696, so he proved irresponsive to Tyrrell's repeated requests to publish his essays on natural law. Admittedly, the converse of the argument we have advanced is equally possible, and we might say that Locke's inability to make known the law of nature as the rule of moral actions and to establish it as the chief premiss of a demonstrable science of ethics was the reason for his failure to treat ethics on the mathematical method. His inability in this direction is shown in the last, unfinished, section of his paper *Of Ethick in General*, where he proposes to 'establish morality upon its proper basis' and to prove the existence of a law of nature. Though the latter line of explanation may appear preferable, the question which is the right one remains a matter of pure conjecture. If we accept the latter explanation and regard Locke's scanty exposition of natural law in the *Essay* as the cause, rather than the effect, of his undeveloped theory of the demonstrable nature of moral principles, we are still left with two reasons which explain why Locke did not more fully discuss natural law in his *Essay*—namely his growing belief in hedonism, and his scepticism about language.

There is, however, one more reason that prevented Locke from making inquiries in the *Essay* into an absolute standard of morality. It is true that in Books I and II he often makes use of such expressions as 'the true ground of morality', 'the unchangeable rule of right and wrong, which the law of God hath established', 'the true boundaries of the law of nature, which ought to be the rule of virtue and vice'. Throughout these parts of the *Essay*, obviously the earliest in order of composition, Locke adheres to the essential ideas set forth in his essays on natural law, and he appeals to the 'light of reason' or the 'candle of the Lord' as the means of arriving at the knowledge of the divine lawmaker and of an eternal morality. None of these notions, however, is properly analysed or even discussed by Locke in the *Essay*; they figure rather as presuppositions of his teaching. In Book II, chapter xxviii, where he distinguishes between three sorts of rules or laws, in accordance with which men generally judge of the moral worth of their actions, he briefly comments on the divine law as one of these rules, and rather fully on the civil law, and the law of fashion. Yet in his two early drafts of the *Essay* and in his paper *Of Ethick in General* it was precisely in this context that he promised his reader to speak

Introduction

elsewhere more fully of God and the law of nature. The promise, we have seen, is fulfilled only to a limited extent in the paper on ethics and nowhere in the drafts; it is not even repeated in the *Essay*. Instead, Locke's aim here is to show how, as a matter of fact, men come by their moral ideas, regardless of whether the rules to which they compare their actions so as to arrive at moral ideas are true or false. This project is part of the novel scheme of the *Essay*: it reflects Locke's 'historical, plain method' and his self-chosen task to inquire into the 'original and nature' of ideas rather than into the ultimate nature of things. Its merit lies in the attempt to define different kinds of moral evaluation rather than to consider morality as the embodiment of absolute standards of truth.

Misunderstandings and criticisms regarding Locke's way of treating morality in this part of his main work arose soon after the *Essay* was published. Some of the difficulties, as they appeared to critics in Oxford, were pointed out to Locke in letters from Tyrrell,[1] who seized the opportunity of urging his friend again to publish his essays on natural law in order thereby to clarify his position and remove any suspicion of Hobbism. Locke, in his reply, laid stress on three points, the last of which is of interest to us here. He explains that by the divine law he means both the law of nature and God's revealed law, that demonstration in matters of morality has its limits,[2] and that the scruples raised by his critics are due to a misunderstanding of his design in the *Essay*. 'I know not how you would still have me, besides my purpose, and against all rules of method, run out into a discourse of the divine law, show how and when it was promulgated to mankind, demonstrate its enforcement by rewards and punishments in another life, in a place where I had nothing to do with all this, and in a case where some men's bare supposition of such a law, whether true or false, served my turn.'[3] And again: 'For I did not design to treat of the grounds of true morality, . . . my business was only to show whence men had moral ideas, and what they were.'[4]

Nevertheless, Locke took his critics' exceptions to heart: in the second edition of the *Essay* (1694) he made two additions to the section

---

[1] MS. Locke c. 22; letters of 30 June 1690, 27 July 1690, 30 Aug. 1690. I have not thought it necessary to reproduce here the relevant passages in these unpublished letters of Tyrrell, since their contents are reflected in Locke's reply to Tyrrell of 4 Aug. 1690, which is printed in Lord King's *Life* (1858), pp. 198–201.

[2] Cf. also Locke's 'Introduction' to the *Essay*, par. 5, fin.

[3] Lord King's *Life* (1858), p. 200.

[4] Ibid., p. 201.

dealing with the divine law,[1] and in one of these he emphasized the point that the divine law 'is the only true touchstone of moral rectitude'. He adopted a similar attitude towards the objections raised by James Lowde in the preface to his *Discourse Concerning the Nature of Man* (1694). He repudiated Lowde's charge that in the chapter of the *Essay* under discussion the author's intention was 'to make virtue vice and vice virtue'.[2] 'In the place he quotes I only report as a matter of fact what *others* call virtue and vice.' Locke felt confident that, if Lowde had considered what was said in another passage of that chapter and elsewhere in the *Essay*, he would have known what the author thought of the 'eternal and unalterable nature of right and wrong', what he called virtue and vice, and that he regarded the law of nature as the 'standing and unalterable rule by which men ought to judge of the moral rectitude and gravity of their actions, and accordingly denominate them virtues or vices'. When Thomas Burnet, in his *Remarks* on the *Essay* (1697), wished to know 'upon what ground [Locke] will build the divine law, when he pursues morality to a demonstration', and insinuated that for Locke 'the distinction of virtue and vice was to be picked up by our eyes, or ears, or our nostrils', Locke snubbed his critic with an evasive reply on the first point and a contemptuous one on the second.[3]

Our impression of the reason and nature of this whole controversy can be summed up in this way. Throughout the *Essay* Locke showed himself a faithful advocate of natural law and in vindicating the novel aspects of his ethical teaching against some of his critics he kept stressing his belief in an eternal and objective morality. He did not, however, develop the details of his natural-law theory nor did he explain the ground on which his moral faith rested. Perhaps, as an ideal law or as a presupposition of his thought, natural law to him was not capable of further explanation. His views of a demonstrable science of morals were not, in their turn, sufficiently clear or elaborated by him to give rise to such an explanation. Besides, his hedonism and his philosophy of language had now made it difficult for him to attempt a full exposition of natural law. Furthermore, in the *Essay* his chief design concerning ethical matters was to consider the ideas of moral

---

[1] II. xxviii. 8; cf. also the addition to a passage in I. ii. 18, where Locke speaks of 'the rule prescribed by God' as 'the true and only measure of virtue'.

[2] *Essay, The Epistle to the Reader* (ed. Fraser, i. 17–19).

[3] *An Answer to Remarks*, appended to Locke's *Second Letter* to Stillingfleet (*Works*, 1801, iv. 187–8). Cf. also Noah Porter's 'Marginalia Lockiana' (*New Englander and Yale Review*, July 1887) and Fraser's extracts from it in his edition of Locke's *Essay* (i. 71, n. 1).

relations, i.e. the range and the different kinds of moral rules to which men refer their actions and valuations in real life. For the purposes of an examination like this God's revealed law and the law of nature occupied no higher rank than any other of such rules nor did divine sanctions carry a greater force than those attached to the civil law or the law of reputation. Within the scheme of the *Essay* Locke's intention was not to deal with the absolute and universal grounds of morality but with the variable moral ideas in men's minds and the several origins of their individual consciences.

In view of all the novel teaching in the *Essay* and of Locke's new lines of approach in matters of morality it is not surprising to find that the thought of publishing his early work on natural law receded from his mind and that the moral doctrines of his youth were not wholly absorbed in the writings of his maturity. There was, however, as we have shown earlier, a variety of material in the early essays which Locke included in his two drafts of the *Essay* of 1671; and this, as is to be expected, was incorporated by him in the final version of the *Essay* of 1690. It is of interest to note, however, that in certain passages of the *Essay* this material must have been derived by Locke directly from the essays, and not from the presentation of it in the drafts of 1671. For instance, his reference to the inhabitants of Saldanha Bay in *Essay*, I. iii. 8, like that in the fifth essay[1] but unlike that in Draft B,[2] is preceded by the remark that there is no law without a law-maker, a fact which does seem to indicate that the reference in the *Essay* was taken by Locke directly from his essays. Besides, several of the borrowings from the essays in the *Essay* of 1690 are altogether new, that is to say they do not appear in the drafts of 1671 at all. This fact would seem to show that Locke's process of exploiting useful material contained in his essays continued while his thought of publishing them separately diminished. Even after 1690, in chapters and passages added in new editions of the *Essay*, he continued to derive from his essays a number of arguments which he had not previously used. There is no need to specify again every detail of Locke's borrowings, but the following few points may be mentioned.

Most of Locke's borrowings from the essays in the *Essay* of 1690 are found in Book I, and here the most exploited essay is the fifth, containing Locke's arguments concerning the general consent of men. These arguments, in fact, together with the many illustrations concerning justice, piety, chastity, polytheism, and men's transgression of

[1] f. 76.   [2] Par. 4, p. 22.

moral rules, could conveniently be reproduced by him in his polemic against innate knowledge in the *Essay*. To say this is not to maintain that Locke's transfer of arguments from one context to the other was justifiable, or that his arguments in either context were good ones. On the contrary, the soundness of his teaching in Book I of the *Essay* is largely impaired by what we can now recognize as the survival of very early, immature notions of his. One of the few interesting and valuable arguments in Locke's fifth essay,[1] however, suggested a passage in Book IV, chapter xx, paragraph 8 in the *Essay* and was again taken up by him at some length in his chapter 'Of Enthusiasm',[2] added in the fourth edition of the *Essay* in 1700. In this chapter, as Fraser has rightly pointed out,[3] Locke appears to argue against the extravagant beliefs of the sects under the Commonwealth, which had vexed him in his early years and against which Henry More[4] had warned his readers a few years before Locke composed his essays on natural law. It is of interest to discover that one argument in this chapter is taken directly from Locke's early essays which were written at the time when his mind had only recently been irritated by the fancies and pretensions of such enthusiasts as the Quakers. In this chapter, as indeed in several others in the latter part of Book IV of the *Essay*, the voice of Culverwel[5] can again be recognized, this time in connexion with the doctrine of faith and reason, a topic not discussed by Locke in his essays, despite the fundamental treatment afforded to it in Culverwel's *Discourse of the Light of Nature* and the substantial influence of this work on the young Locke. In the *Essay* chapter on 'Faith and Reason', however, and also in the chapters 'Of Probability' and 'Of the Degrees of Assent', several of Locke's views concerning testimony and tradition can be traced back to notions expressed by him in his second and fifth essays. Another argument in the *Essay*,[6] which Locke anticipated in his essays,[7] though not in the two drafts of the *Essay* of 1671, is about the final cause of the ideas of pleasure and pain. In this argument Locke explains that, unless God, by His infinite wisdom and goodness, had joined the perception of pleasure to some objects of human thought

---

[1] ff. 79–80.   [2] IV. xix. 10.

[3] In his edition of the *Essay*, ii. 431, n. 2; p. 432, n. 1.

[4] In his *Enthusiasmus Triumphatus*, 1656; cf. also *An Explanation of the Grand Mystery of Godliness*, 1660, bk. III, ch. ix, par. 5.

[5] John Cairns, in J. Brown's edition of Culverwel's *Discourse*, 1857, p. liv, has drawn attention to the close resemblance between a passage in Locke's *Essay*, IV. xix. 4, and a passage in Culverwel's *Discourse*, ch. xvi, p. 222.

[6] II. vii. 3–6.   [7] Cf. the fourth essay, ff. 56 and 59.

and the perception of pain to others, man, despite his faculties of understanding and will, would be left unemployed and unmotivated. Locke's hedonistic development of this argument in another part of the *Essay*,[1] however, formed no part of his early teaching in the essays; he first embarked on it in some shorthand entries in his Journal for 1676, printed at the end of the present volume.

If we turn now to Locke's *Two Treatises of Government* and compare these with his essays on natural law, we are led to the same general conclusions at which we have arrived in the previous discussion.

The *Two Treatises* were published in 1690, the same year as the *Essay*, and, as we shall see presently, they had a share in the spoils of the essays. A point to be first taken notice of, however, is that, despite the basic importance of the idea of natural law for Locke's political theory, there is scarcely a fuller discussion of it in this work than in any other of his mature writings. In a passage of the *Second Treatise*[2] he expressly declines an investigation of the particulars of this law, though of course he still believes that there is such a law. For his purposes in this treatise it was sufficient to have introduced the idea of a law of nature as the declaration of God's will and as the standard of right and wrong.

From the following examples it will be seen that several of Locke's remarks, not only about the law of nature but also other topics dealt with in the *Two Treatises*, especially in the *Second Treatise*, have their original in passages of his early essays.

There is his doctrine that there is a 'plain difference between the state of nature and the state of war', and that 'the state of nature has a law of nature to govern it, which obliges every one and . . . which willeth the peace and preservation of all mankind'.[3]

The law of nature, for Locke, is a law of reason, unwritten, and to be found only in the minds of men;[4] since it is made known by reason only, and since children and idiots are destitute of the use of reason, they cannot be said to be bound by this law.[5] However, on Locke's view, it follows that, if men make promises to one another in the state of nature, they must consider themselves bound by them, 'for truth

[1] II. xx.
[2] Par. 12.
[3] These passages in the *Second Treatise*, pars. 6, 7, and 19, should be compared with the fifth essay, ff. 63–64, and the eighth, ff. 114–15.
[4] *Second Treatise*, par. 136, to be compared with the first essay, f. 18.
[5] *Second Treatise*, pars. 57 and 60, to be compared with the seventh essay, f. 104.

and keeping of faith belong to men as men, and not as members of society'.[1]

Locke also holds that part of God's purpose in making man was to 'put him under strong obligations of necessity, convenience, and inclination to drive him into society, as well as to fit him with understanding and language to continue and enjoy it.'[2] A notable aspect of his teaching concerning conditions subsequent to the state of nature is that 'the obligations of the law of nature cease not in society', and that 'a great part of the municipal laws of countries are only so far right as they are founded on the law of nature'.[3]

Locke likewise maintains that it is according to this law and prior to any positive civil laws that the amount of each man's private property is determined and secured.[4] Though God, he believes, has given the earth and all its fruits to men in common,[5] the law of nature sets bounds to what each man is allowed to appropriate and to keep for himself, and since within these bounds a person's 'right and conveniency go together', there can be little room for quarrels about property thus established.[6] Though in his essays on natural law Locke did not as yet formulate the theory that labour is the origin of the right of property, it is clear from the references given here in the footnotes that several assumptions of his theory of property in the *Second Treatise* are derived from the eighth of his essays—that essay, in fact, which he scarcely, if at all, turned to account in other of his mature works.

Some further, though less important, parallels between the essays and the *Two Treatises* can be found in Locke's distinction between natural right, the right of donation, and the right of contract,[7] in his discussion of the difference between a king and a tyrant,[8] and in his intimation that men would be foolish, when entering into society, to endure the iniquity of an absolute civil power.[9]

With this account of Locke's borrowings from his own essays in his

[1] *Second Treatise*, par. 14, to be compared with the seventh essay, ff. 98 and 102, and the first, f. 20.

[2] *Second Treatise*, par. 77, to be compared with the fourth essay, ff. 60–61.

[3] *Second Treatise*, pars. 135 and 12, to be compared with the first essay, ff. 18–19, the sixth, ff. 89–90, the seventh, f. 102, and the eighth, ff. 115–16.

[4] *Second Treatise*, par. 30, to be compared with the eighth essay, ff. 107–8.

[5] *Second Treatise*, par. 26 and *passim*, to be compared with the eighth essay, ff. 112–13.

[6] *Second Treatise*, pars. 31, 36, 51, to be compared with the eighth essay, ff. 107–8, 114–15.

[7] The distinction is drawn by Locke throughout the *Two Treatises* and in his sixth essay, f. 85.

[8] *First Treatise*, par. 81; *Second Treatise*, par. 200, to be compared with the sixth essay ff. 86 and 90.

[9] *Second Treatise*, par. 93, to be compared with the first essay, f. 19.

two major philosophical works of 1690 we complete our discussion in this section. Our inquiry has led to two main conclusions, which may be summed up as follows:

(1) For a variety of reasons, Locke's doctrine of natural law as expounded by him in his early essays was never in detail reconsidered by him in his later writings, though it became an important premiss of several of his mature theories. (2) A great number of arguments, notions, and illustrations in Locke's early essays, however, found their way into the two drafts of the *Essay* of 1671, the *Essay* of 1690, some of the subsequent editions of the *Essay*, and the *Two Treatises of Government*. Thus, over a period of nearly forty years the essays provided Locke with topics and inspiration which he turned to account in the building up of his philosophy.

A corollary of this conclusion may be stated briefly. There are, as we know, statements in Locke's published works which have puzzled or dissatisfied readers. With the reappearance of the manuscript of his essays it is possible to show that several of these statements are the products of his early thought, and that in relation to their original context they can be explained and perhaps justified.

VIII

The Influence of the Essays on Subsequent Thought: Gabriel Towerson and James Tyrrell

FOR 250 years, so it would seem, Locke's essays on natural law have lain in the Lovelace Collection unidentified and unexplored, thus neither arousing interest nor exercising influence. During Locke's lifetime only two friends of his, Gabriel Towerson and James Tyrrell, knew about the essays; and one of these, to judge by the evidence collected in this section, used the essays to advantage in a book of his own.

In 1676, twelve years after Locke had completed his essays, Towerson published a book entitled *An Explication of the Decalogue or Ten Commandments, with reference to the Catechism of the Church of England. To which are premised by way of Introduction Several General Discourses concerning God's both Natural and Positive Laws.* The first Discourse deals with the 'Law of Nature', and Towerson proposes to inquire into the following four questions, namely (1) 'How it doth appear that there is such a Law', (2) 'What the general Contents of that Law are', (3) 'Of what continuance the obligation thereof is', and (4) 'Of what use the knowledge thereof is, after the superinducing the

Laws of Moses and Christ'. The only authority quoted by Towerson in this Discourse, apart from the Scriptures, is Hooker. Since we know from Towerson's letter to Locke, quoted on pp. 8–9, that the two friends carried on a prolonged discussion on the law of nature in the early sixties, we must now inquire whether Towerson's views in the first Discourse of his book are his own, or Locke's, or perhaps the joint product of the early discussions between the two friends.

In answer to the first question raised by him in his Discourse Towerson infers the existence of a law of nature from two considerations, namely (a) that there is a God who, in His wisdom and by right and of necessity, has given laws to His creatures suitable to their nature and to His design, and (b) that all men regard themselves as bound by the pronouncements of their consciences—a fact to be explained only on the supposition that all men are intimately acquainted with a natural rule of good and evil. Towerson's lines of argument here are mostly the same as those followed by Locke in his first essay.

From Towerson's letter to Locke, quoted on pp. 8–9, it appears that the first of the two considerations stated above was suggested by Towerson and admitted by Locke, and also that the second consideration, the argument from conscience, was proposed by Towerson. Since Towerson in his letter recommends to Locke that, apart from these two arguments, they should not concern themselves with further proofs for the existence of a law of nature, it would seem that the additional arguments we find in Locke's first essay are due to Locke's own initiative. As regards the argument from conscience, there are indeed good reasons for believing that Towerson, rather than Locke, introduced it into the discussion and took upon himself to formulate it. In the first place, Locke's exposition of the argument is less explicit than Towerson's. Secondly, Towerson (and Locke too, though not with equal emphasis) argues that conscience does not make the distinction between good and evil but only judges an action by what it regards as the eternal rule of good and evil. It was not until many years later that this point came to be urged by Locke himself in his *Essay* of 1690 and particularly in his marginal replies to Thomas Burnet's *Remarks* on the *Essay*, of 1697.[1]

The second question discussed in Towerson's Discourse concerns the contents of the law of nature. Like Locke, he prefers to investigate this question by an *a priori* rather than an *a posteriori* method. Like him, he defines the duties that men owe to God, their neighbour, and

---

[1] *Essay*, I. ii. 8, and note 1 (Fraser's ed., i. 71).

themselves, as the worship of and obedience to God, the giving to every man what is his own, and self-preservation. Towerson's treatment in this case is again more detailed and also more compact than Locke's, whose remarks on this topic are cursory and are scattered throughout the essays. We may assume, therefore, that Towerson's exposition of arguments in this part of his book is the result, if not of his own independent research, none the less of his discussions with Locke, and consequently that he must be credited with at least part of it.

Next Towerson discusses the validity of natural law, which for him no less than for Locke continues as long as the human race lasts. When he comes to speak of certain cases which seem to indicate that at God's command the binding force of this law can lapse, he mentions two examples, often cited by traditional authors, namely that of the Israelites taking with them to Palestine the goods of the Egyptians, and that of Abraham sacrificing his innocent son. Locke, in his seventh essay, uses as an illustration only one of these examples, but his arguments showing that in such a case there is not really a change in the law are the same as Towerson's and, in fact, can be traced to traditional sources. In answer to the question why, despite the permanent validity and the certainty of the law of nature, men frequently disobey or misunderstand this law, Towerson produces an orderly set of reasons, the first two of which, but not the last, can be found in Locke's essays, though they are there not grouped together but advanced in different places. The quotation *facile credimus quae volumus*, which Towerson in this connexion cites from Minucius Felix, is absent from Locke's essays, though it occurs in a similar context in his *Essay* of 1690.[1] From all this we again conclude that Towerson's active part in the discussions between the two friends was considerable, and that when he published his views on natural law he had no reason for feeling indebted to Locke's essays.

Towerson's last inquiry in the Discourse concerns the relation between the law of nature on the one hand and the Mosaic law and the Gospel on the other. For this inquiry he alone must be held responsible, for there is no parallel to it in any of Locke's essays. It is true, in his attempt to show that it is mainly on account of the reasonableness of its precepts that natural law has not been replaced by the laws of Moses and Christ, he expresses a latitudinarian attitude, an attitude shared by Locke, which both may have taken over from Whichcote and Culverwel. At the end of his inquiry, however, Towerson refers

[1] iv. xx. 12; also in Locke's Journal for 8 Feb. 1676/7, f. 42 (ed. Aaron, p. 84).

to the law of nature as the 'Candle of the Lord', a metaphor employed by Locke in his *Essay* of 1690,[1] but not in his essays on natural law where, probably influenced by the title of Culverwel's main work, he prefers to use the phrase 'the light of nature' and this only with a reference to reason.

Our general impression, then, is that Towerson's arguments in his Discourse are partly his own, partly derived from traditional sources, and that he published them without necessarily consulting Locke's essays. On account of their similarity with arguments in Locke's essays, however, their origin must be sought in that early series of discussions between himself and his friend, to which Towerson obviously contributed a substantial part. I am inclined to believe that the scheme of these discussions has survived in the fourfold design of the first Discourse in Towerson's *Explication of the Decalogue* and that, while the Discourse to some extent reflects Towerson's share in the discussion, an estimate of Locke's share can conveniently be derived from all those parts of his essays, to which there is no parallel in Towerson's Discourse.

Let us proceed now to a consideration of Tyrrell's book, published in 1692 and entitled *A Brief Disquisition of the Law of Nature, According to the Principles and Method laid down in the Rev. Dr. Cumberland's Latin Treatise on that Subject*. In following Cumberland, Tyrrell's main tasks in his book are to refute Hobbes and to explain the binding force of natural law by its chief purpose, namely to impose the endeavour, enjoined by God, to seek and to establish the common good of rational beings. He had already stressed the urgency of the latter task in the first chapter of his book of 1681, *Patriarcha non Monarcha*, in connexion with his refutation of Filmer.

Tyrrell became acquainted with Locke during their early years in Oxford, before Locke had begun to write his essays on natural law. Throughout their lifelong friendship he knew about Locke's essays. He discussed their subject-matter with him at intervals and repeatedly urged him to publish them, first in 1687, when Locke had finished his *Essay* in manuscript, then in 1690 after the publication of the *Essay*, and then again in 1692, after he had himself published his *Disquisition of the Law of Nature*. In many places of this book Tyrrell acknowledges his indebtedness to Locke's *Essay* and quotes from it. However, we get the impression that his indebtedness to Locke extends further than what he owes to the *Essay*. Several of Tyrrell's chief arguments

[1] IV. iii. 20; 'Introduction', par. 5. For the origin of the term see Proverbs xx. 27.

concerning natural law, to which there is in fact no parallel in Locke's *Essay*, are so much like those in Locke's essays on natural law that there can be little doubt about their derivation. Tyrrell makes no mention of the essays in his *Disquisition*, and in some places where his arguments resemble Locke's he even intimates that he is the first to set them forth. The suspicion that we are here face to face with a case of plagiarism is strong enough to make it necessary to look farther.

In the 'Preface to the Reader', which serves as an introduction to his work, Tyrrell explains that there are objections to employing, like Grotius and Selden, an *a posteriori* method in the discovery of natural law, that is, to the method of proving it from tradition and the general consent of men. Like Locke and Towerson, he prefers to make use of the *a priori* method and to demonstrate the certainty of this law by inquiring into the nature of things and the nature of men. He feels sure that, as a result of such inquiries, the binding force of natural law can be shown to originate from the will and authority of God, and he sets himself the special task of showing how exactly it proceeds from God. In this connexion he rejects the attempt, made (as he says) by the Platonists, to prove the divine origin of natural law by supposing certain innate ideas of moral good and evil, impressed by God upon the souls of men. For a refutation of this assumption Tyrrell refers the reader to Locke's *Essay*, and he proposes to base his own investigation on knowledge derived from the senses. No doubt this reference to Locke's *Essay* meets the requirement of a refutation of innate *ideas*, but Tyrrell's real concern here is to show that natural *law* is not an innate law, and with this point Locke dealt extensively in his second and third essays and only very briefly in the *Essay*.[1] Similarly, at the end of the Preface, when summarizing his reasons for maintaining that 'the law of nature has all things necessary to render it so', Tyrrell again seems to be borrowing from Locke's essays[2] rather than from his mature work. The same impression is conveyed in chapter v,[3] where Tyrrell states certain objections to the belief in natural law and his replies to these objections, and where he repeats his doubt that the existence of this law can be proved by tradition.

None of the examples so far mentioned would carry much weight in answer to the problem we have raised, if there were not one which is decisive. It occurs in chapter iii, paragraph 8,[4] of Tyrrell's book, in

---

[1] I. ii. 13 (Fraser's ed., i. 78).   [2] Cf. the fourth essay, f. 52, and the sixth essay, f. 88.
[3] pp. 208–10, to be compared particularly with the second essay, ff. 33–34.
[4] p. 116.

connexion with his discussion of obligation. Whereas Cumberland, in his *De Legibus Naturae Disquisitio Philosophica*,[1] of which Tyrrell's book is to a large extent a paraphrase, had derived the definition of obligation from Justinian's *Institutes*,[2] Tyrrell does not follow his professed model, but introduces in precisely the same words Locke's somewhat different definition of obligation as it occurs in the sixth essay[3] and, in addition, inserts an almost literal translation of a number of passages in this essay.[4] For the sake of reference Tyrrell's words in paragraph 8 are quoted in full:

> For the further clearing of this, I shall premise somewhat to explain this Word *Obligation*, which the Civilians thus define: *Obligatio est vinculum Juris, quo quis astringitur debitum persolvere.* That is, an Obligation is that Bond of Law, whereby every one is obliged to pay his Debt, or Due: Which Definition doth well include all sorts of Obligations, if by the word *Jus*, or Law, we understand that Law whose Obligation we propose to define. So that by *vinculum Juris* in this Definition, we understand that Bond, or Tye, of the Law of Nature, by which every one is obliged to pay this natural Debt, i.e. to perform that Duty which he owes to GOD his Creator, by reason of his own Rational Nature, or else to undergo those Punishments which are ordained for his Disobedience or Neglect. So that there is a twofold Tye, or Obligation, in all Laws; the one active in the Debt, or Duty; the other passive, in a patient submission to the Punishment, in case of any wilful neglect, or omission thereof: Of both which, we shall speak in their order.

The argument of this passage is one of those which, as I have tried to show earlier in this Introduction, Locke took over from Bishop Sanderson.[5] There can be no doubt that Tyrrell reproduced it from Locke's sixth essay, and not from Sanderson's Lectures, for his version follows Locke's much more closely than Sanderson's in nearly every detail. Besides, his opening sentences in paragraph 9 consist largely in a verbal translation of other passages in that essay.

There is only one explanation that I can suggest to show how this part of Locke's essays found its way into print under Tyrrell's name, though without Tyrrell's intention. A notebook on the law of nature, possibly the one we have named MS. B and from which the essays in the present volume are printed, is listed in an inventory of 1680[6] of Locke's belongings in Christ Church. During Locke's absence in Holland (1683–9) most of his belongings, books, and manuscripts in Christ Church were stored at the home of Tyrrell near Oxford, who

---

[1] Ch. v, par. xi, p. 205; par. xxvii, p. 239.
[2] lib. iii, tit. 13.   [3] f. 83.   [4] Cf. ff. 83–85.
[5] *De Juramenti Obligatione*, i. 11–12.   [6] MS. Locke c. 25, fols. 30–31.

returned them to their owner in the early nineties. If, as is not unlikely, the notebook on the law of nature was among the things in Tyrrell's hands for the nine years preceding the publication of his *Disquisition of the Law of Nature*, there would have been ample time and every reason for him to consult it and possibly to take notes from it for future reference. At all events we may assume that sometime during his lifelong friendship with Locke Tyrrell was allowed to see the essays and on that occasion skimmed from them information about a subject-matter that he had very much at heart. When his own book on natural law came to be written, Tyrrell may have failed to discriminate between the various sources he had drawn from and may thus have transferred into his text, from notes collected over a period of years, passages he had once copied from Locke's essays. That at this final stage he was unaware of the true provenance of these passages is borne out by the fact that in 1692, the year his *Disquisition* appeared in print, he once again urged Locke to publish his own essays on natural law.

Beyond what has been set out in the preceding pages I can find no evidence of any direct influence of Locke's essays upon subsequent thought.

IX

The Latin Text

I PROPOSE in this section to give details about the Latin text of Locke's essays on the law of nature and of his valedictory speech as Censor of Moral Philosophy, and to specify the methods employed in forming the text of the present edition.

As was explained in Section II of this Introduction, the Latin text is preserved in three different manuscripts in the Lovelace Collection. One of these, obviously the earliest, which I have named MS. A, is in Locke's own handwriting, but it is incomplete and unpolished; another, obviously the latest, which I have named MS. C, is a faulty and uncorrected copy of the third, named by me MS. B, which is complete and bears all the marks of a thorough and final revision by Locke. It is MS. B, the only serviceable manuscript among the three and also the best preserved, from which the text printed in this volume is taken.

MS. B. is in the hand of an amanuensis, but it has many corrections and additions in Locke's hand. It would seem that the amanuensis copied MS. B from MS. A, which is Locke's own draft version of the essays, and in the process of transcription—being an illiterate man—

he committed[1] many grave mistakes, some of which escaped even Locke's notice in revising. Some parts of MS. B, however, may have been written at Locke's dictation, for a number of mistakes in the text appear to be due to errors in hearing[1] rather than to errors in reading. Wherever the changes introduced by Locke in MS. B, whether corrections or additions, are substantial—in which case they were written by him on the left-hand pages otherwise left blank—I have indicated the fact in footnotes.

For the solution of difficulties in the text of MS. B a comparison with Locke's draft version (MS. A) has often proved helpful, but since MS. A does not contain the first three essays, such a comparison could be made only with respect to the remaining essays of the series and Locke's valedictory speech. For the first three essays, an attempt has been made in footnotes to explain doubtful words and also to suggest emendations where the text itself is uncertain, e.g. where the amanuensis appears to have dropped a word in the process of transcription or to have committed some other mistake unnoticed by Locke. Important variations between MS. A and MS. B are pointed out in the notes, but differences in the order of words or of phrases are not indicated, unless the sense is affected.

As the reader will notice, Locke's Latin is not faultless. He frequently takes liberties with the rules of grammar and syntax, especially in his use of moods, which at times is inconsistent in the same clause. He also shifts his construction sometimes in the middle of a sentence. In all this I have followed him in the printed text, except in a few places where there can be no doubt that his mistakes were caused by mere inadvertency on his part. I have not preserved the frequent contractions used by Locke[2] but have printed their extended forms.

I have tried to reproduce accurately the spelling of MS. B wherever it conforms to a recognized rule.[3] Eccentric and clearly incorrect spellings, however, have been silently corrected to the normal,[4] and where there are different spellings of the same word in different places I have aimed at uniformity.[5] Where there are differences in spelling

---

[1] e.g. *quibuscam* for *quibuscum*, *dictet* for *dictat*.

[2] e.g. aīā (anima), maā (materia), naā (natura), oīs (omnis), hoīu (hominum), n : (enim), qd (quod), cē (esse), pᵗ (potest), ō (non).

[3] e.g. I have kept *foemina*, which often occurs in manuscripts and prints of the Renaissance period, instead of *femina*.

[4] e.g. *sydus* to *sidus*, *pyrata* to *pirata*, *acuratius* to *accuratius*, *liberimus* to *liberrimus*, *ceremonia* to *cerimonia*.

[5] Thus *cum* and *quum* are not both kept as in MS. B, but *cum* is printed throughout; also

between MS. A and MS. B,[1] preference is given to Locke's spelling in MS. A. As to capitalization, I have followed modern usage, for instance I have always used capitals at the beginning of main sentences. In places where Locke capitalizes an important word (e.g. *Philosophia*) in the middle of a sentence I have followed him only once or twice. *Deus* is capitalized by me throughout, except where the word stands for 'deity' in general or for a non-Christian god.

The punctuation in the printed text preserves neither that of MS. B nor that of MS. A. In MS. B it is abundant and mostly haphazard, confusing rather than helping the reader. In MS. A it is too sparse, and it is often difficult there to distinguish a comma from a semicolon or a full stop. In order to gain in clearness, I have therefore frequently added to Locke's punctuation as it occurs in MS. A and have eliminated some of the amanuensis's punctuation as it occurs in MS. B, aiming throughout at systematization in these matters. As a result, the length of sentences in the printed text differs occasionally from that in the two manuscripts: for the most part the reader will find sentences considerably shortened.

The paragraphing in this edition does not differ from that in MS. B, except in a few places where, as in essay V, the mass of Locke's arguments and illustrations can be conveniently subdivided. Brackets round passages are left unaltered except those enclosing the forms of address in the valedictory speech, where I have preferred to print commas instead. Clauses that are obviously of the nature of a parenthesis I have marked off by adding dashes. Two passages in essay I, and one in essay V, which were deleted by Locke but which may nevertheless be of interest to readers, are printed in the notes. All other words or passages crossed out by Locke are not specially noted. Passages which Locke ostensibly quotes from other authors are italicized in this edition, and since he rarely indicates the title of the work from which the quotation is taken, particulars are given in footnotes. Likewise, for passages which I could identify as quotations, though not marked by Locke as such, I have, wherever possible, supplied the necessary references in footnotes.

In my footnotes to the Latin text, therefore, I have tried to serve more than one purpose. In the first place, I have aimed at making clear the sources of Locke's quotations, of concealed ones no less than of manifest ones, by supplying full references. In the second place, I

---

impossibilis rather than *inpossibilis*, *faelix* rather than *felix*. *Se ipse* is spelled in two words rather than one.   [1] e.g. *praeservatio* in MS. A, *preservatio* in MS. B.

have indicated variant readings. In the third place, I have dealt critically with points of grammar and with words or sentences where the text is doubtful. In the fourth place, I have printed all those passages deleted by Locke which are of interest, and shown which of his corrections and additions are substantial. Lastly, at the end of essays II, IV, and VI, I have added, along with some comments, the titles of essays which were contemplated by Locke but never actually written by him. It may be pointed out here that there are no footnotes by Locke himself in the manuscripts of the essays.

Originally MS. B had no pagination. The folio-numbering to be found in it was done by the Bodleian Library after the purchase of the Lovelace Collection in 1942, and in this edition it is indicated by figures in round brackets inserted in the body of the text. In cases where a page ends in the middle of a word, I have placed the number of the following folio page behind this word.

<h2 style="text-align:center">x</h2>

The English Translation

IT remains to say a few words about the English translation of the essays and the valedictory speech.

The translation, which is given side by side with the Latin text, has been made as literal as possible, and my aim has been to reproduce not only the substance but also the general tone of the original. In this task I had a choice between two alternatives, namely, either to adopt modern idiom and terminology, or to follow that used by Locke in his published writings—which in fact would have been the idiom and terminology of his essays, had he decided to write them in English. For the most part I have preferred to adopt modern idiom, but where Locke's arguments in the essays are of the same technical nature as in his *Essay concerning Human Understanding* I have found it advisable to use his own expressions.

Occasionally, and chiefly on account of the unsatisfactory punctuation in the manuscripts, the Latin text presents difficulties of interpretation and, in consequence, raises problems of translation. I have explained such difficulties in footnotes appended to the translation, but I call attention here to a slightly puzzling, yet obviously important, paragraph in essay V (ff. 79–80), where I have sought to give a coherent version without taking unwarranted liberties with the text. In Locke's valedictory speech I have found a number of allusions that are

difficult to explain and occasionally also a play on words, which I have rendered in the translation as best as I could. Wherever Locke's train of arguments is complex I have sought to clarify its structure by introducing new paragraphs and bracketed numerals at the beginnings of paragraphs. The analytical summary provided will, I hope, serve to clarify the whole series of Locke's essays, and the précis included in the Introductory Note to his valedictory speech is intended for the same purpose.

I have added footnotes to the translation, the nature of which is different from that of the notes appended to the Latin text. Instead of giving particulars about Locke's quotations, they indicate sources of influence on his thought and passages similar to Locke's occurring in the works of other authors or in his own published writings. Footnotes also explain covert references and give cross references and deal with various points arising from the translation and from the subject-matter. I have also given in the notes a translation of the three passages in the essays which Locke deleted and which are themselves reproduced in footnotes to the Latin text. Though there are many parallels to be found between the essays and Locke's *Essay*, and particularly Book I of the *Essay*, I have provided references only in cases where I thought they would be illuminating, and throughout I have purposely kept the number of footnotes small.

ESSAYS ON THE

Law of Nature

ANALYTICAL SUMMARY

1. *An detur Morum Regula sive Lex Naturae? Affirmatur*
Is there a Rule of Morals, or Law of Nature, given to us? Yes

ON the assumption that some divine being presides over the world as
a whole—a fact proved by the 'argument from design', since nature
and the world of living beings are seen to be governed by divine laws—
certain fixed rules of conduct must apply to the life of man in particular.
These rules are the law of nature, and such a law, whether referred to
as 'moral good' by the Stoics, or as 'right reason', or as 'the rule of
living according to nature', is on the one hand to be distinguished from
natural right and on the other should not be called the dictate of reason:
for (*a*) it is the decree of the divine will issuing commands and prohibitions, and (*b*) it is implanted in men's hearts by God so that reason
can only *discover* and *interpret* it. Five arguments can be advanced to
prove the existence of a law of nature, viz.:

(1) The first argument can be derived from two passages in Aristotle's *Nicomachean Ethics* (Bk. I, 1098 a 7, and Bk. V, 1134 b 18),
where it is maintained that 'the special function of man is the active
exercise of the mind's faculties in accordance with rational principle'
and that 'a natural rule of justice is one which has the same validity
everywhere'. It may be objected that, if natural law is defined in such
terms, there can be no such law in existence, because most people live
as though there were no rational ground in life at all nor any law of
such a kind that all men recognize it. The answer to the objection is
twofold, viz.:

(*a*) From the fact that there are people who pay no attention to a
law because they are indifferent, idle, or occupied otherwise, or are
corrupt from birth or by habit, it does not follow that the law does
not exist or is not promulgated. Natural law is not known to any and
every one but only to the more rational and perceptive among men.

(*b*) If even the more rational of men disagree about natural law,
this only shows that a law which can be interpreted differently must in
fact exist.

(2) The second argument can be derived from human conscience,
which, in the absence of any other law, passes judgement upon men's
conduct, thus indicating that there is some law whereby they are in
duty bound.

(3) The third argument is derived from the observation that all

things in the universe are governed by law [Hippocrates, St. Thomas Aquinas, Hooker are quoted or referred to] so that man, too, must be bound by some guiding principle suitable to his nature. God did not endow man with reason and make him supremely susceptible of law in order that he should neither exercise the one nor submit to the other.

(4) The fourth argument is taken from human society which depends on (*a*) a constitution and a form of government, and (*b*) on the fulfilment of contracts, i.e. on obligations independent of human will. Without a law of nature these two bases of human society fall to the ground, and then no man could be bound by his own or other people's positive laws.

(5) The fifth argument is that without natural law there would be no honour in virtue and no baseness in vice; man would have nothing to do but what his will, utility, or pleasure recommends.

11. *An Lex Naturae sit Lumine Naturae cognoscibilis? Affirmatur*

    Can the Law of Nature be known by the Light of Nature? Yes

EXPLANATION that the knowledge of the law of nature is conveyed to men by the light of nature, provided they make proper use of their natural faculties.

There are three sources of knowledge, which may be roughly called 'inscription', 'tradition', and 'sensation'. Supernatural and divine revelation is not pertinent to the present argument, since it forms no part of man's natural endowment; and 'reason' is not named in the list, because the inquiry is concerned with the first principles and sources of knowledge, i.e. with the way in which the first notions of knowledge enter the mind, and reason cannot be said to disclose or establish these; they are either stamped on the mind by inscription, or received second-hand, or they enter by the senses.

(1) 'Inscription': The inquiry as to whether the law of nature, as some have maintained, is inscribed or innate in all men belongs to another place (essay III). At present it suffices to say that men, if properly using their inborn faculties, can arrive at the knowledge of this law without such further help.

(2) 'Tradition': Though the precepts of the law of nature may be, and in actual fact often are, handed on by tradition and inculcated by parents and teachers, tradition itself is not a primary and certain way of knowing this law, *qua* law. For (*a*) traditions differ from one

another, and any attempt to scrutinize them and to discover that which is most worthy of trust *ipso facto* undermines the whole authority of tradition; (*b*) tradition implies trust rather than knowledge; it depends more on a belief in authority than on the evidence of facts; and (*c*) the first author of a tradition is no better qualified to know this law than one who is ignorant of tradition, for he must have either found it inscribed within his heart or come to know it by arguments derived from sense-experience, ways of knowing that are equally open to the rest of mankind.

(3) 'Sensation': Sense-perception is the true and only source from which the knowledge of natural law is derived. From the things perceived through the senses reason advances to the notion of a Deity who is the maker of all these things and so, as will appear later on, to the notion of a universal law of nature. It is thus evident that there is a natural law besides the positive laws made by God and by men, and that this law can be known by the light of nature, i.e. by an inward process of reasoning starting from sense-experience.

The objection that the light of nature does not lead to the knowledge of natural law because many men are ignorant or think differently about this law, can be answered by saying that not all men make proper use of their mental faculties either in ordinary life or in scientific pursuits; for only a few direct their conduct by reason or become good mathematicians, though the employment of their natural faculties should enable them to achieve both.

[At the end of this essay Locke added the title of another which remained unwritten, scil., *An lex naturae per traditionem nobis innotescat? Negatur (Does the law of nature become known to us through tradition? No)*]

III. *An Lex Naturae Hominum Animis inscribatur? Negatur
Is the Law of Nature inscribed in the Minds of Men? No*

FIVE arguments to show that the law of nature is not inborn in the minds of men and that the souls of the newly-born are empty tablets, only afterwards filled in by observation and reasoning, viz.:

(1) The (Cartesian) doctrine of innate ideas is a mere assertion and has so far never been proved.

(2) There can be no natural imprint of the law of nature in men's hearts, because this law is not universally obeyed or even acknowledged. If it be said that this law, after having been stamped by nature on the minds of men, has, on account of the Fall, been either partly or

97

altogether obliterated, the following difficulties arise: (*a*) Supposing, on the one hand, that after the Fall some of the precepts of this law have remained inscribed in the hearts of men, these will either be the same in all and all men then should recognize them as such (but this is by no means the case), or they will differ from person to person and we then could hardly believe that nature, otherwise so uniform in its works, was the cause of these different dictates; nor could we, on account of this difference, ever have knowledge of a definite moral law. (*b*) Supposing, on the other hand, that after the Fall no precept of natural law has remained inscribed in men's hearts, this law will be nothing whatever, unless there is some other way of knowing it than by inscription.

(3) The law of nature does not seem to be written in the minds of men, seeing that untutored and primitive people who, since they are their own teachers and live according to nature, should best of all know this law, are ignorant of it. *Per contra*, if among the more cultured peoples there do exist some definite views about morals, which are taken for the law of nature and believed to be innate, the origin of these can be explained by the influences of early education.

(4) Foolish and insane people are without knowledge of natural law and yet on their minds this law, if it were innate, would impress itself immediately in that it is not subject to the influence of a man's bodily constitution.

(5) If the doctrine of innate ideas is to be accepted, speculative as well as practical principles should be found to be inscribed in men's minds. However, everybody will agree that the primary scientific axiom, the principle of non-contradiction, is not innate but the result of an empirical generalization.

IV. *An Ratio per Res a Sensibus haustas pervenire potest in Cognitionem Legis Naturae? Affirmatur*
    Can Reason attain to the Knowledge of Natural Law through Sense-experience? Yes

DEFINITION of the light of nature in terms of sense-perception and reason. These two faculties are interdependent, sensation furnishing reason with the ideas of particular objects, reason combining the images of these and thus forming new ones. In mathematics as well as in the moral sciences, in speculations concerning the mind as well as the body, reason always advances from things known through the senses to things unknown, and it is on the basis of some truth perceived by the senses that it leads also to the knowledge of natural law.

Analytical Summary

The two presuppositions which are required for knowledge of any and every law are (1) the recognition of a law-maker, and (2) the recognition that there is some will revealed by the law-maker and that he requires us to conduct our life in accordance with it. Sense-experience and reason assist one another in making these two presuppositions known to men.

(1) The senses tell us of bodies and their properties, of motion, and all the wonderful regularity in the orbits of the stars and the changes of the seasons.

Reason then inquires into the origin of all these beautiful and ingeniously ordered phenomena and infers the existence of a powerful and wise Deity who has made the whole universe and created mankind. Man, surely, cannot have been created by inanimate things or by beasts, which are less perfect than he is, nor indeed by his own efforts, for, with the exception of God, nothing is its own cause; and, besides, if he were his own maker, man would not only bestow existence on himself but also preserve it and be immortal. God, then, as our creator, has a powerful and rightful command over us and it is He who determines whether we are to be happy or miserable. There are other proofs of God's existence, such as the argument from conscience and (Descartes's) argument from the idea of God, which are equally certain but not derived from sensation and reason alone (the latter argument, in fact, contains an explicit reference to 'inscription', which is not well founded). Since all men in the world, however, can exercise their senses and reason, they all are sufficiently prepared by nature to discover God for themselves.

(2) From the belief in God as the maker of all things it can be inferred that the world was created with a divine purpose and that God wishes man to do something with all that equipment for action with which he has been endowed. Man's duty is, partly, to worship God and, partly, in virtue of his natural faculties, to contemplate His works and to enter into, and maintain, a life in society with other men. There is no special need to remind man that he has duties towards himself as well as towards God and his neighbours.

[At the end of this essay Locke added the title of another which remained unwritten, scil., *An ex inclinatione hominum naturali potest cognosci lex naturae? Negatur* (*Can the law of nature be known from man's natural inclination? No*). In MS. A the question in the title is *An firma animi persuasio probat legem naturae?* (*Does a strong conviction of the mind prove that there is a law of nature?*)]

v. *An Lex Naturae cognosci potest ex Hominum Consensu? Negatur*
Can the Law of Nature be known from the General Consent of Men? No

'The voice of the people is the voice of God' is a fallacious proverb. History shows that the general consent of men has advocated the most impious deeds and thus cannot be the source of the decrees of reason and nature.

There are various meanings of the term 'general consent', viz.:

(1) Positive consent, which is based on a contract either (*a*) tacit, i.e. prompted by men's common interests, such as the free passage of envoys, free trade, &c., or (*b*) expressly stated, such as the delimitation of frontiers, import prohibitions, &c. Neither form of general consent, since it is not derived from any natural principle, proves a law of nature. In fact, the conditions giving rise to an agreement concerning the safe passage of envoys, for example, are contrary to natural law, which enjoins that all men shall live in peace. Supposing, however, that in the state of nature men are at war with one another, still no reason can be derived from natural law why envoys should have a safer passage than ordinary people, but this is brought about only by a tacit agreement. In that case, of course, the crime of doing violence to envoys is worse than that of injuring any private person; for in addition to wrong being done an agreement is broken.

All forms of general consent based on contract should be called the 'law of nations', which is not commanded by natural law but suggested to men by common expediency.

(2) Natural consent, which is based on a natural instinct, can be of three kinds, viz.:

(*a*) In moral behaviour. This form of general consent, i.e. in the manners and conduct of the majority of men, does not prove a natural law, for in most cases men's actions constitute a life of wickedness, i.e. lawlessness.

(*b*) In opinions, i.e. men's innermost convictions about morality, the verdicts of their consciences.

(i) Many examples, however, from history and contemporary life show that there is no such general consent concerning moral opinions. Men have conflicting views about virtue and vice, and public authority and custom may approve of a shameful code of morals in the interests of religion or for the sake of glory. Thus, in antiquity, piracy and theft

were often regarded as honourable, and for most nations desert consists in force and oppression. What is true of men's views about justice is true of their views about chastity, filial piety, self-preservation. [Illustrations are taken from ancient authors and the reports of travellers.] There is no agreement among men even in the matter of first principles, such as the existence and nature of God and the soul's immortality, both of which are necessary assumptions in doctrines of morality and natural law. There are whole nations which are atheistic or polytheistic and for that reason have no satisfactory notions of duty. To appeal to more civilized peoples or to philosophers is of no avail, for they, too, differ in their moral views and often approve of what is immoral, as does also the Catholic Church.

(ii) Even if there existed among men a general consent in some moral opinions, such a consent would not prove these opinions to be a natural law. For the law of nature can only be inferred by reason from the first principles of nature, and it is not a matter of belief or agreement. Besides, there can be a general consent in things which have nothing to do with natural law and which cannot impose a moral obligation merely because the majority of men assent to them.

(*c*) Agreement in first principles, i.e. self-evident or tautological propositions. These fall outside the present inquiry and have no bearing on ethics.

VI. *An Lex Naturae Homines obligat? Affirmatur*
    Are Men bound by the Law of Nature? Yes

REJECTION of the view that all natural law is based on the principle of self-preservation, the observance of which is advantageous rather than virtuous.

In order to inquire into the binding force of the law of nature, certain terms concerning obligation must first be explained. The jurists' definition of obligation, i.e. that it is the bond of law whereby one is bound to render what is due, can be applied to all kinds of obligation, including that arising from the law of nature. Both legal and natural obligations derive their origin from someone who has right and power over us and to whom we owe a debt or duty.

A debt can be of two kinds, viz.:

(1) A liability to pay dutiful obedience, or to act in conformity with a moral rule, i.e. according to the will of a superior power to which we are subject. Ultimately, all obligation leads back to God, who is omnipotent and our Creator.

(2) A liability to punishment, arising from a failure to pay dutiful obedience. The obligation in this case is evidenced by compulsion and fear of penalty.

However, an obligation is not imposed by fear of punishment by itself, but rather by the recognition that someone has authority over us either by natural right and the right of creation, as God has, or by the right of donation, as in the case of the first-born and monarchs, or by the right of contract. Coercion or fear of punishment is the sole reason for a man to comply with the orders of a pirate, and it is for his own safety and with the approval of his conscience that he will try to free himself. But a rational apprehension of what is right is the ground of a subject's allegiance to a king, and he would violate the right of another and be condemned by his own conscience if he showed himself disobedient.

Further, a thing can bind

(1) 'effectively', as does the will of a superior, which is the first and formal cause of all obligation, or

(2) 'terminatively', as does the declaration of a superior will, a law prescribing the manner and extent of an obligation.

Further, a thing can bind

(1) by its intrinsic force, and such is the divine will, which is known either by the light of nature and then is called natural law, or by revelation and then is called positive divine law; or

(2) by a power external to itself, e.g. the will of a king or parent has power over us by the will of God.

That the law of nature is binding on men by its intrinsic force can be proved by three arguments, viz.:

(1) All that is required to impose an obligation is the rightful power of a superior and the disclosure of his will, and natural law contains these two requirements, for

(*a*) God is supreme over everything in perfect justice, and

(*b*) natural law, which is the will of God, becomes sufficiently known to everyone who is willing to apply his mind to it.

(2) Natural law is as much God's will as positive divine law, differing from it only in the way in which it is disclosed and apprehended. Since God's positive law is binding on men, natural law must be binding as well.

(3) Only because natural law is binding on men can human positive law be binding. In the case of those, and they are the majority, who are without the knowledge of a divine revelation, it is natural law

alone that establishes the authority of civil government and enables a king (unlike a tyrant) to rule over his subjects by right, not by force.

[At the end of this essay Locke added the title of another which remained unwritten, scil., *An lex naturae obliget bruta? Negatur (Are animals bound by the law of nature? No)*]

VII. *An Obligatio Legis Naturae sit Perpetua et Universalis?*
Affirmatur
Is the Binding Force of the Law of Nature Perpetual and Universal? Yes

SINCE there are men, and even whole nations, in whom there is no sense of law or morality, it may be justly doubted whether there is any law of nature at all or, if there is, whether it is binding on all men. A third way of explaining the existing immorality among men is absurd, i.e. to suppose that nature should plant a moral law in human hearts and require its subjects to observe it, while at the same time keeping it dark.

But since it has been proved already that natural law is morally binding, it must now be shown to what extent it is binding. The following are proofs to show that the binding force of this law is (1) perpetual, and (2) universal.

(1) It is perpetual in the sense that there is no time when it would be lawful for a man to act against the precepts of this law, for it is coeval with the human race. This does not mean that men are bound at all times to perform everything that this law commands, for it is surely impossible for them to observe several duties at once. What is meant is that the binding force of this law is continuous, though the action whereby it is observed need not be so. In explanation of this the following four points must be noted, viz.:

(*a*) Some acts, e.g. theft and murder, are absolutely forbidden and men are at all times bound to abstain from them.

(*b*) It is always a duty to fear and revere God, to show affection for one's parents and love of one's neighbour.

(*c*) Men are bound, not continuously, but at particular times and in certain conditions, to worship God outwardly, to bring relief to people in trouble, to feed the hungry, &c.

(*d*) Sometimes, while a particular course of action is not itself commanded, the circumstances which would accompany it are. E.g. no one is bound to talk about his neighbour, but whenever he chooses to do so, natural law bids him talk candidly and unscathingly. The

law's binding force, though perpetual, is here only conditional, not absolute.

(2) The binding force of natural law is universal, though not in the sense that each of its precepts is binding on any and every man, for this is impossible. What is meant is that, according as there are different stations in life and different relations between men, there are definite duties attached to them all over the world. Princes have duties differing from those of the common people; generals have their own duties and so have soldiers: in each case the specific duties are the same everywhere. In all stations of life it is, of course, commanded to abstain from theft and slander and to practise charity and fidelity, and these commands are binding on kings as well as subjects, parents as well as children. The binding force of natural law is thus everywhere the same, only the circumstances of life are different.

Rejection of two possible arguments to show that natural law is not binding on all men, viz.:

(1) It cannot be said that this law is not universally binding because it is not acceptable to some part or the whole of mankind. For ultimately it is so rooted in human nature that before it can be annulled human nature must be changed. Since there is, in fact, a harmony between this law and human nature, in so far as it is rational, and since human nature is essentially the same, forming as it does part of the eternal order of things, it follows that what is proper for some rational men now must needs be proper for all at all times. The moral duties arising out of man's nature are just as necessary and immutable as the deduction from the nature of a triangle that its three angles are equal to two right ones.

(2) It cannot be said that natural law is not binding on all men because it has been repealed. For it is impossible for human beings to alter it, since they are subject to it, and God certainly would not wish to abrogate it, because, on account of the harmony between this law and man's nature, he would then have to undo mankind and create a new race of men.

There are arguments *a posteriori* to show that natural law is universally binding, namely the disappearance of religion, fellowship among men, fidelity, &c., if this binding force were abolished.

Three doubts might be raised about this whole matter, but they can all be resolved, viz.:

(1) That the binding force of the law of nature is not everlasting and universal because it can lapse at God's own command, as actually

happened in the case of the Hebrews who, when leaving for Palestine, were commanded to take with them the goods of the Egyptians. In answer to this it must be observed that if God orders someone to take another's property, He wills that the ownership of it should be changed, not that a theft should be committed.

(2) That natural law is not always binding because in some cases we are not bound to obey parents. Here it must be observed that parents' commands must always be complied with as long as they concern things lawful, but that, if e.g. they conflict with a king's commands, they become unlawful and their binding force ceases. It is not that natural law ceases here to be binding, but that the nature of the case happens to change.

(3) The doubt that natural law is not universally binding because men's manners and moral views differ so widely can be dispelled by the observation that the reason for this diversity lies in men's frailty and their irrational behaviour as a group, rather than in any variation of the law of nature.

The case of children and idiots need not be discussed, because natural law does not bind those to whom it is not given, and it is not given to those who have no means of knowing it.

VIII. *An Privata cujusque Utilitas sit Fundamentum Legis Naturae? Negatur*
Is every Man's own Interest the Basis of the Law of Nature? No

SOME, like Carneades, have attacked natural law by advancing the theories of psychological, or of ethical, egoism, and by vindicating men's natural rights and liberties.

Explanation of the terms (1) 'basis of natural law', and (2) 'each man's private interest'.

(1) The basis of natural law means the standard of all the other and less evident of its precepts.

(2) Each man's personal interest, though far from being the basis of natural law, is nevertheless in keeping with the rules of equity. In fact, the law of nature is the strongest protection of each man's private property. The question to be debated here, however, is whether what each person judges to be in his own interest can be accepted as the standard of what is just and right, and this question must be answered in the negative, for three reasons, viz.:

(1) The private interest of each person cannot be the basis of natural

law because none of the dutiful actions of human life are derived from it; nay, as history shows, the best virtues consist in doing good to others at our own loss. [Illustrations are taken from the conduct of M. Curtius, G. Fabricius, Catilina, and Cicero.]

(2) If the private interest of each person were the primary law of nature, that law would inevitably be broken, for it is impossible to have regard for the interests of all at one and the same time. The natural supplies of the world do not grow in proportion to the number of its inhabitants and their needs or desires, and thus if one man acquires as much as he can, he does this only at another's expense. Hence, from the assumption that every man's self-interest is the basis of natural law, it follows (a) that men are under an obligation to do what cannot be realized, for one man's dutiful action will thwart another's, and (b) that men are in a state of war with one another, forgoing thereby all the benefits of an ordered social life. On the assumption that the opposite of self-interest is the basis of natural law, however, the duties of different people do not clash (for example, the liberality of a prince does not thwart the generosity of his subjects), nor do they engage men in conflict.

(3) If self-interest were the basis of natural law, all justice (for without an undisputed right of ownership in each person there is no justice), friendship, and generosity would be abolished. In fact, if the duties of life were to live by one's appetites and natural instincts, it would be unlawful for a man to renounce his own rights or to impart benefits to another. That the assumption is untenable can thus be seen from the absurdity of what follows from it. If it is argued that the basis of natural law is self-interest because the observance of every duty is always rewarded by happiness, it is clear that in this argument there is a failure to realize the true connexion between causes and effects, for a personal advantage is not the basis of natural law but the consequence of obedience to it.

ESSAYS ON THE

Law of Nature

I

AN DETUR MORUM REGULA SIVE LEX NATURAE? AFFIRMATUR

Cum Deus[1] se ubique praesentem nobis praestat et se quasi oculis hominum ingerit tam in constanti jam naturae tenore quam frequenti olim miraculorum testimonio, neminem fore credo qui aut ullam vitae nostrae habendam esse rationem aut aliquid esse quod aut virtutis aut vitii mereatur nomen agnoscit, qui non Deum esse secum statuerit. Hoc igitur supposito quod dubitare nefas esset, scilicet numen aliquod mundo praesidere, cum caelum perpetua rotatione volvi, terram stare, sidera lucere jusserit, ipsi indomito mari limites posuerit, omni plantarum generi et germinandi et crescendi modos tempestatesque praescripserit, cum animantes omnes illius voluntati morem gerentes suas habeant et nascendi et vivendi leges, nec quicquam sit in tota hac rerum natura tam vagum tam incertum quod[2] ratas fixasque non agnoscit operandi naturae suae convenientes leges, merito quaerendum videtur num solus homo exlex (f. 10) sui omnino juris, sine consilio, sine lege, sine aliqua vitae suae norma in mundum prodierit, quod non facile credet quisquam qui aut Deum O.M.[3] aut universum totius humani generis omni tempore et loco consensum aut denique se ipsum aut conscientiam suam cogitaverit. Sed priusquam ad legem ipsam et illa quibus esse probatur deveniamus argumenta, operae pretium facturus videar si varia illius nomina quibus insignitur indigitavero.

Primo igitur hoc illud est bonum morale vel honestum quod tanto studio quaesiverunt, tantis laudibus prosecuti sunt olim philosophi et inter eos praecipue Stoici; hoc unum illud Seneca bonum quo contentum esse dicit debere hominem, cui inest tantus splendor tantus decor ut illud[4] etiam agnoscat vitiis corrupta mortalium pars et ipsum dum fugiunt probant.[5]

---

[1] The spelling of this word in MS. A (i.e. from essay IV onward) and also in some of Locke's corrections in MS. B is *deus*; in this edition the word is capitalized wherever it stands for the proper name 'God'. [2] *quae* MS. B. [3] i.e. *Optimum Maximum*.
[4] *illum* MS. B.
[5] This may be a reference to Ovid, *Metam.* vii. 20, *Video meliora proboque, deteriora sequor*, quoted by Locke in his *Essay*, II. xxi. 35. Cf. also Rom. vii. 19.

I

IS THERE A RULE OF MORALS, OR LAW OF NATURE GIVEN TO US? YES

Since God shows Himself to us as present everywhere and, as it were, forces Himself upon the eyes of men as much in the fixed course of nature now as by the frequent evidence of miracles in time past, I assume there will be no one to deny the existence of God, provided he recognizes either the necessity for some rational account of our life, or that there is a thing that deserves to be called virtue or vice. This then being taken for granted, and it would be impious to doubt it, namely, that some divine being presides over the world—for it is by His order that the heaven revolves in unbroken rotation, the earth stands fast[1] and the stars shine, and it is He who has set bounds even to the wild sea and prescribed to every kind of plants the manner and periods of germination and growth; it is in obedience to His will that all living beings have their own laws of birth and life; and there is nothing so unstable, so uncertain in this whole constitution of things as not to admit of valid and fixed laws of operation appropriate to its nature—it seems just therefore to inquire whether man alone has come into the world altogether exempt from any law applicable to himself, without a plan, rule, or any pattern of his life. No one will easily believe this, who has reflected upon Almighty God,[2] or the unvarying consensus of the whole of mankind at every time and in every place, or even upon himself or his conscience. But before we come to speak of the law itself and those arguments whereby its existence is proved, it seems to me worth while to indicate the various names by which it is denoted.

First then, we can equate with our law that moral good or virtue which philosophers in former times (and among them especially the Stoics) have searched for with so much zeal and adorned with so many praises; we can equate with it that single good which Seneca says man ought to be content with, to which appertains so much dignity, so much glory, that even those among mortals who are corrupted by vice recognize it and while shunning it approve it.

[1] Locke here adheres to the geocentric theory (cf. *Essay*, II. xiv. 21).
[2] Literally 'the best and greatest'.

Secundo[1] recta ratio vocatur,[2] quam quisquis se hominem putat sibi vindicat; hoc illud est de quo tam acriter inter se digladiantur variae hominum sectae, et quisque (f. 11) opinioni suae praetendit. Per rationem autem hic non intelligendum puto illam intellectus facultatem quae[3] discursus format et argumenta deducit, sed certa quaedam practica principia e quibus emanant omnium virtutum fontes et quicquid necessarium sit ad mores bene efformandos; quod ex his principiis recte deducitur id jure dicitur rectae rationi conforme.

Alii et plurimi vocant legem naturae qua appellatione hujusmodi legem intelligunt quam quisque eo solum lumine quod natura nobis insitum est detegere potest, cui etiam per omnia se morigerum praestare,[4] officii sui rationem postulare sentit; et hoc illud est secundum naturam vivere quod toties inculcant Stoici.

Haec lex his insignita appellationibus a jure naturali distinguenda est: jus enim in eo positum est quod alicujus rei liberum habemus usum, lex vero id est quod aliquid agendum jubet vel vetat.

Haec igitur lex naturae ita describi potest quod sit ordinatio voluntatis divinae lumine naturae cognoscibilis, quid cum natura rationali conveniens vel disconveniens sit (f. 12) indicans eoque ipso jubens aut prohibens. Minus recte enim mihi videtur a nonnullis dici dictatum rationis, ratio enim legem hanc naturae non tam condit dictatque quam a superiore potestate sancitam et pectoribus nostris insitam investigat detegitque, nec legis illius author est sed interpres;[5] nisi supremi legislatoris minuendo dignitatem velimus rationi illam legem acceptam referre quam solum quaerit; nec enim ratio, cum facultas solum animi sit et pars nostri, nobis dare leges potest. Ex his facile patet in ea omnia reperiri quae ad legem requiruntur. Nam primo declaratio est superioris voluntatis, in quo consistere videtur legis ratio formalis; quo autem

---

[1] Here and often elsewhere Locke employs Arabic numerals instead of words.

[2] Cf. Cicero, *De Rep.* iii. 22 (Lactantius, *Inst. Div.* vi. 8, 7); also Grotius, *De Jure Belli ac Pacis*, 1625, lib. i, c. 1, sect. 10, par. 1; and, particularly for the last sentence in Locke's paragraph, Hobbes, *De Cive*, 1642, c. i, par. 1, note (*Works* [Latin], ed. Molesworth, 1839, ii. 169). [3] Possible reading is *qua* which would give a less direct construction.

[4] Text doubtful. Possible reading is *praestat*. In any case either *et* or *quam* ought to be inserted before the next word.

[5] Locke's correction for *scrutator*.

Secondly, there is the title of right reason, to which everyone who considers himself a human being lays claim, and this it is about which the various parties of men contend so fiercely among themselves, and which each one alleges to be the foundation of its doctrine. By reason, however, I do not think is meant here that faculty of the understanding which forms trains of thought and deduces proofs, but certain definite principles of action from which spring all virtues and whatever is necessary for the proper moulding of morals. For that which is correctly derived from these principles is justly said to be in accordance with right reason.

Others, and they are many, refer to a law of nature, by which term they understand a law of the following description: i.e. a law which each can detect merely by the light planted in us by nature, complete obedience to which, he perceives, is demanded by the principle of his obligation; and this is the rule of living according to nature which the Stoics so often emphasize.

This law, denoted by these appellations, ought to be distinguished from natural right: for right is grounded in the fact that we have the free use of a thing, whereas law is what enjoins or forbids the doing of a thing.[1]

Hence, this law of nature can be described as being the decree of the divine will discernible by the light of nature and indicating what is and what is not in conformity with rational nature, and for this very reason commanding or prohibiting.[2] It appears to me less correctly termed by some people the dictate of reason, since reason does not so much establish and pronounce this law of nature as search for it and discover it as a law enacted by a superior power and implanted in our hearts.[3] Neither is reason so much the maker of that law as its interpreter, unless, violating the dignity of the supreme legislator, we wish to make reason responsible for that received law which it merely investigates; nor indeed can reason give us laws, since it is only a faculty of our mind and part of us. Hence it is pretty clear that all the requisites of a law are found in natural law. For, in the first place, it is the decree of a

---

[1] Cf. Hobbes, *Leviathan*, pt. i, ch. 14 (ed. Pogson Smith, p. 99); also Pufendorf, *Elementa Jurisprudentiae Universalis*, 1660, lib. 1, def. xiii, par. 3.

[2] For this sentence and the following definition of natural law as *dictatum rationis* see Grotius, *De Jure Belli ac Pacis*, lib. i, c. 1, sect. 10, par. 1. The idea expressed in the beginning of the sentence reappears in the opening phrase of a passage in Locke's commonplace book of 1661, p. 10, printed in Lord King's *Life* (1858), p. 292. For the idea of 'conformity' or 'harmony' (*convenientia*) between law and man's rational nature, see essay VII, f. 99.

[3] Cf. Culverwel, *Discourse of the Light of Nature*, 1652, ch. ix, p. 99 (ed. Brown, 1857); also Hooker, *Laws of Ecclesiastical Polity*, bk. i. ch. 8, par. 3 (Keble's ed. of Hookers *Works*, 1865, i. 228).

modo humano generi innotescat postea fortassis inquirendi locus erit. Secundo, quod legis est proprium, quid agendum sit vel omittendum praescribit. Tertio homines obligat, omnia enim quae ad obligationem requiruntur in se continet; quamvis enim eo modo quo leges positivae non promulgatur, sufficienter tamen hominibus innotescit (quod sufficit), cum possibile sit solo lumine naturae eam cognoscere. (f. 13) His ita positis hujusmodi dari legem sequentia suadent argumenta.

Primum argumentum desumi potest ex Aristotelis testimonio ad Nicom., lib. 1, c. 7,[1] ubi dicit quod ἔργον ἀνθρώπου ἐστὶ ψυχῆς ἐνέργεια κατὰ λόγον: cum enim prius variis instantiis probasset esse cujusque rei proprium opus, quid sit illud etiam in homine quaesivit; quod per anno-[ta]tionem omnium operationum facultatis et vegetantis et sentientis quae hominibus cum brutis plantisque sunt communes tandem recte concludit officium hominis esse actionem secundum rationem adeo ut ea homini necessario agenda sunt quae dictat ratio. Item lib. 5, c. 7,[2] jus dividens in civile et naturale, τὸ δὲ νομικὸν[3] φυσικόν, inquit, ἔστι τὸ πανταχοῦ τὴν αὐτὴν ἔχον δύναμιν, unde recte colligitur dari aliquam legem naturae, cum sit aliqua lex quae ubique obtinet.[4]

(f. 15) Objicitur hic a nonnullis contra legem naturae, scilicet nullam omnino dari quia nullibi reperitur, quod maxima pars hominum ita vivit quasi nulla omnino vitae esset ratio nec ulla hujusmodi lex quem omnes agnoscunt; imo hac in re maxime dissentire videntur homines. Si enim esset lex naturae lumine rationis cognoscibilis, qui fit quod omnes homines quibus datur ratio eam non sciunt?

Respondemus primo quod uti in rebus civilibus non inde sequitur non esse aut promulgari legem quia tabulam publice prostantem aut caeco legere impossibile (f. 16) sit aut caecutienti difficile, quod[5] aliis in rebus occupato non vacat aut otioso aut improbo non placet oculos ad tabulam attollere et inde officii sui rationem ediscere. Rationem omnibus dari a natura concedo et esse legem naturae ratione cognosci-

---

[1] *Nicomachean Ethics*, i. 7. 14, 1098ª 7. The reference in the Latin text could be given in a more complete form as *ex Aristotelis testimonio in Ethicis ad Nicomachum.*

[2] *Nicomachean Ethics*, v. 7. 1, 1134ᵇ 18. *lib.* 5° MS. B.

[3] τὸ δὲ νομικόν, quoted by Locke before φυσικόν, belongs to the preceding clause, in which Aristotle says that social justice is partly natural and partly conventional; Locke erroneously treated τὸ νομικόν as a substantive characterized by φυσικόν, thus confusing it with τὸ δίκαιον. Aristotle's whole sentence reads (in Burnet's edition): τοῦ δὲ πολιτικοῦ δικαίου τὸ μὲν φυσικόν ἐστι τὸ δὲ νομικόν, φυσικὸν μὲν τὸ πανταχοῦ τὴν αὐτὴν ἔχον δύναμιν.

[4] See note A, p. 282.   [5] *aut* is needed before *quod.*

superior will, wherein the formal cause of a law appears to consist; in what manner, however, this may become known to mankind is a question perhaps to be discussed later on.[1] Secondly, it lays down what is and what is not to be done, which is the proper function of a law. Thirdly, it binds men, for it contains in itself all that is requisite to create an obligation. Though, no doubt, it is not made known in the same way as positive laws, it is sufficiently known to men (and this is all that is needed for the purpose) because it can be perceived by the light of nature alone.

So much being assumed, the existence of such a law is made acceptable by the following arguments:

The first argument can be derived from a passage in Aristotle's *Nicomachean Ethics*, Book I, chapter 7, where he says that 'the special function of man is the active exercise of the mind's faculties in accordance with rational principle'.[2] For since in the preceding passages he had shown by various examples that there is a special sort of work each thing is designed to perform, he tried to find out what this may be in the case of a human being also. Thus, having taken account of all the operations of the vegetal and sentient faculties which men have in common with animals and plants, in the end he rightly concludes that the proper function of man is acting in conformity with reason, so much so that man must of necessity perform what reason prescribes. Likewise in Book V, chapter 7, where he draws a distinction between legal justice and natural justice, Aristotle says 'A natural rule of justice is one which has the same validity everywhere'.[3] Hence it is rightly concluded that there is a law of nature, since there is a law which obtains everywhere.[4]

Some people here raise an objection against the law of nature, namely that there is no such law in existence at all, since it can nowhere be found, for most people live as though there were no rational ground in life at all nor any law of such a kind that all men recognize it; on the contrary, on this point men appear to disagree most of all. If indeed natural law were discernible by the light of reason, why is it that not all people who possess reason have knowledge of it?

My answer to this, first, is that, as in civil affairs, from the fact that it is impossible for a blind man, or difficult for one who sees badly, to read a legal notice displayed in a public place, or from the fact that a

[1] Cf. essays II and ff. [2] Tr. by H. Rackham, 1943, p. 20.
[3] Tr. by H. Rackham, 1943, p. 97. Another distinction drawn by Aristotle (*Rhetoric*, 1373 b 4) between law which is particular and positive and law which is universal and according to nature, is not referred to by Locke.
[4] See note B, pp. 282–3.

bilem dico; inde tamen non necessario sequitur eam cuilibet esse notam. Alii enim lumine hoc non utuntur sed tenebras amant nec se sibi ostendere velint, sol autem ipse viam qua eundum est nulli monstrat nisi qui aperit oculos et se itineri accingit; alii vitiis innutriti vix inter honestum et turpe distinguunt, cum prava consuetudo diuturnitate temporis invalescens peregrinos induxerit habitus et mali mores principia etiam corrupere; aliis etiam vitio naturae acumen ingenii hebetius est quam ut sufficiat eruendis his naturae arcanis. Quotusquisque enim est qui in rebus quotidiani usus aut scitu facilibus rationis se permittit imperio aut illius ductum sequitur, cum aut affectuum impetu in transversum acti aut per incuriam negligentes aut consuetudine degeneres, non quid[1] dictat ratio, sed quid suadet voluptas aut jubent pravi affectus proni sequuntur. Quis pene est in republica qui suae civitatis leges cognoscit promulgatas, publicis in locis appensas, lectu et cognitu faciles et ubique oculis patentes? quanto minus abditas et latentes naturae leges? (f. 17) Hac igitur in re non major pars hominum sed sanior et perspicacior consulenda est.

Secundo respondemus quod licet ipsa sanior pars hominum non prorsus inter se consentiunt quid sit lex naturae, quae illius certa et cognita decreta, non inde sequi nullam omnino dari naturae legem; imo vero magis efficitur esse hujusmodi legem, cum omnes de lege ipsa tam acriter contendunt; quemadmodum enim in civitate male concluditur nullas dari leges quia variae earum apud jurisperitos interpretationes reperiuntur, sic etiam in ethica male sequitur nullam dari legem naturae cum alibi hoc alibi illud pro lege naturae habeatur; unde fortius astruitur legis existentia, cum de lege ipsa omnes eandem tuentur sententiam, interpretando solum differunt, cum omnes agnoscant natura dari turpe et honestum; sed altius paulo hoc repetendum erit argumentum cum de modo cognoscendi hanc legem erit agendum.

[1] In this clause and the next, grammar requires *quod* instead of *quid*, or *quid* followed by the subjunctive mood.

man busy with other affairs is not at leisure, nor an idle or bad man inclined, to lift his eyes to the notice board and learn from it the nature of his duty, it does not follow that a law does not exist or is not published. So I admit that all people are by nature endowed with reason, and I say that natural law can be known by reason, but from this it does not necessarily follow that it is known to any and every one. For there are some who make no use of the light of reason but prefer darkness and would not wish to show themselves to themselves. But not even the sun shows a man the way to go, unless he opens his eyes and is well prepared for the journey. There are others, brought up in vice, who scarcely distinguish between good and evil, because a bad way of life, becoming strong by lapse of time, has established barbarous habits, and evil customs have perverted even matters of principle. In others, again, through natural defect the acumen of the mind is too dull to be able to bring to light those secret decrees of nature. For how few there are who in matters of daily practice or matters easy to know surrender themselves to the jurisdiction of reason or follow its lead, when, either led astray by the violence of passions or being indifferent through carelessness or degenerate through habit, they readily follow the inducements of pleasure or the urges of their base instincts rather than the dictates of reason. Who, as I might almost say, is there in a commonwealth that knows the laws of his state, though they have been promulgated, hung up in public places, are easy to read and to understand, and are everywhere exposed to view? And how much less will he be acquainted with the secret and hidden laws of nature? Hence, in this matter, not the majority of people should be consulted but those who are more rational and perceptive than the rest.

Secondly, I answer that, although even the more rational of men do not absolutely agree among themselves as to what the law of nature is and what its true and known precepts are, it does not follow from this that there is no law of nature at all; on the contrary it follows rather that there *is* such a law, when people contend about it so fiercely. For just as in a commonwealth it is wrong to conclude that there are no laws because various interpretations of laws are to be met with among jurisprudents, so likewise in morality it is improperly inferred that there is no law of nature, because in one place it is pronounced to be this, in another something different. This fact rather establishes the existence of the law more firmly, seeing that all the disputants maintain the same idea about the law itself (for they all know that there is something evil and something good by nature), and they differ only in their interpretations of it.

Secundum argumentum quo probatur dari legem naturae desumi potest ab hominum conscientiis, quod scilicet *se judice nemo nocens absolvitur*.[1] Judicium enim illud quod de se quisque fert testatur dari legem naturae. Si enim non detur lex naturae cui nos nosmet morigeros praestare debere dictat ratio, quomodo evenit quod eorum conscientia qui nullius alterius legis quibus aut diriguntur aut obligantur (f. 18) agnoscunt decreta de sua quidem vita et moribus fert sententiam et vel absolvit vel crimine alligat? cum sine lege aliqua nulla ferri potest sententia; quae lex non scripta est, sed innata.[2]

Tertium deducitur argumentum ab ipsa constitutione hujus mundi in quo reliqua omnia certam operationum suarum legem modumque naturae suae convenientem observant; id enim quod cuique rei formam et modum et mensuram agendi praescribit id demum lex est; *id omne, quod in rebus creatis fit, materia est legis aeternae*, inquit Aquinas,[3] et, τὴν πεπρωμένην μοίρην ἕκαστον ἐκπληροῖ καὶ ἐπὶ τὸ μεῖζον καὶ ἐπὶ τὸ μεῖον dictante Hippocrate,[4] unumquodque a lege sibi praescripta ne latum quidem unguem discedit. Quod cum ita sit, non videtur solum hominem legibus solutum esse dum reliqua tenentur, sed praescriptum habet suae naturae convenientem agendi modum; nec enim primi opificis sapientiae convenire videtur perfectissimum formare animal et irrequietum, mente, intellectu, ratione, et omnibus ad operandum necessariis abunde prae reliquis instruere et tamen nullum ei opus destinare aut ideo solum legis capacem formare hominem ut nulli obtemperaret.

---

[1] Quotation from Juvenal, *Satires*, xiii. 2–3.

[2] Cf. Cicero, *Orat. pro Milone*, sect. 10. Cicero's phrase is quoted in Culverwel's *Discourse of the Light of Nature*, 1652, ch. vi, p. 72 (ed. Brown, 1857).

[3] This is not a quotation but a paraphrase of passages in the *Summa Theol*. Ia IIae, q. 93, art. 4; the paraphrase can be found in Hooker's *Laws of Ecclesiastical Polity*, bk. i, ch. 3, par. 1, note (Keble's ed. of Hooker's *Works*, 1865, i. 205).

[4] περὶ διαίτης, i. 5 (ed. Littré, vi. 478). The quotation occurs in Hooker's *Laws of Ecclesiastical Polity*, bk. i, ch. 3, par. 4 (Keble's ed. of Hooker's *Works*, 1865, i. 209, and n. 29).

However, this argument will have to be discussed again a little farther on, when we shall have to deal with the way in which this law is known.[1]

The second argument which proves the existence of a law of nature can be derived from men's consciences;[2] from the fact, namely, that 'no one who commits a wicked action is acquitted in his own judgement'. Thus the sentence which everyone passes on himself testifies that there is a law of nature. For if there were no law of nature which reason declares we must show ourselves obedient to, how does it come to pass that the conscience of people who recognize the precepts of no other law whereby they are either guided or bound in duty, nevertheless passes judgement upon their life and conduct and either acquits or declares guilty,[3] seeing that without some law no judgement can be pronounced? This law, then, is not written, but innate, i.e. natural.[4]

The third argument is derived from the very constitution of this world, wherein all things observe a fixed law of their operations and a manner of existence appropriate to their nature. For that which prescribes to every thing the form and manner and measure of working, is just what law is.[5] Aquinas says that all that happens in things created is the subject-matter of the eternal law, and, following Hippocrates, 'each thing both in small and in great fulfilleth the task which destiny hath set down', that is to say nothing deviates even by an inch from the law prescribed to it. This being so, it does not seem that man alone is independent of laws while everything else is bound. On the contrary, a manner of acting is prescribed to him that is suitable to his nature; for it does not seem to fit in with the wisdom of the Creator to form an animal that is most perfect and ever active, and to endow it abundantly above all others with mind, intellect, reason, and all the requisites for working, and yet not assign to it any work, or again to make man alone susceptible of law precisely in order that he may submit to none.

---

[1] Essays II and ff.

[2] The argument from conscience was suggested to Locke in a letter by Gabriel Towerson, quoted on pp. 8–9 (Towerson expounded the argument in some detail in his own book, *An Explication of the Decalogue*, 1676, discourse i, pp. 2–3). In his letter to Locke, Towerson also says: 'I shall thinke it incumbent upon you ... to answer in short your owne objections.' This passage seems to refer to the above objection to the first argument for the existence of a law of nature and Locke's answers to it.   [3] Cf. Rom. ii. 14–15.

[4] Cf. Sanderson, *De Obligatione Conscientiae*, 1647, lect. iv, par. 14; also Sanderson's *Judgment in one View for the Settlement of the Church*, 1663, published in I. Walton's *Life of Dr. Sanderson*, 1678, pp. 117–18.

[5] In his Latin treatise on the civil magistrate (p. 6), Locke quotes a passage from Hooker's *Laws of Ecclesiastical Polity*, bk. i, ch. 2, par. 1 (Keble's ed. of Hooker's *Works*, 1865, i. 200), and on this passage the sentence here obviously is modelled.

Quartum argumentum desumitur ab hominum societate, cum sine hac lege hominibus inter ipsos nulla consuetudo aut conjunctio esse potest; duo enim sunt quibus niti videtur hominum societas, (f. 19) certa scilicet reipublicae forma ac regiminis constitutio, et pacti fides; quibus sublatis corruit omnis inter homines communitas, uti sublata hac lege naturae corruunt haec ipsa. Quae nempe civitatis facies esse potest, quae reipublicae constitutio aut rerum suarum securitas, si pars illa reipublicae quae maxime nocere valet omnia pro libitu suo agere possit, si in summa potestate maxima esset licentia? Cum enim principes, quos penes est leges pro libitu suo figere vel refigere et pro imperio suo omnia agere aliorum domini, nec suis nec aliorum positivis legibus astricti sint, aut esse possunt, si alia superior non esset lex naturae, scilicet cui parere debent, quo tandem in loco essent res humanae, quae societatis privilegiae, si ideo solum coirent in civitatem mortales ut aliorum potestati fierent paratior praeda?[1] Nec melior sane principum quam subditorum esset conditio, si nulla esset lex naturae, sine qua populus reipublicae legibus teneri non poterat. Leges nempe civitatum positivae non per se, sua virtute, aut alio modo obligant quam vi legis naturae jubentis superioribus obtemperare pacemque publicam tueri: adeo ut, sine (f. 20) hac lege, vi et armis principes forte ad obsequium plebem cogere poterant, obligare vero non poterant. Alterum etiam humanae societatis fundamentum corruit sine lege naturae, scilicet rerum contractarum fides; non enim in pacto manere hominem expectandum esset quia promiserat, ubi alibi se commodior offerret conditio, nisi promissorum implendorum obligatio esset a natura et non a voluntate humana.

Quintum argumentum est quod sine lege naturae nec virtus esset nec vitium, nec probitatis laus aut nequitiae poena: nulla culpa, nullus reatus, ubi nulla lex; omnia ad voluntatem humanam referenda essent, et cum officium nihil postularet non aliud agendum homini videtur nisi quod suaderet aut utilitas aut voluptas aut ni quod forte impingeret caecus et lege omni solutus impetus; recti et honesti interirent vana nomina aut nihil omnino essent nisi nomen inane; injurius esse non posset, cum lex nulla aut juberet aut vetaret quicquam, homo suarum actionum liberrimus et supremus arbiter. Intemperans vitae et valetu-

---

[1] Here follows a short passage which Locke deleted. It reads: si principes, cum agerent, raperent, truderent, prosternerent, occiderent subditos, jure tantum suo uterentur.

The fourth argument is taken from human society, since without this law men can have no social intercourse or union among themselves. Indeed there are two factors on which human society appears to rest, i.e. firstly, a definite constitution of the state and form of government, and, secondly, the fulfilment of pacts. Every community among men falls to the ground if these are abolished, just as they themselves fall to the ground if the law of nature is annulled.[1] In fact, what is to be the shape of a body politic, the constitution of a state, and the security of its interests, if that part of a community which has the power to do most harm may do everything as it pleases, if in the supreme authority there is the most unrestrained liberty? For since the rulers, in whose power it is to make or remake laws at their will and as the masters of others to do everything in favour of their own dominion, are not, and cannot be, bound either by their own or by other people's positive laws, supposing there is no other, superior, law of nature, i.e. one which they are bound to obey, in what condition, pray, would be men's interests, what would be the privileges of society, if men united in a commonwealth only to become a more ready prey for the power of others? Nor indeed would the condition of the rulers be better than that of the subjects, if there were no natural law, for without it the people could not be restrained by the laws of the state. Certainly, positive civil laws are not binding by their own nature or force or in any other way than in virtue of the law of nature, which orders obedience to superiors and the keeping of public peace. Thus, without this law, the rulers can perhaps by force and with the aid of arms compel the multitude to obedience, but put them under an obligation they cannot. Without natural law the other basis also of human society is overthrown, i.e. the faithful fulfilment of contracts, for it is not to be expected that a man would abide by a compact because he has promised it, when better terms are offered elsewhere, unless the obligation to keep promises was derived from nature, and not from human will.[2]

The fifth argument is that without natural law there would be neither virtue nor vice, neither the reward of goodness nor the punishment of evil: there is no fault, no guilt, where there is no law.[3] Everything would have to depend on human will, and, since there would be

[1] Cf. here Grotius's notion of nature or the law of nature as the great-grandmother of municipal law (*De Jure Belli ac Pacis*, proleg., par. 16).

[2] Cf. Pufendorf, *Elementa Jurisprudentiae Universalis*, 1660, lib. i, def. xii, par. 16 (fin.).

[3] The phrase is reminiscent of Hobbes, *Leviathan*, pt. i, ch. 13 (ed. Pogson Smith, p. 98), but see also Rom. iv. 15, quoted by Culverwel, *Discourse of the Light of Nature*, ch. vi, p. 77 (ed. Brown, 1857).

dini suae minus forte consuluisse videatur, honestatem aut officium neglexisse minime; quamcunque nempe honestatem aut (f. 21) turpitudinem habent virtutes et vitia eam omnem legi huic naturae debent, cum earum natura aeterna sit et certa, nec decretis hominum publicis nec privata aliqua opinione aestimanda.

nothing to demand dutiful action, it seems that man would not be bound to do anything but what utility or pleasure might recommend, or what a blind and lawless impulse might happen perchance to fasten on. The terms 'upright' and 'virtuous' would disappear as meaningless or be nothing at all but empty names. Man would not be able to act wrongfully, since there was no law issuing commands or prohibitions, and he would be the completely free and sovereign arbiter of his actions. Granted that, undisciplined as he would then be, he would seem, perhaps, to have taken but little thought for his life and health,[1] yet he seems in no way to have disregarded honour and duty, since whatever honour or baseness our virtues and vices possess they owe it all to this law of nature; for the nature of good and evil is eternal and certain, and their value cannot be determined either by the public ordinances of men or by any private opinion.

---

[1] Cf. here a passage on intemperance in Locke's commonplace book of 1661, printed in Lord King's *Life* (1858), p. 293.

II

AN LEX NATURAE SIT LUMINE NATURAE COGNOSCIBILIS? AFFIRMATUR

Cum turpis et honesti aliqua apud omnes homines agnoscatur ratio, nec ulla gens sit tam barbara tam ab omni humanitate remota quae aliquam non habeat virtutis et vitii notitiam, laudis et vituperii conscientiam, proxime inquirendum videtur quibus modis innotescat hominibus lex illa naturae cui unanimi adeo consensu praestant obsequium, nec illius omnem sensum exuere possunt nisi simul exuant humanitatem; amolienda enim prorsus natura est priusquam aliquis in omnimodam se asserere potest libertatem. Modum autem per quem in legis hujus cognitionem devenimus dicimus esse lumen naturae ut opponitur aliis cognoscendi modis; dum autem lumen naturae hujus legis indicem esse asserimus, non id ita accipi velimus quasi aliqua esset homini interna lux (f. 23) a natura insita quae illum officii sui perpetuo admoneret et quo illi eundum esset recto tramite et sine omni errore duceret: legem hanc naturae tabulis inscriptam in pectoribus nostris patere non dicimus quae, uti admota tabulae publice prostanti in tenebris face, adventante aliqua luce interna, illius demum radiis legitur, intelligitur, et innotescit. Sed per lumen naturae aliquid esse cognoscibile nihil aliud velimus quam hujusmodi aliqua veritas in cujus cognitionem homo recte utens iis facultatibus quibus a natura instructus est per se et sine ope alterius devenire potest.

Tres autem sunt modi cognoscendi quos sine scrupuloso nimis vocabulorum delectu liceat mihi appellare inscriptionem, traditionem, et sensum, quibus quartus addi potest, revelatio scilicet supernaturalis et divina quae ad praesens non pertinet argumentum, dum inquirimus non quid homo divino spiritu afflatus scire, (f. 24) quid lumine e caelis delapso illuminatus conspicere valet, sed quid naturae vi et sua ipsius sagacitate eruere et investigare potest homo mente, ratione, et sensu instructus; quae omnis cognitio quantacunque est, quae certe magnos

II

CAN THE LAW OF NATURE BE KNOWN BY THE LIGHT OF NATURE? YES

SINCE some principle of good and evil is acknowledged by all men, and since there is no nation so savage and so far removed from any humane feelings that it does not have some notion of virtue and vice, some consciousness of praise and blame, it seems we must next inquire in what ways men come to know that law of nature to which they pay deference by so general a consent, and of which they cannot eradicate all feeling without at the same time eradicating humanity itself; for nature must be altogether negated before one can claim for himself absolute liberty. Now we maintain that the way in which we arrive at the knowledge of this law is by the light of nature as opposed to other ways of knowledge. But while we assert that the light of nature points to this law, we should not wish this to be understood in the sense that some inward light is by nature implanted in man, which perpetually reminds him of his duty and leads him straight and without fail whither he has to go. We do not maintain that this law of nature, written as it were on tablets, lies open in our hearts, and that, as soon as some inward light comes near it (like a torch approaching a notice board hung up in darkness), it is at length read, perceived, and noted by the rays of that light. Rather, by saying that something can be known by the light of nature, we mean nothing else but that there is some sort of truth to the knowledge of which a man can attain by himself and without the help of another, if he makes proper use of the faculties he is endowed with by nature.

However, there are three kinds of knowledge which, without an over-careful choice of terms, I may call inscription,[1] tradition,[2] and sense-experience. To these may be added a fourth kind, namely supernatural and divine revelation, but this is no part of our present argument. For we do not investigate here what a man can experience who is divinely inspired, or what a man can behold who is illuminated by a light from heaven, but what a man who is endowed with understanding, reason, and sense-perception, can by the help of nature and his

[1] i.e. innate knowledge.
[2] i.e. second-hand knowledge by way of information or instruction.

123

fecerit progressus, quae totam pervadens rerum naturam nec inter limites mundi circumscripta caelum ipsum contemplatione ingreditur, et spiritus mentesque, quid sint, quid agant, quibus legibus tenentur, accuratius inquisivit, haec, inquam, tota cognitio una e tribus illis sciendi modis ad animum pertingit, nec alia praeter haec dantur principia et fundamenta cognoscendi; quicquid enim scimus id omne vel beneficio naturae et quodam nascendi privilegio pectoribus nostris inscriptum est, vel fando auditum, vel sensibus haustum.[1] Sed cum de modis cognoscendi agere proposuerim, miretur hic fortasse aliquis cur rationem, magnum illud et uti videtur praecipuum omnis cognitionis lumen, omiserim, praesertim cum lex naturae a plerisque vocetur ipsa ratio recta[2] et dictatum rectae rationis. Dicimus autem nos hic inquirere de primis principiis et primordiis omnis scientiae, quomodo primae notiones et cognitionis fundamenta in animum illabuntur; illa autem a ratione non accipi asserimus: vel enim per inscriptionem imprimuntur animis nostris, vel traditione accipimus, vel per sensus intrant; nihil enim agit ratio, magna illa argumentandi facultas, nisi aliquo prius posito et concesso; utitur fateor hisce scientiae principiis ad majora et altiora eruenda, sed ea minime ponit; non jacit fundamentum, etsi augustissimam saepenumero erigat structuram et ad caelum usque attollat scientiarum apices; aeque enim facile poterit quisquam sine praemissis conclusionem inferre ac sine aliqua prius cognita et concessa veritate ratiocinari; ipsam autem originem cognitionis jam investigamus.

Primo inscriptionem quod attinet,[3] quidam sunt qui existimant hanc legem naturae nobis innatam esse et omnium animis ita a natura infixam ut (f. 25) nemo sit qui in mundum prodit, cujus mens nativos hosce officii sui characteres et indices sibi insculptos non gerat, cujus animus practica haec principia et vivendi regulas sibi connatas notasque non habeat; nec aliunde quaerere necesse sit extraneas et mutuatitias morum leges, cum homo suas intus semperque patentes habeat pandectas quae omne illius complectuntur officium. Haec fateor facilis est et percommoda cognoscendi methodus, et optime cum humano genere

---

[1] The following passage from *sed* to *investigamus* was added by Locke on f. 23[v].
[2] e.g. Cicero, *De Rep.* iii. 22 (Lactantius, *Inst. Div.* vi. 8. 7).   [3] *attinent* MS. B.

own sagacity search out and examine. For all this sort of learning, whatever its extent (and it certainly has made great progress), traverses the whole world and is not confined within any of its limits but leads even to the contemplation of the sky, and has inquired with no little care into the nature and functions of spirits and minds and the laws that apply to them; all this learning, I repeat, reaches the mind altogether from those three ways of knowing,[1] and besides these there exist no other principles and foundations of knowledge. For whatever we know is all either inscribed in our hearts by a gift of nature and a certain privilege of birth, or conveyed to us by hearsay, or drawn by us from the senses.

However, since I have proposed to deal with ways of knowing, someone perhaps may wonder in this connexion why I have omitted to mention reason, that great and, as it seems, chief light of all knowledge, especially because the law of nature is most often called right reason itself and the dictate of right reason. Our explanation is that we investigate here the first principles and sources of all kinds of knowledge, the way in which primary notions and the elements of knowledge enter the mind. Yet all these, we maintain, are not apprehended by reason: they are either stamped on our minds by inscription, or we receive them second-hand, or they enter by the senses. Nothing indeed is achieved by reason, that powerful faculty of arguing, unless there is first something posited and taken for granted. Admittedly, reason makes use of these elements of knowledge, to amplify and refine them, but it does not in the least establish them. It does not lay a foundation, although again and again it raises a most majestic building and lifts the summits of knowledge right into the sky. As easily, indeed, will a man be able to construct a syllogism without premisses as find use for his reason without anything first being known and admitted as true. It is, however, the actual origin of knowledge we are inquiring into just now.

(1) As regards inscription, there are some who are of the opinion that this law of nature is inborn in us and is so implanted by nature in the minds of all, that there is none who comes into the world whose mind does not carry these innate characters[2] and marks of his duty engraved upon it, who has not in his thoughts these moral precepts

---

[1] The meaning of this last sentence is clear, but on account of some ambiguity in the construction of it I cannot think of a satisfactory translation. I have taken *una* as an adverb.

[2] In his *Essay*, i. i. 1, Locke speaks of 'primary notions' or 'characters'; in i. ii. 27, he speaks of 'marks' and 'characters'.

actum esset si ita edocti essent homines, ita a natura instructi, ita nati ut quid deceret, quid minus, dubitare non possint. Hoc si concedatur stat certe theseos[1] nostrae veritas: legem scilicet naturae lumine naturae esse cognoscibilem. An vero aliqua hujusmodi detur legis naturae in pectoribus nostris inscriptio, an hoc modo humano generi innotescat, alibi fortassis inquirendi erit locus. Ad praesentem quod spectat quaestionem sufficiet probasse (f. 26) posse hominem, si recte utatur ratione sua et nativis facultatibus quibus a natura instructus est, devenire in hujus legis cognitionem sine praeceptore aliquo qui erudiret, sine monitore qui doceret officium. Si autem legem hanc alio modo cognosci praeterquam traditione probaverimus, constabit illam lumine naturae et interno principio cognosci, cum quicquid sciat homo id omne vel ab aliis vel a se discat necesse est.

Secundo itaque dicimus traditionem, quam ideo a sensu distinguimus, non quod traditiones per sensum ad animum non ingrediuntur, fando enim audimus, sed quod auribus tantum sonum accipimus, fide rem amplectimur; ut, dum Ciceroni de Caesare loquenti fidem habemus, nos credimus fuisse Caesarem quem cognovit Cicero fuisse; traditionem, inquam, dicimus non esse cognoscendi modum quo ad nos pervenit lex naturae, non quod negamus aliqua etiam pene omnia illius praecepta nobis (f. 27) tradi a parentibus, praeceptoribus, et illis omnibus qui juventutis mores efformare et teneros adhuc animos virtutis amore et cognitione imbuere satagunt; ne enim animi in voluptatem nimium proclives, vel corporis illecebris capti, vel malis quae ubique occurrunt exemplis seducti, saniora rationis dictata negligant, maxime cavendum putant omnes qui de erudiendis juvenum animis quicquam cogitant, adeoque in prima adhuc aetatula virtutum fundamenta jaciunt et omni opera numinis reverentiam et amorem erga superiores obsequium, promissorum implendorum fidem, veracitatem, clementiam, li-

---

[1] Greek genitive.

and rules of conduct born with him and known to him; and that it is not necessary to seek information from any other source, consulting moral laws borrowed from somewhere without oneself, since man has his pandects within himself[1] and always open before his eyes, and they contain all that constitutes his duty. Admittedly this is an easy[2] and very convenient way of knowing, and the human race would be very well off if men were so fully informed and so endowed by nature that from birth they were in no doubt as to what is fitting and what is less so. If this view is accepted, the truth of our assertion is firmly established, namely that the law of nature can be known by the light of nature. Whether in fact there is any such imprint of the law of nature in our hearts, and whether it becomes known to mankind in the manner described, will perhaps be discussed at another place.[3] As regards the present question, it will suffice to have proved that, if man makes use properly of his reason and of the inborn faculties with which nature has equipped him, he can attain to the knowledge of this law without any teacher instructing him in his duties, any monitor reminding him of them.[4] However, if we shall hereafter prove that this law is known otherwise than by tradition, it will be certain that it is known by the light of nature and by an inward principle, since, whatever a man knows, he necessarily learns it all either from others or from himself.

(2) We come next to tradition, which we distinguish from sense-experience not because traditions do not enter the mind by sense—for it is through hearsay that they are received—but because the ears hear the sound only, and it is belief which embraces the fact. For example, provided we place confidence in Cicero when he speaks of Caesar, we believe that Caesar, whom Cicero knew to have lived, has lived. Now, of tradition we say that it is not a way of knowing whereby the law of nature comes to us; and this we do not say because we deny that some, nay almost all, precepts of that law are transmitted to us by parents, teachers, and all those who busily fashion the manners of young people and fill the still tender souls with the love and knowledge of virtue. For, indeed, that we must take special care lest human souls become too prone to pleasure, or get caught by the enticements of the body, or are led aside by bad examples that occur everywhere, and thus make light of the more wholesome precepts of reason, is held by all those

---

[1] Cf. Culverwel, *Discourse of the Light of Nature*, ch. ix, p. 99 (ed, Brown, 1857), quoting from Hierocles.   [2] Cf. *Essay*, I. iii. 25.   [3] Essay III.
[4] The last part of the sentence is reminiscent of a phrase in Cicero's definition of natural law, *De Republica*, iii. 22 (Lactantius, *Inst. Div.* vi. 8. 8).

beralitatem, morum castitatem, reliquasque inculcant virtutes. Quae omnes cum praecepta sint legis naturae non negamus posse nobis ab aliis tradi; sed id solum asserimus, scilicet traditionem non esse primarium et certum modum cognoscendi legem naturae; quae enim ab aliis fando audimus, si ideo solum (f. 28) amplectimur quia alii honesta esse dictitarunt, haec licet fortasse mores nostros recte satis dirigant et intra officii nostri cancellos contineant, nobis tamen hominum dictata sunt, non rationis. Nec dubito quin maxima hominum pars, mutuatitiis hisce morum regulis quas a traditione accipiunt contenti, ad exemplum et opinionem eorum hominum inter quos nasci et educari contigit mores suos componunt, nec aliam habent recti et honesti regulam quam civitatis suae consuetudines et communem hominum quibuscum versantur sententiam; ideoque legem naturae ab ipsis fontibus haurire et officii sui ratio quibus nitatur principiis, quomodo obligat, unde primo promanat, investigare minime laborant, opinione et laude, non naturae lege ducti. Legem autem naturae, prout lex est, nobis traditione non innotescere sequentia probare videntur argumenta.

Primo quia in tanta traditionum inter (f. 29) se pugnantium varietate impossibile esset statuere quid sit lex naturae, difficile admodum judicare quid verum, quid falsum, quid sit lex, quid opinio, quid dictet[1] natura, quid utilitas, quid suadeat ratio, quid doceat politia. Cum enim tam variae sint ubique traditiones, tam contrariae plane et inter se pugnantes hominum sententiae, non solum in diversis nationibus sed eadem civitate, unaquaeque enim opinio quam ab aliis discimus traditio est, cum denique pro sua quisque sententia tam acriter contendat et sibi credi postulat,[2] impossibile plane esset, si traditio solum officii nostri dictaret rationem, quae nam illa sit cognoscere vel in tanta varietate verum eligere, cum nulla assignari potest ratio cur huic homini potius quam alteri contrarium plane asserenti majorum traditionis deferenda sit authoritas aut pronior adhibenda

---

[1] *dictat* MS. B; Locke obviously intended the subjunctive *dictet*.
[2] Inconsistent moods of the two verbs.

who reflect a little on the education of young minds and who indeed early in that as yet youthful age lay the foundations of the moral virtues and do their best to inculcate sentiments of respect and love for the deity, obedience to superiors, fidelity in keeping promises and telling the truth, mildness and purity of character, a friendly disposition, and all the other virtues. Since all these are precepts of the law of nature, we do not deny that such precepts can be transmitted to us by others, but only this: that tradition is a primary and certain way of knowing the law of nature. For what we take over from other people's talk, if we embrace it only because others have insisted that it is good, may perhaps direct our morals well enough and keep them within the bounds of dutiful action, yet it is not what reason but what men tell us. And I am in no doubt that most persons, content with these second-hand rules of conduct which they derive from tradition, build up their morals after the manner and belief of those among whom they happen to be born and educated, and that they have no other rule of what is right and good than the customs of their society and the common opinion of the people with whom they live. And for this reason they least of all strive to derive the law of nature from its very fountain-head and to investigate on what principles the ground of their duty rests, in what manner it creates obligations, and what its first origin is; for they are, after all, guided by belief and approval, not by the law of nature. But that the law of nature, in so far as it is a law, does not become known to us by means of tradition, is shown, if I mistake not, by the following arguments.

First, in the presence of so much variety among conflicting traditions it would be impossible to determine what the law of nature is, and it would be difficult to decide completely what is true and what is false, what is law and what is opinion, what is commanded by nature and what by utility, what advice reason gives and what instructions are given by society. For since traditions vary so much the world over and men's opinions are so obviously opposed to one another and mutually destructive, and that not only among different nations but in one and the same state—for each single opinion we learn from others becomes a tradition—and finally since everybody contends so fiercely for his own opinion and demands that he be believed, it would plainly be impossible—supposing tradition alone lays down the ground of our duty—to find out what that tradition is, or to pick out truth from among such a variety, because no ground can be assigned why one man of the older generation, rather than another maintaining quite the

fides, nisi ratio in ipsis rebus quae traduntur aliquam reperiat differentiam (f. 30) et ideo alteram amplectitur alteram rejicit opinionem quod in hac minor in illa major sit evidentia lumine naturae cognoscibilis; quod sane non est traditioni credere sed de rebus ipsis judicare, quod tollit omnem traditionis authoritatem. Aut igitur in cognoscenda lege naturae traditione promulgata adhibenda est ratio et judicium, et tunc cessat omnis traditio, aut lex naturae per traditionem innotescere non potest, aut nulla erit. Cum enim lex naturae ubique una eademque sit, traditiones autem variae, necesse sit ut nulla omnino sit lex naturae aut hoc modo non cognoscibilis.

Secundo, si a traditione discenda esset lex naturae, fides hoc potius esset quam cognitio, cum penderet potius ex authoritate loquentis quam ipsius rei evidentia, et ita demum mutuatitia potius esset quam innata lex.

Tertio, qui legem naturae traditione cognosci dicunt sibimet ipsis contradicere videntur; qui enim retro oculos convertere velit et ad originem ipsam traditionem persequi, necesse sit ut alicubi (f. 31) gradum sistat et aliquem tandem agnoscat primum hujus traditionis authorem qui legem hanc aut intus in pectore inscriptam invenerit vel ad ejus cognitionem a rebus sensu haustis argumentando pervenerit. Hi autem cognoscendi modi reliquis etiam hominibus aeque competunt, nec opus est traditione ubi quisque in se eadem habeat cognoscendi principia; quod si author ille primus hujus traditionis oraculo aliquo edoctus, spiritu divino afflatus, mundo promulgaverit, haec lex ita promulgata nequaquam lex naturae est sed positiva.

Concludimus igitur, si qua sit lex naturae, quod nemo negaverit, ea quatenus lex sit traditione cognosci non potest.

Tertius et ultimus qui remanet cognoscendi modus sensus est, quod principium constituimus hujus legis cognoscendae; quod tamen sic accipi non debet (f. 32) quasi ita alicubi prostaret lex naturae ut vel oculis legere vel manibus explorare vel sese promulgantem audire possimus; sed, cum jam de principio et origine hujus legis cognoscendae quaerimus et quo modo humano generi innotescat, dico fundamentum omnis illius

opposite, should be credited with the authority of tradition or be more worthy of trust; except it be that reason discovers a difference in the things themselves that are transmitted, and embraces one opinion while rejecting another, just because it detects more evidence recognizable by the light of nature for the one than for the other. Such a procedure, surely, is not the same as to believe in tradition, but is an attempt to form a considered opinion about things themselves; and this brings all the authority of tradition to naught. Thus there are three possibilities: either that in trying to become acquainted with the law of nature as promulgated by tradition one has to employ reason and understanding, and then the whole of tradition becomes void, or that the law of nature cannot become known by tradition, or that it does not exist at all. For since the law of nature is everywhere one and the same, but traditions vary, it follows either that there is no law of nature at all, or that it cannot be known by means of tradition.

Secondly, if the law of nature could be learnt from tradition, it would be a matter of trust rather than of knowledge, since it would depend more on the authority of the giver of information than on the evidence of things themselves, and would therefore be a derived rather than an inborn, i.e. natural, law.

Thirdly, those who maintain that the law of nature is known by tradition apparently contradict themselves. For anyone who is willing to look back and trace a tradition to its very source must necessarily come to a stand somewhere and in the end recognize someone as the original author of this tradition, who either will have found the law of nature inscribed within his heart or come to know it by reasoning from the facts perceived by the senses. These ways of knowing, however, are equally open to the rest of mankind also, and there is no need of tradition as long as everyone has within himself the same basic principles of knowledge. But if that first author of the tradition in question has laid down a law to the world, because he was instructed by some oracle or inspired by a divine message, then a law of this kind and promulgated in this manner is by no means a law of nature, but a positive law.

Therefore we conclude that, if there is a law of nature (and this nobody has denied), it cannot be known in so far as it is a law by means of tradition.

(3) The last way of knowledge that remains to be discussed is sense-perception, which we declare to be the basis of our knowledge of the law of nature. However, this must not be understood in the sense that

cognitionis hauriri ab iis rebus quas sensibus nostris percipimus; e quibus ratio et argumentandi facultas, quae homini propria est, ad earum opificem progrediens, argumentis a materia, motu, et visibili hujus mundi structura et oeconomia necessario emergentibus, tandem concludit et apud se pro certo statuit Deum esse aliquem harum rerum omnium authorem; quo posito necessario sequitur universa lex naturae qua tenetur gens humana, uti in posterum patebit. Ex dictis autem satis constat legem naturae esse lumine naturae cognoscibilem, cum quicquid apud homines vim legis (f. 33) obtineat necesse est ut aut Deum aut naturam aut hominem agnoscat authorem, quicquid autem aut homo jusserit aut Deus oraculo mandaverit id omne lex positiva est; lex autem naturae, cum traditione cognosci non potest, remanet ut solo lumine naturae hominibus innotescat.

Contra hanc nostram sententiam haec facile occurrit objectio, scilicet si lex naturae lumine naturae cognoscatur, quomodo evenit, cum interna haec lex omnibus a natura insita sit, quod ubi omnes illuminati sunt tot sunt caeci; qui fit quod plurimi mortales hanc legem ignorant et omnes pene de ea diversa sentiunt, quod fieri non posse videtur, si omnes lumine naturae ad illius cognitionem ducerentur?

Haec objectio aliquam in se vim haberet, si diceremus legem naturae pectoribus nostris inscribi; hoc enim supposito necessario sequeretur eandem ubique de lege hac esse sententiam, cum lex haec eadem in omnibus inscriberetur et intellectui pateret. (f. 34) Respondemus autem quod licet facultates nostrae intellectivae nos in hujus legis cognitionem deducere possunt, non tamen inde sequi omnes homines iis facultatibus necessario recte uti: figurarum numerorumque natura et proprietates obviae videntur et lumine naturae sine dubio cognoscibiles, non tamen inde sequitur quod quicunque mente compos sit geometres evadat aut artem arithmeticam penitus calleat; attenta animi meditatione, cogitatione, et cura opus est, ut quis a rebus sensibilibus obviisque argumentando et ratiocinando in reconditam earum[1]

---

[1] *eorum* MS. B.

the law of nature appears somewhere so conspicuously that we can either read it off with our eyes, examine it with our hands, or hear it proclaiming itself. But since we are searching now for the principle and origin of the knowledge of this law and for the way in which it becomes known to mankind, I declare that the foundation of all knowledge of it is derived from those things which we perceive through our senses. From these things, then, reason and the power of arguing, which are both distinctive marks of man, advance to the notion of the maker of these things (there being no lack of arguments in this direction such as are necessarily derived from the matter, motion, and the visible structure and arrangement of this world) and at last they conclude and establish for themselves as certain that some Deity is the author of all these things. As soon as this is laid down, the notion of a universal law of nature binding on all men necessarily emerges; and this will become clear later on.[1] From what has been said, however, it is quite certain that there is a law of nature that can be known by the light of nature. For whatever among men obtains the force of a law, necessarily looks to God, or nature, or man as its maker; yet whatever man has commanded or God has ordered by divine utterance, all this is positive law. But since the law of nature cannot be known by tradition, all that remains is that it becomes known to men by the light of nature alone.

Against this conclusion of ours the following objection readily presents itself: if the law of nature becomes known by the light of nature, how does it happen that where all are enlightened there are so many blind, since this inward law is implanted by nature in all men? How does it arise that very many mortals are without knowledge of this law and nearly all think of it differently, a fact that does not seem possible if all men are led to the knowledge of it by the light of nature?

This objection would have some force in it if we asserted that the law of nature is inscribed in our hearts. For, if this were assumed, it would necessarily follow that what is thought about this law would be everywhere the same, since this law would be written down in all men and be disclosed to the understanding as one and the same. Our answer, however, is that, granted that our mental faculties can lead us to the knowledge of this law, nevertheless it does not follow from this that all men necessarily make proper use of these faculties. The nature and properties of figures and numbers appear obvious and, no doubt, know-able by the light of nature; yet from this it does not follow that who-

[1] Essay IV.

133

naturam penetrare possit. Latent in terrae visceribus auri et argenti ditiores venae, dantur etiam hominibus quibus effodi possunt brachia et manus, et machinarum inventrix ratio, non tamen inde omnes homines divites concludimus; operi se accingant prius necesse est, et multo labore eruendae sunt illae opes quae in tenebris latent reconditae, otiosis et oscitantibus sese (f. 35) non offerunt, nec vero omnibus qui quaerunt, cum aliquos etiam incassum sudantes videamus. Quod si in rebus ad communis vitae usum pertinentes paucos admodum inveniamus qui ratione dirigantur, cum homines raro admodum in sese descendunt ut inde vitae suae causam, modum rationemque eruant, non mirandum est quod tam diversae sint de lege hac non adeo cognitu facili mortalium sententiae, cum plurimi hominum de officio suo parum soliciti, aut aliorum exemplis aut patriis institutis et loci consuetudine aut denique eorum quos bonos et prudentes viros judicant authoritate potius quam ratione ducti, non aliam quaerunt vitae morumque regulam, sed mutuatitia illa contenti sunt quam aliorum mores, opiniones, aut consilia sine gravi aliqua meditatione aut studio incautis facile suggerunt. Non igitur sequitur naturae legem naturae lumine (f. 36) non esse cognoscibilem quia pauci admodum sunt qui nec vitiis corrupti nec per incuriam negligentes lumine illo recte utuntur.[1]

---

[1] At the end of this essay Locke added the title of another which remained unwritten, namely, *An Lex Naturae per Traditionem Nobis Innotescat? Negatur.* ('Does the law of nature become known to us through tradition? No.') This question has already been dealt with in this last essay and Locke's answer to it has been in the negative. Culverwel dealt with tradition in his *Discourse of the Light of Nature*, ch. viii, and p. 102 (ed. Brown, 1857); he, too, denied that the law of nature is discovered by tradition. Behind this discussion of tradition in connexion with natural law lies the long-lived controversy with papists who endeavoured to secure for tradition an equal authority with the written word of God by accepting it as part of His unwritten word (cf. Hooker's *Laws of Ecclesiastical Polity*, bk. i, ch. 13, par. 2).

ever is in possession of mental faculties turns out a geometer or knows thoroughly the science of arithmetic. Careful reflection, thought, and attention by the mind is needed, in order that by argument and reasoning one may find a way from perceptible and obvious things into their hidden nature. Concealed in the bowels of the earth lie veins richly provided with gold and silver; human beings besides are possessed of arms and hands with which they can dig these out, and of reason which invents machines. Yet from this we do not conclude that all men are wealthy. First they have to equip themselves; and it is with great labour that those resources which lie hidden in darkness are to be brought to the light of day. They do not present themselves to idle and listless people, nor indeed to all those who search for them, since we notice some also who are toiling in vain. But if in matters that relate to the practice of ordinary life we meet but few who are directed by reason, since men only seldom delve into themselves in order to search out from thence the condition, manner, and purpose of their life, then it is not to be wondered at that of the law of nature, which is much less easy to know, men's opinions are so different. For most people are little concerned about their duty; they are guided not so much by reason as either by the example of others, or by traditional customs and the fashion of the country, or finally by the authority of those whom they consider good and wise. They want no other rule of life and conduct, being satisfied with that second-hand rule which other people's conduct, opinions, and advice, without any serious thinking or application, easily supply to the unwary. It does not therefore follow that the law of nature cannot be known by the light of nature because there are only few who, neither corrupted by vice nor carelessly indifferent, make a proper use of that light.

III

AN LEX NATURAE HOMINUM ANIMIS INSCRIBATUR? NEGATUR

CUM dari legem naturae, eamque legem non traditione sed lumine naturae esse cognoscibilem superius probavimus, quid sit illud lumen naturae dubitari potest, quod, ut lux solis, dum res caeteras radiis suis nobis ostentat, ignoratur tamen ipsa et natura illius in occulto latet. Cum vero nihil homini cognoscatur cujus cognitionis principium aut animae in ipsis natalibus non imprimatur aut ab extra per sensus intret, hujus cognitionis primordia investigare operae pretium videtur et quaerere an hominum nascentium animae sint rasae tantum tabulae, observatione et ratiocinio postmodum informandae, an leges naturae officii sui indices connatas sibique inscriptas habeant.[1] Dum autem quaerimus an lex naturae hominum animis inscribatur, id volumus, scilicet an dentur aliquae propositiones practicae menti connatae et quasi insculptae, ut tam naturales sint animae et ei intimae quam ipsae facultates, voluntas scilicet et intellectus, et sine studio omni aut ratiocinatione immutabiles semperque patentes nobis innotescant. Verum hujusmodi nullam dari legis naturae in pectoribus nostris inscriptionem sequentia suadent argumenta.

(f. 38) Primo, gratis tantum dictum est et a nemine hactenus probatum, etiamsi in eo laborarunt multi,[2] scilicet nascentium[3] hominum animas aliquid esse praeter rasas tabulas quorumlibet characterum capaces nullos tamen a natura inscriptos sibi gerentes.

Secundo, si lex haec naturae hominum animis naturaliter tota simul in ipsis natalibus imprimatur, quomodo evenit quod homines ad unum omnes, qui suas secum habeant animas lege hac instructas, de ea statim sine haesitatione omni non consentiunt ad obsequium parati? cum circa hanc legem tam in diversum abeunt, cum alibi hoc alibi illud

---

[1] The following passage from *Dum* to *innotescant* was added by Locke on f. 36ᵛ.

[2] *laborarunt multi* was substituted by Locke for *laborat acutissimus Car[t]esius*. From the phrase before correction it appears that Locke originally regarded Descartes as the chief exponent of the doctrine of innate ideas.   [3] *noscentium* MS. B.

III

IS THE LAW OF NATURE INSCRIBED IN
THE MINDS OF MEN? NO

SINCE we have proved earlier that there is a law of nature and that this law can be known, not indeed by tradition but by the light of nature, doubts can be raised as to what this light of nature is: for while like sunlight it reveals to us by its rays the rest of reality, it is itself unknown and its nature is concealed in darkness.[1] Since in fact nothing is known to man without the principle of that knowledge being either imprinted in the original nature of the soul or imparted from outside through the senses, it appears worth our labour to investigate the first beginning of this knowledge and to inquire whether the souls of the newly-born are just empty tablets afterwards to be filled in by observation and reasoning, or whether they have the laws of nature as signs of their duty inscribed on them at birth. But by our inquiry whether the law of nature is written in the souls of men we mean this: namely, whether there are any moral propositions inborn in the mind and as it were engraved upon it such that they are as natural and familiar to it as its own faculties, the will, namely, and the understanding, and whether, unchangeable as they are and always clear, they are known to us without any study or deliberate consideration. The following arguments, however, show that there exists no such imprint of the law of nature in our hearts.

(1) It has been only an empty assertion and no one has proved it until now, although many have laboured to this end, that the souls of men when they are born are something more than empty tablets capable of receiving all sorts of imprints[2] but having none stamped on them by nature.

(2) If this law of nature were stamped by nature upon the minds of men as a whole at their very birth, how does it come about that human beings, who would have their souls furnished with that law, do not forthwith all to a man agree about it without hesitation and show readiness to obey it? For in respect to this law they differ so very widely, one rule of nature and right reason being proclaimed here,

---

[1] Cf. *Essay, Introduction*, par. 1.
[2] 'Characters', 'primary notions', cf. *Essay*, 1. i. 1.

dictatum naturae et rectae rationis praedicatur, idem apud hos hone-stum quod apud alios turpe, cum legem naturae hi aliam hi nullam omnes obscuram agnoscunt. Hic (quod a nonnullis fieri scio) siquis responderet legem hanc a natura pectoribus nostris inscriptam lapsu primi hominis aut partim obliterari aut prorsus et in universum deleri (f. 39) (quod sane argumentum maximae mortalium parti penitus ignotum, qui de primo homine aut illius lapsu ne semel quidem cogi-taverint), hujusmodi responsum praeterquam quod ad philosophos mi-nus pertineat nodum minime solveret nec dubium eximeret; dum enim hanc legem in cordibus hominum primitus inscriptam deletam asserunt, alterum horum affirment necesse est, scilicet legem hanc naturae aut partim amissam, aliqua nempe illius praecepta prorsus intercidisse, aut omnia; si aliqua hujus legis praecepta omnino deleta sunt ex hominum pectoribus, quae inscripta remanent aut eadem sunt in omnibus aut diversa; si eadem dicant tum de his cognitu facilibus inter se facile consentirent omnes qui ubique sunt homines, quod minime factum videmus; si diversa esse quae in hominum animis relicta sunt naturae decreta asserant et inter se differre nativas has (f. 40) inscriptiones, rogo hic quaenam sit hujus differentiae causa, cum natura in operibus suis ubique eadem sit et uniformis? deinde an non absurdum videtur asserere hominum mentes inter se principiis ipsis differre? quo etiam pacto cognosci poterat lex naturae et certa recti et honesti regula, si concedatur semel in diversis hominibus diversa et alia esse dictata naturae et actionum principia? Quod si legem hanc primitus inscriptam prorsus deletam asserunt, ubi tandem erit lex illa naturae de qua quaerimus? nulla sane erit hoc concesso nisi alium[1] praeter inscriptionem reperiamus cognoscendi modum.

Tertio, si lex haec naturae hominum mentibus inscribatur, qui fit quod pueruli juniores, indocti, et barbarae illae nationes, qui sine institutis, sine legibus, sine eruditione omni secundum naturam vivere

---

[1] *aliam* MS. B.

another there, one and the same thing being good with some people, evil with others, some recognizing a different law of nature, others none; but all see in it something obscure.[1] If anyone at this juncture should reply (and I know that several have done so)[2] that this law which nature has inscribed in our hearts has, on account of the Fall, been either partly erased or absolutely and altogether effaced (an argument which, to be sure, is wholly unknown to the majority of men, who may not even once have thought about Adam or his fall), such an answer, besides being one that does not particularly concern philosophers, would by no means remove the difficulty nor take away the doubt. For since they maintain that this law originally written in the hearts of men has been effaced, they must affirm one or the other of two things, namely that this law of nature has been either partly lost, that is to say that some of its precepts have entirely perished, or that all its precepts have become lost. If only some of the precepts of this law have been utterly effaced from the hearts of men, those that remain inscribed therein are either the same in all or are different. If it is said that they are the same, then all men in the world would easily agree among themselves about these precepts, for they would readily be known; but this we can see is by no means the case. If it is said that the decrees of nature which are left behind in the souls of men are different and that these innate impressions are unlike one another, what I ask here is the cause of this difference, since nature in its works is everywhere the same and uniform? And then, does it not seem unreasonable to assert that the minds of men differ from one another about the very first principles? Again, by what means could the law of nature and a definite rule of moral rectitude and goodness be known, if it is once admitted that the dictates of nature and the principles of action vary from person to person? But if it is asserted that this law originally impressed is altogether effaced, where, pray, will be that law of nature for which we search? Surely on this admission it will be nothing, unless we can find a way of knowledge other than by inscription.

(3) If this law of nature is inscribed in the minds of men, how does it happen that younger boys, illiterate people, and those primitive races which, having no institutions, laws, and knowledge, are said to live in accordance with nature, do not best of all know and understand this

---

[1] Cf. Hobbes, *Leviathan*, pt. ii, ch. 26 (ed. Pogson Smith, p. 212).

[2] Locke's reference here might be to St. Augustine's doctrine of the partial depravity of 'fallen' man (*De Civ. Dei*, xix. 13, and xxii. 24) and the more pessimistic and severe Fall-doctrines of Calvin (*Institutes*, ii. i. 8–9), Luther, and the Jansenists. Cf. also Robert Sanderson, *De Obligatione Conscientiae*, 1647, iv. 24.

dicuntur, hanc non optime omnium cognoscant callentque[1] legem? qui ab adventitiis (f. 41) liberrimi sunt notionibus quae alio animos avocare possint, qui mutuatitias aliunde non imbibunt opiniones quae dictata naturae aut pervertere aut obliterare aut delere possunt, cum non alios habeant praeceptores praeter se ipsos nec aliud sequuntur quam naturam. Si lex naturae pectoribus hominum inscriberetur, inter hos homines illam sine lituris sine mendis repertam[2] iri credendum esset; verum quam longe horum hominum mores a virtute distent, quam alieni sunt ab omni humanitate, dum nullibi tam incerta fides, tanta perfidia, tam immanis crudelitas dum caesis hominibus cognato sanguine et diis et genio suo simul sacrificant, facile patebit consulenti et veteris et novi orbis historias et peregrinantium itineraria, nec quis credet inter barbaras hasce et nudas gentes cognosci maxime (f. 42) et observari legem naturae, cum inter plurimas harum pietatis, mansuetudinis, fidei, castitatis, et reliquarum virtutum appareat nec vola nec vestigium, sed inter rapinas, furta, stupra, et homicidia misere vitam transigunt; lex igitur naturae hominum pectoribus inscribi non videtur, cum illi qui non alium habent ducem praeter ipsam naturam, in quibus dictata naturae a positivis morum institutis minime corrumpuntur, ita vivunt omnis legis ignari quasi nulla omnino recti et honesti habenda esset ratio.

Fateor ego inter moratiores populos et eruditione et morum institutis perpolitos dari aliquas certas indubitatasque de moribus opiniones quas licet pro lege naturae agnoscunt et pectoribus suis a natura inscriptas credant,[3] vix tamen puto a natura acceptas sed aliunde promanasse; quae licet sint fortasse legis naturae aliqua praecepta, non tamen a natura edocti sunt sed ab hominibus; hae enim opiniones de recto et honesto quae tam (f. 43) arcte amplectimur hujusmodi plerumque sunt quae in tenera adhuc aetatula, antequam de iis quicquam judicare adhuc possimus vel observare quomodo se insinuent, animis nostris parum cautis infunduntur instillanturque a parentibus vel praeceptoribus nostris aliisque quibuscum versamur; qui dum eadem credunt ad vitam

---

[1] Inconsistent moods of the two verbs.   [2] Grammar would require *repertum*.
[3] Inconsistent moods of the two verbs in this clause.

law? They are all free from notions coming from without which may divert the minds elsewhere; they do not imbibe opinions borrowed from some other source, which can either corrupt, or blot out or destroy the dictates of nature; for they have no other teachers than themselves and follow nothing but nature. If the law of nature were written in the hearts of men, one would have to believe that among these people it will be found undiminished and unspoiled.[1] But yet anyone who consults the histories both of the old and the new world, or the itineraries of travellers, will easily observe how far apart from virtue the morals of these people are, what strangers they are to any humane feelings, since nowhere else is there such doubtful honesty, so much treachery, such frightful cruelty in that they sacrifice to the gods and also to their tutelary spirit by killing people and offering kindred blood. And no one will believe that the law of nature is best known and observed among these primitive and untutored tribes, since among most of them there appears not the slightest trace or track of piety, merciful feeling, fidelity, chastity, and the rest of the virtues; but rather they spend their life wretchedly among robberies, thefts, debaucheries, and murders. Thus the law of nature does not appear to be written in the hearts of men, if those who have no other guide than nature itself and among whom the decrees of nature are least spoiled by arbitrary moral customs live in such ignorance of every law, as though there were no principle of rightness and goodness to be had at all.

I myself admit that among the peoples which are better mannered and polished through training and moral instruction there exist some definite and undoubted views about morals, but although they may take these for the law of nature and believe that they are written in their hearts by nature, nevertheless I hardly think they are derived from nature but suppose that they have come from some other source. Though they may be perhaps some of the precepts of the law of nature, they are not learned from nature but from men. For these opinions about moral rightness and goodness which we embrace so firmly are for the most part such as, in a still tender age, before we can as yet determine anything about them or observe how they insinuate themselves, stream into our unguarded minds and are inculcated by our parents or teachers or others with whom we live. For since these believe that such opinions are conducive to well ordering of life, and

---

[1] Cf. Culverwel, *Discourse of the Light of Nature*, ch. x, pp. 118–19 (ed. Brown, 1857), quoting from Salmasius's *De Coma*.

bene efformandam conferre, ipsi etiam eodem forsan modo eadem edocti, proni sunt his opinionibus recentes adhuc puerulorum animos imbuere, quas necessarias putant ad bene beateque vivendum; in hac enim re maxime cauti sunt et seduli qui putant his quae primo jacta sunt morum fundamentis totam futurae vitae spem niti. Et hoc demum modo cum opiniones hae animis nostris parum attentis sine observatione nostra irrepserint, in pectoribus nostris radices agentes, nobis interim aut quomodo aut quando ignorantibus, suamque etiam confirmant authoritatem communi hominum quibuscum nobis (f. 44) consuetudo est consensu et laude, illico concludendum putamus, cum non aliam illarum observemus originem, hasce opiniones a Deo et natura pectoribus nostris inscriptas; et dum eas quotidiano usu vitae regulas constituimus, si has dubitaremus esse legem naturae, et futurae vitae incerti essemus et paeniteret[1] anteactae, cum judicare necesse esset, si haec non sit lex naturae quam hactenus observavimus, nos male et sine ratione adhuc vixisse; hanc igitur ob rationem has primae juventutis opiniones ab aliis infusas quam arctissime amplectimur, pluris aestimamus, credimus obstinate, nec in dubium vocari a quoquam patimur, et dum haec principia esse praedicamus, de iis nosmet ipsos nec dubitare nec contra negantem (principia enim credimus) disputare permittimus; ex his igitur patet multa esse posse quae quis credat a natura menti suae inscripta, quae tamen aliunde mutuantur (f. 45) originem, nec ideo sequi quod quicquid proni credimus et pro principio amplectimur, cujus tamen fontem ignoramus, id esse legem naturae a natura pectoribus nostris inscriptam.

Quarto, si lex haec naturae pectoribus nostris inscriberetur, cur stulti et mente capti nullam hujus legis habent cognitionem? cum dicatur immediate ipsis mentibus imprimi quae minime pendent ex constitutione et structura organorum corporis, quam solam esse differentiam inter sapientes insipientesque in confesso est.

[1] *paeniterit* MS. B.

perhaps have also themselves been brought up in them in the same manner, they are inclined to imbue the still fresh minds of the young with opinions of this kind, which they regard as indispensable for a good and happy life. For in this matter the most cautious and zealous are those who think that the whole hope of after-life rests upon the moral foundations which are laid in the beginning. And at last, because in this way and without our notice these opinions have crept into our minds with but little attention on our part, striking roots in our breasts while we are unaware either of the manner or the time, and also because they assert their authority by the general consent and approval of men with whom we have social intercourse, we immediately think we must conclude that they are inscribed in our hearts by God and by nature, since we observe no other origin of them. And since by daily practice we are firmly establishing these opinions as rules to live by, we should both be uncertain of our future life and repent of our past life, if we were to doubt that these represent the law of nature. For if the law of nature were not what we have hitherto observed, it would be necessary to conclude that thus far we have lived badly and without reason. On that account, therefore, we embrace as firmly as possible these opinions of early youth which have been instilled into us by others, we think of them the more highly, believe in them obstinately, and do not suffer them to be called in question by anybody. And since we proclaim them as principles, we do not allow ourselves either to doubt them or to argue about them against anyone denying them (for we believe them to be first principles). From all this, therefore, it is clear that there can exist many things which anyone may believe to be inscribed in his mind by nature, which nevertheless derive their origin from some other source, and that it does not follow that, just because we eagerly believe in something and cherish it as a principle, though we are ignorant of its source, this is the law of nature, written in our hearts by nature.

(4) If this law of nature were written in our hearts, why do the foolish and insane have no knowledge of it, since the law is said to be stamped immediately on the soul itself and this depends very little upon the constitution and structure of the body's organs?[1] Yet therein admittedly lies the only difference between the wise and the stupid.

---

[1] There is an ambiguity in the construction of the Latin sentence from *cum* to *corporis*; if compared with a very similar passage in Locke's *Essay*, I. i. 27 (Fraser's ed. i. 61), the clause might be translated thus: 'since (as they say) it is on the soul itself that those principles are immediately impressed which least depend on the constitution and structure of the body's organs'.

Quinto, si lex naturae pectoribus nostris inscribatur, concludendum foret speculativa principia aeque inscribi ac practica, quod tamen vix probandum videtur; si enim primum illud et celeberrimum scientiarum principium excutere velimus, impossibile scilicet est idem simul esse et non esse, facile constabit axioma illud pectoribus nostris a natura non inscribi nec a quoquam pro concesso haberi (f. 46) priusquam aut ab alio didicerit aut inductione et particularium rerum observatione, quae legitima est axiomatum stabiliendorum methodus, sibimet ipsi probaverit; nulla igitur mihi aut practica aut speculativa principia hominum animis a natura inscribi videntur.

(5) If the law of nature were written in our hearts, it would have to be inferred that speculative as well as practical principles are inscribed. But this seems difficult to prove; for if we try to search out the first and best known principle of the sciences (namely, that it is impossible that the same thing should at the same time both be and not be), it will be readily[1] agreed that this principle is not inscribed by nature as an axiom in our hearts nor taken for granted by anyone before he has either learned it from another or (which is the proper method of establishing principles) proved it to himself by induction and by observing particulars.[2] Thus it appears to me that no principles, either practical or speculative, are written in the minds of men by nature.

---

[1] The whole of the first chapter of Bk. I of the *Essay* of 1690 is devoted to a defence of this assertion.

[2] Cf. *Essay*, IV. vii. 9–11, xii. 3. In Bk. IV of the *Essay*, however, Locke distinguishes empirical generalizations from self-evident truths. The interpretation of logical principles as inductive truths or empirical hypotheses was accepted by J. S. Mill and other empiricists. Locke, in this passage, was probably influenced by Culverwel's *Discourse of the Light of Nature*, ch. xi, pp. 125–7 (ed. Brown, 1857).

IV

AN RATIO[1] PER RES A SENSIBUS HAUSTAS PERVENIRE POTEST IN COGNITIONEM LEGIS NATURAE? AFFIRMATUR

LEGEM naturae lumine naturae esse cognoscibilem supra probavimus. Cum vero lumen illud naturae, quod unicum nos vitae hujus iter ingressuros dirigit quodque per varios officiorum anfractus devitatis hinc vitiorum salebris illinc errorum deviis[2] ad id virtutis faelicitatisque fastigium nos deducit quo et vocant dii et tendit natura—cum, inquam, lumen illud in obscuro lateat et difficilius longe cognitu[3] videtur quid sit quam quo dirigat, operae pretium videtur has etiam excutere tenebras et in sole ipso non caecutire; decet sane non tantum brutorum more ad vitae usum luce frui et ad dirigendos gressus adhibere sed quid lumen illud sit, quae ejus natura et ratio altiore indagine investigare. Quandoquidem vero lumen hoc naturae (ut alibi ostensum est) nec traditio sit nec internum aliquod practicum principium mentibus nostris a natura inscriptum, (f. 48) nihil remanet quod lumen naturae dici possit praeter rationem et sensum, quae solum duae facultates hominum mentes instruere et erudire videntur et id praestare quod luminis proprium est, scilicet ut res aliter ignotae prorsus et in tenebris latentes animo obversentur et cognosci et quasi conspici possint. Quae dum mutuas sibi invicem tradunt operas, dum sensus rerum particularium sensibilium ideas rationi administrat et suggerit discursus materiam, ratio e contra sensum dirigit et ab eo haustas rerum imagines inter se componit, alias inde format, novas deducit, nihil tam obscurum est tam reconditum[4] tam ab omni sensu remotum quod his adjutus facultatibus cogitando et ratiocinando assequi non possit omnium capax animus. Quod si alterutram tollas, altera (f. 49) certe frustra est; sine ratione enim sensibus instructi ad brutorum naturam vix assurgimus, cum sus et simia et plura inter quadrupedes animalia sensuum acumine homines longe superent; sine sensuum autem ope et ministerio nihil magis prae-

---

[1] *Ratio] sive Facultas Discursiva* added and again cancelled in MS. A.

[2] The passage from *deviis* to *natura*, contained in MS. A but omitted by the amanuensis in MS. B, was added by Locke on f. 46ᵛ.

[3] The passage from *cognitu* to *has*, contained in MS. A but omitted by the amanuensis in MS. B, was added by Locke on f. 46ᵛ.   [4] *recognitum* MS. B; *reconditum* MS. A.

IV

CAN REASON ATTAIN TO THE KNOWLEDGE OF NATURAL LAW THROUGH SENSE-EXPERIENCE? YES

WE have proved above that natural law can be known by the light of nature, which, indeed, is our only guide when we are entering the course of this life, and which, amid the various intricacies of duty, avoiding the rough roads of vice on one side and the by-ways of error on the other, leads us to that height of virtue and felicity whereto the gods invite and nature also tends. But since, I say, this light of nature lies hidden in darkness and it seems far more difficult to know what it is than whither it leads, it appears worth our labour both to dispel this darkness also and to be no longer blind in the light of the sun itself. Certainly it is fitting not only, like beasts, to derive advantage from light for the service of life and to use it to guide one's steps, but also to inquire by deeper investigation what is this light, its nature and its source. But since, as has been shown elsewhere, this light of nature is neither tradition nor some inward moral principle written in our minds by nature, there remains nothing by which it can be defined but reason and sense-perception. For only these two faculties appear to teach and educate the minds of men and to provide what is characteristic of the light of nature, namely that things otherwise wholly unknown and hidden in darkness should be able to come before the mind and be known and as it were looked into. As long as these two faculties serve one another, sensation furnishing reason with the ideas of particular sense-objects and supplying the subject-matter of discourse, reason on the other hand guiding the faculty of sense, and arranging together the images of things derived from sense-perception, thence forming others and composing new ones, there is nothing so obscure, so concealed, so removed from any meaning that the mind, capable of everything, could not apprehend it by reflection and reasoning, if it is supported by these faculties. But if you take away one of the two, the other is certainly of no avail, for without reason, though actuated by our senses, we scarcely rise to the standard of nature found in brute beasts, seeing that the pig and the ape, and many of the quadrupeds, far surpass men in the sharpness of the senses. On the other hand, without the help and assistance of the senses, reason can achieve nothing more

stare potest ratio quam clausis fenestris in tenebris operarius; nisi illic transeant rerum ideae nulla erit ratiocinandi materia, nec plus possit ad extruendam cognitionem animus quam ad aedificanda domicilia architectus cui desunt saxa, arbores, arena, et reliqua aedificiorum materia. Per rationem hic intelligimus non practica aliqua principia vel propositiones quasvis in animo repositas, quibus dum vitae nostrae actiones apte respondent dicuntur conformes rectae rationi; hujusmodi enim recta ratio est ipsa lex naturae jam cognita, non modus vel lumen illud naturae quo cognoscitur, et est (f. 50) tantum objectum rationis non ratio ipsa, hujusmodi scilicet veritates quas quaerit ratio et investigat ad vitam dirigendam moresque efformandos necessarias. Ratio autem hic sumitur pro facultate animae discursiva quae a notis ad ignota progreditur et unum ex alio certa et legitima propositionum consecutione deducit. Haec est illa ratio cujus ope gens humana in cognitionem legis naturae pervenit. Fundamentum autem cui innititur[1] tota illa cognitio quam ratio in altum extruit et ad caelum usque attollit sunt objecta sensuum; sensus enim omnium primi suggerunt et ad secretos animi recessus intromittunt totam et primariam discursus materiem; ex cognitis enim et concessis semper procedit omnis argumentatio, nec sine posita et intellecta aliqua veritate magis discurrere vel ratiocinari potest animus quam agillimum quodvis e quadrupedibus animal (f. 51) sese movere vel e loco in locum progredi sine stabili aliquo vestigiorum fulcimento. Mira sunt fateor quae in scientiis mathematicis invenit et investigat ratio sed quae omnia de linea pendent, superficiei inaedificantur, et corpus habent pro fundamento cui innitantur; haec enim operationum suarum objecta et alia insuper communia principia et axiomata sibi dari postulat, non invenit nec probat mathesis. Eadem plane in aliis etiam disciplinis tradendis tractandisque

---

[1] *innitur* MS. B.

than a labourer can working in darkness behind shuttered windows.[1] Unless the ideas of objects penetrate the mind there will be no subject-matter of reasoning, nor could the mind do more towards the construction of knowledge than an architect can towards the building of houses if he falls short of stones, timber, sand, and the rest of building material. By reason here we do not mean some moral principles or any propositions laid up in the mind such that, if the actions of our life fitly correspond to them, these are said to be in accordance with right reason; for right reason of this sort is nothing but the law of nature itself already known, not the manner whereby, or that light of nature whereby, natural law is known; it is only the object of reason, not reason itself; that is to say, it is such truths as reason seeks and pursues as necessary for the direction of life and the formation of character. On the contrary, reason is here taken to mean the discursive faculty of the mind, which advances from things known to things unknown and argues from one thing to another in a definite and fixed order of propositions. It is this reason by means of which mankind arrives at the knowledge of natural law. The foundations, however, on which rests the whole of that knowledge which reason builds up and raises as high as heaven are the objects of sense-experience; for the senses primarily supply the entire as well as the chief subject-matter of discourse and introduce it into the deep recesses of the mind. In fact, at all times every argumentation proceeds from what is known and taken for granted,[2] and the mind cannot discourse or reason without some truth that is given and perceived, any more than the swiftest animal whatsoever among the quadrupeds can move or advance from place to place without something stable to uphold its steps. I admit it is astonishing what reason finds and tracks out in mathematical science, but all this is dependent upon a line, is built within a plane, and has a solid substance as foundation to rest on. Surely mathematics presupposes these objects of its operations together with other general principles and axioms as its data;[3] it does not discover them nor prove them true.

[1] Cf. here Culverwel, *Discourse of the Light of Nature*, ch. xi, pp. 125-7 (ed. Brown, 1857), referring to Aristotle's doctrine of *tabula rasa* and the 'windows of sense'. The simile is taken up in one of the drafts of the *Essay* of 1671 (ed. Rand, 1931, p. 84), and in the *Essay* itself (II. xi. 17).

[2] Cf. Aristotle, *Nic. Ethics*, bk. i, ch. 4, 1095^{a}30 sq.; cf. also bk. vi, ch. 3, 1139^{b}26 sq., and *An. Post.*, bk. i, chs. 1-2, 71^{a}1 sq.; also *Met.* A. 9, 992b30; the scholastic rule (to which Locke refers and objects in his *Essay*, IV. vii. 8) that all reasonings are *ex praecognitis et praeconcessis* made all knowledge depend on maxims.

[3] Cf. Aristotle, *Topics*, bk. vi, ch. 4, 141^{b}5 sqq.; *An. Post.*, bk. i, ch. 18. The word *principium* (Greek ἀρχή) can here mean 'starting-point', a very usual signification of it.

ratio utitur methodo, in quibus ornandis excolendisque, et si abscondita, sublimia, et digna, quae et ratio ipsa miretur inventa proferatque prodatque, nulla tamen est si singulas percurrere velis scientias speculativas in qua non aliquid semper supponitur et pro concesso habetur et a sensibus aliquo modo mutuo accipitur. Omnis (f. 52) conceptus animi uti et corporis fit semper ex aliqua praeexistente materia, nec minus in moralibus et practicis disciplinis eodem modo progreditur et eadem sibi concedi postulat ratio. Ut vero cognoscatur quomodo sensus et ratio dum sibi mutuo opitulentur nos deducere possunt in cognitionem legis naturae, praemittenda sunt aliqua quae ad legis cujusvis cognitionem necessario supponuntur. Primo igitur, ut se lege teneri quisquam cognoscat, scire prius oportet esse legislatorem, superiorem scilicet aliquam potestatem cui jure subjicitur. Secundo scire etiam oportet esse aliquam superioris illius potestatis voluntatem circa res a nobis agendas, hoc est legislatorem illum, quicunque is demum fuerit, velle nos hoc agere illud vero omittere, et exigere a nobis ut vitae nostrae mores suae voluntati (f. 53) sint conformes; ut vero haec duo supposita ad legis naturae cognitionem necessaria nobis innotescant, quid sensus confert quid ratio in sequentibus patebit.

Primo igitur dicimus patere ex sensu esse in rerum natura res sensibiles, hoc est revera existere corpora et eorum affectiones, scilicet levitatem, gravitatem, calorem, frigus, colores, et caeteras qualitates sensui obvias, quae omnes aliquo modo ad motum referri possint; esse mundum hunc visibilem mira arte et ordine constructum, cujus etiam pars nos sumus genus humanum; videmus enim perpetuo certoque cursu circum rotari sidera, volvi in mare flumina, et se certo ordine sequi anni et tempestatum vicissitudines. Haec et infinita pene plura nos docet sensus.

Reason, plainly, adopts the same way of procedure also in the transmission and investigation of other forms of knowledge and in the embellishment and perfecting of anything whatsoever. And if there are things obscure, sublime, and noble, which even reason itself may marvel at and bring forth and proclaim as a discovery, yet, if you would run through each single speculative science, there is none in which something is not always presupposed and taken for granted and derived from the senses by way of borrowing. Every conception in the mental, no less than in the physical, sense always arises out of some pre-existing material, and reason proceeds in the same manner in the moral and practical sciences also and demands to be allowed this material. But in order that we may know how sense-experience and reason, as long as they assist one another mutually, can lead us to the knowledge of natural law, certain facts must first be set forth, because they are necessarily presupposed in the knowledge of any and every law. First, in order that anyone may understand that he is bound by a law, he must know beforehand that there is a law-maker, i.e. some superior power to which he is rightly subject. Secondly, it is also necessary to know that there is some will on the part of that superior power with respect to the things to be done by us, that is to say, that the law-maker, whoever he may prove to be, wishes that we do this but leave off that, and demands of us that the conduct of our life should be in accordance with his will. In what follows it will become clear what sense-experience contributes and what reason does, in order that these two presuppositions, which are required for knowledge of the law of nature, may become known to us.

In the first place, then, we say it is evident from sense-experience that in the natural world there are perceptible objects, i.e. that there really exist solid bodies and their conditions, namely lightness and heaviness, warmth and coldness, colours and the rest of the qualities[1] presented to the senses, which can all in some way be traced back to motion;[2] that this visible world is constructed with wonderful art and regularity, and of this world we, the human race, are also a part. We certainly see the stars turning round in an unbroken and fixed course, rivers rolling along into the sea, and the years and changes of the seasons following one another in a definite order. This and almost infinitely more we learn from the senses.

[1] In Draft A of the *Essay* of 1671 (ed. Aaron and Gibb, 1936, p. 8, n. 1), Locke explains that 'by quality I would be understood to meane that which is the cause of any simple Idea in my minde' (cf. Locke's more detailed explanation at the end of Draft A, p. 73).

[2] Cf. *Essay*, II. viii. 11–12.

Secundo, dicimus, cum mens acceptam[1] hujus mundi machinam secum accuratius perpenderit et rerum sensibilium speciem, ordinem, (f. 54) ornatum, et motum contemplaverit, inde progreditur ad eorum originem inquirendam,[2] quae causa, quis author fuerit tam egregii operis, cum certo constet id casu et fortuito in tam justam tam undique perfectam affabreque factam compagem coalescere non potuisse: unde certe colligitur oportere esse potentem sapientemque harum rerum omnium opificem qui totum hunc fecit fabricavitque mundum et nos homines, non infimam in eo partem: cum autem inanimatorum bruto-rumque caetera turba efficere non possint hominem se ipsis longe perfectiorem, nec se ipsum homo; nos enim nobismet ipsis originem no-stram non debere vel inde constat non solum quod sui ipsius nihil causa sit, nam id axioma non prohibet quo minus credamus aliquid esse quod non est ab alio si Deum agnoscere velimus, sed etiam quod homo eas omnes in se non invenit perfectiones quas animo concipere potest; (f. 55) nam (ut[3] omittam omnium rerum perfectam cognitionem et in res naturales majorem potentiam) si homo sui ipsius author esset qui sibi dare poterat essentiam, qui se produceret in rerum naturam daret etiam sibi suae existentiae durationem sempiternam, cum concipi non potest aliquid sibi adeo infensum adeo inimicum fore quod, cum sibi tribuere poterat existentiam, non simul eandem conservaret vel peracto brevis aetatulae curriculo eam libenter amittere vellet sine qua reliqua omnia, chara, utilia, jucunda, beata retineri[4] non possunt et frustra quaeruntur; cum certe minoris vel saltem ejusdem sit potentiae con-servare ac constituere et qui quovis momento aliquid incipere jussit id ne quovis momento desinat efficere possit. His ita positis necessario sequitur alium esse praeter nos potentiorem et sapientiorem authorem (f. 56) qui pro libitu suo nos producere, conservare, ac tollere potest. His ita a sensuum testimonio deductis dictat ratio aliquam esse superio-

---

[1] *a sensibus acceptam* MS. A.
[2] *inquirendum* MS. A; the reading in MS. B seems to be *inquirendam*, which gives a pre-ferable construction.
[3] The bracketed passage begins with *nam* in MS. B.
[4] *reteneri* MS. B.

Secondly, we say that the mind, after more carefully considering in itself the fabric of this world perceived by the senses and after contemplating the beauty of the objects to be observed, their order, array, and motion,[1] thence proceeds to an inquiry into their origin, to find out what was the cause, and who the maker, of such an excellent work, for it is surely undisputed that this could not have come together casually and by chance into so regular and in every respect so perfect and ingeniously prepared a structure. Hence it is undoubtedly inferred that there be a powerful and wise creator of all these things, who has made and built this whole universe and us mortals who are not the lowest part of it. For, indeed, all the rest of it, inanimate things and brute beasts, cannot create man who is far more perfect than they are. Nor, on the other hand, can man create himself; for that we do not owe our origin to ourselves is surely undisputed, not merely for the reason that nothing is its own cause—for obviously this axiom does not prevent us, if we are willing to acknowledge God, from believing that something exists which does not depend upon another—but also because man does not find in himself all those perfections which he can conceive in his mind. For (omitting perfect knowledge of all things and a greater authority over things in nature) if man were the maker of himself, able to give himself being, then he who could bring himself forth into the world of nature would also give himself an existence of everlasting duration. For it cannot be conceived that anything will be so unfriendly, so hostile to itself that, while able to bestow existence on itself, it would not at the same time preserve it, or would willingly let it go, when a little life's brief course had ended; for without it all other precious, useful, agreeable, and blessed things cannot be retained and are sought for in vain. Certainly it requires a lesser power to preserve something than to create it, or at any rate only the same power,[2] and whoever at any moment has ordered something to come into being, he can effect that it does not cease to exist at some other moment. After the case has been put thus it necessarily follows that above ourselves there exists another more powerful and wiser agent who at his will can bring us into the world, maintain us, and take us away. Hence, having inferred this on the evidence of the senses, reason lays down that there must be some superior power to which we are

[1] The proof of God's existence advanced here combines the argument from motion with that from design. A few lines lower he adds to it the anthropological argument.

[2] For the whole of this anthropological argument see Descartes, *Meditation III* (*The Philosophical Works of Descartes*, ed. Haldane and Ross, i. 168).

rem potestatem cui merito subjicimur, Deus scilicet qui in nos justum habet et ineluctabile imperium, qui prout sibi visum fuerit nos erigere potest vel prosternere, eodem nutu faelices vel miseros reddere; qui cum animam ipse creavit corpusque mira arte contexuit, utriusque facultates, vires, et secretam fabricam naturamque probe perspectam habet,[1] illam aerumnis vel gaudio, hoc dolore vel voluptate implere et exagitare potest et utrumque simul ad summam beatitudinem tollere vel miseriam poenamque detrudere. Unde liquido apparet rationem sensu monstrante viam nos deducere posse in cognitionem legislatoris sive superioris alicujus potestatis cui necessario subjicimur, quod primum (f. 57) erat requisitum ad cognitionem alicujus legis. Fateor equidem alios numen esse et mundo huic praesidere ex conscientiae testimonio probare aggressos, alios ex idea illa Dei quae nobis innata videtur, quae utraque argumentandi methodus [si][2] Deum esse certo probet, etsi (quod rem accuratius intuenti forsan apparebit) vim suam omnem utriusque argumenta a nativis nostris facultatibus, sensu scilicet et ratione, circa res sensibiles operantibus et inde deductis argumentorum momentis non mutuentur. Sufficit tamen ad confirmandam argumenti nostri veritatem posse hominem sensu simul et ratione utens[3] pervenire in cognitionem summi alicujus numinis uti supra ostensum est, ut omittam in praesens merito dubitari posse utrum idea illa Dei omnibus hominibus a natura insit, cum (si qua peregrinantibus adhibenda fides aliquas esse in orbe (f. 58) terrarum gentes quae nullum omnino numen agnoscant[4] uti testantur eorum itineraria) [cum][5] nulla ubique sit gens tam barbara tam ab humanitate omni remota quae sensuum usu non gaudeat, quae rationis privilegio et argumentandi facultate belluas non superat, licet forsan facultates illas nativas parum excoluerit adhibita disciplina, et adeo omnes ubique homines sufficienter a natura instructi sunt ad Deum in operibus suis investigandum, si nativis hisce facultatibus uti non negligant et quo ducat natura sequi non dedignentur. Patet igitur posse homines a rebus sensibilibus colli-

---

[1] *habeat* MS. A.

[2] *si* appears redundant.

[3] The case here seems wrong and the reading should be *utentem*.

[4] *agnoscunt* MS. A.

[5] This word should be deleted as a repetition of the same word two lines above. I have inserted round brackets.

rightly subject, namely God who has a just and inevitable command over us and at His pleasure can raise us up or throw us down, and make us by the same commanding power happy or miserable. And since He has Himself created the soul and constructed the body with wonderful art, and has thoroughly explored the faculties and powers of each, as well as their hidden constitution and nature, He can fill and stir the one with sorrow or delight, the other with pain or pleasure; He also can lift both together to a condition of the utmost happiness or thrust them down to a state of misery and torment. Hence it appears clearly that, with sense-perception showing the way, reason can lead us to the knowledge of a law-maker or of some superior power to which we are necessarily subject. And this was the first thing needed for the knowledge of any law. Certainly I grant that some have undertaken to prove from the testimony of conscience[1] that there is a Deity presiding over this world; others have done so from the idea of God,[2] regarded as innate in us, either of which ways of argument would certainly prove that God exists, even if (and this will perhaps become clear to anyone considering the case more carefully) the argument of neither method derives its whole force from our inborn faculties, i.e. from sense-perception and reason, operating upon objects of sense, and from points of arguments thence deduced. However, for the purpose of confirming the truth of our argument it suffices that man, as has been shown above, by exercising the senses and reason at the same time, can attain to the knowledge of some supreme godhead. Let me for the present abstain from pointing out that it can be justly doubted whether that idea of God pertains to all men by nature, because, even if travellers abroad are to be trusted that there are in the world, as the records of their journeys testify, some peoples which recognize no deity at all, yet there is nowhere a nation so uncivilized and so far removed from any culture as not to rejoice in the use of the senses and not to surpass brute animals in the use of reason and the faculty of arguing, though perhaps it has not sufficiently perfected those inborn faculties by training as well. In fact, all men everywhere are sufficiently prepared by nature to discover God in His works, so long as they are not indifferent to the use of these inborn faculties and do not refuse to follow whither nature leads. Thus it is clear that men can infer from sense-experience that there exists

---

[1] For an exposition of the argument from conscience see Calvin, *Institutes*, bk. i, ch. 3; Henry More, *An Antidote against Atheisme*, 1653, ch. x, pp. 29–31.

[2] Cf. Descartes, *Meditation V* (ed. Haldane and Ross, i. 180 f.); Henry More, *An Antidote against Atheisme*, 1653, chs. viii–ix.

gere superiorem esse aliquem potentem[1] qui in homines ipsos jus habet et imperium; quis enim negabit lutum figuli voluntati esse subjectum, testamque eadem manu qua formata est (f. 59) posse comminui?

Secundo igitur, cum ex sensuum testimonio concludendum sit esse aliquem harum rerum omnium opificem quem non solum potentem sed sapientem agnoscere necesse sit, sequitur inde illum non frustra et temere fecisse hunc mundum; repugnat enim tantae sapientiae nullo destinato fine operari, neque enim credere potest homo, cum se sentiat mentem habere agilem, capacem, ad omnia promptam et versatilem, ratione et cognitione ornatam, corpus insuper agile et pro animae imperio huc illuc mobile, haec omnia ad agendum parata sibi a sapientissimo authore dari ut nihil agat, his se[2] facultatibus omnibus instrui ut eo splendidius otietur et torpescat: unde liquido constat Deum velle illum aliquid agere, quod secundum erat requisitum ad legis cujusvis cognitionem, scilicet voluntas superioris potestatis (f. 60) circa res a nobis agendas, hoc est velle illum nos aliquid agere. Quid vero illud sit quod nobis agendum est partim ex fine rerum omnium, quae cum a beneplacito divino suam mutuentur originem et opera sint authoris summe perfecti et sapientis non videntur ab eo ad alium destinari finem quam ad sui ipsius gloriam ad quam omnia referri debent, partim etiam officii nostri rationem certamque regulam colligere possumus ex hominis ipsius constitutione et facultatum humanarum apparatu; cum enim nec temere factus sit homo nec in nihilum his donatus facultatibus quae exerceri et possunt et debent, id videtur opus hominis ad quod naturaliter agendum instructus est, id est cum in se sensus et rationem reperit pronum se et paratum sentit ad Dei opera ejusque in iis sapientiam potentiamque contemplandam et laudem deinde honorem et gloriam tanto tamque benefico authore (f. 61) dignissimam tribuendam reddendamque; deinde ad vitae conjunctionem cum aliis hominibus conciliandam et conservandam non solum vitae usu et necessitate impelli, sed ad societatem ineundam propensione quadam naturae incitari eamque tuendam sermonis beneficio et linguae commercio instrui, quantum vero ad se ipsum conservandum obligetur. Cum ad eam

---

[1] *potentem*] *sapientemque* add. MS. A.
[2] *se*, in MS. A, seems necessary but is omitted in MS. B.

some powerful superior who has right and authority over themselves; for who will deny that the clay is subject to the potter's will, and that a piece of pottery can be shattered by the same hand by which it has been formed?

In the second place, then, since on the evidence of the senses it must be concluded that there is some maker of all these things, whom it is necessary to recognize as not only powerful but also wise, it follows from this that he has not created this world for nothing and without purpose. For it is contrary to such great wisdom to work with no fixed aim; nor indeed can man believe, since he perceives that he has an agile, capable mind, versatile and ready for anything, furnished with reason and knowledge, and a body besides which is quick and easy to be moved hither and thither by virtue of the soul's authority, that all this equipment for action is bestowed on him by a most wise creator in order that he may do nothing, and that he is fitted out with all these faculties in order that he may thereby be more splendidly idle and sluggish. Hence it is quite evident that God intends man to do something, and this was the second of the two things required for the knowledge of any and every law, namely, the will on the part of a superior power with respect to the things to be done by us; that is, God wills that we do something. But what it is that is to be done by us can be partly gathered from the end in view for all things. For since these derive their origin from a gracious divine purpose and are the work of a most perfect and wise maker, they appear to be intended by Him for no other end than His own glory, and to this all things must be related. Partly also we can infer the principle and a definite rule of our duty from man's own constitution and the faculties with which he is equipped. For since man is neither made without design nor endowed to no purpose with these faculties which both can and must be employed, his function appears to be that which nature has prepared him to perform. That is to say, when he in himself finds sense-experience and reason, he feels himself disposed and ready to contemplate God's works and that wisdom and power of His which they display, and thereupon to assign and render praise, honour, and glory most worthy of so great and so beneficent a creator. Further, he feels himself not only to be impelled by life's experience and pressing needs to procure and preserve a life in society with other men, but also to be urged to enter into society by a certain propensity of nature, and to be prepared for the maintenance of society by the gift of speech and through the intercourse of language, in fact as much as he is obliged to preserve

officii partem interno instinctu nimium quam impellatur, nemoque repertus sit qui se negligit, se ipsum abdicet,[1] et in hanc rem omnes forte magis attenti sint[2] quam oportet, non opus est ut hic moneam; sed de his tribus quae omne hominum erga Deum, vicinum, et se ipsum complectuntur officium alibi forte sigillatim disserendi erit locus.[3]

[1] *abdicet* in MS. A and Locke's correction in MS. B.
[2] *sint* in MS. A and Locke's correction for *sunt* in MS. B.
[3] At the end of this essay Locke added the title of another which remained unwritten, namely, *An ex Inclinatione Hominum Naturali potest cognosci Lex Naturae? Negatur.* ('Can the law of nature be known from man's natural inclination? No.') In MS. A the question in the title is *An Firma Animi Persuasio probat Legem Naturae?* ('Does a strong conviction of the mind prove that there is a law of nature?'). At the end of this, the fourth, essay Locke has made it clear that man is urged to the performance of some of his duties by a certain propensity of nature, but he has not committed himself to the view that man's natural instincts lead him to the knowledge of natural law. For a statement of this view see Samuel Parker, *A Demonstration of the Divine Authority of the Law of Nature and of the Christian Religion*, 1681, pt. i, par. 7, pp. 42 ff.

himself.[1] But since man is very much urged on to this part of his duty by an inward instinct, and nobody can be found who does not care for himself or who disowns himself, and all direct perhaps more attention to this point than is necessary, there is no need for me here to admonish. But there will be room perhaps elsewhere to discuss one by one these three subjects which embrace all that men owe to God, their neighbour, and themselves.[2]

[1] To preserve oneself, to know the truth about God, and to live in society are the main precepts of the law of nature according to St. Thomas Aquinas, *Summa Theol.* Ia IIae, q. 94, art. 2.

[2] The task is partly fulfilled in essay VII. The three classes of duty mentioned by Locke are discussed by Gabriel Towerson in his *Explication of the Decalogue*, 1676, discourse i, pp. 3–4.

V

AN LEX NATURAE COGNOSCI POTEST EX HOMINUM CONSENSU? NEGATUR

Vox[1] *populi vox Dei*:[2] quam incerta quam fallax sit haec regula et malorum ferax, quanto partium studio, quam atroci consilio in vulgus jactatum[3] sit hoc mali ominis[4] proverbium, nos certe infaelici nimis documento didicimus, adeo ut si huic voci tanquam legis divinae praeconi auscultare velimus vix aliquem tandem crederemus esse Deum. Quid enim est tam nefarium tam impium tam contra jus omne fasque quod non aliquando suaderet multitudinis insanientis consensus sive potius conjuratio? Hinc spoliata deorum templa, confirmatam audaciam et turpitudinem, violatas leges, eversa regna accepimus. Et certe si haec sit vox Dei contraria plane est primo illi Fiat quo ornatam hanc compagem creavit et e nihilo eduxit, nec unquam sic homines alloquitur Deus nisi cum omnia iterum miscere et in chaos redigere velit; frustra igitur in hominum consensu quaereremus rationis dictata aut decreta naturae.

Consensus autem hominum diversimode considerari (f. 63) potest: primo enim dividi potest in consensum positivum et naturalem; positivum eum vocamus qui ex pacto fit, vel tacito, suadente scilicet communi hominum necessitate et commodo, qualis est legatorum liber commeatus, mercatura libera, et id genus alia, vel expresso, ut inter

---

[1] The passage from *Vox* to *Deum* was added by Locke on f. 61ᵛ, in place of the amanuensis's version of it in MS. B, which is a faulty and incomplete transcription from MS. A.

[2] This ancient saying occurs in Culverwel's *Discourse of the Light of Nature*, ch. x, p. 112 (ed. Brown, 1857); see also Locke's *Conduct of the Understanding*, par. 24 (*Works*, 1801, iii. 226).

[3] Above this word in MS. A Locke wrote *non ita pridem*; I have bracketed the English equivalent of this phrase in the translation.

[4] *omnis* MS. A.

V

CAN THE LAW OF NATURE BE KNOWN FROM THE GENERAL CONSENT[1] OF MEN? NO

'THE voice of the people is the voice of God.' Surely, we have been taught by a most unhappy lesson[2] how doubtful, how fallacious this maxim is, how productive of evils, and with how much party spirit and with what cruel intent this ill-omened proverb has been flung wide [lately] among the common people. Indeed, if we should listen to this voice as if it were the herald of a divine law, we should hardly believe that there was any God at all. For is there anything so abominable, so wicked, so contrary to all right and law, which the general consent, or rather the conspiracy, of a senseless crowd would not at some time advocate? Hence we have heard of the plunder of divine temples, the obstinacy of insolence and immorality, the violation of laws, and the overthrow of kingdoms. And surely, if this voice were the voice of God, it would be exactly the opposite of that first fiat whereby He created and furnished this world, bringing order out of chaos; nor does God ever speak to men in such a way—unless He should wish to throw everything into confusion again and to reduce it to a state of chaos. In vain, therefore, should we seek the dictates of reason and the decrees of nature in the general consent of men.[3]

But the general consent of men can be considered in different ways, for, firstly, it can be divided into positive and natural consent.

We call positive consent one that arises from a contract, either from a tacit contract, i.e. prompted by the common interests and convenience of men, such as the free passage of envoys,[4] free trade, and other things of that kind; or from an expressly stated contract, such as the fixed

[1] Locke is speaking of universal and general consent or assent in Bk. I, ch. 1 of the *Essay*; throughout this essay, therefore, I have preferred to render the Latin *consensus* by 'general consent' rather than by 'consensus'.　　　[2] i.e. the Civil War and its aftermath.

[3] Grotius (*De Jure Belli ac Pacis*, lib. i, c. 1, sect. 12) and, following him, Culverwel (*Discourse of the Light of Nature*, ch. x) maintained that the general consent of men can serve as an argument *a posteriori* for the existence of natural law.

[4] It is Hobbes's fifteenth Law of Nature (*Leviathan*, pt. i, ch. 15, p. 119, ed. Pogson Smith) 'That all men that mediate Peace, be allowed safe Conduct'. Cf. also Grotius, *De Jure Belli ac Pacis*, lib. ii, c. 18, and Pufendorf, *Elementa Jurisprudentiae Universalis*, lib. I, Def. xiii, par. 26. Later in this paragraph Locke, it would seem, follows arguments advanced by Pufendorf (ibid., Def. iii, par. 5); but there are important differences between his view concerning the law of nations and those of Pufendorf (ibid., Def. xiii, par. 24) and Hobbes.

finitimas gentes terminorum constituti limites, certas merces emendi et importandi prohibitio, et alia plurima; qui uterque consensus cum totus ex pacto pendeat nec ex principio quovis naturae fluat legem[1] naturae minime probat. Nam, verbi gratia, consensum illum de legatis recipiendis qui apud omnes pene gentes obtinuit positivum esse nec inferre legem naturae inde constat quod ex lege naturae omnes homines inter se amici sint et communi necessitate conjuncti, nisi, quod aliqui volunt, in statu naturae commune sit bellum et hominibus inter ipsos perpetuum et internecinum odium. Sive autem hoc sive illud statueris, sive homines infensos inter se sive amicos esse velis, nulla tamen ex lege naturae dari potest ratio cur legati apud exteros populos quam privati cujuspiam (f. 64) tutior sit commeatus aut potior conditio, nisi ex tacito id fieret hominum pacto ex necessitate orto, ut scilicet res per injuriam ablatas unius potius postulationibus quam multorum aperta vi repetere possint. Cum sane lex naturae privatum quemvis aeque ac legatum sine causa laedere aut violare omnino prohibeat, fateor equidem supposito hujusmodi pacto majus est legatorum quam privati cujuspiam violati crimen, cum duplex sit reatus, facta scilicet injuria et laesa fides. Quod igitur sanctior sit apud homines legatus quam alter quispiam, id non ex lege naturae sancitum est, cum lex illa homines inter se odio flagrantes, in hostiles civitates divisos nec supponit nec permittit; nec sane consensus ille positivus dictus in aliis rebus tantus est ut ad omnes pertineat populos, quod enim forte inter finitimas hasce et vicinas Europae gentes pro rato et ab (f. 65) omnibus comprobato habetur, alii et Asiae et Americae populi longo terrarum tractu sejuncti nec moribus nostris aut opinionibus assueti negligunt prorsus et nihili aestimant nec iisdem legibus se teneri arbitrantur. Hic igitur totus ex pacto consensus legem naturae non probat, sed potius jus gentium dicendus est quod lex naturae non jussit sed communis utilitas persuasit hominibus.

---

[1] The passage from *legem* to *quod* was added by Locke on f. 62ᵛ.

boundary-lines between neighbouring peoples, the prohibition of the purchase and import of particular goods, and many other such things. Neither form of general consent, since both wholly depend on a contract and are not derived from any natural principle, proves at all a law of nature. For, to take an example, it is evident that the agreement about envoys having safe passage which is kept among almost all nations is positive and does not imply a law of nature, precisely because according to the law of nature all men alike are friends of one another and are bound together by common interests, unless (as is maintained by some) there is in the state of nature a general war and a perpetual and deadly hatred among men. But whether you decide for this alternative or for that, whether you would have it that men are hostile or friendly to one another, no reason can yet be given by natural law why the passage of an envoy among foreign peoples is safer, or his position more important, than that of some private person, unless this is brought about by a tacit agreement among men, arising out of a pressing need—an agreement, that is, that men should be able to reclaim property unjustly taken from them at the request of a single man rather than by open force on the part of great numbers. While, however, the law of nature altogether forbids us to offend or injure without cause any private person as well as an envoy, I for my part admit of course that, if a contract such as we have described is assumed, the crime of doing violence to envoys is worse than that of injuring any private person: for the guilt is twofold, i.e. wrong is done and an agreement is violated.[1] Thus, although an envoy in foreign countries is held more inviolable than another person, this rule is not ordained by the law of nature; for this law neither supposes nor allows men to be inflamed with hatred for one another and to be divided into hostile states. Nor indeed is that consent, which we have called positive, so general in other matters that it would apply to all nations. For what perhaps is firmly believed in among the neighbouring and kindred nations of Europe and wholly approved of by all is utterly disregarded and set at nought by other peoples both of Asia and America, who do not consider themselves to be bound by the same laws, separated from us as they are by long stretches of land and unaccustomed to our morals and beliefs. Therefore, all this general consent derived from contract does not prove a natural law, but should rather be called the law of nations, which is not imposed by the law of nature but has been suggested to men by common expediency.

[1] Cf. Suarez, *Tractatus de Legibus ac Deo Legislatore*, 1613, lib. ii, c. 19. 7, p. 128.

Secundo, consensus naturalis, in quem scilicet homines feruntur instinctu quodam naturae sine alicujus foederis interventu, triplex esse potest:

Primo morum sive actionum, ea scilicet convenientiâ quae in hominum moribus et communis vitae usu reperitur.

Secundo opinionum, quibus homines varium praebent assensum, aliis firmum et constantem aliis tenuem et instabilem.

Tertio principiorum, quae hujusmodi plane sunt ut facilem a quovis homine mentis suae compote extorqueant assensum, nec quivis unquam sanus repertus est qui de eorum veritate intellectis terminis dubitare possit.[1]

(f. 66) Primo igitur de morum consensu dicimus eum minime probare legem naturae, actum enim esset de morum rectitudine et honestate si ex hominum vita jus fasque aestimandum esset. Quae turpitudo non modo licita sed etiam necessaria non esset si legem nobis darent majoris partis exempla, in quam nos infamiam, nequitiam, et omne genus flagitiorum[2] deduceret lex naturae si illuc eundum esset quo a pluribus itur? Quotusquisque enim est inter moratiores populos certis sub legibus quas omnes agnoscunt et quibus se teneri fatentur enutritos, qui moribus suis vitia non comprobat et malo exemplo alios saepissime errare non docet, cujus frequentes numerari non possunt lapsus? Adeo jam omne genus malorum inter homines excrevit et per universum orbem se diffudit rebusque omnibus se immiscuit. (f. 67) Tanta jam olim fuit hominum in moribus corrumpendis solertia et vitiorum tanta varietas ut posteris quod reperiri possit, quod superaddi, nihil relictum sit, nec possibile est quemquam jam nullo exemplo crimen quodvis admittere: adeo ut qui ad hunc actionum humanarum consensum morum rectitudinem exigere velit et inde legem naturae colligere, nihilo plus agit quam si det operam ut cum ratione insaniat.[3] Nemo

---

[1] Here follows a passage which was bracketed and deleted by Locke and which reads: quae omnia (f. 66) principia communi ita consensu comprobata mihi videntur hujusmodi esse quae manifestam in se continent repugnantiam, quale est illud *idem non potest esse et non esse*, aut plane identica.

[2] It seems that the sense requires a negative here and another in the last clause of the next sentence.

[3] The last clause is taken from Terence, *Eun.* i. 1. 17–18 (similarly in R. Sanderson, *De Obligatione Conscientiae*, 1647, iv. 35).

Secondly, natural consent, namely one to which men are led by a certain natural instinct without the intervention of some compact, can be of three kinds:

(1) In customs or actions, that is, the conformity to be found in the moral conduct of men and in the practice of social life.

(2) In those opinions to which men give assent in various ways, firmly and invariably to some, feebly and unsteadily to others.

(3) In first principles, which are precisely such as to elicit ready assent from any man of sound mind, and such that there is no sane person who could be doubtful of their truth after having understood their terms.[1]

(1) First, then, concerning general consent in matters of morals, we say that it by no means proves a natural law. For if what is rightful and lawful were to be determined by men's way of living, moral rectitude and integrity would be done for. What immorality would not be allowable and even be inevitable, if the example of the majority gave us the law? Into what disgrace, villainy, and all sorts of shameful things would not the law of nature lead us astray, if we had to go whither most people go? In fact, how few are there among the more civilized nations, brought up under definite laws recognized and acknowledged by all as binding, who do not by their way of life set the mark of their approval upon vices and very often by bad example teach others to go astray, and whose frequent lapses cannot be counted? Nay, by this time every kind of evil has grown up among men and spread over the world and become mixed with everything. In the past men have already shown so much ingenuity in the corruption of morals and such a variety of vices that nothing has been left for posterity to invent or to add, and it is impossible for anyone to commit any crime whatsoever of which there has not been an example already. It comes to this, that if anyone wants to judge moral rectitude by the standard of such accordance of human actions among themselves, and thence to infer a law of nature, he is doing no more than if he bestowed his pains on playing the fool according to reason. No one,

---

[1] The deleted passage reads in translation: 'And all these principles thus approved by universal consent appear to me to be of such a kind as either to involve the use of clearly contradictory terms as in the proposition "It is impossible for the same thing to be and not to be", or else to be plainly tautological.' In this passage Locke appears to be borrowing again from Culverwel's *Discourse of the Light of Nature*, ch. xi, p. 127 (ed. Brown, 1857). The principle of contradiction becomes Locke's stock example of acquired self-evident truths in Bk. I of the *Essay* of 1690. For further examples of what Locke takes to be the nature of self-evident principles, cf. *Essay*, I. i. 18, and IV. vii. 4.

igitur ex hac pessima hominum concordia legem naturae astruere conatus est. Dici sane potest non ex hominum moribus sed sententiis colligendam esse legem naturae—non vitas hominum sed animas scrutari debemus—illic enim inscribi naturae decreta illic latere morum regulas et principia illa quae mores corrumpere non possunt: quaeque cum in omnibus eadem sint, alium authorem habere non possunt praeter Deum et naturam; et hinc esse quod illam legem internam quam negant saepe (f. 68) vitia fateatur hominum conscientia, et illi ipsi qui perverse agunt recte sentiant. Transeamus igitur ad consensum illum quem in hominum opinionibus repertum iri speramus.

Secundo dicimus igitur[1] non dari inter homines de rebus moralibus universalem et communem consensum, secundo si daretur constans et unanimis omnium qui ubique sunt hominum de rebus agendis consensus, ex eo tamen colligi et certo cognosci non posse legem naturae.

Primo non datur inter homines de morum rectitudine communis consensus. Et hic, priusquam ad singula descendero, breviter dicam nullum pene esse vitium, nullam legis naturae violationem, nullam morum turpitudinem, quam non facile patebit mundi historias consulenti et hominum res gestas observanti alicubi terrarum non solum privatim admissam sed publica authoritate et consuetudine comprobatam; nec aliquid tam sua natura turpe fuisse quin aut religione alicubi consecratum aut virtutis loco habitum et laudibus cumulatum (f. 69) fuerit. Unde facile est scire quaenam fuit ea de re hominum sententia, cum hujusmodi rebus aut se deos sancte colere aut se heroas fieri arbitrarentur. Nam, ut omittam varias populorum religiones, alias cerimoniis ridiculas alias ritibus impias et cultu ipso nefandas, quarum ipsam mentionem reliquae gentes perhorrescerent et sacros eorum ritus cum ipsa naturae lege manifesto pugnantes novis sacrificiis expiandos crederent—ut haec, inquam, omittam, cum religionem non tam lumine naturae quam revelatione divina hominibus innotescere credendum sit, si singula virtutum et vitiorum genera recensere velimus, quae[2] nemo dubitat esse ipsam legem naturae, facile constabit nullum[3] esse de quo variae non sunt hominum opiniones publica authoritate et

---

[1] *igitur*] *primo* MS. A.

[2] Locke corrected *quae*, which refers to *genera*, to *quas*, which would refer to *virtutum*, thereby confusing the syntax. In MS. A the reading is doubtful.

[3] *nullam* MS. B; *nullum* MS. A.

therefore, has attempted to build up a law of nature upon this most unfortunate agreement among men. It may be said, however, that the law of nature is to be inferred not from men's behaviour but from their innermost ways of thinking—we must search not the lives of men but their souls—for it is there that the precepts of nature are imprinted and the rules of morality lie hidden together with those principles which men's manners cannot corrupt; and that, since these principles are the same in every one of us, they can have no other author than God and nature. And it is for this reason that the internal law, whose existence is often denied by vices, is acknowledged by men's conscience and the very men who act perversely feel rightly. Let us pass therefore to that general consent which we hope will be found in men's opinions.

(2) We say, then, in the first place, that no universal and general consent is found among men about morals. In the second place, we say that, if there did exist an invariable and unanimous consent concerning dutiful actions among all men in the world, still from this the law of nature could not be inferred and known for certain.

First, then, there does not occur among men a general consent concerning moral rectitude. And here, before I proceed to details, I shall say briefly that there is almost no vice, no infringement of natural law, no moral wrong, which anyone who consults the history of the world and observes the affairs of men will not readily perceive to have been not only privately committed somewhere on earth, but also approved by public authority and custom. Nor has there been anything so shameful in its nature that it has not been either sanctified somewhere by religion, or put in the place of virtue and abundantly rewarded with praise. Hence it is easy to see what has been the opinion of men in this matter, since they believed that by such deeds they either reverently honoured the gods or were themselves made godlike. I shall say nothing here of the various religions of the nations, some of which are ridiculous in their ceremonies, others irreverent in their rites and impious in respect of the cult itself, so that the other nations shudder at the very name of them and believe that the sacred rites of those peoples, since they are clearly at variance with natural law itself, are to be purged by fresh sacrifices. All this, I repeat, I shall pass over, because we must believe that religion becomes known to men not so much by the light of nature as by divine revelation. But if we would review each class of virtues and vices—and nobody doubts that this classification is the actual law of nature—it will easily appear that there is none of them of which men do not form different opinions

consuetudine stabilitae: adeo ut si hominum consensus sit morum regula habendus, aut nulla erit lex (f. 70) naturae aut diversis in locis diversa, id hic honestum quod alibi turpe, et vitia ipsa transibunt in officia, quod nemo dixerit; dum enim homines ea quae obtinuit opinione ducti hoc vel illud pro more gentis suae perpetrarunt, quod forte aliis nec sine ratione inhonestum et impium videretur, non se legem naturae violasse sed potius observasse putarunt, nulla senserunt conscientiae verbera nec internum illud animi flagellum quod ulcisci et exagitare solet criminis conscios, dum existimarunt[1] id, quicquid fuerit, sibi non modo licere sed etiam laudi fuisse. Unde manifesto colligere licet non solum qui hominum mores sed quaenam etiam de moribus illis opinio fuerit.

Quid de justitia, eximia illa lege naturae et omnis societatis vinculo, sensisse homines putemus? cum accepimus ab authoribus fide dignis totas gentes ex professo piratas fuisse (f. 71) et praedones: οὐ παράδοξον ἦν τοῖς παλαιοῖς τὸ λῃστεύειν, ἀλλ' ἔνδοξον, inquit in suo in Homerum scholio Didymus.[2] *Apud veteres Aegyptios, quod genus hominum constat et in artibus reperiendis solertes extitisse et in cognitione rerum indaganda sagaces, furta omnia fuisse licita et impunita,* affirmat Aristo ab A. Gellio[3] citatus. *Apud Lacedaemonios quoque, sobrios illos ac acres viros, cujus rei non adeo ut Aegyptiis fides longinqua est, non pauci neque ignobiles scriptores jus atque usum fuisse furandi dicunt,* inquit idem Gellius.[4] Et vero ipsi Romani, qui universo orbi virtutum exempla exhibere perhibentur, qua ex re sibi honores, triumphos, gloriam, et immortalis nominis sui memoriam conquisiverunt nisi ex furto et latrociniis quibus totum orbem terrarum devastarunt? quid aliud apud illos tantis encomiis celebrata virtus illa, quid aliud, inquam, quam vis et injuria? Nec (f. 72) adhuc exolevit inimica illa justitiae opinio, cum plurimis adhuc populis spoliare, fallere, circumvenire, rapere, et vi et armis quantum possunt possidere ea demum laus sit et vera gloria et inter artes imperatorias habeatur summa; justitiamque credunt, qualem sibi

---

[1] *existimarent* MS. A.

[2] It appears from MS. A that Locke intended to place *inquit* after *scholio*. The scholium occurs on the *Odyssey*, iii. 71. Locke probably derived it from memory (for the quotation is inexact) from Aldus's edition of the *Scholia minora* (1528, 21ᵛ) erroneously ascribed to Didymus. The scholium can be found in G. Dindorf, *Scholia Graeca in Homeri Odysseam*, Oxford, 1855, vol. i, p. 125, ll. 18–19. Cf. also Thucydides, i. 5. 1–2.

[3] *Noctes Atticae*, xi. 18. 16.

[4] Ibid. 17.

buttressed by public authority and custom. Hence, if the general consent of men is to be regarded as the rule of morality, there will either be no law of nature at all or it will vary from place to place, a thing being morally good in one place and wrong in another, and the vices themselves will become duties. But this no one will maintain. For while men, led by the prevailing opinion, have performed this or that according to the moral practice of their country (though perhaps, and not without reason, it appeared to others wrong and wicked) they did not think they had transgressed the law of nature but rather had observed it; they felt no pangs of conscience nor that inward mental scourge which usually punishes and torments the guilty, for they believed that their action, whatever it may have been, was not only lawful but laudable. From this review, evidently, one can infer not only what were the morals of men, but also what men thought about those morals.

What are we to believe has been men's notion of justice, that chief law of nature and bond of every society, when we have learned from reliable authors that whole nations have professedly been pirates and robbers? 'Among the ancients piracy was not of ill repute but of good', Didymus says in a marginal note by him on Homer. Aristo,[1] in a passage quoted by Aulus Gellius, maintains that 'among the ancient Egyptians, a race of men known to have been both ingenious in the invention of the arts and shrewd in pursuing the knowledge of things, thefts of all kinds were lawful and free from punishment'. And Gellius himself says, 'Among the Spartans too, temperate and brave men they (a matter for which the evidence is not so far back in time as in the case of the Egyptians), many, nay, distinguished writers affirm that stealing was lawful and customary.' In what way, in fact, have even the Romans, who are alleged to present to the whole world examples of virtue, procured for themselves honours, triumphs, glory, and the memory of their immortal name, if not by the robbery and brigandage by means of which they devastated the whole earth? What else did that virtue, so highly praised and celebrated, mean to them—what else, I say, but force and violence? And this injurious view of justice has not yet disappeared, since even now for most nations desert consists precisely in plunder, deceit, oppression, assault, and in gaining as many possessions as they can by force of arms: all this is regarded as true glory and the height of generalship. They also believe that justice, such as they have come to conceive it, is blind and armed with a sword.

---

[1] A Roman jurist of the time of Trajan.

finxerunt, caecam esse et gladio armatam. *Fures,* inquit Cato,[1] *privatorum furtorum in nervo atque in compedibus aetatem agunt, fures publici in auro atque in purpura.*

Quid de pudicitia et castitate? cum apud Assyrios foeminae nudo penitus corpore et omnium oculis exposito conviviis interesse cum laude consueverunt, dum apud alias gentes foeminas licet tectas in publicum prodire aut faciem aperire et ab ignotis conspici nefas sit; apud alias innuptis puellis stupra facere licet, ad nuptas solum castitatem pertinere arbitrantur et a libidine mulieres solo matrimonio coerceri; alii sunt qui genialem torum stupris consecrant et maritales taedas libidinis (f. 73) flammis accendunt, ubi nova nupta hospites omnes excipit, cujus prima nox tot numerat quot Messalina adulteros; sunt alii apud quos princeps alii ubi sacerdos sponsae virginitatis spolium pro more obtinet. *Garamantes Aethiopes matrimonia privatim nesciunt, sed omnibus vulgo in venerem licet,* inquit Solinus,[2] quam turpitudinem de iis etiam affirmat P. Mela[3]—et[4] talibus sacris propitiaretur deum mater quibus offenderetur matrona—ut omittam polygamiam quae his privilegium illis piaculum habetur, quae illic lege jubetur hic morte mulctanda est.

De pietate erga parentes quid putandum est? cum repertae sint totae gentes apud quas[5] adulta progenies parentes occidit, liberi Parcis ipsis saeviores eam adimunt vitam quam adhuc Fata largiuntur, ubi non solum statutum est omnibus mori sed certa mortis praefinitur hora nec expectanda est sera dies et tarde marcescentis senii mora, ubi (f. 74) quisque parentis sui carnifex et inter pietatis officia numeratur parricidium. Νόμος ἐστὶ Σαρδῷος, inquit Aelianus,[6] τοὺς ἤδη γεγηρακότας τῶν πατέρων οἱ παῖδες ῥοπάλοις τύπτοντες ἀνῄρουν καὶ ἔθαπτον, αἰσχρὸν ἡγούμενοι τὸν λίαν ὑπέργηρων ὄντα ζῆν ἔτι, et eodem in loco[7] Derbices omnes septuagesimum annum egressos interficiunt, nec major alios erga liberos suos tenet cura, cum nuper natos pro libitu exponunt

[1] Cf. Aulus Gellius, ibid., xi. 18, 18.

[2] *Collectanea Rerum Memorabilium,* c. 30. 2, p. 130 (ed. Mommsen, 1895). Solinus has *Garamantici* in his text instead of *Garamantes.*

[3] *De Chorographia,* lib. i, c. 8, ll. 49–50, p. 11 (ed. Frick, 1935).

[4] The passage from *et* to *matrona* was added by Locke on f. 72ᵛ; the clause is an almost literal quotation from St. Augustine, *De Civ. Dei,* ii. 5 (*Corp. Script. Eccl. Lat.,* vol. 40, 1, p. 65, ll. 10–11).

[5] *quas* MS. A; *quos* MS. B, which might be defended as a sense construction.

[6] *Varia Historia,* lib. iv. 1, p. 60, ll. 13–16 (ed. Hercher, 1887).

[7] Ibid., p. 60, ll. 27–28.

'Thieves committing private theft', says Cato, 'spend their lives in prison and in chains; public thieves, in gold and in purple.'

What is one to say of modesty and chastity, if among the Assyrians women were accustomed and encouraged to take part in banquets stark naked and exposed to the view of all present, while among other nations it is unlawful for women to go out in public, even though veiled, or to show the face, or be seen by strangers? Among others it is lawful for unmarried girls to live dissolutely, and it is thought that chastity belongs only to married women, and that females are restrained from lust only by matrimony. There are others who consecrate the bridal bed by lechery and kindle the nuptial torches with the flames of lust, and where the bride lies with all the wedding guests, having in her first night as many adulterers as Messalina had. There are some where it is the custom that the prince, others that the priest, obtains the spoil of the bride's virginity. According to Solinus 'the Garamantes in Ethiopia do not know of private marriage, on the contrary all may form promiscuous unions', and this immorality is also ascribed to them by Pomponius Mela (and the mother of the gods would be placated by such rites as would give offence to a decent woman!). Let me pass over polygamy, which here is regarded as a right, there as a sin, which in one place is commanded by law, in another is punished by death.

What is one to believe about duty towards parents, if whole nations have been met with where grown-up offspring kill their parents, where children, fiercer even than the goddesses of Fate, take away the life which the Fates continue to bestow, where it is not only ordained that all must die but a particular time of death is appointed beforehand, where no ripe old age and no lingering on of slowly declining years are to be expected, where each is the executioner of his parent and parricide is considered as one of the duties of piety. Aelianus says, 'There is a custom in Sardinia that children kill their aged fathers by beating them with sticks, and then bury them, believing that it would be wrong if those who are already too old remained alive any longer'. He says in the same place that the Derbices[1] kill all those who have advanced beyond the age of seventy, and other tribes show no more concern for their children, since at their will they expose the newly-born, and seem to have given life only in order that they may take it away. There are others who utterly discard their female progeny as if it were bastard and a mistake of nature, and purchase wives from their neighbours in

---

[1] An ancient people of Asia, near the Caspian Sea.

ideoque solum vitam dedisse videntur ut auferant; sunt qui sobolem foemineam tanquam spuriam et naturae erratum prorsus negligunt et a finitimis suis in spem prolis suas mercantur uxores: adeo ut quam legem etiam in brutorum animis sanxisse videtur natura ea se obligari non sentiant homines et feritate belluas superent.[1]

Si qua autem maxime sancta apud omnes videatur lex naturae, ad cujus observationem instinctu quodam naturae et suo commodo impelli videtur universum humanum genus, ea certe est sui ipsius praeservatio, quam (f. 75) nonnulli ideo primariam et fundamentalem legem naturae constituunt. Sed ea est consuetudinis et opinionis a moribus domesticis mutuatae vis ut homines etiam in se ipsos armet, ut sibi violentas manus inferant et eodem studio mortem quaerant quo alii fugiunt. Subditi inventi sunt qui vivum regem non solum colunt proteguntque sed sequuntur mortuum, servi qui dominos ad umbras comitantur et ibi praestare obsequium velint ubi omnes sunt aequales. Nec hoc solum audent viri, animosior pars mortalium, apud Indos enim imbellis et timidus foeminarum sexus audet lethum contemnere et ad demortuos maritos per flammas, per mortem properare; conjugales taedas non nisi rogi flammis extingui patiuntur et novos potius optant in ipso sepulchro quaerere thalamos quam viduos pati toros et conjugis desiderium: cujus rei testem se oculatum profitetur Mandelslo in nupero illo Olearii itinerario,[2] qui (ut narrat ipse) foeminam vidit juvenem formosam quae (f. 76) defuncto marito cum nullis amicorum monitis, precibus vel lachrymis vinci poterat et in vita retineri, tandem post invitam sex mensium moram permittente magistratu ornata tanquam ad nuptias ovans[3] et hilari vultu pyram in medio foro extructam ascendit et in mediis flammis laeta expiravit.

Longum esset singula persequi. Nec mirandum est tam diversas esse hominum de recto et honesto sententias, cum in principiis ipsis differant et Deus et animarum immortalitas in dubium vocetur; quae licet non sint propositiones practicae et leges naturae, necessario tamen ad legis

---

[1] *superent* MS. A; *superant* MS. B.

[2] Cf. Adam Olearius, *The Voyages and Travels of the Ambassadors sent by Frederick Duke of Holstein to the Great Duke of Muscovy, and the King of Persia* (1633–39), &c.; *whereto are added The Travels of John Albert de Mandelslo,* &c., *into the East-Indies* (1638–40). *Rendered into English by John Davies, of Kidwelly,* London, 1662. The reference is to Bk. I of Mandelslo's *Travels,* pp. 40–41. There were earlier editions of the book in French, German, and Dutch.

[3] *orans* MS. B; *ovans* MS. A.

hope of offspring from them. Thus men do not regard a law which nature seems to have established even in the souls of animals as binding on themselves, and they surpass brutes in savageness.

But if any law of nature would seem to be established among all as sacred in the highest degree, which the whole of mankind, it seems, is urged to observe by a certain natural instinct and by its own interest, surely this is self-preservation, and therefore some lay this down as the chief and fundamental law of nature.[1] But in fact the power of custom and of opinion based on traditional ways of life is such as to arm men even against their own selves, so that they lay violent hands upon themselves and seek death as eagerly as others shun it. Subjects have been met with who not only worship and defend their king while alive but also follow him into death. And there are slaves who attend their masters beyond the grave and desire to discharge their duty of obedience in a place where all are equal. Nor have only male persons, the more spirited portion of mortals, the courage to do this, for among the Indians the weak and timid female sex dares to make light of dying and to hasten to rejoin departed husbands by passing through the flames and through the gate of death. They allow the nuptial torches to be extinguished only in the flames of the funeral pyre, and they prefer to seek a new marriage-chamber in the grave itself rather than to endure a widow's couch and mourning for a lost spouse. Of this fact Mandelslo, in the recently published itinerary of Olearius, declares himself an eye-witness. As he himself relates, he saw a beautiful young woman who after the death of her husband could not be prevailed upon, or restrained from murdering herself, by the advice, entreaties, and tears of her friends. At length, after an involuntary delay of six months, with the permission of the magistrate, she dressed as if for a wedding, triumphantly and with a joyous face ascended a pyre set up in the middle of the market-place, and cheerfully perished in the flames.

It would be tedious to describe further instances. Nor is it surprising that men think so differently about what is right and good, since they differ even in the matter of first principles, and doubt is thrown upon God and the immortality of souls. Even if God and the soul's immortality are not moral propositions and laws of nature, nevertheless they must be necessarily presupposed if natural law is to exist. For there is no law without a law-maker, and law is to no purpose without punishment. For example, some nations in Brazil and the inhabitants of

---

[1] e.g. St. Thomas Aquinas, *Summa Theol.* Ia IIae, q. 94, art. 2, and also Hobbes, *Leviathan*, pt. i, ch. 14 (ed. Pogson Smith, p. 99).

naturae existentiam supponi debent, nulla enim lex si nullus legislator, aut frustra si nulla poena. Nam aliquos Brasiliae populos et Soldaniae incolas deum omnino nullum agnoscere aut colere ferunt illi qui haec loca adire operae pretium duxerunt. Quod si nemo tam sensus omnis tam rationis et humanitatis expers extiterat unquam qui numen nullum haberet, quanto, quaeso, potior est polytheorum sententia? quid Graecorum, Latinorum, et totius mundi (f. 77) ethnici de diis opinio? qui cum plures deos sibi finxerunt eosque inter se pugnantes uti in bello Trojano, inter se varie affectos, crudeles, fures, adulteros, non mirum videtur si ex deorum talium voluntate officii sui rationem colligere non poterant. Quam illa vitae regulam doceret religio ubi quisque quem et qualem velit deum sibi eligeret et cultum, ubi in hortis crescerent numina et quotannis expectare possint deorum messem, bos et canis divinos meruerunt honores? Talem[1] hominum de diis consensum ad mores recte instituendos nihil omnino profecisse quid miremur? Quid hi, quaeso, nisi alio nomine athei? aeque enim impossibile est multa aut esse aut concipere numina ac nullum, et qui deorum auget numerum tollit divinitatem. Nec, si moratiores gentes aut sanioris mentis philosophos appelles, quicquam proficies, cum Judaeis reliquae omnes gentes ethnicae sint et profanae, Graecis barbarae; Sparta severa illa gens furtum probet, et nefanda Jovis Latialis sacrificia Romana (f. 78) religio. Quid juvat philosophos adire? cum eorum plus quam ducentas de summo bono sententias recenseat Varro,[2] nec pauciores esse possunt de via quae ad faelicitatem deducit opiniones, hoc est de lege naturae; et inter philosophos extiterit[3] Diagoras Melius,[4] Theodorus Cyrenaicus, et Protagoras atheismo infames. Si Christianam religionem professos consulere velis, quid de iis existimandum erit? qui magnum illud humani generis rescindunt vinculum dum doceant fidem non esse servandam cum haereticis, hoc est qui Papae dominatum non agnoscunt et in

---

[1] *Talis . . . consensus* MS. B; Locke forgot to correct the nominatives after shifting his construction in the middle of a sentence originally governed by *constat*.

[2] In his book *De Philosophia* (cf. St. Augustine, *De Civ. Dei*, xix. 1).

[3] *extiterint* MS. A.

[4] *Milesius* MSS. A and B.

---

be R. Sanderson's *De Juramenti Promissorii Obligatione*, 1646, iv. 8 (ed. 1686, p. 70). Cf. also Marlowe, *The Jew of Malta*, ii. iii. 312; 2 *Tamburlaine*, ii. i. 33 f.; also an entry in Locke's Journal for 1676 (MS. Locke f. 1, p. 46), his *Essay concerning Toleration* (in Fox Bourne's *Life*, i. 188), and his *Letter concerning Toleration* (ed. Gough, 1946, p. 155).

Saldanha Bay[1] acknowledge or worship no god at all, as is reported by those who have considered it worth while to go to these places.[2] But even if no one had ever been so devoid of every sense, so destitute of reason and humane feelings as not to have a god in his heart, to what extent, pray, is the belief of polytheists in a better position? What sort of thing is the opinion of the Greeks, the Romans, and the whole heathen world concerning the gods? For since all these have conceived of many gods and represented them as fighting among themselves, as they did in the Trojan War, as being variously affected towards one another, as cruel, thieves, adulterers, it does not appear surprising if they were unable to derive the ground of their duty from the will of such gods. What rule of life would that religion teach, where each person picked out for himself any sort of god and worship he liked, where deities grew up in gardens, where a harvest of gods was to be expected every year, and where ox and dog received divine honours? Is it surprising that such a general consent about gods on the part of men has contributed nothing at all to the proper foundation of morals? What are these people, pray, if not disguised atheists? For it is just as impossible that many gods either exist or can be apprehended, as that there is no God. In fact, to increase the number of gods means to abolish Divinity. Nor will you gain anything if you appeal to more civilized peoples[3] or to philosophers of a sounder mind. For to the Jews all the other nations are heathen and unholy, to the Greek they are barbarous, and while Sparta, that austere nation, approves of theft, Roman religion approves of the atrocious sacrifices of the Latin Jupiter. What use is it to turn to philosophers? For Varro produces more than two hundred of their notions about the highest good, and there can be no fewer opinions about how to reach happiness, that is, about the law of nature. And also such philosophers as Diagoras of Melos, Theodorus of Cyrene, and Protagoras were notorious for atheism. If you wish to consult those professing Christianity, what is one to think of those who break the great bond of humanity by their teaching that faith is not to be kept with heretics,[4] that is, with people who do not recognize

---

[1] An inlet on the south-western coast of South Africa, north of Cape Town.

[2] Cf. *Essay*, 1. iii. 8 (Fraser's ed. i. 97).

[3] Cf. Grotius, *De Jure Belli ac Pacis*, lib. i, c. 1, sect. 12, par. 1, and Culverwel, *Discourse of the Light of Nature*, ch. x, pp. 116 and 118 (ed. Brown, 1857).

[4] This point of Catholic doctrine was widely discussed in the sixteenth and seventeenth centuries. Martinus Becanus, S.J. (*Manuale Controversiarum hujus Temporis*, lib. v, c. 15) endeavoured to show that it was because of the calumny of a Dutch Calvinist that Catholics were accused of teaching that faith need not be kept with heretics. Locke's source here may

[contd. opposite

eandem se tradunt societatem: adeo ut cum civibus forsan servandam fidem putent, erga exteros fraudem et dolum licere. Quid Graecorum Romanorumque sapientissimi (ne plures referam) Socrates et Cato? Ad thalamos suos alios admiserunt, amicis accomodarunt uxores et alienae libidinis facti sunt ministri. Ex quibus omnibus liquido constat ex illo qui inter homines est consensu nequaquam colligi posse legem naturae.

(f. 79) Secundo dicimus, si daretur inter homines unanimis et universalis opinionis alicujus consensus, ille tamen consensus non probaret eam opinionem esse legem naturae, cum certe ex principiis naturalibus non ex fide aliena unicuique deducenda sit lex naturae, et hujusmodi consensus de ea re possit esse quae nequaquam sit lex naturae, ut si apud omnes homines majori in pretio esset aurum quam plumbum, non inde sequeretur id lege naturae esse sancitum; si omnes cum Persis humana cadavera canibus voranda exponerent aut cum Graecis comburerent, non probaret hoc aut illud legem esse naturae et homines obligare, cum hujusmodi consensus minime sufficiat ad inducendam obligationem; hujusmodi fateor consensus indicare poterat legem naturae probare non poterat, efficere ut vehementius credam, non ut certius sciam eam esse legem naturae; certo enim scire non possum utrum haec sit privati cujusque sententia, fides enim est sed non cognitio. Si enim eandem mei animi reperio esse opinionem (f. 80) ante cognitum hujusmodi consensum, consensus illius cognitio non mihi probat quod ante ex principiis naturalibus cognoscerem; quod si eam esse animi mei sententiam ante cognitum hujusmodi hominum consensum non constat, merito etiam dubitare possim an illa sit et aliorum opinio, cum nulla ratio dari potest cur id omnibus aliis a natura inesse credam quod mihi deesse sentio. Nec sane illi ipsi homines qui consentiunt scire possunt aliquid bonum esse quia consentiunt, sed ideo consentiunt quia ex principiis naturalibus aliquid esse bonum

the supremacy of the Pope and join in the one society? They go so far as to believe that faith is to be kept perhaps with their own fellow citizens, but that fraud and cunning are permissible if directed against foreigners. What sort of men, to say nothing of many others, were Socrates and Cato, the wisest of the Greeks and Romans? They admitted others to their bridal-bed, they lent their wives to friends and made themselves abettors of another man's lust. From all this it is quite evident that natural law can in no wise be inferred from the general consent to be found among men.

In the second place, we say that if there existed among men a unanimous and universal consent in some opinion, that consent would not prove this opinion to be a natural law. For surely, each single person has to infer the law of nature from the first principles of nature, not from another person's belief. Besides, such a consent can be about a thing which is in no wise a law of nature; for instance, if among all men gold were more highly valued than lead, it would not follow that this is decreed by natural law. If all men, following the practice of the Persians, were to expose human corpses to be eaten by dogs, or, along with the Greeks, were to burn them, this would not prove that either the one or the other practice is a law of nature nor that it is binding on men, for such a general agreement is by no means a sufficient reason for creating an obligation. Admittedly, such a general consent might point to a natural law, but it could not prove it; it might make me believe more ardently, but could not make me know with greater certainty, that this opinion is a law of nature. For I can never know for certain whether this[1] is the opinion of every individual. That would be a matter of belief, not of knowledge. For (1) if I discover this opinion in my own mind before ascertaining the fact of such general consent, then the knowledge of the general consent will not prove to me what I knew already from natural principles; and (2) if I cannot be sure that it really is the opinion of my own mind until I have first ascertained that there is such a general consent among men, then I can also reasonably doubt whether it is the opinion of others; since it is impossible to suggest a reason why something should be accorded by nature to all other men which I feel to be wanting in myself. Nor, indeed, can those very people who think alike know that something is good because they think alike; rather they think alike because from natural principles they know that something is

---

[1] To make sense of Locke's argument here I take *haec* in this sentence and *eandem* in the next to mean 'any given opinion'.

cognoscunt, et cognitio praecedit consensum. Nam aliter idem esset simul causa et effectus et omnium consensus produceret omnium consensum, quod plane absurdum.

De tertio, scilicet principiorum, consensu non est quod multa dicam, cum principia speculativa ad rem non attinent (f. 81) nec res morales ullatenus attingunt. De principiis autem practicis qualis sit hominum consensus ex supra dictis facile est colligere.

good. And truly, knowledge precedes general consent, for otherwise the same thing would at the same time be cause and effect, and the consent of all would give rise to the consent of all, a thing which is plainly absurd.[1]

(3) Lastly, it is not necessary for me to say much about the third kind of general consent, i.e. agreement in first principles, because speculative principles do not pertain to the matter under discussion and do not affect moral facts in any respect whatever.[2] From what has been said above, however, it is easy to gather what is the nature of the general consent of men with regard to practical principles.

---

[1] The main ideas in this paragraph were developed by Locke in the chapter 'Of Enthusiasm' added in the fourth edition of the *Essay* (1700).

[2] The question of a general consent concerning speculative principles is discussed by Locke in his early drafts of the *Essay* of 1671, and more fully in his *Essay* of 1690, bk. i, ch. i.

VI

AN LEX NATURAE HOMINES OBLIGAT?
AFFIRMATUR

CUM aliqui reperti sint qui omnem legem naturae ad suam cujusque praeservationem referunt nec altius illius fundamenta petunt quam ab amore et instinctu illo quo unusquisque se amplectitur sibique quantum potest ut tutus et incolumis sit prospicit, cum quisque se sentit in se conservando satis sedulum et industrium, operae pretium videtur inquirere quae et quanta sit legis naturae obligatio, cum, si sui ipsius cura et conservatio sit omnis hujus legis fons et principium, virtus non tam officium hominis videretur quam commodum, nec homini quid honestum erit nisi quod utile, neque legis hujus observatio tam munus nostrum esset et debitum ad quod natura obligamur quam privilegium et beneficium ad quod utilitate ducimur: adeoque sine incommodo forsan non possumus, sine crimine certe eam possumus (f. 83) negligere et violare quandocunque nobis cedere jure nostro libitum fuerit.

Ut vero cognoscatur quomodo et quantum obligat lex naturae, pauca de obligatione praemittenda sunt, quam sic definiunt juris consulti, scilicet quod sit vinculum juris[1] quo quis astringitur debitum persolvere, ubi per jus intelligunt legem civilem; quae etiam definitio omnimodam obligationem satis commode describit si per jus legem illam intelligas cujus obligationem definiendam proponis: adeo ut hic per vinculum juris intelligendum sit vinculum legis naturalis quo quis astringitur persolvere debitum naturale, id scilicet praestare officium quod cuivis ex naturae suae ratione praestandum incumbit, vel poenam admisso crimini debitam subire. Ut vero cognoscamus unde oriatur illud juris vinculum, sciendum est neminem nos ad quodvis agendum obligare vel astringere posse nisi qui in nos jus et potestatem habet; et

---

[1] Justinian, *Institutiones*, lib. III, tit. xiii (ed. Krueger, 1872).

VI

ARE MEN BOUND BY THE LAW OF NATURE? YES

SINCE there are some who trace the whole law of nature back to each person's self-preservation and do not seek its foundations in anything greater than that love and instinct wherewith each single person cherishes himself and, as much as he can, looks to his own safety and welfare, and since everyone feels himself zealous and industrious enough in self-preservation, it seems worth our labour to inquire what and how great is the binding force of the law of nature. For if the source and origin of all this law is the care and preservation of oneself, virtue would seem to be not so much man's duty as his convenience, nor will anything be good except what is useful to him; and the observance of this law would be not so much our duty and obligation, to which we are bound by nature, as a privilege and an advantage, to which we are led by expediency. And thus, whenever it pleases us to claim our right and give way to our own inclinations, we can certainly disregard and transgress this law without blame, though perhaps not without disadvantage.

But in order that it may be known how and to what extent the law of nature is binding, a few facts concerning obligation must first be set forth. The jurists define obligation in the following manner, namely that it is the bond of law whereby one is bound to render what is due,[1] and by law they mean the civil code. Yet this definition also describes well enough all kinds of obligation, if by law you understand that particular law the binding force of which you propose to define. Hence, by the bond of law we must mean here the bond of natural law whereby one is bound to discharge a natural obligation,[2] that is, to fulfil the duty which it lies upon one to perform by reason of one's nature, or else submit to the penalty due to a perpetrated crime. But in order that we may know whence this bond of law takes its origin, we must understand that no one can oblige or bind us to do anything, unless he has

---

[1] Locke's version of the definition is almost the same as Robert Sanderson's in his *De Juramenti Promissorii Obligatione*, 1646, i. 11 (ed. 1686, p. 12). In the next sentence Locke also follows Sanderson (loc. cit., pp. 13–14).

[2] The expression occurs in Culverwel who borrowed it from Suarez (cf. *Discourse of the Light of Nature*, ch. vi, p. 77, ed. Brown, 1857).

dum imperat quid fieri velit, quid non, jure tantum utitur suo: adeo ut vinculum illud sit (f. 84) ab illo dominio et imperio quod superior quivis in nos actionesque nostras obtinet, et in quantum alteri subjicimur in tantum obligationi obnoxii sumus. Vinculum autem illud nos ad debitum persolvendum astringit, quod debitum duplex est:

Primo debitum officii, scilicet quod quis ex edicto superioris potestatis tenetur facere vel amittere;[1] cum enim voluntas legislatoris nobis cognita sit aut ita sufficienter promulgata ut, nisi impedimenti quid a nobis sit, cognosci potest, ei morem gerere et per omnia obsequi tenemur, et hoc est illud quod vocatur debitum officii, conformitas scilicet inter actiones nostras et earum regulam, scilicet superioris potestatis voluntatem. Et haec obligatio videtur fluere tum a sapientia legislatoris divina, tum a jure illo quod creator habet in creaturam suam; in Deum enim ultimo resolvitur omnis obligatio, cujus voluntatis imperio nos morigeros praestare ideo tenemur quia, cum ab eo accepimus et esse et operari, ab ejus voluntate utrumque dependet, et eum modum quem ille praescribit observare debemus, nec minus aequum est (f. 85) ut id agamus quod omniscienti et summe sapienti visum fuerit.

Secundo debitum supplicii, quod oritur ex officii debito non persoluto, ut illi qui ratione duci et potestati superiori moribus et vitae rectitudine se subjectos fateri nolint vi et poenis coacti potestati illi se subditos agnoscant illiusque sentiant vim cujus sequi nollent voluntatem, et hujus obligationis vis in potestate legislatoris fundari videtur, ut quos monita movere non possint cogat potentia. Nec vero omnis obligatio videtur consistere et ultimo terminari in potentia illa quae delinquentes coercere possit et punire nocentes, sed potius in potestate

---

1 *amittere*: possibly a slip for *omittere*, as on p. 112, 2.

right and power over us; and indeed, when he commands what he wishes should be done and what should not be done, he only makes use of his right. Hence that bond derives from the lordship and command which any superior has over us and our actions, and in so far as we are subject to another we are so far under an obligation. But that bond constrains us to discharge our liability, and the liability is twofold:

First, a liability to pay dutiful obedience,[1] namely what anyone is bound to do or not to do at the command of a superior power. For when the will of a law-maker is known to us, or so sufficiently promulgated that it can be known unless there is some impediment on our part, then we are bound to obey it and to submit to it in everything, and it is this which is called liability to pay dutiful obedience, namely to conform our actions to the rule imposed upon them, i.e. the will of a superior power. And this obligation seems to derive partly from the divine wisdom of the law-maker, and partly from the right which the Creator has over His creation. For, ultimately, all obligation leads back to God, and we are bound to show ourselves obedient to the authority of His will because both our being and our work depend on His will, since we have received these from Him, and so we are bound to observe the limits He prescribes; moreover, it is reasonable that we should do what shall please Him who is omniscient and most wise.

Secondly, a liability to punishment,[2] which arises from a failure to pay dutiful obedience, so that those who refuse to be led by reason and to own that in the matter of morals and right conduct they are subject to a superior authority may recognize that they are constrained by force and punishment to be submissive to that authority and feel the strength of Him whose will they refuse to follow. And so the force of this obligation seems to be grounded in the authority of a law-maker, so that power compels those who cannot be moved by warnings. However, not all obligation seems to consist in, and ultimately to be limited by, that power which can coerce offenders and punish the wicked, but

[1] In the English translation of Robert Sanderson's *De Juramenti Promissorii Obligatione*, entitled *De Juramento* (London, 1655, lect. i, sect. xii, p. 25), *debitum officii* is rendered thus: '. . . debt, according unto which every man is bound by the precept of the Law to act'. Locke derived this distinction between two kinds of duty from Sanderson. In accordance with his voluntarist theory of law, however, he substituted the expression *ex edicto superioris potestatis* for Sanderson's phrase *ex praecepto juris* (*De Juramenti Promissorii Obligatione*, 1646, i. 12).

[2] In the translation of Sanderson's work, loc. cit., *debitum supplicii* is rendered thus: '. . . debt, according to which every man is bound by the decree of the Law to suffer if he neglect his duty'.

et dominio illo quem in alium aliquis habet, sive jure naturae et creationis, cum ei merito omnia subjiciuntur a quo et primo facta sunt et perpetuo conservantur, vel jure donationis, cum Deus cujus omnia sunt partem imperii sui in aliquem transtulit et jus imperandi tribuit, ut primogenitis et monarchis, vel jure pacti, cum quis volens alteri se emancipavit et se alterius voluntati subjecit; omnis enim obligatio conscientiam alligat et animo ipsi vinculum injicit, (f. 86) adeo ut non poenae metus sed recti ratio nos obligat, et conscientia de moribus fert sententiam et admisso crimine nos merito poenae obnoxios esse judicat; verum enim illud poetae *se judice nemo nocens absolvitur,*[1] quod plane aliter esset si poenae solum metus obligationem induceret, quod quis in se facile sentiret et aliam obsequii sui rationem perciperet cum piratae captivus serviret, aliam cum principi obediret subditus, aliudque esset apud se neglecti erga regem obsequii judicium, aliud cum piratae aut praedonis mandata sciens transgrederetur, cum hic permittente conscientia jure usus suo saluti tantum consulerit, illic condemnante conscientia jus alterius violaret.

Deinde de obligatione observandum est alia obligare effective, alia solum terminative. Effective id obligat quod est prima causa omnis obligationis et a qua fluit formalis illius ratio, et id est voluntas superioris; ideo enim obligamur ad aliquid quia is sub cujus ditione sumus id velit. Terminative id obligat quod praescribit modum et mensuram obligationis et officii nostri; (f. 87) quod nihil aliud est quam declaratio istius voluntatis, quam alio nomine legem vocamus; a Deo enim optimo maximo obligamur, quia vult, hujus vero voluntatis obligationem et

---

[1] Juvenal, xiii. 2–3.

rather to consist in the authority and dominion which someone has over another, either by natural right and the right of creation,[1] as when all things are justly subject to that by which they have first been made and also are constantly preserved; or by the right of donation, as when God, to whom all things belong, has transferred part of His dominion to someone and granted the right to give orders to the first-born, for example, and to monarchs; or by the right of contract, as when someone has voluntarily surrendered himself to another and submitted himself to another's will. Indeed, all obligation binds conscience and lays a bond on the mind itself, so that not fear of punishment, but a rational apprehension of what is right, puts us under an obligation, and conscience passes judgement on morals, and, if we are guilty of a crime, declares that we deserve punishment. Of a surety, the poet's saying is true that 'no one who commits a wicked action is acquitted in his own judgement'; but it would clearly be otherwise, if fear of punishment alone imposed an obligation. Anyone would easily discern in himself that this is so and perceive that there was one ground of his obedience when as a captive he was constrained to the service of a pirate, and that there was another ground when as a subject he was giving obedience to a ruler; he would judge in one way about disregarding allegiance to a king, in another about wittingly transgressing the orders of a pirate or robber. For in the latter case, with the approval of conscience, he rightly had regard only for his own well-being, but in the former, though conscience condemned him, he would violate the right of another.

Further, regarding obligation, it must be noted that some things bind 'effectively', others only 'terminatively', i.e. by delimitation.[2] That thing binds 'effectively' which is the prime cause of all obligation, and from which springs the formal[3] cause of obligation, namely the will of a superior. For we are bound to something for the very reason that he, under whose rule we are, wills it. That thing binds 'terminatively', or by delimitation, which prescribes the manner and measure of an obligation and of our duty and is nothing other than the declaration of that will, and this declaration by another name we call law. We are indeed bound by Almighty God because He wills, but the declaration of His will delimits the obligation and the ground of our obedience;

---

[1] The expression occurs in Calvin's *Institutes*, bk. i, ch. 2, par. 2.

[2] This distinction, again, was derived by Locke from Sanderson (*De Obligatione Conscientiae*, 1647, v. 5; Engl. tr., 1660, p. 153).

[3] Cf. Culverwel, *Discourse of the Light of Nature*, pp. 45 and 77 (ed. Brown, 1857).

obsequii nostri rationem terminat declaratio, quia ad aliud non obligamur nisi quod legislator aliquo modo notum fecerit et promulgavit se
velle.

Obligant insuper aliqua per se et vi sua, aliqua per aliud et virtute
aliena. Primo per se et vi sua et sic solum obligat voluntas divina, sive
lumine naturae cognoscibilis et tunc est de qua disputamus lex naturae,
vel per viros θεοπνεύστους vel alio modo revelata et tunc est lex divina
positiva. Secundo per aliud et virtute mutuatitia obligat voluntas
superioris cujusvis alterius, sive regis sit sive parentis, cui ex voluntate
divina subjicimur; totum illud imperium quod in alios obtinent et jus
leges[1] ferendi et ad obsequium obligandi a solo Deo mutuantur legisla-
tores reliqui, quibus ideo tenemur obedire quia Deus sic vellet sic
jubet,[2] adeo ut illis obtemperando Deo etiam paremus. His ita positis
dicimus (f. 88) quod lex naturae obligat omnes homines primo et per
se et virtute sua, quod sequentibus argumentis confirmare conabimur.

Primo, quia haec lex omnia habet quae ad obligationem alicujus
legis requiruntur. Deus enim legis hujus author hanc voluit esse
morum et vitae nostrae regulam et sufficienter promulgavit, ut quivis
si studium si industriam adhibere mentemque ad illius cognitionem
advertere velit scire possit: adeo ut, cum nihil aliud ad inducendam
obligationem requiratur praeter dominium et justam imperantis potestatem et patefactam illius voluntatem, nemo dubitare potest legem
naturae homines obligare. Primo, cum Deus super omnia summus sit
tantumque in nos jus habet et imperium quantum in nosmet ipsos
habere non possimus, cumque corpus, animam, vitam, quicquid sumus,
quicquid habemus, quicquid etiam esse possumus, ei soli unice debemus,
par est ut ad praescriptum voluntatis illius vivamus. Deus nos ex nihilo
fecit et in nihilum si libet iterum redacturus: (f. 89) ei igitur summo
jure et summa necessitate subjicimur. Secundo lex haec est hujus
omnipotentis legislatoris voluntas nobis ex lumine et principiis naturae

---

[1] *legis* MS. B; *leges* MS. A.
[2] *jubet*: possibly a slip for *juberet*.

for we are not bound to anything except what a law-maker in some way has made known and proclaimed as his will.

Besides, some things bind of themselves and by their intrinsic force, others indirectly and by a power external to themselves:[1]

(1) Of itself and by its intrinsic force (and only so) is the divine will binding, and either it can be known by the light of nature, in which case it is that law of nature which we are discussing; or it is revealed by God-inspired men or in some other manner, in which case it is the positive divine law:

(2) Indirectly and by delegated power the will of any other superior is binding, be it that of a king or a parent, to whom we are subject by the will of God. All that dominion which the rest of law-makers exercise over others, both the right of legislation and the right to impose an obligation to obey, they borrow from God alone, and we are bound to obey them because God willed thus, and commanded thus, so that by complying with them we also obey God. The case having been put thus, we say that the law of nature is binding on all men primarily and of itself and by its intrinsic force, and we shall endeavour to prove this by the following arguments:

(1) Because this law contains all that is necessary to make a law binding. For God, the author of this law, has willed it to be the rule of our moral life, and He has made it sufficiently known, so that anyone can understand it who is willing to apply diligent study and to direct his mind to the knowledge of it. The result is that, since nothing else is required to impose an obligation but the authority and rightful power of the one who commands and the disclosure of his will, no one can doubt that the law of nature is binding on men.

For, in the first place, since God is supreme over everything and has such authority and power over us as we cannot exercise over ourselves, and since we owe our body, soul, and life—whatever we are, whatever we have, and even whatever we can be[2]—to Him and to Him alone, it is proper that we should live according to the precept of His will. God has created us out of nothing and, if He pleases, will reduce us again to nothing: we are, therefore, subject to Him in perfect justice and by utmost necessity.

In the second place, this law is the will of this omnipotent law-maker, known to us by the light and principles of nature; the know-

[1] For this distinction see Sanderson, *De Obligatione Conscientiae*, 1647, iv. 6 (Engl. tr., 1660, pp. 110–11).
[2] This phrase is reminiscent of one used by St. Thomas Aquinas, *Summa Theol.* Ia IIae, q. 21, art. 4, ad 3um.

innotescens, cujus cognitio neminem latere potest nisi qui caecitatem tenebrasque amat et ut officium suum effugiat exuit naturam.

Secundo, si lex naturae homines non obligat, obligare etiam non potest lex divina positiva, quod nemo dixerit; fundamentum enim obligationis utrobique eadem est, scilicet voluntas supremi numinis: differunt solum promulgandi ratione et diverso cognitionis nostrae modo, hanc enim lumine naturae et ex principiis naturalibus certo scimus, illam fide apprehendimus.

Tertio, si lex naturae homines non obligat, nec lex quaevis humana positiva eos obligare potest, cum magistratus civilis leges vim suam omnem ex hujus legis obligatione mutuentur, certe quoad maximam mortalium partem; ad quos cum revelationis divinae certa cognitio non pervenerit, nullam aliam divinam et virtute sua obligantem legem habent praeter naturalem, adeo ut inter eos (f. 90) legem naturae si tollas omnem inter homines civitatem, imperium, ordinem, et societatem simul evertis; non enim ideo ex metu regi obtemperandum est quia potentior cogere potest, hoc enim esset tyrannorum, latronum, et piratarum imperium stabilire, sed ex conscientia, quia jure in nos imperium obtinet, jubente scilicet lege naturae obtemperari[1] principibus et legislatori vel quocunque demum nomine superiorem voces: adeo ut legis civilis obligatio ex lege naturae pendeat, nec tantum ad obsequium magistratui praestandum potestate illius cogimur quantum jure naturae obligamur.[2]

---

[1] *ut obtemperemus* MS. A; *ut obtemperari* MS. B. While changing to the infinitive construction in MS. B, Locke omitted to delete *ut*.

[2] At the end of this essay Locke added the title of another which remained unwritten, namely, *An Lex Naturae obliget Bruta? Negatur.* ('Are animals bound by the law of nature? No.') Ulpian's definition of natural law as 'that which nature has taught all animals' (*Digest*, I. i. I) was rejected by Canon law, which regarded the law of nature as confined to the human race. That animals are not bound by this law was taught by Grotius (*De Jure Belli ac Pacis*, I. i. 11), Selden (*De Jure Naturali et Gentium juxta Disciplinam Hebraeorum*, I. i. 4), and Culverwel (*Discourse of the Light of Nature*, ch. vi, pp. 59–66, ed. Brown, 1857). In his next essay Locke affirms that natural law came into existence with the creation of man as a rational being.

ledge of it can be concealed from no one unless he loves blindness and darkness and casts off nature in order that he may avoid his duty.

(2) If natural law is not binding on men, neither can positive divine law be binding, and that no one has maintained. In fact, the basis of obligation is in both cases the same, i.e. the will of a supreme Godhead. The two laws differ only in method of promulgation and in the way in which we know them: the former we know with certainty by the light of nature and from natural principles, the latter we apprehend by faith.

(3) If natural law is not binding on men, neither can any human positive law be binding. For the laws of the civil magistrate derive their whole force from the constraining power of natural law, certainly so far as the majority of men is concerned. In fact, since the definite knowledge of a divine revelation has not reached them, they have no other law, both divine and binding by its very nature, than natural law; so that, if you abolish the law of nature among them, you banish from among mankind at the same time the whole body politic, all authority, order, and fellowship among them. For we should not obey a king just out of fear, because, being more powerful, he can constrain (this in fact would be to establish firmly the authority of tyrants, robbers, and pirates), but for conscience' sake, because a king has command over us by right; that is to say, because the law of nature decrees that princes and a law-maker, or a superior by whatever name you call him, should be obeyed. Hence the binding force of civil law is dependent on natural law; and we are not so much coerced into rendering obedience to the magistrate by the power of the civil law as bound to obedience by natural right.

VII

AN OBLIGATIO LEGIS NATURAE SIT PERPETUA ET UNIVERSALIS? AFFIRMATUR

VARIAS et multiplices esse hominum de lege naturae et officii sui ratione opiniones unica forsan res est de qua idem sentiunt omnes mortales, quod etiam si tacerent linguae satis loquerentur mores tam in diversum abeuntes, cum passim reperiantur non solum pauci et privatae sortis homines sed totae gentes, in quibus nullum legis sensum, nullam morum rectitudinem observare licet. Alii etiam sunt, et plurimi populi, qui aliqua saltem legis naturae praecepta sine criminis conscientia negligunt, quibus non solum in more sed et laude positum est ea patrare et probare scelera quae aliis recte sentientibus et secundum naturam viventibus maxime sunt detestanda. Hinc furta apud hos licita et laudata, nec rapaces latronum manus ullis conscientiae vinculis a vi et injuria coercentur. Apud alios nullus stupri (f. 92) pudor; hic nulla deorum templa aut altaria illic humano sanguine conspersa. Quod cum ita sit, dubitari merito possit an totum genus humanum, vagum et incertum, institutis diversissimis assuetum, motibusque plane contrariis actum, obliget lex naturae, cum vix credi possit tam obscura esse naturae dictata ut universas lateant gentes. Nonnullos nasci homines tam mente quam oculis captos, quibus duce opus est quique quo eundum sit nesciunt, facile conceditur, universos autem populos caecos natos quis dixerit? aut id esse secundum naturam quod totae gentes et hominum multitudo prorsus ignorat, lumenque pectoribus humanis inditum aut a tenebris omnino non differre aut ignis fatui[1] instar incerta luce in errores seducere? Hoc esset naturae convicium facere, cujus dum indulgentiam praedicamus saevissimam experiremur tyrannidem; quae enim unquam tanta fuit vel Sicula crudelitas ut eam sub-

---

[1] A favourite phrase with Chillingworth and the Cambridge Platonists. Cf. also Locke's *Essay*, iv. xix. 10 (ed. Fraser, ii. 436). Hobbes, *Leviathan*, ch. 5 (ed. Pogson Smith, p. 38).

VII

IS THE BINDING FORCE OF THE LAW OF NATURE PERPETUAL AND UNIVERSAL? YES

THE only thing, perhaps, about which all mortals think alike is that men's opinions about the law of nature and the ground of their duty are diverse and manifold—a fact which, even if tongues were silent, moral behaviour, which differs so widely, would show pretty well. Men are everywhere met with, not only a select few and those in a private station, but whole nations, in whom no sense of law, no moral rectitude, can be observed. There are also other nations, and they are many, which with no guilty feeling disregard some at least of the precepts of natural law and consider it to be not only customary but also praiseworthy to commit, and to approve of, such crimes as are utterly loathsome to those who think rightly and live according to nature. Hence, among these nations, thefts are lawful and commendable, and the greedy hands of robbers are not debarred from violence and injury by any shackles of conscience. For others there is no disgrace in debauchery; and while in one place there are no temples or altars of the gods, in another they are found spattered with human blood. Since such is the case, it may be justly doubted whether the law of nature is binding on all mankind, unsettled and uncertain as men are, accustomed to the most diverse institutions, and driven by impulses in quite opposite directions; for that the decrees of nature are so obscure that they are hidden from whole nations is hard to believe. That some men are born defective in mind as well as in eyesight, and are in need of a guide and do not know whither they ought to go, can readily be admitted; but who will say that entire nations are born blind, or that a thing is according to nature, of which whole nations and a multitude of men are absolutely ignorant, or that the light infused into human hearts either differs not at all from darkness or like an *ignis fatuus* leads into error by its uncertain gleam? To say this would be to insult nature, for while praising her gentleness we should be experiencing her most terrible tyranny. For has there ever been cruelty, even Sicilian cruelty,[1] so savage as that nature should demand of her subjects observance of a law which in the meantime she would conceal—that

---

[1] Possibly a reference to Phalaris, tyrant of Agrigentum.

191

ditos (f. 93) observare vellet legem quam interim occultaret, ei morem gerere voluntati quam scire non poterant? Draconis leges sanguine scriptas legimus, sed et scriptae fuerunt ut sciri possint. Tam crudelis certe esse non potest omnium mater natura ut ei[1] legi mortales parere velit quam non docuit, non sufficienter promulgavit. Unde concludendum videtur aut legem naturae alicubi nullam esse aut ea aliquos saltem populos non teneri, adeoque obligationem legis naturae non esse universalem.

His nequicquam obstantibus, asserimus legis naturae obligationem perpetuam esse et universalem.

Dari hujus legis obligationem jamjam probavimus; ista vero obligatio quanta sit venit nunc discutienda. Dicimus igitur legis naturae obligationem esse primo perpetuam, hoc est nullum esse tempus in quo liceret homini hujus legis praecepta violare; nullum hic datur interregnum, nulla Saturnalia aut libertatis sive licentiae in hoc imperio intervalla. Aeterna sunt hujus legis vincula et humano generi coaeva, simul nascuntur (f. 94) et simul intereunt. Non autem ita sumi debet perpetua haec obligatio quasi homines tenerentur semper praestare omnia quae lex naturae jubet: hoc plane impossibile esset, cum diversis simul actionibus non sufficit unus homo, nec magis pluribus simul potest adesse officiis quam corpus pluribus locis. Sed obligationem naturae ita perpetuam esse dicimus ut nullum sit tempus aut esse potest in quo lex naturae homines aut hominem quemvis quicquam agere jubet, in quo ad praestandum obsequium non tenetur: adeo ut obligatio sit perpetua, actus vero non requiritur perpetuus; nunquam mutatur legis obligatio, quamvis saepe mutentur et tempora et circumstantiae actionum, quibus circumscribitur obsequium nostrum; cessare aliquando possumus ab agendo secundum legem, agere vero contra legem non possumus; in hoc vitae itinere quies aliquando conceditur, error nunquam. Verum de legis naturae obligatione haec observanda sunt.

(f. 95) Primo aliqua esse quae omnino prohibentur, et ad haec obligamur ad semper, uti loqui amant Scholastici, hoc est nullum esse

---

[1] The passage from *ei* to *promulgavit*, contained in MS. A but omitted by the amanuensis in MS. B, was added by Locke on f. 92ᵛ.

they should be obedient to a will which they could have no knowledge of? Draco's laws, we read, were written in blood, but even so they were written so that they could be known. Surely, nature, the mother of all things, cannot be so cruel that she would bid mortals submit to a law which she has not taught and sufficiently promulgated. Hence it seems necessary to conclude, either that there is no law of nature in some places, or that some nations at least are not bound by it, so that the binding force of natural law is not universal.

In spite of these objections, we maintain that the binding force of the law of nature is perpetual and universal.[1]

We have already proved that this law is given as morally binding, and we must now discuss to what extent it is in fact binding. We say then that in the first place the binding force of the law of nature is permanent, that is to say, there is no time when it would be lawful for a man to act against the precepts of this law; no interregnum is provided here, in this realm there are no Saturnalian holidays given to either freedom or licence. The bonds of this law are perpetual and coeval with the human race,[2] beginning with it and perishing with it at the same time. However, this permanently binding force must not be supposed to be such that men would be bound at all times to perform everything that the law of nature commands. This would be simply impossible, since one man is not capable of performing different actions at the same time, and he can no more observe several duties at once than a body can be in several places. Still, we say that the binding force of nature is perpetual in the sense that there neither is, nor can be, a time when the law of nature orders men, or any man, to do something and he is not obliged to show himself obedient; so that the binding force is continuous though it is not necessary that the action be so. The binding force of the law never changes, though often there is a change in both the times and the circumstances of actions, whereby our obedience is defined. We can sometimes stop acting according to the law, but act against the law we cannot. In this life's journey rest is sometimes allowed, but straying at no time. However, the following points must be noted concerning the binding force of the law of nature:

(1) There are things which are altogether forbidden and to these we are bound—as the Schoolmen are wont to say—for ever; in other

[1] Cf. Cicero's definition of natural law, *De Republica*, iii. 22 (Lactantius, *Inst. Div.* vi. 8, 7 and 9).

[2] For this conception, which is part of Canon law, see *Decretum Gratiani*, dist. v, pars i, par. 1, col. 7 (ed. Friedberg, 1879).

temporis momentum in quo hujusmodi aliquid sine crimine admittere licet, uti furtum, homicidium, et id genus alia, adeoque aliquem fortunis suis per vim aut fraudem evertere perpetuum habet in se crimen, nec quisquam sine reatu se alieno sanguine polluere potest; ab his et hujusmodi aliis perpetuo abstinere tenemur.

Secundo alia sunt quorum habitus a nobis lege naturae requiruntur, qualia sunt reverentia et timor numinis, pietas erga parentes, amor vicini, et id genus alia; ad haec etiam obligamur ad semper, nec quodvis datur momentum temporis in quo hos licet exuere mentis habitus aut aliter quam lex naturae praescribit esse erga res illas affectos.

Tertio alia sunt quorum externi actus jubentur, verbi gratia, cultus numinis externus, afflicti vicini consolatio, laborantis sublevatio, esurientis cibatio, in quibus non obligamur ad semper sed certo solum (f. 96) tempore et modo; non enim quemlibet hominem aut quovis tempore tecto excipere et cibo reficere tenemur, sed tunc solum quando miseri calamitas eleemosynam a nobis postulat et res nostra familiaris charitati subministrat.

Quarto alia denique sunt in quibus substantia actionis non jubetur sed solum circumstantiae. Verbi gratia, in hominum inter se consuetudine et communi vita, de vicino suo sermonem habere et alienis rebus se immiscere quis tenetur? Nemo sane; aut loqui aut tacere quis potest sine crimine. Quod si forte alterius mentionem quis facere velit, jubet sane lex naturae ut candide, ut amice loquatur, eaque dicat quae alterius famam aut existimationem laedere non possunt. In his materia actionis indifferens est, circumstantiae determinatae. In his non obligamur absolute sed tantum ex hypothesi, et in nostra situm est potestate nostraeque prudentiae permissum, an aliquas hujusmodi actiones praestare velimus in quibus obligamur. In his omnibus, uti patet, obligatio legis aeque perpetua est, (f. 97) officii nostri munera non aeque perpetua; in duobus prioribus semper obligamur ad actualem obedientiam,

words, there is no single moment when one is at liberty to perform anything of this kind without incurring guilt; for example theft, murder, and other acts of that sort. Thus to force or cheat a man out of his property is at all times a crime, and no one can stain himself with another man's blood without incurring guilt. From these and other such acts we are for ever bound to abstain.

(2) There are other things towards which the law of nature requires us to maintain certain sentiments, such as reverence and fear of the Deity, tender affection for parents, love of one's neighbour, and other such sentiments. To these, too, we are obliged for ever, and there is no single moment when one is allowed to throw off these mental dispositions or be disposed towards those objects otherwise than the law of nature prescribes.

(3) There are things of which the outward performance is commanded, for example the outward worship of the Deity, the consoling of a distressed neighbour, the relief of one in trouble, the feeding of the hungry: in these matters we are not under obligation continuously, but only at a particular time and in a particular manner. For we are not obliged to provide with shelter and to refresh with food any and every man, or at any time whatever, but only when a poor man's misfortune calls for our alms and our property supplies means for charity.

(4) Lastly, there are cases where the action in itself is not commanded but only circumstances accompanying it. For example, in customary intercourse among men and in communal life who is bound to hold a conversation about his neighbour and to meddle with other people's affairs? No one, surely. Anyone can without harm either talk or be silent. But if perchance one wants to talk about another person, the law of nature undoubtedly enjoins that one's talk be candid and friendly and that one should say things that do not harm that other person's reputation and character.[1] In cases like these, the 'matter' of the action is neither good nor bad, but the circumstances accompanying it are so determined. We are not bound here absolutely, but only conditionally,[2] and it depends on our ability, and is entrusted to our prudence, whether or not we care to undertake some such actions in which we incur obligation. In all these cases, as is obvious, the binding force of the law is equally permanent; the requirements of our duty, however, are not equally permanent. In cases I mentioned in the first two sections we are always bound to actual obedience; in cases mentioned in

---

[1] Cf. S. Pufendorf, *Elementa Jurisprudentiae Universalis*, 1660, lib. II, obs. iv, par. 26.
[2] Op. cit., lib. I, def. xiii, par. 16.

in duobus posterioribus obligamur etiam semper ad ea praestanda quae solum per intervalla et successive, habita ratione loci, temporis, et circumstantiarum, agere debemus: adeo ut cessat aliquando actio, obligatio nunquam.

Deinde legis naturae obligationem universalem esse dicimus, non quod quaelibet lex naturae quemlibet obligat hominem; hoc enim fieri non possit, cum plurima legis hujus praecepta diversas hominum inter se relationes respiciunt et in iis fundantur: multa sunt principum privilegia plebi haud concessa, multa subditorum officia, qua subditi sunt, quae in regem convenire non possunt; imperatoris est gregariis suas destinare stationes, et militum tenere; nec deceret parentem liberos suos officiose et humiliter salutare. De quibus sic breviter statuendum est. Praecepta illa legis naturae quae absoluta sunt, in quibus continentur furta, stupra, calumniae, et altera ex parte religio, (f. 98) charitas, fides, etc.—haec, inquam, et hujus modi alia, omnes qui[1] ubique sunt homines aeque obligant, tam reges quam subditos, cum plebe patres, parentes simul et liberos, nec minus barbaros quam Graecos; nec quivis populus aut homo tam ab omni humanitate remotus est, tam efferus tam exlex, qui hisce legis vinculis non tenetur. Quae vero naturae decreta diversas respiciunt hominum sortes et inter se relationes non aliter homines obligant quam prout munera, sive privata sive publica, exigunt; aliud regis officium aliud subditi; unusquisque subditus tenetur parere principi, sed unusquisque homo non tenetur esse subditus, quidam enim nascuntur reges; nutrire et educere liberos patris officium est, nemo autem cogitur esse pater: adeo ut obligatio legis naturae eadem est ubique, vitae solum conditio varia; idemque plane est officium subditi apud Garamantas et Indos ac apud Athenienses aut Romanos.

His ita positis dicimus legis naturae obligationem et per omnia saecula et per universum terrarum orbem vim (f. 99) suam illibatam et inconcussam obtinere. Quia si omnes homines non obligat, ratio est vel quia alicui parti generis humani aut omnino lata non sit, aut iterum abrogata; sed neutrum horum dici potest.

---

[1] *quae* MS. B.

the last two sections we are likewise always bound to undertake the things which we have to do, but these things occur at intervals only and successively, and regard is paid to place, time, and circumstances, so that while the action comes to an end at some time, the obligation never does.

Next we say that the binding force of natural law is universal, but not because any and every law of nature is binding on any and every man, since this is impossible. For most precepts of this law have regard to the various relations between men and are founded on these. Princes have many privileges which are not granted to the common people, and subjects, in their capacity as subjects, have many duties which cannot be appropriate to a king. While it is a general's duty to assign soldiers their posts, it is the soldiers' duty to hold them; and it would not become a parent to salute his children ceremoniously and humbly. Of these matters we have to lay down our view briefly thus: Those precepts of the law of nature which are absolute and which embrace thefts, debaucheries, and slanders, and on the other hand religion, charity, fidelity and the rest, these I say, and others of that kind, are binding on all men in the world equally, kings as well as subjects, noblemen as well as the common people, both parents and children, barbarians no less than Greeks. And no nation or human being is so removed from all humanity, so savage and so beyond the law, that it is not held by these bonds of law. But those decrees of nature which are concerned with the various conditions of men and the relations between them are binding on men exactly in proportion as either private or public functions demand; the duty of a king is one thing, the duty of a subject is another. Each single subject is bound to obey the prince; but each single man is not bound to be a subject, for certain men are born kings. It is a father's duty to feed and bring up his children, but no one is compelled to be a father. The result is that the binding force of natural law is everywhere the same, only the circumstances of life are different. Clearly, the duty of a subject is the same among the Garamantes and the Indians as among the Athenians or the Romans.[1]

On these assumptions we say that the binding force of the law of nature holds its power undiminished and unchanged both throughout all ages and over the whole world. Because if this law is not binding on all men the reason is either that it has never been given at all to any part of mankind, or that it has been repealed. Neither of these two things, however, can be maintained.

---

[1] Cf. Cicero's definition of natural law in *De Republica*, iii. 22 (Lactantius *Inst. Div.* vi. 8. 9). For the Garamantes see p. 171.

Primo, quia dici non potest aliquos homines ita liberos natos esse ut huic quidem legi minime subjiciantur; non enim privatum hoc aut positivum jus pro temporum occasione et praesenti commodo natum, sed fixa et aeterna morum regula, quam dictat ipsa ratio, adeoque humanae naturae principiis infixum[1] haeret; et mutetur prius oportet humana natura quam lex haec aut mutari possit aut abrogari; convenientia enim est inter utramque, quodque jam convenit naturae rationali, quatenus rationalis est, in aeternum conveniat est necesse, eademque ratio easdem dictabit ubique morum regulas. Quandoquidem igitur omnes homines sint natura rationales, et convenientia sit inter hanc legem et naturam rationalem, quae convenientia lumine naturae cognoscibilis est, necesse est omnes rationali natura praeditos, id est omnes ubique (f. 100) homines hac lege teneri: adeo ut, si aliquos saltem homines obliget lex naturalis, eodem plane jure et omnes obliget necesse sit, cum par sit apud omnes homines ratio obligationis, idem cognoscendi modus, eademque natura. Non enim ex fluxa et mutabili voluntate pendet haec lex, sed ex aeterno rerum ordine; mihi enim videntur quidam immutabiles esse rerum status et quaedam officia ex necessitate orta, quae aliter esse non possunt, non quod natura vel (ut[2] rectius dicam) Deus non potuit aliter fecisse hominem, sed cum ita factus sit, ratione et aliis suis facultatibus instructus, ad hanc vitae conditionem natus, sequuntur necessario ex nativa ipsius constitutione aliqua illius et certa officia, quae aliter esse non possunt. Mihi enim videtur tam necessario sequi ex natura hominis, si homo sit, quod tenetur amare et venerari Deum, et alia etiam praestare naturae rationali convenientia, hoc est observare (f. 101) legem naturae, quam sequitur ex natura trianguli, si triangulus sit, quod tres illius anguli sunt aequales duobus rectis,[3] quamvis plurimi forsan sunt homines adeo

---

[1] The gender is surprising, but perhaps it refers back to *jus*.
[2] The bracketed passage begins with *vel* in MS. B.
[3] See St. Thomas Aquinas, *Summa Theol.*, Ia IIae, q. 94, art. 4.

For, in the first place, it cannot be said that some men are born so free that they are not in the least subject to this law, for this is not a private or positive law created according to circumstances and for an immediate convenience; rather it is a fixed and permanent rule of morals, which reason itself pronounces, and which persists, being a fact so firmly rooted in the soil of human nature. Hence human nature must needs be changed before this law can be either altered or annulled. There is, in fact, a harmony[1] between these two, and what is proper now for the rational nature, in so far as it is rational, must needs be proper for ever, and the same reason will pronounce everywhere the same moral rules. Since therefore all men are by nature rational, and since there is a harmony between this law and the rational nature, and this harmony can be known by the light of nature, it follows that all those who are endowed with a rational nature, i.e. all men in the world, are morally bound by this law. Hence, if natural law is binding on at least some men, clearly by the same right it must be binding on all men as well, because the ground of obligation is the same for all men, and also the manner of its being known and its nature are the same. In fact, this law does not depend on an unstable and changeable will, but on the eternal order of things. For it seems to me that certain essential features of things are immutable,[2] and that certain duties arise out of necessity and cannot be other than they are. And this is not because nature or God (as I should say more correctly) could not have created man differently. Rather, the cause is that, since man has been made such as he is, equipped with reason and his other faculties and destined for this mode of life, there necessarily result from his inborn constitution some definite duties for him, which cannot be other than they are.[3] In fact it seems to me to follow just as necessarily from the nature of man that, if he is a man, he is bound to love and worship God and also to fulfil other things appropriate to the rational nature, i.e. to observe the law of nature, as it follows from the nature of a triangle that, if it is a triangle, its three angles are equal to two right angles, although perhaps very many men are so ignorant and so thoughtless that

---

[1] The idea of 'harmony' or 'conformity' (*convenientia, congruentia*) between law and man's rational nature, indicated already by Cicero (*De Rep.* iii. 22) and other writers in antiquity, reappears in Gabriel Vasquez, Suarez, Grotius (*De Jure Belli ac Pacis*, lib. i, c. 1, x. 1 and xii. 1), and Sanderson (*De Obligatione Conscientiae*, iv. 24). Locke probably derived the notion from Culverwel (*Discourse of the Light of Nature*, ch. vi, pp. 71–77, ed. Brown, 1857).

[2] Cf. ibid. p. 77, referring, in note 4, to the phrase *essentiae rerum sunt immutabiles*.

[3] The last two sentences recall arguments advanced by Pufendorf in his *Elementa Jurisprudentiae Universalis*, 1660, lib. 1, def. ii, par. 1.

ignari, adeo socordes qui, dum animum non advertant, utramque hanc ignorant veritatem tam perspicuam tam certam ut nihil magis: adeo ut legem hanc homines ad unum omnes obligare dubitare nemo possit; unde etiam constat

Secundo, jus hoc naturale nunquam abrogatum iri, cum homines legem hanc obrogare[1] non possint; ei enim subjiciuntur, subditorum autem non est pro libitu suo leges refigere; nec certe Deus velit, cum enim ex infinita et aeterna sua sapientia ita fecit hominem ut haec illius officia ex ipsa hominis natura necessario sequerentur, haud certe mutabit factum et novam producet hominum progeniem, quibus alia sit lex et morum regula, quandoquidem cum humana natura, quae jam est, lex naturae stat simul caditque.[2] Potuit Deus homines ita creasse ut oculis carerent nec iis opus esset; dummodo vero oculis utuntur[3] eosque aperire velint et sol luceat, necesse est cognoscant noctis et diei vicissitudines, colorum percipiant differentias, et inter curvum et rectum quid intersit oculis videre.

Alia argumenta ad probandam universalem legis naturae obligationem deduci poterant (f. 102) a posteriori, ab incommodis scilicet quae sequerentur si supponeretur alicubi cessare hanc obligationem; nulla enim esset religio, nulla inter homines societas, nulla fides, et id genus innumera: quae vel leviter attigisse satis est. Restat jam ut dubiis nonnullis hac de re breviter occurramus.

Primo enim sic probari potest legis naturae obligationem non esse perpetuam et universalem: haec scilicet omnibus consentientibus lex est naturae ut suum cuique tribuatur,[4] vel nemo quod alienum est abripiat et sibi habeat; hujus legis obligatio jubente Deo cessare potest, ut ab Hebraeis dum Aegypto decederent et invaderent Palaestinam factum legimus. Ad hoc respondemus negando minorem; nam si Deus juberet aliquem mutuo acceptum non restituere, non cessaret legis

---

[1] *obrogare* and *abrogare* both occur in the passage containing Cicero's definition of natural law, *De Republica*, iii. 22 (Lactantius, *Inst. Div.* vi. 8. 8).

[2] The following passage from *potuit* to *videre* was added by Locke on f. 100ᵛ.

[3] *utuntur*: obviously a slip for *utantur*.

[4] Cicero, *De Legibus*, I. vi. 19; Justinian, *Institutiones*, I. i. 3 (ed. Krueger, 1872).

for want of attention they ignore both these truths, which are so manifest and certain that nothing can be plainer. Hence, no one can doubt that this law is binding on all human beings, to a man, and it is also clear from this that

In the second place, this natural duty will never be abolished; for human beings cannot alter this law,[1] because they are subject to it, and it is not the business of subjects to abrogate laws at their liking, and because God certainly would not wish to do so. For since, according to His infinite and eternal wisdom, He has made man such that these duties of his necessarily follow from his very nature, He surely will not alter what has been made and create a new race of men, who would have another law and moral rule, seeing that natural law stands and falls together with the nature of man as it is at present.[2] God could have created men such that they would be without eyes and not need them; but so long as they use their eyes and want to open them, and so long as the sun shines, they must of necessity come to know the alternations of day and night, be aware of the differences of colours, and see with their eyes the difference between a curved and a straight line.[3]

Other arguments to show that the binding force of natural law is universal could be derived *a posteriori*, namely from the inconveniences that would follow on the assumption that this binding force came somewhere to an end. For there would be no religion, no fellowship among men, no fidelity, and countless other such things. But it is sufficient to mention this merely in passing. It remains now to cope briefly with some doubts about this matter.

(1) A proof that the binding force of the law of nature is not ever-lasting and universal can be given in this way: namely by showing that, though by general agreement it is a law of nature that every man should be allowed to keep his own property, or, if you like, that no one may take away and keep for himself what is another's property, yet at God's command the binding force of this law can lapse, for this actually happened, as we read, in the case of the Israelites when they departed from Egypt and journeyed to Palestine.[4] To this we reply by denying the minor premiss; for if God should order someone not to restore something he has received on loan, the ownership of the thing

---

[1] Cf. Suarez, *Tractatus de Legibus ac Deo Legislatore*, 1613, lib. ii, c. 14, 8, p. 106. The doctrine forms part of Canon law (cf. W. Ullmann, *Medieval Papalism*, 1949, ch. ii, p. 46).

[2] Cf. here Pufendorf, op. cit., lib. i, def. xiii, par. 14.

[3] Cf. *Essay*, iv. xiii. 1 and 4.

[4] Taking with them the goods of the Egyptians, Exod. xii. 35 f.

naturae obligatio sed rei ipsius dominium, non violatur lex sed mutatur dominus; prior enim dominus cum possessione rei amittit simul et jus ad rem; bona enim fortunae nunquam ita nostra sunt ut Dei esse desinant; ille supremus rerum omnium dominus cuilibet pro arbitrio suo sine injuria de suo (f. 103) donare potest.

Secundo, si ad idem obsequium parentibus praestandum aliquando tenemur aliquando non tenemur, ergo perpetua non est legis naturae obligatio, sed aliud jubente principe non tenemur obsequi parentibus, ergo respondemus quod tenemur observare mandata parentum in licitis tantum, quae obligatio nunquam tollitur; si enim aliud imperet rex, parentis jussa fiunt illicita, verbi gratia, domi manere et rei familiaris curam gerere, cum rex ad militiam evocat: adeo ut non cesset omnino legis naturae obligatio, sed mutatur rei ipsius natura.

Tertio, si quis dubitet an universalis sit obligatio, quia tam variae sint de officio suo inter homines sententiae, tam diversi mores, sciendum est istum mortalium et in vita et in opinionibus dissensum non esse quia alia ac alia est lex naturae apud diversas gentes, sed quia aut diuturna consuetudine et domesticis exemplis seducti aut passionibus in transversum acti tradunt se in aliorum mores, et dum sibi rationis (f. 104) suae usum non permittunt sed appetitui parent brutorum more gregem sequuntur; aeque enim erroribus obnoxius est qui aperire nolit oculos ac qui caecus nascitur, etsi forsan via impedita non sit et oculorum acies satis sit acuta.

De infantibus et fatuis non est quod laboremus; etsi enim omnes obliget lex quibus datur, non tamen eos obligat quibus non datur, nec datur iis a quibus cognosci non potest.

---

[2] Cf. here Suarez, *Tractatus de Legibus etc.*, 1613, lib. ii, c. 15, 21, p. 115. Similar arguments in Grotius, *De Jure Belli*, lib. ii, c. 26, iii; Jeremy Taylor, *Ductor Dubitantium*, bk. iii, ch. 5, rule 7. For the view that, in certain cases, disobedience may not only be a possibility but a duty, see *Decretum Gratiani*, i. viii. 2 (ed. Friedberg), and Calvin, *Institutes*, bk. ii, ch. 8, par. 38.

[3] This is what the Scholastics called *mutatio materiae*.

[4] Cf. St. Thomas Aquinas, *Summa Theol.* Ia IIae, q. 94, articles 4 and 6.

[5] Cf. Sanderson, *De Obligatione Conscientiae*, 1647, lect. iv, par. 21 (fin.); also Pufendorf, *Elementa Jurisprudentiae Universalis*, 1660, lib. i, def. xii, par. 18.

itself, but not the binding force of natural law, would cease; the law is not violated, but the owner is changed, for the previous owner loses together with the possession of the thing his right to it. In fact, the goods of fortune are never so much ours that they cease to be God's: that supreme Lord of all things can, without doing wrong, give of His property to anyone as He pleases by His sovereign will.[1]

(2) If sometimes we are, and sometimes we are not, bound to render the same obedience to parents, then this shows that the binding force of natural law is not perpetual; nay, rather, if a prince commands differently, we are not bound to obey parents. Then, in that case we reply that we are no doubt bound to comply with the orders of parents but only in things lawful, and this obligation is never annulled; but if a king commands otherwise, a parent's orders become unlawful; for instance, an order to stay at home and show concern for the family, when the king is summoning a man for military service.[2] Thus the binding force of natural law does not by any means cease, yet the nature of the case itself changes.[3]

(3) If anyone doubts whether that binding force is universal on the ground that the opinions about their duty vary so much from men to men and their habitual actions are so different, it ought to be remembered that this diversity among mortals, both in their manner of life and in their opinions, does not occur because the law of nature varies among different nations, but because men are either carried off by inveterate habit and traditional examples or led aside by their passions, thus yielding to the morality of others; also they follow the herd in the manner of brute beasts, since they do not allow themselves the use of their reason, but give way to appetite.[4] In like manner, in fact, he who will not open his eyes, as well as he who is born blind, is liable to errors, though possibly the road is unobstructed and his eyesight is sufficiently sharp.

There is no reason that we should deal with the case of children and idiots. For although the law is binding on all those to whom it is given, it does not, however, bind those to whom it is not given, and it is not given to those who are unable to understand it.[5]

---

[1] Cf. here St. Thomas Aquinas, *Summa Theol.* Ia IIae, q. 94, art. 5; also Grotius, *De Jure Belli*, lib. i, c. 1, x. 6; William Ames, *De Conscientia etc.*, 1630, lib. v, c. 1, viii–x, p. 189; Edward Stillingfleet, *Irenicum*, 1659, ch. 2, par. 1 (fin.); Jeremy Taylor, *Ductor. Dubitantium*, 1660, bk. ii, ch. 1, rule 9. Gabriel Towerson, with whom Locke exchanged views on the law of nature, discussed the point in his *Explication of the Decalogue*, 1676, Discourse I, par. 3, p. 5.
[2], [3], [4], [5]. *See opposite.*

VIII

AN PRIVATA CUJUSQUE UTILITAS SIT
FUNDAMENTUM LEGIS NATURAE?
NEGATUR

ALIQUI sunt qui legis naturae oppugnationem aggressi illud sibi assumpserunt argumentum: *jura*, scilicet, *homines utilitate sibi sanxisse varia pro moribus, et apud eosdem pro temporibus saepe mutata; jus autem naturale esse nullum: omnes enim et homines et animantes ad utilitates suas natura ducente ferri; proinde aut nullam esse legem naturae aut, si sit aliqua, summam esse stultitiam, quoniam sibi nocet alienis commodis consulens.*[1] Haec et ejusmodi alia in Academia sua disputavit olim Carneades, cujus acerrimum ingenium et eloquentiae vis nihil intactum nihil pene inconcussum praetermisit; nec defuerunt ab illa (f. 106) usque aetate qui summo studio ad hanc sententiam accesserunt; quibus cum defuerunt virtutes et eae animi dotes quarum ope ad honores et divitias sibi munirent aditum, inique cum humano genere actum querebantur et res publicas non sine injuria geri contenderunt, dum communibus et nativis commodis et in commune bonum natis prohiberentur: adeoque excutienda esse imperiorum juga libertatem naturalem asserendam clamarunt, et jus omne et aequum non aliena lege sed propria cujusque utilitate esse aestimandum. Huic vero tam iniquae opinioni sanior mortalium pars, cui aliquis inerat humanitatis sensus, aliqua societatis cura, semper obstitit. Verum ut accuratius[2] rem definiamus, praemittenda est aliqua terminorum explicatio, quid nempe per (f. 107) fundamentum legis naturae velimus, et quid deinde per privatam cujusque utilitatem.

Primo per fundamentum legis naturae id volumus cui innituntur et cui tanquam fundamento superstruuntur alia omnia et minus patentia illius legis praecepta, et ab eo aliquo modo deduci possunt: adeoque vim suam omnem et obligationem ex eo obtinent, quod cum ea tanquam primaria et fundamentali lege conveniunt quae omnium aliarum legum inde pendentium regula est et mensura.

---

[1] This account of Carneades's argument is taken, almost literally, from a passage in Lactantius (*Inst. Div.* v. 16. 3), which in its turn is taken from a part, now lost, of Cicero's *De Republica* (iii. 12. 21). There is reason to believe, however, that Locke derived the quotation from Grotius, *De Jure Belli ac Pacis*, proleg., par. 5. Towards the end of the quotation Locke substitutes *lex naturae* for *justitia*.

[2] *paulo accuratius* MS. A.

VIII

IS EVERY MAN'S OWN INTEREST THE BASIS OF THE LAW OF NATURE? NO

THERE are some who in their attack upon natural law have adopted the following argument: 'It is on a basis of utility that men have laid down for themselves legal codes varying in accordance with their manners and customs, and often changed with changing times among the same people; there is, however, no law of nature, for all men as well as other living creatures are driven by innate impulse to seek their own interests; and there is likewise no such thing as a natural law of justice, or, if it exists, it is the height of folly, inasmuch as to be mindful of the advantages of others is to do harm to oneself.' This and other such arguments Carneades once maintained in his Academy. His very sharp intellect and power of speech left nothing untouched, almost nothing unshaken, and there have been a number of people ever since who have assented to this doctrine very eagerly. Since these people have lacked virtues and those gifts of the mind whereby they might prepare for themselves the way to honours and wealth, they have complained that mankind has been treated unfairly and have contended that civil affairs were not conducted without injustice, as long as they were debarred from general and natural advantages destined for the common good. They went so far as to proclaim that the yoke of authority should be shaken off, and natural liberty be vindicated, and every right and equity be determined not by an extraneous law but by each person's own self-interest. This most harmful opinion has, however, always been opposed by the more rational part of men, in whom there was some sense of a common humanity, some concern for fellowship. However, in order that we may define the matter more carefully, we must first give some explanation of the terms, namely what we mean firstly by the basis of natural law, and then, by each man's private interest.

First, by the basis of natural law we mean some sort of groundwork on which all other and less evident precepts of that law are built and from which in some way they can be derived, and thus they acquire from it all their binding force in that they are in accordance with that, as it were, primary and fundamental law which is the standard and measure of all the other laws depending on it.

Secundo, cum dicimus privatam cujusque utilitatem non esse fundamentum legis naturae, non ita accipi volumus quasi opposita essent inter se jus commune hominum et utilitas cujusque privata; maximum enim munimentum rei cujusque privatae lex est naturae, sine cujus observatione rem suam possidere suisque commodis inservire nemini licet: adeoque cuivis humanum genus hominumque mores (f. 108) recte secum perpendenti certum erit nihil aeque communi cujusque utilitati conducere, nihil aeque res hominum tutas et securas custodire ac observatio legis naturae. Verum negamus id cuique licere quod ipse pro re nata judicet sibi commodum fore; frustra enim statuis privatam cujusque utilitatem esse aequi et recti regulam, nisi privato cuique permittis ut pro se ipse judicet, ut quid sibi sit utile ipse aestimet; nemo enim alterius commodi aequus et justus esse potest aestimator; et illum illudis solum specie utilitatis cui id licitum asseris quod utile est, in alterius vero potestate situm velis ut statuat quid sit utile quid non: adeo ut status quaestionis hic demum sit: an quod privatus quisque pro re nata judicet sibi rebusque suis utile fore id esse secundum legem naturae, eoque nomine sibi non solum licitum esse sed et necessarium nec quicquam in natura (f. 109) obligare nisi quatenus aliquam immediate prae se ferat utilitatem? quod negamus.

Primo, quia id non potest esse fundamentum legis naturae sive primaria lex ex qua[1] obligatio aliarum ejusdem naturae legum minus universalium non pendet. Sed ex hoc fundamento non pendet aliarum legum obligatio; si enim percurrere velis omnia vitae humanae officia, nullum invenies ex sola utilitate natum quodque obligat ex hoc solum quod commodum sit: cum multae sint et maximae virtutes quae in eo solum consistunt ut cum dispendio nostro aliis prosimus; hujusmodi virtutibus ad astra olim evecti et in deorum numerum ascripti sunt

---

[1] *quo* would more correctly link up with the antecedent *id*.

Secondly, when we say that each man's personal interest is not the basis of natural law, we do not wish to be understood to say that the common rules of human equity and each man's private interest are opposed to one another, for the strongest protection of each man's private property is the law of nature, without the observance of which it is impossible for anybody to be master of his property and to pursue his own advantage. Hence it will be clear to anyone who candidly considers for himself the human race and the practices of men, that nothing contributes so much to the general[1] welfare of each and so effectively keeps men's possessions safe and secure as the observance of natural law.[2] Nevertheless we do deny that each person is at liberty to do what he himself, according to circumstances, judges to be of advantage to him. You have certainly no reason for holding that each person's own interest is the standard of what is just and right, unless you let every single man be judge in his own case and himself determine what is in his own interest, seeing that no one can be a fair and just appraiser of another's advantages; and you deceive a man with what is only a semblance of utility, if you say he is permitted to do what is useful and yet would let another man have the power to determine what is and what is not useful. Hence the point of the question is precisely this: Is it true that what each individual in the circumstances judges to be of advantage to himself and his affairs is in accordance with natural law, and on that account is not only lawful for him but also unavoidable, and that nothing in nature is binding except so far as it carries with it some immediate personal advantage? It is this we deny, for three reasons:

First, it is impossible for something to be the basis of natural law or to be the principal law, which is not the ground of the binding force of other, less universal, laws of that same nature. But the binding force of other laws does not rest on the principle of utility as its foundation, for if you should run over all the dutiful actions of human life, you will find none that arises out of mere utility and is binding for the sole reason that it is advantageous. In fact a great number of virtues, and the best of them, consist only in this: that we do good to others at our own loss. By virtuous actions of this kind heroic men in former times were raised to the sky and placed among the number of gods,[3] purchasing

---

[1] Locke here has used a word which properly implies 'shared with other people'.
[2] Cf. Grotius, De Jure Belli ac Pacis, proleg., pars. 16 and 18.
[3] The phrase is reminiscent of St. Augustine, De Civ. Dei, lib. ii, c. 5 (Corp. Script. Eccl. Lat., vol. 40, 1, p. 65, l. 2).

heroes, qui caelum congestis et undique conquisitis pecuniis non eme-
runt, sed labore, sed periculis, sed liberalitate; non privatis studuerunt
commodis, sed utilitati publicae et totius humani generis; alii laboribus,
alii lucubrationibus, alii morte immortalitatem meruerunt; nemo
ignavia aut avaritia (f. 110) aut magnus aut probus factus est. Quod
si primaria esset lex naturae ut sibi quisque rebusque suis privatis con-
suleret, magna illa virtutum exempla literarum monumentis consecrata
oblivioni danda essent, ut interiret prorsus tantae insaniae tantae
nequitiae memoria. Ii enim ipsi quos jam pro summis optimisque viris
miramur non solum stulti sed et nefarii ac sceleratissimi essent habendi,
qui tanto cum studio se suasque res contempserunt ut majori solum
pretio mercarentur turpitudinem, ut rem suam simul abjicerent et
innocentiam, et in eo sibi laborandum putarent ut damna simul crescerent et crimina. Si utilitatem recti regulam esse volumus, tui, Alcides,
labores crucem potius meruerunt quam apotheosim, et naturae ipsi
magis quam monstris bellum indixisti. Curtii, qui patriae causa in
patentem insiluit voraginem et, ne suis Roma minis sepeliretur, vivus
terram subivit, non (f. 111) tam virtus fuit quam insania; vitae simul
valedixit et innocentiae, eodemque tempore intravit sepulchrum et
meruit mortem. Benignissima certe merito dicenda est omnium mater
natura, cum officia nostra non solum necessaria esse vellet sed jucunda
et ditia nec ullas esse virtutes nisi fructuosas; optime cum humano
genere actum est, ut tantum crescat virtus quantum ipsa pecunia
crescit! Quorsum igitur laudamus Fabritii inopiam et verborum splendore nefarias ejus ornamus sordes? qui fortunam suam et virtutem
vendere mallet quam patriam, qui rempublicam stulte sibi anteposuit
et se ipso habuit cariorem. Quanto rectius magnus Catilinae animus,
qui naturae praeceptis optime imbutus suum mundi capiti praetulit nec
timuit hostile ipsius Romae muris aratrum imprimere,[1] dummodo sibi

---

[1] Cf. Horace, *Od.* i. 16. 20.

heaven not with a mass of riches brought together from all sides, but with toil, hazards, and generosity. They did not pursue their own advantage but the interests of the commonwealth and of all mankind. Some earned immortality by their works, some by their studies, some by their death; none achieved either greatness or excellence by being idle or covetous. Yet if it were the principal law of nature that each man should be mindful of himself and his own affairs, those noble examples of virtue which the records of history have hallowed would have to be consigned to oblivion, so that the memory of so much folly, of so much perversity, would be completely blotted out. The very same people, in fact, whom we now admire as the best and the most eminent of men would have to be regarded not only as foolish but even as wicked and most pernicious. For they were so zealously contemptuous of themselves and of their own affairs only to purchase infamy at a higher price and, by throwing away their own property, by the same act to cast off their innocence; and they believed they were bound to exert themselves thus in order that injuries should multiply and crimes too. If we wish utility to be the standard of what is right, your labours, Hercules, deserved a felon's cross rather than a place in heaven, and you declared war on nature itself rather than on monsters. What Curtius[1] did when for the sake of his country he leaped into the yawning chasm and plunged into the earth alive lest Rome should be engulfed in the grave of her own forebodings, was not so much virtue as madness: he bid both life and innocence farewell and he deserved his death the moment he entered his grave. To be sure, nature undoubtedly deserves to be called the most kindly mother of all, if she wishes our duties to be not only unavoidable but also pleasant and lucrative and no actions to be virtuous unless they are profitable! Well indeed is it for mankind that virtue should increase in proportion to the increase of wealth itself! Why, then, do we praise the indigence of Fabricius[2] and paint that abominable stinginess of his in bright colours? He preferred to sell his fortune and his virtue rather than his country, and he foolishly held the Roman republic in greater esteem, and loved it more dearly, than himself. How much more fitly should we praise the fine spirit of Catilina who, perfectly instructed in the precepts of nature, preferred his own interest to that of the world's capital and did not fear to drive the foeman's plough over the walls of Rome itself, so long

[1] Marcus Curtius, in the year 362 B.C. (cf. Livy, vii. 6. 5).
[2] C. Fabricius Luscinus, leader of the Romans against Pyrrhus, famous for his frugality and for his noble conduct towards Pyrrhus (cf. Cicero, *De Off*. iii. 22. 86).

inde sperare liceret messem? Audiat forsan Cicero (f. 112) pater patriae, hic certe genuinus naturae filius, et imperium orbis dum Romam invasit magis meruit quam Tullius qui defendit! Pudet sane hanc infamiam naturae inurere et tantam turpitudinem illius institutis imputare; cumque nihil tam sanctum sit quod aliquando non violaverit avaritia, officii rationem in lucro ponere et recti regulam utilitatem statuere, quid aliud esset quam omni nequitiae fenestram aperire?

Secundo ea non potest esse lex naturae primaria cujus violatio necessaria est; sed si utilitas cujusque privata sit fundamentum istius legis, eversum iri necesse est, cum omnium simul utilitati consulere impossibile sit; unica enim est et eadem semper universae stirpis humanae haereditas nec pro nascentium numero augetur.[1] Ad hominum commoditates et usus certam rerum ubertatem natura largita est, et ea quae gignuntur certo modo et numero donata sunt consulto, non fortuito nata, nec cum hominum necessitate aut avaritia crescunt. Nobiscum non nascitur vestitus, nec homines more testudinum cognata habent et secum una crescentia domicilia (f. 113) circumgerunt. Quoties inter homines crescit aut cupido aut necessitas habendi, non protenduntur illico mundi limites. Victus, vestitus, ornamenta, divitiae, et caetera omnia hujus vitae bona in communi posita sunt; et dum sibi rapit quantum quisque potest, quantum suo addit acervo tantum alieno detrahit, neque cuivis licet nisi per alterius damna ditescere. Regeret hic fortasse aliquis,[2] cum dicimus utilitatem cujusque esse legis naturae fundamentum, id non ita intelligi debere quasi quisque teneretur faelix esse et beatus et rebus omnibus abunde affluere, sed unusquisque homo quantum in se est obligatur sibi consulere: adeoque recti mensuram esse utilitatem propriam, in eaque fundari omnia (f. 114) vitae officia. Quo posito sequitur primo quod ad id obligantur homines quod fieri non potest; tenetur enim quisque sibi rerum utilium parare et possidere quam maximam copiam, quod dum fit necesse est

[1] The following passage from *ad* to *crescunt* was added by Locke on f. 111ᵛ.

[2] While changing from *quod . . . debet* to the infinitive construction in MS. B, Locke omitted to delete *quod* after *aliquis*.

as he could hope thereby to reap a harvest! Cicero may perhaps be called a father to his country,[1] Catilina certainly was a true son of nature and, the while he attacked Rome, he rather than Cicero who defended it deserved to rule the world. Surely, one feels ashamed to fasten such infamy upon nature and to impute so much evil to her ordinances. Besides (since there is nothing so sacred that avarice has not at one time or other treated it with violence), if the ground of duty were made to rest on gain and if expediency were acknowledged as the standard of rightness, what else would this be than to open the door to every kind of villainy?

Secondly, it is impossible that the primary law of nature is such that its violation is unavoidable. Yet, if the private interest of each person is the basis of that law, the law will inevitably be broken, because it is impossible to have regard for the interests of all at one and the same time. In point of fact, the inheritance of the whole of mankind is always one and the same, and it does not grow in proportion to the number of people born. Nature has provided a certain profusion of goods for the use and convenience of men, and the things provided have been bestowed in a definite way and in a predetermined quantity; they have not been fortuitously produced nor are they increasing in proportion with what men need or covet. Clothes are not born with us, nor do men, like tortoises, possess and carry about shelters that have originated with them and are growing up together with them. Whenever either the desire or the need of property increases among men, there is no extension, then and there, of the world's limits. Victuals, clothes, adornments, riches, and all other good things of this life are provided for common use. And so, when any man snatches for himself as much as he can, he takes away from another man's heap the amount he adds to his own, and it is impossible for anyone to grow rich except at the expense of someone else. Someone here will possibly amend the statement by saying that if we make every man's self-interest the basis of natural law, this must not be understood in the sense that each person would be required to be prosperous and happy and to have everything in abundance, but that every one is obliged, as much as he can, to have regard for himself, so that the standard of rightness is private interest and all the duties of life are founded on it. From this assumption it follows, first, that men are under an obligation to do what cannot be realized. For in such a case each person is required to procure for himself and to retain in his possession the greatest possible

---

[1] The title bestowed on Cicero for saving the republic in 63 B.C.

211

ut alteri relinquatur quam minima, cum certum sit quod nihil emolumenti tibi accrescit quod alteri non aufertur: quod plane contrarium est si alia ponamus virtutum fundamenta; virtutes enim ipsae inter se non pugnant nec homines committunt: accendunt se mutuo foventque. Mea justitia alterius non tollit aequitatem, nec principis munificentia officit subditorum liberalitati; sanctitas patris non corrumpit liberos, nec Catonis temperantia efficere potest ut minus severus sit Cicero. Inter se non pugnant (f. 115) vitae officia nec homines invicem armant, quod secundo ex hoc supposito necessario sequitur et homines (uti loquuntur) lege naturae in statu belli sunt; tollitur omnis societas et societatis vinculum fides. Quae enim promissorum implendorum ratio, quae societatis custodia, qui hominum convictus, cum id omne aequum justumque sit quod utile? Quid enim aliud esse poterit hominum inter se consuetudo quam fraus, vis, odium, rapina, caedes, et id genus alia, cum cuilibet homini non solum liceret sed necesse esset id quovis modo ab alio abripere quod ille pariter tenetur defendere?

Unde tertio oritur argumentum, nempe id non potest esse fundamentum legis naturae, quo posito omnis justitia, amicitia, liberalitas (f. 116) e vita tollitur. Quae enim justitia ubi nulla proprietas aut dominium, aut quae proprietas ubi cuivis licet non solum id possidere quod suum est, sed id suum cujusque est quod possidet, quod utile est? Verum hic breviter observare licet hujus sententiae propugnatores petere morum principia et vitae regulam potius ex appetitu et inclinatione hominum naturali quam ex legis obligatione, quasi id moraliter optimum esset quod plures appetunt. Unde etiam hoc insuper sequitur, aut legis naturae nullam esse obligationem—quod nemo dixerit, tum enim lex non est—aut eam esse vitae humanae conditionem ut non liceret homini cedere jure suo aut alteri benefacere sine certa spe lucri. Si enim rectitudo alicujus actionis nascatur ex utilitate et (f. 117)

number of useful things; and when this happens it is inevitable that the smallest possible number is left to some other person, because surely no gain falls to you which does not involve somebody else's loss. But obviously a contrary result follows if we lay down another foundation for the virtues. In fact, virtues themselves do not clash nor do they engage men in conflict: they kindle and cherish one another. Justice in me does not take away equity in another, nor does the liberality of a prince thwart the generosity of his subjects. The moral purity of a parent does not corrupt his children, nor can the moderation of a Cato lessen the austerity of a Cicero. The duties of life are not at variance with one another, nor do they arm men against one another —a result which, secondly, follows of necessity from the preceding assumption, for upon it men are, as they say, by the law of nature in a state of war; so all society is abolished and all trust, which is the bond of society. For what reason is there for the fulfilment of promises, what safeguard of society, what common life of man with man, when equity and justice are one and the same as utility? What else indeed can human intercourse be than fraud, violence, hatred, robbery, murder, and such like, when every man not only may, but must, snatch from another by any and every means what the other in his turn is obliged to keep safe.

Hence there arises a third argument, namely, that it is impossible for any principle to be the basis of natural law, whereby, if it is laid down as true, all justice, friendship, and generosity are taken away from life. For what justice is there where there is no personal property[1] or right of ownership, or what personal property where a man is not only allowed to possess his own, but what he possesses is his own, merely because it is useful to him. In truth, one may observe here briefly that the upholders of this doctrine seek the principles of moral action and a rule to live by in men's appetites and natural instincts rather than in the binding force of a law, just as if that was morally best which most people desired. Hence it furthermore follows either that the law of nature is not binding (but this no one will be found to say, for then there would be no law), or that human life is so constituted that it would be unlawful for a man to renounce his own rights or to impart benefits to another without a definite hope of reward. In fact, if the rightness of a course of action be derived from expediency and men are

---

[1] The same phrase occurs in *Essay*, iv. iii. 18, as one of the examples whereby Locke wants to show the possibility of demonstration in ethics. Cf. also Hobbes, *Leviathan*, pt. i, ch. 15 (ed. Pogson Smith, p. 110). Also Locke's *Some Thoughts Concerning Education*, § 110.

homines obligantur ad eam rectitudinem, nescio quo pacto liceret cuiquam aliquid amico largire, donare, impendere, vel quovis alio modo gratis beneficium conferre sine legis hujus violatione, quod quam absonum sit, quam a ratione et humana natura et vita honesta alienum aliorum judicio permitto. Verum objici potest, si ex observatione legis naturae et ex omni vitae officio semper sequatur commodum, nec quicquam agere possumus secundum legem naturae quod magnam post se non trahat vel immediate vel mediate utilitatem: ergo fundamentum legis naturae est cujusque utilitas; sed minor patet; ex hujus enim legis observatione nascitur pax, concordia, amicitia, impunitas, securitas, (f. 118) rerum nostrarum possessio, et, ut omnia uno verbo complectar, faelicitas. Ad haec sic respondemus. Utilitas non est fundamentum legis aut ratio obligationis, sed obsequii consequentia; aliud enim est si actio per se aliquod afferat emolumentum, aliud si ea ratione prosit quod conformis sit legi, qua lege abrogata nullum in ea esset omnino commodum—verbi gratia, promissis stare licet sit incommodum. Distinguendum enim est inter actionem ipsam et obedientiam; actio enim ipsa incommoda esse potest—exempli causa, depositi restitutio quae rem nostram minuit—obedientia utilis quatenus poenam sceleri debitam averruncat, quae poena debita non esset adeoque non fugienda, (f. 119) si recti regula praesens esset commodum: adeo ut actionis rectitudo non pendet ex utilitate, sed utilitas consequitur ex rectitudine.

Sic Cogitavit

1664   J. Locke

bound to comply with that sort of rectitude, I know not in what way it would be possible for anyone, without breaking this law, to grant or give anything to a friend, incur expenses on his behalf, or in any other manner do him a favour out of pure kindness. I leave others to judge the absurdity of this and how contrary it is to reason, to human nature, and to an honourable conduct of life. An objector, however, might say that if the observance of natural law and of every duty of life always leads to what is useful and if whatever we do according to the law of nature cannot but create, either directly or indirectly, great advantages, then the basis of natural law is each man's own interest. But (he goes on) the truth of the minor premiss is evident, for the observance of this law gives rise to peace, harmonious relations, friendship, freedom from punishment, security, possession of our property, and—to sum it all up in one word—happiness. Our answer to the objector is this: Utility is not the basis of the law or the ground of obligation, but the consequence of obedience to it. Surely, it is one thing for an action of itself to yield some profit, another for it to be useful because it is in accordance with the law, so that if the law were abolished it would have in it no utility whatever: for example, to stand by one's promise, though it were to one's own hindrance. In fact we must distinguish between an action as such and obedient action, for an action itself can be inexpedient—for example, the restitution of a trust that diminishes our possessions—whereas obedient action is useful in so far as it averts the penalty due to a crime. But this penalty would not be due and hence need not be shunned, if the standard of rightness were immediate advantage. And thus the rightness of an action does not depend on its utility; on the contrary, its utility is a result of its rightness.

Thus thought

1664   J. Locke

Locke's Valedictory Speech

AS CENSOR OF
MORAL PHILOSOPHY
(1664)

INTRODUCTORY NOTE

THIS speech was written by Locke in 1664, when he was Censor of Moral Philosophy at Christ Church, and probably he delivered it himself at the end of his year of office, in December 1664, in the presence of the Dean and Chapter and the whole College. It is Locke's valedictory speech as Censor, a 'funeral' oration in Latin demanded of him as part of the traditional ceremony of 'burying the Censor'. This hitherto unpublished speech, which is more fully discussed in the General Introduction to the present volume, pp. 11–12, is of considerable biographical interest; it shows that Locke as Censor delivered a series of lectures on the law of nature, probably identical with the essays printed in this volume or some extended version of them. His interest in natural law, an interest shared by his students, is twice referred to in the speech, and from the original title of it in MS. A we can gather that in his mind the speech must have been closely linked with the essays. The bare contents of this valedictory address, which is not without humour and felicitous phrases and is throughout highly rhetorical, can be summed up as follows:

In the first part Locke dwells on the futility of life, urging men to accept death as a deliverance. These are his reasons: Life is full of hopes and desires, hardship and pain, and is totally devoid of happiness. Not even philosophy can make men truly happy, as can be seen from the example of Aristotle and the teaching of the Stoics and Epicureans. Philosophical speculation incites men against one another and offers no repose. Men were wretched even in the Golden Age (if ever there was such a time) under the rule of the malevolent Saturn. Happiness can be found in bygone times as little as it can be found in the small compass of a lifetime. With advancing years a man appears terrifying to himself and to others ludicrous. If ever he reaches a state of good fortune, he is at once filled with anxiety, and thus constantly disillusioned. Yet man is fond of life, even at its worst; therefore we must pity not so much his condition as his refusal to quit it. More distressing is it that men, despite their common plight, do not console, but rather hate, one another. Thus, since the pleasures of life are burdensome and life itself brutish and the body the source of all pain and the world a prison, man is best advised to make an end of himself.

In the second part of his speech Locke bids farewell to the various

218

members of the House. The Dean's rule over the College is compared to the omnipotence of Jupiter; even if there were unpropitious influences in the House, these could not shake the Dean's everlasting dominion: Jupiter himself in his Olympian height is at times in conjunction with Saturn.

The Sub-dean is applauded for the inspiration of his poetic genius.

The presence of the Prebendaries on this occasion, the favours they have bestowed on Locke, and their readiness to support him throughout the term of office undertaken at their bidding are acknowledged with gratitude.

The Masters' accomplishments are set forth as a model worthy of emulation rather than as deserving the criticism that apparently they had received.

The Junior Censor with whom Locke has shared the burden of administration and, as Castor did with Pollux, a life of affection and friendship is bid Godspeed for the remaining three days of his term of office.

The pall-bearers are thanked for the munificent display they have lavished on the funeral rites of an otherwise undistinguished man.

The dialectical skill of the Bachelors is acknowledged as being superior to Locke's own, and though by argument they have endeavoured to disprove the natural law, by their morals they have confirmed it.

Locke is full of praise for the diligence, ability, and good manners of the Scholars, to whom he has been more of a counsellor than a taskmaster, forgiving rather than censuring their shortcomings. None the less, he exhorts them all to bring learning to the support of their mission by becoming good philosophers as well as good theologians.

Finally Locke has a few words to say of himself in his capacity as Censor. Laying aside the appurtenances of his lofty station, he reviews the course of his year of office without stressing any particular incident except one regrettable occurrence at the end of the period. His sole consolation is that he has lived and died honourably, according to the law of nature and the law of the House, and that after his death no one will bear him malice. Therefore he accepts death gladly.

ORATIO CENSORIA FUNEBRIS
1664

AN SECUNDUM NATURAM[1] QUISQUAM POTEST ESSE FAELIX IN HAC VITA? NEGATUR

QUISQUIS e pectoribus hominum penitus insitum hujus vitae amorem delere conabitur et persuadere mortalibus summum malorum quae in hac vita patiuntur esse vitam ipsam videbitur certe aut ipse insanus aut alios velle insanire. Quantam autem promittat natura faelicitatem, quam tenuem quam nullam praestat[2] satis docent totius humani generis querelae, spes inanes et in futurum semper protensae quibus animus tanquam in eculeo positus semper extenditur, expletur nunquam. Leges quidem nobis dedit natura, sed quae non sunt tam faelicium privilegia quam miserorum vincula quibus in hac vita detinentur; omnes enim mortales in hanc vitam conclusit natura tanquam in commune ergastulum, ubi legum et mandatorum satis, tranquillitatis et otii nihil: fessae illic laboribus manus et terga loris concisa, nulla pars aut labore vacat aut supplicio, et ipsi industriae imminet flagellum. Haec est vitae nostrae conditio: quam infimam esse satis docuit natura cum e terra nos fabricavit, cui in hoc etiam similes agnoscimur quod sentibus sumus abunde feraces. Et si qua forsan insit caelestis originis flammula, tremulo illo (f. 121) et irrequieto motu quo ad nativas sedes continuo tendit, plus molestiae et anxietatis nobis affert quam lucis, et hoc solum luto huic nostro confert ut sentiat se ardere et tacito inclusi ignis tormento consumi simul et vexari: adeo ut Promethei furtum nobis non minus quam ipsi authori dolendum, cum vita nostra duret solum in poenas nec alium in finem viscerum reparentur damna quam ut crescant et semper supersit aliquid quod crucietur. Sic votis nostris illudit natura nec in hac vita faelicitatis quicquam nobis largitur praeter desiderium. Nec benignior hac ex parte philosophia, inter cujus magnifica verba inopem se et miseram sentit infaelix mortalitas. Multas suas ostentat

---

[1] The title in MS. A begins *An secundum legem naturae quisquam*, &c.
[2] *praestet* MS. A.

CENSOR'S VALEDICTORY SPEECH
1664

CAN ANYONE BY NATURE BE HAPPY IN THIS LIFE? NO

WHOEVER shall attempt to efface from the hearts of men the deeply
rooted love of life and persuade them that the greatest of the evils they
suffer in this life is life itself, will certainly seem either to be mad himself or to wish others to be mad. And yet, however much happiness
nature may promise, what she in fact offers is little and trifling, as can
be seen well enough from the complaints of the whole of mankind,
and from the hopes, vain and directed always to the future, whereby
the mind, as if set on a rack, is continually stretched out but never
satisfied. No doubt nature has given us laws, but they are not so much
the privileges of the happy as the fetters whereby the wretched are
detained in this life. Nature in fact has confined all men alike to this
life as to a convict prison, where there are laws and commands enough
but no tranquillity and peace: hands there are wearied by work and
backs are stricken beneath the lash, no one is free from hardship or
suffering, and the scourge is a threat even to the industrious. Such is
the condition of our life, and nature has shown pretty well how very
mean it is by creating us out of earth, which we are seen to resemble in
this also, that we bear briars and brambles in great profusion. And if
perchance there is in us a small flame of divine origin, yet by that
flickering and restless motion whereby it strives perpetually towards its
original dwelling-place, it gives us more trouble and anxiety than light,
and it bestows on this clay of ours merely the awareness that it is
ablaze and is both consumed and tormented with the silent torture of
an imprisoned fire. Hence Prometheus' theft must be deplored by us
no less than by him who committed it, since our life only drags on
from pain to pain, and the injuries done to our vitals are repaired for
no other purpose than that they may be increased and something
always left to be plagued. Thus nature mocks our prayers and grants
us in this life no happiness at all except the desire for it.[1] Nor is philosophy in this respect more kindly; in the midst of its noble utterances
unhappy mankind feels itself powerless and pitiable. Philosophy holds

---

[1] In a more serious mood, Locke expressed some similar views in his *Essay*, II. xxi. 32–46.

221

divitias, sed quae omnes orationis potius sunt quam hominum. Acres illae et subtiles de summo bono disputationes humanis malis non magis medentur quam pugna aut ferro sanantur vulnera. Tam procul ab hac vita semota est faelicitas ut ubi sit ex hac faece naturae[1] conspici non possit; nec quaerendo faelicitatem ultra profecerunt philosophi quam ut nobis ostenderent reperiri non posse. Aristoteles quam alios docuit faelicitatem ipse frustra quaesivit: et tum demum fluctuare tum demum jactari desiit cum in mare se projecit et majorem quam in vita sua perfecta in Euripo invenit tranquillitatem. Porticum si ingrederis, reperies illic Stoicos virum suum beatum magno molimine effingentes et, ut contra omnes fortunae ictus satis indurescat et quam natura effingere potuit perfectior exeat, (f. 122) ad incudem saepius revocantes; quem omnibus affectibus exutum dum beatum vellent efficere, tollunt hominem et pro faelici stipitem tandem producunt speciosa verborum pompa ornatum: et eam demum humano generi tradunt faelicitatem qua frui qua laetari non possit. Diverso plane itinere ad faelicitatem suam tendunt Epicurei, qui eodem eventu cupiditates suas satiare conantur quo Stoici tollere, nec in amoenis Epicuri hortis melior nascitur faelicitas quam in Aegyptiorum Deus, etsi utrique non defuerunt cultores devotissimi; quisque enim pro sectae suae summo bono tanquam pro summo numine digladiatur, et dum tanta animorum contentione tanto ingenii acumine pugnarunt inter se philosophi, facta est omnia complectens Philosophia Oceano similis, cui salis inest plurimum, quietis nihil.[2] Multa illic reperiuntur jucunda varietate altitudine stupenda, quibus animum oblectes; ubi vero te sistas cui certo innitaris, stabile et fixum nihil, et infinitae illae quae circumfluunt quae obruunt

[1] *natura* MS. B.
[2] A partial echo of Isaiah 57, 20.

out her many riches, but they all are mere words rather than the property of men. Those pointed and shrewd discourses concerning the highest good do not heal human misfortunes any more than fist and sword cure wounds. Happiness is so far removed from this life that it is impossible from out of these dregs of nature to see where it is, and philosophers in their search for happiness have not accomplished more than to tell us that it cannot be found. The happiness that Aristotle taught others he himself looked for in vain; and he did not cease to be storm-tossed and perturbed until he had at last thrown himself into the sea and had found a greater tranquillity in the Euripus[1] than in his fully lived life. If you enter the Porch, you will find there the Stoics fashioning with great effort their happy man. In order that he may become sufficiently inured to all the strokes of fate and turn out a more accomplished product than nature could have formed, they frequently call him back to their forge and to make him happy despoil him of all his passions; they destroy the man, and in the end produce, in place of a tree of happy growth,[2] a barren stump decked with a pompous show of words: they bequeath to the human race only a sort of happiness which it cannot make use of and enjoy. The Epicureans strive towards their happiness along a completely different course; they endeavour to gratify their passions and they reach the same result as do the Stoics, who try to eradicate them, and happiness does not better come to birth in the pleasant gardens of Epicurus than God does in those of Egypt, though both have been well supplied with devoted attendants; each school in fact contends fiercely for the highest good of its sect as if it were the supreme godhead. And since philosophers have fought among themselves with minds so strenuous and intellects so keen, all-embracing philosophy has become like the encompassing sea, in which there is a great deal of salt[3] but no repose. Many things are found there, delightful in variety, stupendous in depth, with which you may divert the mind, but wherever you betake yourself so as to rest there with certainty, you will find nothing stable, nothing firmly fixed, and the endless waves, abounding on all sides and overwhelming,

[1] Procopius (*Bell. Goth.* iv. 66, p. 485, ed. Bonn), among others, reports the legend that Aristotle, incapable of solving the problem of the violent flux and reflux in the strait between Euboea and Boeotia, threw himself headlong into that narrow sea, the Euripus. Locke probably derived the information from Thomas Stanley's *History of Philosophy*, 4 vols., 1655–62, a copy of which he possessed (the passage in question occurs on p. 236 of the third edition in one volume, 1701). Cf. also J. Glanvill, *The Vanity of Dogmatizing*, 1661, p. 66.

[2] Locke is playing here on two meanings of *faelix*.

[3] The Latin *sal* equals (1) salt, and (2) sharp wit, and Locke is playing here on the two meanings of the word.

undae incertum et anxium jactant animum, sitientem et faelicitatis avidum explere non possunt. Sic natura et sic philosophia ab ipsis quidem incunabulis querula et irrequieta; et si nascenti humano generi et pene jam vacuo orbe, in ipsa mundi infantia, plus forte esset crepundiorum, lachrymarum certe non minus. Sunt, fateor, qui prioris saeculi laudes perpetuo crepant, quibus nihil exiinium nihil mediocre nisi quod antiquum audit, in quibus omnia[1] forte antiqua reperies praeter mores; quasi (f. 123) majores nostri tantum faelicitate nos praeirent quantum tempore. Aurea fuisse retro saecula fando audivimus, sed quae in iisdem quibus primo nata sunt poetarum cerebris latuisse semper videantur. Quod si aurea illa de qua tantum laboratur iterum rediret aetas, perpendite (quaeso), Auditores, quae esset illius faelicitas, si in ea dominaretur senex et tardus et malevolus Saturnus paterno illo in filios animo,[2] hoc est ad juniores devorandos parato: praestat sane quale dicitur saeculum sub Jove plumbeum. Miretur senectus praeterita et quae amisit fruatur bonis, praesentibus ingemiscens: nemo praeterito faelix, seni invidendum non est si sit laudator temporis acti se puero;[3] quid enim mirum si perspicillis utenti conspectiora omnia et majora videantur e longinquo posita? In nobis et nostrum esse debet quicquid efficit faelicem, nec ἀκριτόμυθον[4] illum Thersiten meliorem virum aut faeliciorem quis dixerit, quod heroum tempore vixerit aut Pelidae et Ulyssi fuerit coaetaneus. Majus sane quiddam est faelicitas quam ut brevi aetatulae nostrae compendio contineri possit. Quod si natura Nestoris daret annos, nihilo magis efficeret faelices, si cum longitudine vitae afferret et senectutem. Quis credat hominem faelicitatem tum possidere

---

[1] Possible reading *omina*.
[2] A faint echo of Horace, *Od.* ii. 2. 6.
[3] Quotation from Horace, *A.P.* 173–4.
[4] ἀκριτόμυθος: Homer, *Il.* ii. 246.

224

toss the uneasy and anxious mind without being able to appease its thirst and its longing for happiness. Thus nature and thus also philosophy are from their very cradles disquieted and fretful. When mankind took its rise and the earth was almost empty and the world was then very young, there were perhaps more children's rattles, yet certainly no fewer tears. Admittedly, there are some who continually rattle off[1] the praises of former times,[2] for whom there is nothing excellent, nothing even moderately good, except what is called ancient (men in whom you will perhaps find the whole of antiquity except its morals); as if our ancestors excelled us as much in happiness as they do in age. We are told that there have been golden ages in the past, but which ones they were seems always to have been concealed in the same poetic minds in which they first originated. And if that golden age which one is so concerned about were to return again, please consider, Gentlemen, what would be its state of felicity, if the aged, sluggish, and malevolent Saturn ruled over it with that paternal feeling of his for his sons—to wit, a readiness to devour his young. Certainly, what is called the age of lead under Jupiter is preferable. Let old age admire the past and, while lamenting the present, enjoy the good things it has lost: no one was happy in time past, but we should not begrudge it to an old man, if he is full of praise for a bygone time when he himself was a boy. For is it surprising, if to a man wearing spectacles everything at a distance looks more conspicuous and larger? Nay, whatever it is that makes a man happy, it must lie in us and be ours. And no one will say that the scurrilous Thersites was a better or happier man because he lived in an heroic age or because he was a contemporary of Achilles and Odysseus. Surely, happiness is something too big to be encompassed by the narrow limits of our feeble age. And if nature were to grant Nestor's long life, she would make us none the happier, if along with length of days she brought also senility. Who could believe

---

[1] *crepant* recalls *crepundia* in the last sentence.

[2] Here Locke alludes to the famous seventeenth-century dispute about ancient and modern learning. In France, at the end of the century, the controversy culminated in the 'Querelle des anciens et des modernes' with Boileau deciding the contest in favour of ancient times and Perrault in favour of modern times. In England, about the same time, Sir William Temple and the Hon. Charles Boyle stood up as defenders of traditional authorities, while William Wotton and Richard Bentley extolled modern achievements (cf. Swift's *Battle of the Books*, written in 1697). Earlier, before Locke wrote his valedictory speech of 1664, Bodin and Descartes in France, and Bacon and Hobbes in England, had sided with the 'moderns'. The controversy lost its relish with the emergence of a truly historical notion of development. Locke himself, in his later years, dismissed the whole question as unreasonable in his *Conduct of the Understanding*, par. 24 (*Works*, 1801, iii. 225).

cum sese amiserit et ipse sibi subtrahitur, qui si in conspectum sui adduceretur, non minus terrori esset sibi quam aliis ludibrio? Videre enim est in quibus humanam speciem delevit (f. 124) vetustas, quorum vultum larvam dixeris, quasi ludos faceret natura eademque quae poetas facit faceret et histriones serio ridiculos. Nunquam aliquem ad illud perduxit haec vita quo se ipso possit esse contentus, ad remota et futura hiantem semper et vacuum mittit bona. Quod si esset uti audit natura mater benignissima donisque suis plorantes cumularet filios, quid prosunt beneficia quae exagitant quae occidunt? Anxietatem, fastidium, crapulam secum affert rerum affluentia; flatibus maxime expositae et tempestatibus opportunae illae undae quae latissimae patent; et in magna fortuna majores semper tumultus et majores miseriae. Quid juvat naturae benignitas, si qui novercantis severitatem fugiunt pereant indulgentia? Mallem ego furcas quam amplexus officiose strangulantes. Saevius illud factum quod perfugio suo fidentem et mediis in gaudiis securum opprimit; nec simplici morte contentus is videtur qui spem faelicitatis injicit, ut utramque magis invito et magis sentienti abripiat. Ferre vitam tot calamitatibus onustam miserum est, miserius certe amare; et e carcere et ergastulo tot patentibus undique portis nolle exire ostendit nos non solum conditione sed voluntate miseros esse. Hoc enim in se gravissimum habent hujus vitae miseriae quod placent; ea maxime metuenda (f. 125) aegritudo quae adblanditur; cujus dum quis succumbit magnitudini, nec ipse doloris sensum habet nec alter miseretur. Hoc unum erat quod tantis superaddi poterat malis: quod fallimur, quod gaudemus. Tam misera enim est haec vita ut ipsa corrumpat gaudia, nec cuiquam licet sine insania laetari. Quae enim dementia est ut quam quisque cogente natura invitus lachrymansque ingreditur vitam eam sciens, prudens, laetusque retineat et illud miretur et toto animo amplectatur naturae donum quod sine dolore sine fletu non poterat accipere! Sic stulte in limine haeremus et querimur, ingressi tripudiamus quasi nihil in carcere incommodum esset praeter

that a man would possess happiness only when he has lost himself and his true self is withdrawn from him, and when, if he were induced to look upon himself, he would be no less a terror to himself than an object of mockery to others? For one can see people in whom old age has destroyed the outward appearance of man, whose face you would describe as a mask, just as if nature were putting on stage-plays and the same nature who makes poets were making also actors who are in sober truth ridiculous. This life never brings anyone to a point where he can be content with himself, but sends him away, panting and ever empty, after remote and future goods. But if nature were the most kindly mother, as she is called, and overloaded her wailing children with her gifts, of what use are favours that pester and slay? A profusion of good things carries with it anxiety, nausea, and a drunken surfeit; those waters that are widest in extent are most exposed to the winds and offer a favourable occasion for storms: so in a state of great good fortune upheavals are always greater and sorrows greater. What is the benefit of nature's kindness if those who escape from the harshness of a step-motherly treatment die through being spoiled by her? I would rather be hanged on the gallows than officiously suffocated by embraces. A thing is the more cruel if it crushes a man when he is confident in his refuge and carefree in the midst of joy. Nor does the oppressor seem content with simple death, if he inspires the hope of happiness only that he may snatch away both life and hope from one who is thus the more unwilling and the more sensitive. To endure a life burdened by so many ills is pitiable enough, to love it is surely more pitiable. And the desire not to leave the prison and convicts' cells, though so many doors are open on all sides, shows that we are pitiable not only on account of our condition but also of our will. In fact, the miseries of this life have in themselves this most painful feature, namely that they are welcome. That illness is to be dreaded most which soothes us: when anyone yields to its pressure he feels no pain nor does another feel pity. This only could be added as a climax to such grievous ills: namely, that we are cheated and rejoice in them. For so miserable is this life that it makes pleasures go bad and it is impossible for anyone to be joyful without being insane. What folly indeed it is that anyone should purposely, deliberately, and gladly preserve a life which he enters at nature's bidding tearfully and unwillingly, and that he should respect, and cherish whole-heartedly, a gift of nature which he could not receive without grief and lamentation! Thus on the threshold we linger like fools and lament, but once in, dance as if there was nothing

aditum et ea mala quae primo aspectu ferre non potuimus propter diu-
turnitatem essent amanda. Inter haec deest commune miserorum solatium, eosdem quos pari fortuna conjunxit calamitas distrahit animorum
dissensio et invicem armat; odimus non solamur doloris socios et pari
jure nobis adulamur et aliis invidemus. O quam beata illorum sors qui
nihil faelicitatis habent nisi quod in ea molestum est et maxime fugien-
dum, dum quisque et suo morbo laborat et invidia aliena! Valeant
igitur tristes vitae voluptates; nihil habet terrarum orbis quod dare
potest votis nostris dignum praeter sepulchrum. Viventibus ipsae graves
sunt deliciae, mortuis vel terra levis. Fruges et herbas et quicquid
(f. 126) in externo telluris cortice nascitur quasi projicit natura et
bestiarum pabulum esse voluit; illic homines cum brutis tanquam in
communi caenaculo versantur, nec egregium quicquam sperandum est
tam iniquam societatem passis; illic quasi domo ejecti precario vivimus
et mendicorum more prae foribus alimur; quicquid enim splendidum
quicquid pretiosum intus in secretiore recessu abscondidit natura, nec
minus faelicitatem quam divitias quaerentibus subeunda tellus. Cujus
munificentia tunc vere ditescimus et satiamur, tunc se totam nobis
tradit cum suos nobis pandit sinus et in gremium redeuntes placide
recipit. Ab aevo condito unica illa faelix aetas in qua mundus ipse
invenit sepulchrum, nec tanto quo in hac vita obruitur humanum
genus malorum diluvio minus quam diluvium poterat mederi: in communi illo fato, cum exularet e rerum natura totumque amiserat orbem,
solus qui vixit Deucalion passus est naufragium lachrymisque suis
quibus jactabatur auxit undas.[1] Amolienda igitur aliquando est natura,
exuenda fragilia haec et caenosa animae integumenta; in tam turpi et
angusto domicilio habitare nescit magnum illud faelicitatis numen.
Quicquid nobis molestum est e corpore oritur, et ei soli tempestates
metuendae non sunt qui terras reliquit; malorum si quaeras (f. 127)
exitum necesse est ut ipse desinas; hujus lucis usura ad labores solum et
aerumnas nos evocat, quae extinguenda est quietem optantibus; sol est
qui facit umbras, et quicquid nobis luctuosum id omne vitae nostrae

[1] Some resemblance to Sophocles's *Trachinian Women*, 114–16.

disagreeable in prison except the entrance, and as if the ills that at first sight we could not bear were to be cherished because we had become accustomed to them. Meanwhile there is no solace in distress for all alike to share, but the very people whom misfortune has joined in suffering a like fate are torn asunder and set in arms against one another by discord in their hearts. We hate rather than console our fellow sufferers, and we flatter ourselves with as much or as little right as we bear ill will against others. Blessed, forsooth, is the lot of those who know nothing of happiness except what is harmful in it and most to be avoided, when each endures both his own plague and the ill will of others! Farewell, then, to the tristful pleasures of life; the world has nothing to give that is worthy of our prayers except the grave. To the living even pleasures are burdensome; upon the dead, however, the earth lies lightly. Fruits and herbs and whatever grows on the crust of the earth, these nature as it were flings abroad and has meant to be fodder for beasts. There on this earth men live with the brutes as in a common feeding-place, nor is there hope of any mark to distinguish them while they endure such uncongenial society. There on earth's crust we live on sufferance like outcasts, and like beggars we feed on doorsteps. For whatever splendour, whatever treasure nature has hidden deep in some secret lurking-place, these must be sought beneath the earth, not less certainly by those who search for happiness than by those who search for riches. Then we shall truly grow rich by her bountifulness and be satisfied; then and only then she will give herself up to us completely, when she throws her bosom open to us and takes back those who return quietly to her breast. From the beginning of time the only happy age has been that in which the world itself has found its grave, and nothing less than a deluge could give relief from such a deluge of evils as that by which mankind is overwhelmed in this life. Deucalion of old, the sole survivor of that universal doom, when he was an exile from all that is and had lost the world, was shipwrecked and added his tears to the waves on which he was tossed. Therefore at some time or other nature must be done away with; these perishable and muddy coverings of the soul must be cast off. That great deity, happiness, cannot dwell in so foul and limited a habitation. Whatever is hurtful to us takes its origin from the body, and only he who has left the world need not fear the storms of misfortune. If you seek the end of evils you must yourself cease to be. So long as we use this light of day it summons us only for drudgery and hardship, and they must extinguish it who desire rest. It is the sun which makes shadows, and we have

debemus. Quis eo contentus esse potest mundo qui animo magno minor est, qui unius sufficere non potuit victoriis? Id cuilibet faelicitatem anhelanti orbis terrarum quod fuit Alexandro: carcer est et animo ad majora nato nimis angustus.[1] Hinc saepe in morte[2] corpus exagitat et membra concutit, dum morae impatiens quaerit exitum; morientium enim tremuli et convulsivi motus non sunt animae labores sed carceris sui vincula diffringentis et vicina libertate exultantis tripudia.

Decano D[ri] Fell

Sed quid ego diu expectata mortis gaudia praedicando differo? Liberet hic certe mortem occupare et tacite ad silentes abire, nisi quod minime deceret per quem maxime in hanc vitam ingressus sum eo insalutato exire. Majora enim Tua in me, Vir Reverendissime,[3] sunt beneficia quam ut ipsa mors eorum delere possit memoriam. Aliarum rerum quas in hac vita aut ipse gessi aut ab aliis passus sum libenter patior obrepere mihi in morte oblivionem, sed dabunt Fata veniam si Lethen transgressus et inter umbras Tuas memorem laudes; neque enim (f. 128) virtutibus Tuis aut imitandis aut praedicandis una sufficere potest vita. Latissimus autem ille dicendi campus anhelanti mihi et jam expiranti fugiendus, non solum quod me deficerent et vires et tempus et ingenium, sed ne moribundus ita delirare[4] videar ut putem Tuis meritis opus esse encomio. Verum dicam quod sentio quodque mecum hi omnes una sentiunt, illam scilicet quam alibi anxie et frustra quaerunt mortales faelicitatem hic solum sub Tuo imperio reperiri, quam tantam esse agnoscant omnes ut credant necesse fore ut aliquid interveniat quod illam Tuam benignam temperet influentiam, ne tranquillitate loci decepti putent aliqui has esse beatorum sedes ubi in aeternum esset commorandum. Nec tamen eo minus existimamus hunc locum esse caelo proximum et ei simillimum, cum scimus et in ipso caelo inter planetas qui res inferiores moderantur esse aliquos minus benignos et conjunctum aliquando cum Jove Saturnum. Hoc certe, quicquid de nobis fiat, laetamur omnes, nempe dum, quod immodicis fieri solet,

---

[1] Cf. Seneca, *Suas.* 1. 3.

[2] Either *se* has dropped out here or *corpus* should be construed as accusative.

[3] Here and in similar places, the forms of address are enclosed within brackets in MSS. A and B, but I prefer to print commas.

[4] *delirare* may be meant as a pun in connexion with *campus* above, 'ploughing awry'.

to thank our life for everything, no matter what, that causes us sorrow. Who can be contented with this world which is less than one great soul and not enough for one man to conquer? For to anyone striving after happiness the earth is just what it was to Alexander: it is a prison, and too narrow for a mind destined for higher ends. Hence the body is often agitated at the time of death and its limbs shake, because it is impatient of delay and longs for the end. In fact the jerks and spasmodic movements of dying people are not the sufferings of the soul but her dance as she breaks the bonds of her prison-house and revels in freedom nigh at hand.

But why do I put off by talking the long looked-for joys of death? To be sure, at this juncture I should like to enter the grave and without a word to join the silent shades, were it not that it would be most unseemly to depart this life without paying my respects to him who more than any other helped me into it. In fact, your kindnesses to me, Very Reverend Sir,[1] are too great for death itself to blot out their memory. On other things that in this life I have done myself or others have done to me, I gladly let forgetfulness fall at my hour of death. But the fates will pardon me, if I should sing your praises after having joined the shades across the river Lethe; and indeed one lifetime is not enough either to copy or to extol your perfections. I must, however, at my last gasp and at the point of death quit that wide field of discourse, not only because strength and time and talents fail me, but also lest at the point of death I appear to be so far out of my mind as to believe that your merits stand in need of praise. Still, I shall say what I feel and what all those present here feel with me, namely, that the happiness which elsewhere men look for anxiously and in vain is found only here under your rule, and that all regard this happiness as so great that they think it necessary something should intervene to set bounds to your propitious influence, lest some, deceived by the serenity of the place, imagine that these are the seats of the blessed to be dwelt in for ever. And yet we do not judge this place to be less nigh to heaven and like thereto for that, since we know that in heaven itself among the planets that guide affairs in the world below some are less benign, and sometimes Saturn is in conjunction with Jupiter. In this, assuredly, we all rejoice, whatever may happen to ourselves: namely that, while, as usually happens to the froward, all we other lesser men,

[1] Here Locke addresses Dr. John Fell (1625–86), Dean of Christ Church since November 1660, and Bishop of Oxford (1675). He was the son of Samuel Fell, former Dean of Christ Church.

nos reliqui omnes brevis aetatis et potentiae homunciones subinde nascimur, vivimus, et mox interimus, Te unum esse immortalem, nec solum mansuetudine sed etiam diuturnitate imperii esse Jovi simillimum.

(f. 129) *Subdecano D. Main*

Ad Tuos ego pedes, Vir Optime, projicio consulatus mei fasces, easque quibus impar fuit tremula haec nostra manus Tibi trado virgas fortiore dextra vibrandas, et spero tum demum reviviscet fatiscentis hujus aedis genius cum Tu antiquae et jam diu conclamatae disciplinae et defunctorum ingeniorum manes magica Tua virga evocaveris. Nam quis illam non ambitiose exercere vellet artem quae venerandas huc majorum nostrorum reduceret saltem umbras? utilior enim est et innocentior hujusmodi magia quam ut timere debeat aut cognitionem judicis aut Dominicae precis repetitionem. Majora jam olim a Te peracta vidimus, nec quis nunc dubitaverit posse Te cum Orpheo domare feras si quae hic sunt,[1] cum Amphione movere lapides et animare truncos, cum magico Tuo permota carmine locuta etiam sunt et muta animalia et quam natura negavit vocem Tuum donavit ingenium.

Praebendariis

Hunc ego anteactae vitae fructum hodie capio amplissimum quod Vos, Viri Colendissimi, qui nascenti olim huic meae dignitati praefuistis, expiranti jam adesse velitis et vitae labores mortis gloria compensare. Fatum enim Caesare dignum est imperium simul et vitam (f. 130) in senatu finire et inter tot veneranda capita interire; qua in re hoc mihi magis augustum accidit quod in Vobis cum pari dignitate majorem sentio benevolentiam. Multa enim et maxima sunt beneficia quae privatim singuli quae universi publice in me contulistis, inter quae hanc meam imprimis censuram acceptam refero; quae si forte praeter morem aliquid in se habuit molestum, id forte eorum quae nactus sum temporum fato meae certe voluntati minime imputandum.

---

[1] *sint* MS. A (possibly more pointed).

whose years and power alike are brief, are born in quick succession, live and soon die, you alone are immortal and are very like to Jove not only in his clemency but also in the long continuance of his rule.

At your feet I lay, most honourable Sir,[1] the fasces of my consulship and I resign to you this bundle of rods, which our trembling hand was unfit to wield, to be brandished by a stronger one. And I feel sure the genius of this crumbling house will come to life again as soon as you call up with your magic wand the spirit of ancient learning, long since mourned as dead, and the spirits of scholars now deceased. For who would not wish to make a display of that art which would bring back to this place at least the venerable shades of our ancestors? This kind of magic, in fact, is too useful and too harmless to have to fear either the inquisition of a judge or an oft-repeated Paternoster. Greater things we have seen you perform once upon a time and no one now will doubt that you can, like Orpheus, tame wild beasts, if there are any here, and like Amphion, move stones and bring timber to life; for roused by your magical charm even mute animals have talked indeed,[2] and the voice that nature has denied, your genius has granted.

Today I experience this the greatest reward of my past life in that you, most worshipful Sirs,[3] who once presided over the beginning of this office of mine, should wish to be present now at the end of it and to compensate me for the travails of life with the glory of my death. It is certainly a fate worthy of Caesar to end both empire and life in the Senate and to perish among so many venerable persons. And in such a situation a more honourable privilege falls to me inasmuch as I note in you, who hold an equally high office, a greater friendliness of feeling; for the favours which each one of you in private and all of you in public have conferred on me are many and vast, and among them I mention first the bestowal of this censorship of mine. If, contrary to custom, the censorship has had perchance some unpleasantness in it,[4] this has to be ascribed perhaps to the fate of the times which I have met with, but certainly not in the least to my own wish.

---

[1] Here Locke addresses Dr. Jasper Mayne (1604–72), Sub-dean and Canon of Christ Church, Archdeacon of Chichester, poet and dramatist.

[2] This may be meant as a general allusion to Mayne's dramatic art, or it may refer to a speech by him to undergraduates acting in a play at Christ Church on 8 Jan. 1663/4. In his speech Mayne had given encouragement to the actors and commended them for their ingenuity, telling them 'he liked well an acting student' (cf. A. Wood, *Life and Times*, ed. A. Clark, ii. 2).

[3] Here Locke addresses the Prebendaries of Christ Church. For a list of the members of the Chapter as reconstituted in 1660, see H. L. Thompson, *Christ Church*, 1900, pp. 84–85.

[4] This may well refer to the prevalence of dissolute habits in the University at this time.

233

Existimavi semper, fateor, onus hoc humeris meis impar, quod tamen Vobis jubentibus invitus licet qua potui constantia tuli; sicubi gravius incubuit, paratum semper habui in Vobis imbecillitatis meae subsidium: adeo ut, cum rei bene gerendae Vestra tanta sit laus, alios sublevandi non sit minor gloria. Quicquid forte aliis, Vobis certe affectati imperii reus videri non possum, quippe quem reluctantem nihil aliud cogere potuit aliis imperare nisi Vestri obsequium. Quod si alii quos per Vos adepti sunt honores faelicius gesserint, nemo certe animo magis grato aut accepit unquam aut deposuit.

Magistris

Valete Vos, Ornatissimi Magistri, doctissima capita, quae cum nullus unquam senserit meus solum (f. 131) infaustus annus insulsa vocavit; verum aliis suos relinquamus sales et suas veneres, nobis non licet esse tam disertis; est autem in Vestra illa inopia unde alii abunde ditescant, et sane putarem ego me hac mea morte immortalem futurum, si quemlibet Vestrum possem imitare[1] dicendo.

M^{ro} Woodroffe collegae

Vale Tu etiam, Frater Charissime, vitae meae et laborum omnium comitem dicam imo ducem et solatium. Gratulor mihi Te relictum in hac vita cum imperio superstitem, ut sciant omnes Tuum imperium minus desiderare socium quam aliorum solent ferre; cumque necessitudo me in laudis Tuae societatem adjunxit, quicquid ex ea mea vita decerpsit in integrum mors restituat. Ego enim dum vixi umbra fui; in Te omnis vis et vigor imperii, et quod de Castore et Polluce fabulantur in nobis compertum est, ut cum duo essemus fratres unica tantum

---

[1] *imitari* MS. A. Locke may have chosen the active form to lessen spondaic close.

Admittedly, I have always considered my shoulders to be unequal to this burden, yet at your bidding, though against my will, I have borne it as steadfastly as I could. If at any point it weighed upon me more heavily than usual, I have always found in you a ready support for my feebleness, so that, while your fame for able administration is so great, you should be not less renowned for your support of others. Whatever other people may think, I am certain I cannot appear to you guilty of a lust for power, for in fact only obedience to you had power to compel me against my will to govern others. But if others may have filled more happily the offices they have obtained through you, surely no one has ever more gratefully accepted or resigned them.

Farewell, you most distinguished Masters and well-learned Sirs, who, though no one ever before perceived it, in this ill-favoured year of mine have been called witless[1]—but let us leave to others their quips and graces, for it becomes us not to be so fluent—yet in your small store of wit I find the means by which others may richly abound, and indeed I myself should think that I by copying any one of you in his way of speaking shall become immortal through this my death.

Farewell to you too, most beloved brother,[2] nay more, let me say, companion of my life and all my labours, my guide and consoler. I congratulate myself that you are left behind in this life, a survivor in full command,[3] so that everyone may know that your reign feels the loss of a partner less acutely than the reign of others is wont to feel the endurance of one; and if friendship has made me a partner in your desert, whatever benefit I have derived from that friendship in life let my death pay back wholly. For I was a shadow while I lived; in you lay all the strength and power of command, and what is told of Castor and Pollux is found in our relationship, namely that, though we were two brothers, there was only one single life and that was yours. Hence

---

[1] *insulsa* (unsalted, insipid) is taken up in the next clause by *sales* (pungent quips).

[2] Benjamin Woodroffe (1638–1711), M.A., Locke's junior by six years, was educated at Westminster School and elected to Christ Church, Oxford, in 1656. 'From about 1662 he was a noted tutor at Christ Church, and in 1663 he studied chemistry with Antony Wood, John Locke, and others, at Oxford under Peter Sthael from Strasburg' (*D.N.B.* lxii. 405–6). He was Censor for the same period as Locke, as can be seen from this section in Locke's speech as also from letters written to Locke and Woodroffe by William Coker (Bodleian Rawl. MS. D. 286, ff. 6–7). Since Locke, as Censor of Moral Philosophy, was the Senior Censor, Woodroffe must have been the Junior Censor, or Censor of Natural Philosophy.

[3] According to custom, Locke as the Senior Censor would deliver his farewell speech on the last Wednesday before Collections in Michaelmas Term; Woodroffe as the Junior Censor would relinquish his office with a speech on the following Saturday.

esset vita et illa Tua. Non igitur mirum si eadem utrisque mens et eadem semper sententia cumque viribus non potuimus animis certe paribus omnia gessimus; decuit enim ut cum nihil aliud potui parem saltem afferrem concordiam. Vale igitur officiis et voluntate conjunctissime,[1] (f. 132) vive faelix, sitque Tuum hoc triduum, quod temporis duratione nimis angustum est, rebus Tuis gestis aeternum.

Dum aliis valedico, Vobis, Humanissimi Vespillones mei, agendae sunt gratiae, qui meum sumptibus Vestris sic exornatis[2] funus ut solenniores celebrari consueverant exequiae, quarum minima pars est illud quod effertur cadaver; quae enim praelucent faces et splendent ornamenta non tam mortuorum ostentant merita quam vivorum munificentiam. Vos liberalitate effecistis Vestra, ut obscuri hominis splendeat rogus et qui sua vita non potuit pyrae saltem flammis inclarescat. Sic terrestria meteora potentiore influentia praeter naturam in sublime evecta dum cadunt lucent, quaeque inter nubila et tempestates jactata latuerunt, non sine aliquo splendore in antiquas iterum et humiliores relabuntur sedes. Juvat sane sic cecidisse ut quorum laudes in lubrico hoc fastigio et alieno loco mereri non poteram jam propior[3] factus mores imitarer.

Baccalaureis

Valete et Vos, Commilitones meos dicam an Dominos? toties enim triumphatus agnosco victores: in arena hac philosophica tales Vos praestitistis ut quilibet Vestrum videretur Aristoteles, qui naturam et humanum (f. 133) genus intime cognosceret, quilibet Alexander, qui potuit superare. Sic ego Vestris hoc anno interfui velitationibus ut victus simul et locupletatus semper abirem; ea enim fuit Vestrae victoriae humanitas ut quantum argumenta Vestra, quibus toties succubui, famae meae detraherent tantum adderent cognitioni. Legem illam de qua omnis dimicatio saepius amissam frustra quaesiveram, nisi quam lingua Vestra mihi extorsit eandem restitueret vita: adeo ut dubitari

---

[1] For the phrase cf. Cicero, *Pro P. Sulla Or.* 20. 57.
[2] *exornastis* MS. A.
[3] *proprior* MS. B.

236

it is not surprising that we were both of the same mind and always of the same opinion, and that when we could not act with equal force, we certainly did all in the same spirit; for, when I could do nothing else, it behoved me at least to bring complete agreement to the common effort. Farewell, then, friend, who are closely bound to me by ties of duty and inclination; may you live happily and may these three days of yours,[1] which are so brief in length of time, be made everlasting by the things you do in them.

In bidding good-bye to others, I have to give thanks to you who most kindly bear me forth to burial. At your own expense you so furnished my funeral rites as more solemn obsequies are wont to be performed, the smallest part of which is the corpse that is carried out. In fact the torches that shine and the ornaments that glitter reveal not so much the merits of the dead as the munificence of the living. By your generosity you have made the pyre of an undistinguished man to shine abroad, so that he who could not become illustrious by his life may at least become so by the flames of his funeral pile. It is thus that earth-born meteors, lifted into the sky against the course of nature by a more powerful influence, shine forth as they fall, and, though out of sight while tossed about among clouds and thunderstorms, sink back again not without splendour to their previous lowlier abode. Glad indeed am I to have fallen thus, so that, now made nearer to them, I follow in the paths of those whose praises I could not earn while on this slippery height and in this alien place.

Farewell, you too, my fellow soldiers,[2] or should I say my masters? For having been overmastered by you so many times I acknowledge you as victors: in this philosophical arena you have so distinguished yourselves that anyone of you would be thought to be an Aristotle, since he had an intimate knowledge of nature and mankind, or an Alexander, able to conquer all. I took part this year in your disputations on such terms that I always went out at once beaten and enriched. Such indeed was the grace of your victory that your arguments, to which I so often yielded, added as much to my knowledge as they detracted from my reputation. That law[3] about which was all our strife had often eluded my fruitless quest, had not your way of life restored that very same law which your tongue had wrested from me. Hence it

---

[1] See last note on p. 235.   [2] Locke addresses the Bachelors of Arts.

[3] In this sentence and the next Locke refers to his essays on the law of nature, which, it appears, he discussed with his students during 1664 in lectures or in a class. Another reference occurs on f. 136.

possit utrum disputationes Vestrae legem naturae acrius oppugnarent an mores defenderint.

Scholaribus

Valete tandem et Vos, Ingeniosissimi Juvenes, quibuscum hoc anno prout potui vixi; difficili enim in loco versatur et iniquo jure imperat cui in praemiis poenisve libero judicio uti non licet, quem diversus utrinque clamor distrahit, hinc venia et illinc virgae, quas[1] etsi forsan vetus disciplina postulaverit, meae tamen certe non conveniunt dextrae aut Vestris moribus; ita enim optimarum rerum studio operam dedistis ut pluribus Vestrum non tam Censor fuerim et laborum exactor quam industriae testis et laudator. Delicta, si qua fuerint, ita expiastis ut solum praeberent et Vobis bene merendi et mihi laudandi (f. 134) ansam et, ut solent non nunquam offendicula, caespitantibus gradum accelerarunt. Eorum omnium, prout per me hactenus tecta et tacita fuerunt, mecum interibit memoria, mecum una sepelientur, nec cuiquam terrori erit Censoris umbra. Obstinatum et contumacem neminem memini; libet enim inter tot bene merentes paucissimorum oblivisci: ea est plurimorum industria, probitas, doctrina, ingenium ut facile possit reliquorum ignaviam expiare et efficere ut, cum in ipso sole non desint, in tanto tamen splendore lateant maculae: omnes igitur ingenuos, sedulos, morigeros pronuncio. Ne quis autem male sibi conscius putet me haec pro more locutum et, uti valedicentes solent, ea laudare quae non probavi; sed discat potius eam amare et colere virtutem cujus tanta est laus ut se diffundat in vicinos et prosit etiam non habenti. Quam[2] si suam esse velint, duo sunt praecipue loca mature semper frequentanda: aula ubi disputare templum ubi orare discant; sic enim fiunt Philosophi et sic Theologi; si quis enim inter Vos, cum

---

[1] *quam* MS. B.
[2] For some reason the following sentences are underlined in MS. B, though not in MS. A. For a parallel see Erasmus, 'Enchiridion Militis Christiani', ch. ii (*Opera*, 1703–6, v, col. 5).

can be doubted whether your disputations assaulted the law of nature or your behaviour defended it, more keenly.

Farewell, finally, to you also, most brilliant young men,[1] with whom I spent this year as well as I could. Certainly he finds himself in a tight corner and rules under an unfair law who is not allowed to use his free judgement in matters of reward or punishment, who is distracted by discordant cries on either side, for pardon on one hand and the rod on the other. Though perhaps ancient tradition might call for the latter, it certainly does not befit my right hand nor your behaviour. For you have devoted yourselves so well to the study of the best things that to most of you I have been not so much a Censor and taskmaster as a witness and applauder of your hard work. Faults, if faults there were, you have so atoned for that they only offered an opportunity to us both—for you to earn and for me to give praise; and, as is the way sometimes with small obstacles, they have quickened our step as we trod the turf. The memory of all such things, just as they have so far been kept secret and silent in me, will die with me and will all be buried with me, nor will the Censor's shade be a terror to anyone. I remember no one who was obstinate and insolent, for I am glad to forget the very few such among so many who have deserved well. Such is the diligence, the worthiness, the learning, and the ability of by far the most of you that it can easily make good the laziness of the rest, and cause the spots, which are not absent even in the sun, to be hidden in so much splendour. And so I pronounce you all well-bred, diligent, obedient. But let no one, should he have a guilty feeling, imagine that I have said this as a formality and that, as those who bid farewell are wont to do, I praise those things which have not really met with my approval; but let him rather learn to love and cherish that virtue whose merit is so great that it overflows upon those around and profits even him who has it not. But if anyone should wish to make this virtue his own, there are two chief places that must be frequented early and often: the hall where men may learn to debate and the temple where they may learn to pray; for thus they become philosophers and thus theologians.[2] If in fact anyone among you, when once

---

[1] Locke addresses the Scholars of the College.

[2] At Christ Church, the first twenty Students of the foundation were the 'Theologi', who were as a rule in priest's orders. From 1665 to 1674, even Locke's name, though he was a layman, occurs in the list of the 'Theologi'. At Christmas 1675, however, we find him lower on the list, among the next twenty Students, the 'Philosophi' (cf. H. L. Thompson, *Christ Church*, 1900, p. 101). The importance of the philosophical training is stressed by Locke in the next sentence.

olim fuerit Ecclesiae Doctor, mediis in precibus mutus haeserit, existimabunt omnes, etsi ab ipso Paulo niteretur, Timotheum illum non piscatorem Evangelicum sed piscem. Sed quid ego, magnus ardelio, cum moriturus (f. 135) nihil aliud possum, satis peritis tamen do consilium? Circumspicienti autem mihi nihil videtur quod aut hisce aedibus faelicius aut Vobis majus jam moriens optare possum quam ut maxima pars sit sui similis et reliqui velint aemulari.

Et jam ultimo Censorem valere jubeo; omnes ego hic minas, impositiones, severitatem exuo, depono etiam fastum et insolentiam et grande supercilium; quae licet in me nunquam fuerint, in Censore tamen esse a nonnullis existimantur. Vixi etsi forte reipublicae huic literariae et faelicitati meae parum Vobis certe omnibus et mihimet nimium. Nollem ego jam in limine mortis positus et faelicitatis confinio unde ad beatas sedes prospicere licet revocare animum ad praeterita mala et repetendo iterare; satis est semel passum fuisse; sed consuetudini, in funeribus praecipue, mos gerendus est. Sic igitur breviter accipite. Hoc ego vitae curriculum uti infantes solent imbellis et tremulus nec sine dolore ingressus sum; prima aetas uti vivere incipientium satis erat jucunda nec proxima aliquid praeter quas ipsa secum affert hujus vitae conditio curas habuit in se molestum; senescentem tandem et jam morti vicinum (f. 136) invasit morbus et aegritudo non sine aliqua malignitatis suspitione, cum tanti ardoris satis sontica reperiri non possit causa. Hunc habuit mea aetas exitum, initiis male respondentem sic volentibus fatis, ut meus annus desineret in piscem. Verum his ego curis et hisce sedibus in aeternum valedico; satis est semel miserum fuisse, hoc est semel vixisse. Unum est quod me in hoc meo fato et in ipso funere consolatur, quod scilicet licet mihi secundum

he has become a teacher of the Church, shall be stricken dumb in the midst of his prayers, all will think this Timothy, even if Paul himself support him, to be no fisherman of the Gospel[1] but a mere dumb fish. But what am I about, gross intermeddler that I am, when at the point of death I can do no more, that I should nevertheless give advice to you who lack no learning? But as I look round in this hour of death, it seems that I could wish nothing more propitious for this House or better for you than that most of you should remain like yourselves and the rest should vie with them.

And now, finally, I bid farewell to the Censorship. I here lay aside all threats, impositions, and severity; I also renounce my pride, arrogance, and lofty haughtiness; for though these have never been in me personally, they are thought by some to pertain to the Censor. Though perhaps I have lived too short a time to serve this republic of letters and to win my own felicity, I have certainly lived too long for you all and for myself. Now that I am at death's door and on the threshold of happiness, whence it is possible to behold the seats of the blest, I should not like to turn my back to the misfortunes of the past and to renew them again. It is sufficient to have suffered once. But custom, particularly in funeral rites, is to be observed. Therefore, accept briefly this much: I entered this life's course, as babes usually do, weak and trembling, and not without pain. The early time of my life, like the life of all beginners, was pleasant enough, and that which followed had in it nothing disagreeable either, apart from the anxieties which the very terms on which we live bring with them. But at the last, in my old age, when I am already near death, illness and sickness have attacked me, and that not without some suspicion of malice: for a sufficiently serious cause of such high fever cannot be found.[2] Such is the ending of my life—an end in ill accord with the beginning, for the gods wish it so: my year (like Triton's body) tails off into a fish.[3] Still, I am saying farewell to this office and place for ever; it is enough to have been miserable once, that is, to have lived once. There is one thing that consoles me in this doom of mine and in the funeral itself, and this is that I am allowed to pass away and succumb to an honourable

[1] Cf. Mark, i. 17.

[2] Perhaps this refers to an incident that took place during Locke's year of office, when he was summoned before the Dean and Chapter 'to answer for the sconcing of one of the servants of the House' (cf. H. L. Thompson, *Christ Church*, 1900, p. 101).

[3] The passage in parentheses is added in the translation to make clear the reference to, for example, Virgil, *Aeneid*, x. 209–11. Possibly Locke here also alludes to the sign of the fishes, the last sign of the zodiacal year. Alternatively, the allusion is to *pisces*, line 3 above; thus: I become henceforth a dumb dog.

quam ut potui vixi secundum eandem et naturae et hujusce aedis legem interire et honesta morte occumbere. Jam facile submitto cervices tot periculis ereptas; nondum enim ad restim res rediit, nec quidquam in vita aut in morte mea repertum iri confido a quo quis merito exigat fatalem illum nummum aut stipem carnifici debitam; augustius certe et faeliciore omine extructum est hoc domicilium quam ut transeat in carnificinam, nec opus est ei victimae mandare laqueum aut minari suspendium quae sua sponte accedit ad aras et libenter mortem oppetit. En igitur tandem, si cujus supersit ira, illius (f. 138)[1] vindictae, meae certe quieti, et omnium expectationi paratum sacrificium. Si quem alium mea non minus quam me ipsum vita offenderit, mors credo omnes placatos reddet nec post cineres ardebit ira. Nemini nunquam negata fuit quies in sepulchro quaerenti. Ad eam igitur anhelus festino. Desinam aliquando et Vobis et mihimet molestus esse; omnem simul cum anima efflo solicitudinem nec diutius differam omnium malorum remedium, quod mihi praestare possum unico hoc verbo: Morior.

---

[1] f. 137 is left blank.

death according to the same law of nature and the same law of this House by which I have lived my life as well as I could. I now readily offer to the knife a throat which has been saved from so many perils; for the noose is not yet at hand,[1] and I trust nothing at all will be found either in my life or in my death for which anyone could justly demand that grim alms-penny due to the hangman. Certainly, this House is too august and has been built under too favourable an omen to be changed into a gallows. Nor is there any need to bid a victim go and be hanged, or to threaten him with a hanging, who is such that he approaches the altar of his own accord and gladly dies. So, then, at last, if anyone's anger against me still survives, here is a sacrifice to hand which will fulfil his vengeance and, of a surety, my own desire for rest and the expectation of all. If my life has offended anyone no less than it has myself, death, I believe, will appease all and no rage will flare up after my corpse is burned. For rest has been denied to no one who has looked for it in his grave. To rest, then, I hasten, panting the while. May I hereafter cease to be troublesome both to you and to myself. Together with my last breath I breathe out all my cares, nor will I longer delay the remedy for all evils, which I can supply myself in this single word: 'I die'.

[1] i.e. hanging is a less honourable form of execution.

Philosophical
Shorthand Writings

INTRODUCTION

Locke's Shorthand

THE last part of this volume consists of a selection of entries in Locke's Journal for 1676 and a note by him of 1677 on his method of translating three of Pierre Nicole's *Essais de Morale*. The Journal entries and the note were written by Locke in shorthand during his long visit to France, and they have never been published hitherto, though most of the longhand entries in his journals have appeared in print. The first to publish excerpts from Locke's journals was Lord King in 1829, in his *Life and Letters of John Locke*. Professor R. I. Aaron and Mr. J. Gibb followed, in 1936, with a publication of all the philosophical longhand entries in the journals (including some of those previously published by Lord King), appended to *An Early Draft of Locke's Essay*. In 1953 Professor J. Lough re-edited Locke's journals written in France and transcribed several of his shorthand entries, in *Locke's Travels in France (1675–1679)*. The shorthand writings transcribed in the present volume are, in the main, philosophical: in fact, they comprise all there is of philosophical shorthand writings in Locke's journals, and indeed in the whole of the Lovelace Collection. Had Professor Aaron and Lord King also been familiar with Locke's shorthand, it is reasonable to believe that they would have printed transcripts of these Journal entries in their own editions.

A few of the questions discussed by Locke in the following shorthand entries recur in longhand entries in the journals published by Lord King and Professor Aaron, and in the two drafts of the *Essay* of 1671. The shorthand entries on idolatry, pleasure and pain, the passions, power, faith, and reason, however, contain Locke's earliest thoughts on these topics, and they have no parallel in his longhand entries or in the drafts of the *Essay*. On the other hand, Locke's shorthand discussions of most of these topics found their way—sometimes in an elaborated form—into the *Essay* of 1690: they can thus be regarded as an early draft of parts of the *Essay*. Transcripts of Locke's shorthand notes on spelling and on translating Nicole, though of no philosophical interest, have been included in this volume; since Locke thought them worth writing, others may think them worth reading.

Each of the Journal entries published here has been provided with an introductory note and footnotes. It remains to explain the nature of

Locke's shorthand and the methods employed in transcribing it. A reproduction of Locke's shorthand note on Nicole has been supplied for the reader's convenience.

Locke used shorthand in his journals, account-books, and medical notebooks, and occasionally in the margin of a manuscript. Wherever he used it he interpolated words or phrases written in longhand—a fact which would seem to indicate that he found it difficult at times to write a particular word in shorthand, and that he never acquired a perfect skill in this art. He himself said, in a letter to William Moly-neux,[1] that he did not learn to write in shorthand before he was grown up: in fact, the earliest examples of his shorthand occur in papers written by him in 1664, when he was thirty-two years old. From the same letter we learn that the only other remark Locke made about the subject of shorthand in his writings, namely the one in paragraph 161 of his *Some Thoughts concerning Education*, was an afterthought, sug-gested to him by Molyneux[2] and not included in the first edition of that work (1693). Locke, it thus appears, felt little inclination to be communicative with regard to his knowledge and use of shorthand. Therefore in attempting to throw light on his practice as a shorthand writer we must take advantage of every clue that offers itself.

First let us quote Locke's words in paragraph 161 of *Some Thoughts concerning Education*.

> Shorthand . . . may perhaps be thought worth the learning, both for dis-patch in what men write for their own memory, and concealment of what they would not have lie open to every eye. For he that has once learned any sort of character, may easily vary it to his own private use or fancy, and with more contraction suit it to the business he would employ it in. Mr. Rich's, the best contrived of any I have seen, may, as I think, by one who knows and considers grammar well, be made much easier and shorter. . . .

There are three important statements in this passage, one about the value of shorthand, another about the possibility of modifying any conventional shorthand system, and the third about Locke's preference of the system invented by Jeremiah Rich. Illustrations of the first two statements will be given shortly from Locke's own practice of short-hand, and I turn therefore to an immediate consideration of Rich's shorthand in relation to Locke's.

The fact that Locke recommended Rich's system in a passage written late in life does not establish, though it may suggest, that he

---

[1] 23 Aug. 1693, printed in 'Familiar Letters' (*Works*, 1801, ix. 325).
[2] Cf. Molyneux's letter to Locke of 12 Aug. 1693, in 'Familiar Letters' (ibid. 321).

himself adopted it in shorthand writings of an early period. As I shall show presently, he consulted more than one system during his life and may have used first one and then another. Besides, Rich's system does not differ considerably from a number of other systems that were in use during the seventeenth century, so that for this reason, too, the clue provided in the passage quoted is not altogether safe. However, it is possible to prove beyond doubt that Rich's shorthand system is the one used throughout by Locke himself. The following references to, and examples of, shorthand, to be found in Locke's papers, may help to illustrate and establish this fact.

One shorthand alphabet, entered by Locke in one of his early account-books[1] but never employed by him in his own shorthand writings, has defied all my attempts to identify it. An alphabet in his notebook of 1664–6,[2] however, and a set of contractions signifying combinations of consonantal sounds or whole words are precisely those invented by Rich, and Locke's shorthand version of the first Psalm, contained in the same notebook, is closely analogous to that suggested by Rich in his broadside of the alphabet of 1659 and in his *Psalms in Shorthand*.[3] Several of Locke's own observations in this notebook are likewise written in Rich's shorthand. It would seem, then, that Locke began to practise Rich's shorthand between 1664 and 1666. We can date his first attempts even more precisely, for the draft version of his valedictory speech as Censor of Moral Philosophy,[4] which was written during the latter half of 1664, contains a number of signs in Rich's shorthand,[5] for which Locke afterwards substituted longhand words in Latin. It may be that the reason why Locke thought it advisable to learn shorthand at this time was that he intended to leave college after his term of office as Censor and to become a man of affairs—in fact, in the winter of 1665–6 he became secretary to Sir Walter Vane and accompanied him on a mission to the Elector of Brandenburg. His drafts of letters sent from Cleves to his friend John Strachey,[6] containing personal information about matters of religion and politics, have several signs in Rich's shorthand, which on this occasion would seem

---

[1] MS. Locke f. 11, fol. 2. The account-book covers the years 1649–57 and 1661–6; the entry probably falls within the latter period.　　　　[2] Ibid. f. 27, pp. 14–15.

[3] In Pepys's *Diary* (16 Apr. 1661) mention is made of the psalms in shorthand, most probably those by Rich or by Thomas Shelton.

[4] In MS. Locke e. 6, entitled *Lemmata*, and part of what I have named MS. A.

[5] e.g. on fol. 7.

[6] Three of Locke's letters to Strachey from Cleves were published by Lord King (*Life*, ed. 1858, pp. 13 ff.) not from Locke's drafts but from the letters actually sent by Locke and returned to him later; these as well as the drafts are preserved in the Lovelace Collection.

to have been used by Locke for reasons of disguise. Most of his note-books and journals of the years following have entries in Rich's short-hand, and one has signs indicating Latin words, while three others contain lists of alternative signs for one and the same word.[1] Occasion-ally we meet with an alphabet in strange symbols, and in 1679 Locke bought two books on shorthand by Shelton,[2] though not, it would seem, for his own use, since shortly afterwards he sent three books on shorthand to his friend Nicolas Thoynard.[3] We know, however, that a copy of one of Rich's shorthand manuals was in Locke's possession in 1680, for an inventory of his belongings in Christ Church, dated December 1680, lists 'J. Rich's shorthand system'.[4]

Now let us look at Locke's shorthand itself. If we list the separate symbols he uses and compare these with the different alphabets in-vented in the seventeenth century,[5] we find that his symbols come nearest to those of Jeremiah Rich. Turning to the manual by which Rich's shorthand system was taught,[6] we see that Locke adopts not only Rich's alphabet of consonants but also his method of indicating vowels and some of his contractions. However, we meet with difficul-ties if we try to transcribe Locke's shorthand on no other basis than that of Rich's system, for there are some signs used by Locke which form no part of Rich's teaching. Presumably these are Locke's own invention, and for the most part they represent a method of indicating tenses. There are also a number of contractions in his shorthand which differ from Rich's, and throughout he appears to vary Rich's system in the manner recommended by him in the statement previously quoted. Fortunately there are some passages in Locke's papers which are available in both shorthand and longhand, and thus the occasional difficulties in deciphering can be removed. The passages in question are excerpts from lectures of Thomas Sydenham on dysentery, small-pox, pleurisy, and intermittent fevers, entered by Locke in shorthand in a notebook of 1669 and in longhand on loose leaves that form part of his medical papers.

On the whole it would seem that Locke used shorthand for the sake

---

[1] e.g. in a notebook of 1667 (MS. Locke, f. 15, pp. 1-2).

[2] Journal for 27 June 1679, p. 107 (Brit. Museum, Add. MS. 15642).

[3] Locke's letter to Thoynard of 15 July 1679 (Brit. Museum, Add. MS. 28728), printed by Fox Bourne (*The Life of John Locke*, 1876, i. 430) and H. Ollion (*Lettres inédites de John Locke*, 1912, p. 28).

[4] MS. Locke c. 25, fols. 30-31

[5] Tables of alphabets are found in most shorthand histories, e.g. in J. E. Rockwell's *Teaching, Literature and Practice of Shorthand*, 1884.

[6] i.e. *The Pen's Dexterity*, in several editions.

of convenience. In some cases, however, as in his drafts of letters to Strachey and in some notes concerning money in his journals, he appears to have used shorthand for purposes of secrecy. That this special purpose was in his mind at least on one occasion can be shown from the following example. The only shorthand that occurs in Locke's Journal for 1677 is an entry for 1 October.[1] It has no title, and there are no marginal keywords in longhand indicating its contents as there are in the case of most other shorthand entries in Locke's journals. There is, however, no demarcation line between this entry and another, under the same date, which precedes it and is in longhand.[2] This latter entry deals with 'sensation', 'delight', and the 'senses' and has been printed by Professor R. I. Aaron and Mr. J. Gibb.[3] One would expect that the shorthand entry immediately joined to it would be a continuation of Locke's philosophical discussion and would have been transcribed and printed in Professor Aaron's book, had it been in longhand. The last words of the longhand entry, as printed by Professor Aaron, are 'after we are hurt'. In the manuscript, however, Locke adds in longhand, with a comma after 'hurt', 'and when we are secure of any danger we may at more[4] leisure examin'. Here the shorthand begins, of which the following is a transcript: 'what good there is in that new thing. Thus I think. I did not intend to have spoken one word in this business; but something has been objected and laid to my charge by the King's counsel, Mr. Attorney and Mr. Solicitor, . . .' Evidently Locke discusses here an altogether new subject, beginning after 'Thus I think'. As I have shown, he introduces shorthand before starting on the new subject-matter. Can we doubt that Locke uses shorthand here as a means of disguising what he has to say, and that he places the shorthand entry thus inconspicuously for purposes of secrecy? Any doubt arising will certainly be dispelled by the discovery that this part of Locke's shorthand entry contains the speech by the first Earl of Shaftesbury in the King's Bench on 29 June 1677 in support of his application to be released on bail from the Tower.[5]

---

[1] MS. Locke f. 2, pp. 282–6.   [2] pp. 280–2.

[3] *An Early Draft of Locke's Essay, together with Excerpts from his Journals*, 1936, pp. 96–97.   [4] *more* is in shorthand.

[5] A longhand version of the speech is printed in W. D. Christie's *A Life of Anthony Ashley Cooper, First Earl of Shaftesbury*, 1871, vol. ii, appendix vi, pp. xciv–xcvi. Locke evidently received during the summer of 1677 a copy of the speech, which he then copied in shorthand in his Journal. The shorthand version is almost identical with the printed version, but since it is more detailed in some places, the printed version would seem to be based on an incomplete manuscript. Locke's shorthand, too, is imperfect in places, and one should consult both versions, the one in shorthand and the one in print, in order to reconstruct the speech.

Philosophical Shorthand Writings

At times Locke is careless in his shorthand: he omits syllables or whole words, and fails to distinguish between similar signs.[1] Nor does he provide signs to indicate the articles, definite or indefinite, and there is no punctuation apart from full stops, which are indicated by three dots arranged in the form of a triangle. In transcribing and editing Locke's shorthand writings I have therefore sought (a) to fill in obvious lacunae (the missing parts being in most cases easily discoverable from the context), (b) to correct casual mistakes, (c) to supply the articles as they would seem to be required in each individual case, and (d) to provide full punctuation. For the sake of uniformity I have also modernized the spelling of words in longhand with which Locke interspersed his shorthand scripts. The pagination is that of the manuscript, i.e. of Locke's Journal for 1676,[2] and in this edition it is indicated by figures in parentheses inserted in the body of the text.[3]

In conclusion I may point out that there is other shorthand material in the Lovelace Collection, written not by Locke but by his cousin, the Lord Chancellor, Peter King. It is preserved, for instance, in seventeen law-reporters' notebooks, and in a diary of events in the House of Commons from the first meeting of the Convention Parliament on 25 April 1660 to the dissolution of Parliament on 28 March 1681. The diary may have been compiled by King from official records, and its wording is the same as, though more summary than, the text printed in the *Journals* of the House of Commons. King's shorthand is based on Rich's system, but it contains many new signs and is different from Locke's.

---

[1] e.g. between the signs for *which* and *with*.

[2] MS. Locke f. 1.

[3] In the excerpts from Locke's journals, as published by Professor R. I. Aaron and Mr. J. Gibb (*An Early Draft of Locke's Essay*, &c., 1936), a few gaps occur where Locke used shorthand signs in the manuscript. I have taken the liberty here to give transcripts of these signs (the page references are to Aaron's edition).

Entry for 20 June 1676 (p. 77), line 1: instead of 'their', there is in the manuscript a shorthand sign for 'having'. Line 4: 'But distance seemes' is followed by signs meaning 'to be nothing but bare'. Line 5: 'ariseing' is followed by a sign meaning 'between'.

Entry for 29 July 1676 (p. 81), line 1: 'the proofs' is followed by two signs meaning 'of our'. 'Our author' refers to Pierre Nicole and his *Essais de Morale*, 1671, vol. ii, containing the *Discours contenant en abrégé les preuves naturelles de l'Existence de Dieu et de l'Immortalité de l'Ame*.

Entry for 19 Feb. 1682 (p. 120, l. 9): the sign printed there in brackets is not in the manuscript.

I

A NOTE ON TRANSLATING THREE OF
PIERRE NICOLE'S *ESSAIS DE MORALE*

MS. Locke c. 28, fol. 42. A reproduction of the shorthand page appears between pp. 254 and 255. The title is mine.

The note is entered on the first of a bundle of small octavo leaves (ff. 42–44ᵛ), endorsed by Locke '1677'. Folios 42ᵛ–44ᵛ contain more notes in longhand, two of which, concerning the loadstone and the art of printing, are drafts of passages occurring in Locke's translation of Nicole's *Essais*; these two notes have been printed by Lord King[1] as excerpts from Locke's Journal. Other longhand notes deal with the cogency of Nicole's arguments for the existence of God and the immortality of the soul. On f. 44ᵛ there is a reference by Locke to p. 367 of his Journal for 1676, where, under the date of 29 July, he entered a lengthy essay on the subject.[2]

Locke's first mention of Nicole, in his notebook of 1664–6,[3] is brief: 'Petrus de Nicol'. The name here may record Nicole as a member of the school of Port-Royal, the friend of Arnauld and Pascal, and the collaborator in the *Lettres Provinciales* and the *Logique ou l'art de penser*. Locke went to France for a few weeks' holiday in the autumn of 1672 and again for a stay of four years in 1675. Between 1672 and 1680 he must have become acquainted with Nicole's *Essais de Morale*, of which the first two volumes appeared in 1671. We do not know exactly when Locke made his translation of three of these essays[4] and presented it in manuscript, together with a dedicatory letter, to Lady Shaftesbury.[5] In the letter he intimates that he brought home these translations on his recent return from France. He returned from France twice, in the autumn of 1672 and at the end of April 1679.

---

[1] *The Life and Letters of John Locke*, ed. 1858, pp. 130–1.
[2] Printed by R. I. Aaron and J. Gibb in *An Early Draft of Locke's Essay*, &c., 1936, pp. 81–82.
[3] MS. Locke f. 27, p. 91.
[4] i.e. 'On the Existence of God and the Immortality of the Soul', 'On the Weakness of Man', 'On the Way of Preserving Peace with Men'.
[5] Pierpont Morgan Library (New York), M.A. 232 (Bodleian MS. film 70). Published by Thomas Hancock in 1828, under the title *Discourses, translated from Nicole's Essays*; extracts quoted by Fox Bourne, *The Life of John Locke*, 1876, i. 296 ff.

Note on Translating Three of Pierre Nicole's Essais de Morale

Considering that his first visit was short and that the three essays translated by him make a volume of some length, it may be reasonable to assume that he worked on the translation during his second visit to France and presented it to Lady Shaftesbury in 1679 or 1680. The bundle of notes in the Lovelace Collection, endorsed by Locke '1677', now makes it possible to define more precisely the date of his translation. There is even reason to suppose that Locke started on the translation as early as 1676, for he appears to have designed his Journal entry for 15 August 1676, which is printed below on pp. 254 ff. of this volume, to form part of a preface to his translation. From the note printed here we can gather that his original intention was to publish the translation, and that the note was to have been part of the original preface. When Locke decided to leave the work unpublished and to present a manuscript copy of it to Lady Shaftesbury instead, he again remarked on his method of translating Nicole in the dedicatory letter addressed to her, but his remarks there are not the same as in the note or in his Journal entry for 15 August 1676.

In 1677 some of Nicole's *Essais*, including two of those selected by Locke but not that on God's existence, were again translated by 'A Person of Quality' and published as *Moral Essays* in London. The fact that Locke chose Nicole's essay on God, an inconspicuous discourse as compared with the other two essays, which were generally appreciated at the time and are indeed masterpieces of psychological analysis, suggests that this essay was of special interest to him. He himself touched upon arguments for God's existence in the fourth of his early essays on natural law and again in his drafts of the *Essay* of 1671 and in his journals in France between 1676 and 1682. It would seem that Nicole's essay on God appealed to him because he found in it a confirmation of his own views and also of his attitude towards Descartes. Traces of Locke's interest in Nicole, in fact, can be found in the *Essay* of 1690, Book IV, chapter 10.[1] There are good reasons, in any case, for regarding Nicole as a bond between Descartes and English philosophy, particularly Locke's.[2]

The note printed below informs us about Locke's designs as a translator; the Journal entry printed next tells us about his plans as a reformer of spelling.

[1] Cf. my 'Locke and Nicole', *Sophia*, January–March 1948, pp. 41–55.
[2] Cf. S. P. Lamprecht, 'The rôle of Descartes in Seventeenth-Century England', in *Studies in the History of Ideas*, ed. by the Dept. of Philosophy of Columbia University, iii (1935), 197, n. 42.

Note on Translating Three of Pierre Nicole's Essais de Morale

This Translation, whether as an innocent diversion of some dull hours or a not unprofitable way of improving my French, being at first designed only for private use, strictly followed the original. But now it being to serve to another purpose, I have thought fit sometimes to dispense with the strict formalities of a translator, and, having no intention in publishing to show to the world the proprieties or agreements of these two languages or how well I might render the one into the other, but to do good to my country and to bring what aid I had met with abroad to the assistance of truth and virtue which is not free from opposition amongst us, it will not seem strange if I have in some places kept so close to that design that I have wholly changed the scheme of the discourse; and I doubt not but the author, whose great pity appears in his writings, will have charity enough to pardon me who, to keep close to his argument, have sometimes deviated from his words. All that is to be feared is that it will appear a great insolence to go about to correct the writing of one of so extraordinary parts and to publish my alterations, though never so little, under his name, which cannot be without a great injustice to him. As a remedy to this, I have thought fit, in all passages where I have been too bold, to print the author's own words, whereby a reader ignorant of French may be able to distinguish the place where my hand has made those faults and those who understand it be able to judge how far I have trespassed, and whether as I have put it does not better suit with our English than it may be in a literal translation.

Essay observation
Essay de Morale

II

SPELLING

MS. Locke f. 1, pp. 402–6: Journal for 15 August 1676. Locke's title is 'Speling'.

This entry, it would seem, is a continuation of the preceding note on Nicole. 'Faults' in the concluding sentence there is taken up by 'another fault' in the first line of the present entry, and in a reference to 'our author' farther on (p. 404 fin.) Locke undoubtedly has in mind Nicole and Nicole's essay on the weakness of man. For these reasons it is tempting to believe that Locke's note on Nicole, though

Locke's shorthand note of 1677 on his method of translating three of Pierre Nicole's *Essais de Morale*

the bundle of leaves of which it forms the first page is endorsed '1677', was itself written in 1676, before this Journal entry for 15 August. I have therefore printed the Journal entry immediately after the note on Nicole, despite the fact that it is preceded in the Journal by three shorthand entries for July 1676, which in the present volume are printed after it.

From what has been said it may be inferred that a longhand version of the Journal entry, just as of the note on Nicole preceding it, was meant by Locke for insertion in a preface to his translation of Nicole's *Essais*. From the last sentence on p. 402 it appears that his intention, originally, was to apply simplified spelling in the paragraph containing his own proposals for it. No simplified spelling was mentioned or applied by him in the manuscript he sent to Lady Shaftesbury, which is preserved in the Pierpont Morgan Library.

We need not deal here with the question as to the value of Locke's suggestions for reforming English spelling. What is important is to realize the close connexion between them and his interest in shorthand. No doubt he was impressed by the numerous attempts at spelling reform made in France during the sixteenth and seventeenth centuries,[1] and these, as he himself admits at the beginning of his entry, provided a stimulus for his own proposals. But just because in both English and French the spelling does not accord with the pronunciation, and because attempts at reforming it were made on a phonetic basis, Locke's early interest in shorthand, in which the sound,[2] not the orthography, of the word is represented, must be regarded as the prime factor influencing his suggestions for spelling reform. Locke's own model in the art of shorthand, Jeremiah Rich,[3] laid great emphasis on the fact that 'the intent of this practice of Short and Swift Writing is only aiming at Sounds of Words, not the Truth of Spelling'. This connexion between shorthand and spelling reform can be traced in most of the 200 shorthand systems published since John Willis's *The Art of Stenographie* of 1602 and before Isaac Pitman's *Stenographic Sound-hand* of 1837.[4] All attempts at reforming English spelling on a phonetic basis, however, in our own day as well as in the past, have come to nothing, mainly, perhaps, on account of the total lack of general interest in the question.[5]

[1] For an historical account of the various attempts see Larousse, *Grand Dictionnaire Universel du XIXe siècle*, vol. xi, s.v. 'Orthographie', 'Néographie'.
[2] See p. 257, bottom.   [3] *The Pen's Dexterity*, 1669, p. 6.
[4] Cf. *Spelling*, published by the Simplified Spelling Society, 1925, i. 54.
[5] Cf. H. C. Wyld, *A Short History of English*, 1921, p. 130.

Spelling

In conclusion the reader may be reminded of another of Locke's progressive views, little known generally but not without interest in this connexion. He entered into conversations about the reformation of the calendar on one occasion,[1] and on another himself suggested an 'easy way'[2] in which a change could be effected from the Julian calendar (Old Style) to the Gregorian calendar (New Style). In spite of his and other people's attempts, the inaccurate Julian calendar was perpetuated in England down to the middle of the eighteenth century and in Russia to the Revolution of 1917.

(p. 402). There is another fault which I know not whether it will be pardoned, because I confess I wholly committed it and which a critical reader will soon find in the spelling. How little a lover soever I am of French fashions, I cannot but take up this which convenience makes them every day more and more follow[3] in their writing, and methinks if the end was extravagant and never so useless, yet it coming from thence should sufficiently justify it without any reason. But yet the opinion I have long had that things ought to be regulated by their ends made me go into it more than their example. For, considering that letters are but the lasting marks of sounds, I think we might avoid much confusion and great many needless difficulties, if we would always apply as near as we could the same characters to the same pronunciation. It would perhaps look a little strange and awkward at first to make a change all at once as in this paragraph,[4] so much is custom able to confirm us in the love and admiration even of inconveniencies, though it cannot but be acknowledged that it would be much better if it were reformed, and nobody can (p. 403) deny but it may be done by degrees and must have a beginning. It would prevent a great many mistakes and make languages, of which we have so great a need and so constant a use, much easier to be learnt, read, and written by all strangers, by the women and illiterate of the same country, nay, in truth, all, for it costs all that are not born learned time and pains to master these difficulties, and children must once have charged their memories, which would be more usefully employed, with all these varieties, and learnt how to set down the same sound with different

---

[1] *Nouvelles de la République des Lettres*, May 1699, art. 9.

[2] Letter to Sloane, 2 Dec. 1699, printed in T. Forster, *Original Letters of Locke*, &c., 1830, pp. 68–69, and Fox Bourne, op. cit. ii. 477–8.

[3] Locke first wrote in longhand *practise*.

[4] Locke apparently thought of applying here in longhand his idea of simplified spelling.

marks, as *isle, guile, mile; to, too, two,* or render the same character, as
in *we, when; me, men; gin, begin,* by different pronunciations. And
perhaps we should think we had reason to complain of a foreign
language that had but five characters, one at least whereof must make
part of every syllable, if they confound three of them,[1] one with
another, in any words. Which may give us ground to consider (p. 404)
whether we have not some reason, too, in several cases to bring our
spelling nearer to our pronunciation; whether, for so real and great an
advantage (and which next to religion and virtue is a great end of all
learning and knowledge) as is this of easing men of a great deal of
useless pain and shortening their labour, we cannot be content to
mend our writing again, though it were with a neglect of the etymolo-
gies of words and leaving out sometimes the marks of their pedigrees.
For what stresses soever I have found so many[2] to lay on these, which
was their only reason against varying from our old writing, I cannot
forbear to think that charity to men may well make us less tender of
the genealogies of words. And when we a little consider what our
author[3] says and experience vouches concerning the shortness of our
lives and the weakness of our understandings, (p. 405) what small progress men of the quickest parts make in real knowledge, and how little
of useful truth we discover after a long search and infinite labour, we
shall find there was reason enough to desire all needless difficulties
should be removed out of the way. We should have enough still to do
to penetrate into the inside and truth of things, though all knowledge
were wrapped up in one simple plain language, as easy as we should
wish it, and so rid us at once of the necessity as well as the perplexity
of criticism, which is so engaged in old copies and moth-eaten records
that the skilfullest hand seldom meddles with it without raising a dust
and sometimes leaving us more in the dark than we were before. But
since such hope in us would be as extravagant as was theirs who brought
this misery upon us[4] at Babel, what hinders to do what we can to
write as we speak, and to pare off this which is but the outside of the
husk of knowledge, which always gives trouble and sometimes disgust
to[5] those who (p. 406) might penetrate deeper?

[1] In the margin Locke wrote in shorthand: *first, worst, cursed.*
[2] *many* omitted in manuscript.
[3] i.e. Nicole, in his essay 'On the Weakness of Man'.
[4] *us* added by Ed.
[5] *to* omitted in manuscript.

[2] (from p. 255) Locke treats words as sounds, not marks in his *Essay* (III. ix. 2; IV. viii.
13; xi. 7; xxi. 4).

III

EXTENSION

MS. Locke f. 1, pp. 313–14: Journal for 9 July 1676.

'Extension, L.2, c.4' is written in the margin at the beginning of the page. The reference is to Locke's *Essay*, Book II, chapter iv, where extension is briefly discussed by him in the central part of paragraph 4, at which point he may have intended to insert the entry printed here. However, there is a closer connexion between this entry and a number of other places in Book II of the *Essay*,[1] where the idea of extension together with that of duration is treated by Locke in detail. The topic was in his mind already when he wrote the two early drafts of the *Essay* of 1671, and he dealt with it in Draft B[2] in much the same manner and almost as extensively as in Book II, chapter xiv of the *Essay* of 1690. Five longhand entries in his Journals for 1676–8[3] show his continued interest in the subject and the persistence of his view that distance in space and in time is nothing but a pure relation. The entry printed here is similar to all these longhand entries in point of doctrine, and particularly to that for 20 June 1676,[4] written only three weeks earlier; it is advisable therefore to read the two in conjunction. All these passages on space in Locke's Journals are valuable, not only because they contain different illustrations of the same doctrine, but also because without them, as Professor Aaron has remarked,[5] it is not possible to understand Locke's account of space and, we may add, of infinity and eternity, in the *Essay*.

(p. 313) As the idea of time is got by the observed motion of bodies,[6] so the idea of extension is got by the observation of them in rest. And as by some constant and equal motion of bodies we get the measure of time, so by observing some bodies of equal length we get the measure of extension. And as we can in our imagination apply that measure of time, which is but the motion of some body, to duration, where there

---

[1] For example, ch. xiv, pars. 24–25, 27–29; ch. xv, par. 7.

[2] Edited by Rand, 1931, pars. 103–25.

[3] Cf. 27 Mar. and 20 June 1676, 16 Sept. 1677, 20 Jan. and 24 Jan. 1678.

[4] Printed by R. I. Aaron and J. Gibb, *An Early Draft of Locke's Essay*, &c., 1936, pp. 77–80.   [5] Op. cit., Introduction, p. xxv.

[6] This statement is qualified in the *Essay* of 1690 (II. xiv, xvi, and xix) and also in one of the drafts of the *Essay* of 1671 (Draft B, ed. Rand, par. 108), where Locke maintains that the idea of duration is not necessarily derived from the perception of motion.

is neither body nor motion, so we can apply that measure of extension, which is only in bodies, to space, where there is no body at all, though that duration and that space without the existence of any other thing be in itself really nothing. But when things really are, both duration and space, i.e. considered as so much space between them, are really a relation commensurable to our measures of time and extension. For supposing God had created (p. 314) a world before this and annihilated it again at the beginning of the Julian account, it is certain that a relation of distance equal to[1] . . . annual revolutions of the sun[2] had resulted from the existence of these two worlds, though, supposing nothing else at all to exist, this relation, which arises only from the existence of two things, would be nothing too. The same is also in space: if God should create another world separate wholly from this, or at first had created only two pebbles with no other body between, neither of which includes a contradiction, there had presently resulted a relation of such a distance between them as was capable to receive other bodies of so many yards, ells, miles, &c. So though[3] this extension be the ranging of real particles of matter united or in rest one by another, yet the distance considered between any two of them without regard to the interjacent particles is nothing but a mere relation which, though it be real, yet being but the result from the being of other things, requires no new act of creation, no more than it was necessary that paternity, which was not before in the world, would be created upon Adam's begetting Cain.

IV

IDOLATRY

MS. Locke f. 1, pp. 320–5, 354–5: Journal for 15 July and 20 July 1676.

Locke left a blank space after the first word of this entry, where he omits to mention the name of an author whose book he discusses in the following lines. Immediately afterwards he refers to another author whose name he indicates by the initial *S*. The discussion in this entry

---

[1] *to* is followed by a blank, meant for the insertion of some number.

[2] The geocentric conception indicated by this phrase (cf. also Locke's first essay on natural law, f. 9) is rectified by Locke in the *Essay* of 1690 (II. xiv. 21).

[3] The sign for *this* in the manuscript comes before that for *though*.

Idolatry

took its rise from a controversy between these two authors, and it is therefore essential to establish their identities.

Dr. S. is Edward Stillingfleet, who in 1671 published *A Discourse of the Idolatry practised in the Church of Rome*. An answer to this, entitled *Catholicks no Idolaters*, &c., and published anonymously in the same year, was written by Thomas Godden[1] (or Godwin), whose real name was Tylden. It is this name which is to be inserted in the blank space at the beginning of this entry; Locke could not fill it in, because for him Godden was an anonymous author. Stillingfleet wrote an answer to Godden in 1676, in reply to which he received from him another anonymous pamphlet[2] in 1677, which he answered in 1679.

Godden (1624–88) was a Roman convert and, in 1661, became chaplain to Catherine of Braganza, the consort of Charles II; his *Catholicks no Idolaters* is dedicated to her. His controversy with Stillingfleet concerning the idolatry of Catholics arose out of his controversy with him concerning salvation. In 1678 Godden was accused of complicity in the murder of Sir Edmund Berry Godfrey. He escaped to France, and was reinstated under James II.

Stillingfleet, later Bishop of Worcester and Locke's literary opponent in the years 1697–9, needs no further introduction.

In his *Catholicks no Idolaters* Godden advances a definition of idolatry in such terms that it enables him to attempt a vindication of Roman Catholicism from the charge of idolatry. In the Journal entry printed here Locke criticizes and rejects this definition. His discussion of the question is particularly valuable in that there is no parallel to it in any of his other writings except for a short entry, dated 1694, in his commonplace book of 1661 (p. 314), now in the Houghton Library at Harvard.

(p. 320) When[3] .... answer to Dr. S.[4] about the idolatry of the Church of Rome came out, I wondered to find some say that he had the better of Dr. S. in some things; that made me look in his book, where reading three or four leaves I found that the great stress of his argument was concerning the notion of idolatry, which methought he had stated so that by it either all idolatry of the heathen would be taken away or a great deal be found even amongst Christians that had no

---

[1] Halkett and Laing, *Dictionary of Anonymous and Pseudonymous English Literature*, 1926, i. 302.　　　　[2] Ibid. iii. 210.
[3] *When* is followed by a blank to be filled by the name of Thomas Godden, who published his book anonymously.　　　　[4] *S.* stands for Stillingfleet.

images at all, it (p. 321) consisting wholly according to his notion in having a wrong idea of God and terminating our worship there. This set me upon thinking what was idolatry; which upon consideration I thought to consist in performing outward worship, i.e. bowing, kneeling, prostrating, or praying, &c., before an image, where either the place, time, or other circumstances give the spectator reason to presume that one is employed in some act of religion or divine worship. For God, being the Lord and maker both of the body and the soul, requires the homage and worship of both the body and the soul. That inward one[1] of the mind is principally acceptable to Him, whereby we acknowledge His power and sovereignty and our dependence and thankfulness and also dispose our own minds to faith and obedience. And He requires also the homage of our bodies, both to testify that inward one to men and by our example to draw them to the worship of Him likewise. Now God being, as He has declared Himself, jealous of His honour might not suffer any part of this homage to be performed, were it[2] suspected to be paid to any thing but the true God. For knowing the grossness of men's (p. 322) apprehension, especially of the ignorant part of mankind which is much greater, and how apt we are all to rest our thoughts upon sensible objects, He forbade His people, that was to own Him among the nations, to do anything upon any pretence whatsoever that had the appearance of, or would be thought to be, divine worship before any image or representation, lest bystanders of the ordinary people among the Jews or those of other nations seeing them would be brought to think the God of[3] Israel like the other gods of nations and not one only, infinite, invisible God; the use of images in worship naturally introducing gross thoughts of God, misapprehensions of Him, superstitious reverence of images, and by that means polytheism. Hence we find falling down before images, i.e. worship, so often forbidden and complained of in the Old Testament. And if idolatry were nothing but terminating our worship, i.e. thought, on something that is not God, I do not see how there could be a law to punish (p. 323) idolaters, seeing their thought cannot be known. And it is not likely God should make so severe a law and declare Himself so often against an idolatry which was to consist in so nice and refined a notion, which was so much in the dark that I do not find that any of the learned Jews or Christians, much less ignorant, found it out or

[1] *one* added by Ed.
[2] *it* is followed by two shorthand signs meaning *not be*, which is not grammatical and, if inserted, would reverse the apparent meaning.　　　[3] *of* added by Ed.

understood it, till of late some of those who chose rather to have images to excite their devotion than Scripture to direct it have discovered idolatry to be some thing which God Himself never explained so to His people, nor gave them the least reason to understand so, which yet one might well expect He would do in a matter of so much moment, of which He speaks so often and on which He lays so much stress. And those that have reason to be friends to this notion seem to me so far to suspect that the Second Commandment will destroy it, and that the plain words of it will be apt to be understood in the but contrary sense by those who are not corrupted and have not done violence to their (p. 324) understandings with studied and useless niceties. I say this seems so to me, because I find in their books of devotion, wherein they give direction about confession and make use of the Commandments as a touchstone of their lives and a rule whereby to examine their transgressions, they wholly leave out the Second Command and divide the Tenth into two, thereby confounding the Seventh with the first part of the Tenth (*vid. Méthode pour la confession et communion*, à Paris, 1671; *Heures royales par les révérends PP. de la Compagnie de Jésus*, à Paris, 1668); and in all their enumeration of sins there we find not the least mention of idolatry, which surely is not so small a peccadillo that it ought not to be confessed among others. And in other books of devotion, where they pretend to give us the Commandments at large, they glutton the First and Second Command together and give the Second in shorter and other words than God gave it in and divide the Tenth into two (*vid. L'office de l'Eglise en latin et en français*, à Paris, 1668, dédic. (p. 325) au Roi). (p. 354) In the *Manual of Prayer and Litanies*, printed at Paris, 12°, *permissu superiorum*, 1672, the Second Command is set down a little more at large than in the French books of devotion, because it is more like to fall into the hands of heretics in England and so with shame to be discovered. But yet here they have made the First and Second but one, and divided the Tenth into two, and have rendered different from (p. 355) our translation and from the true sense of the original especially these words 'Thou shall not adore nor worship them'. Which yet how it agrees with what I find in another book of their devotions, called *La perpétuelle Croix, traduit du latin du P. Judoque Andiez de la Compagnie de Jésus par un Père de la même Compagnie*, à Paris, 12°, 1671, Approbation et privilège du Roi! *vid.* art. 5, p. 13: 'Méthode pour bien profiter des images et figures', at the end of which, 'Avis au dévot Chrétien', in these words: 'O le vrai et parfait amoureux de Jésus . . .

voyez quelle commodité . . . vous avez d'amplifier sa gloire et son honneur, non seulement parmi ceux de votre famille mais encore parmi &c. . . . Bref parmi tous ceux qui adorent les images et veulent participer aux mérites de sa sainte passion.'

V

PLEASURE AND PAIN. THE PASSIONS

MS. Locke f. 1, pp. 325–47: Journal for 16 July 1676.

In several places there are marginal key-words by Locke in longhand, indicating the various topics discussed by him in this entry. He deals with pleasure and pain, the passions in general, some particular passions, happiness, desire, power, and the will. The entry is edited here under the general title 'Pleasure and Pain. The Passions'. The marginal key-words are not reproduced, since it is clear from the text where a new topic begins. The paragraphing is Locke's.

(*a*) *Pleasure and pain.* Locke's chief discussion in this entry turns upon the ideas of 'pleasure and pain'. His short remark about the final cause of these ideas (p. 326), elaborated by him in the *Essay* of 1690 (II. vii. 2–6), can be traced to his fourth essay on natural law (ff. 56 and 59), but the hedonistic development of this remark in other parts of the entry has no parallel in any of his writings except in the *Essay*, II. xx. The *Essay* chapters on pleasure and pain, as Professor Aaron[1] has remarked, are indeed noteworthy in that they have no counterpart in Draft B, which in other respects contains much of the scheme and many of the details of Book II of the *Essay*. Since this entry is in shorthand and its contents have remained unknown, the belief has generally been accepted that Locke discussed the ideas of pleasure and pain for the first time in his *Essay* of 1690 and had not considered them previously, either in his drafts of the *Essay* of 1671 or in his journals, as was his practice with regard to most other topics discussed by him in the *Essay*. As will be seen, Locke's earliest thoughts on pleasure and pain are contained in the Journal entry for 16 July 1676, printed here.[2] However, in a longhand entry for 13 July

[1] *John Locke*, 1937, pp. 56–57.
[2] I pass over the question whether any of these thoughts were suggested to Locke by Gassendi's teaching in the *Philosophiae Epicuri Syntagma* (pt. i, ch. 4; pt. ii, sect. iii, ch. 19; pt. iii, chs. 2–5), a work which he may have begun to study soon after he left for France, where he made the acquaintance of François Bernier, the leader of the Gassendists.

1676,[1] i.e. three days before the present entry, Locke briefly mentions the will, pleasure and pain, and perception as forming 'the four simple ideas we have from the mind'. The passage is covertly referred to towards the end of the present entry (p. 343), and Locke's concluding remark (p. 347) is that his discussion of the *five* simple ideas of pain, pleasure, thinking, power, and will, contained in the present entry, should be placed in the *Essay* before the chapter on the passions— obviously because pleasure and pain, as he himself says,[2] 'are the hinges on which our passions turn'.[3]

(*b*) *The passions.* Several passages in this entry concerning the passions recur in a similar, though sometimes more, sometimes less detailed form in the *Essay*, II. xx and xxi. Other passages do not occur in the *Essay* at all, and they are thus of singular interest. Undoubtedly, Locke had in mind the fuller treatment of the passions in the present entry, when he wrote the concluding paragraph of the chapter on the passions in the *Essay*, which opens with the words: 'I would not be mistaken here, as if I meant this as a Discourse of the Passions; they are many more than those I have here named: and those I have taken notice of would each of them require a much larger and more accurate discourse.'[4] Some of the 'other modes of pleasure and pain', which he says he 'might have instanced' in the *Essay* chapter, are mentioned by him in the first part of the present entry, in his description of love.

(*c*) *Desire.* In connexion with his discussion of love Locke speaks of desire (p. 331, continued on pp. 339–42). The account of desire in the present entry is important for two reasons: (1) desire is not men- tioned by Locke in any of his writings before 1676, and (2) the account of it here is one of the sources of the important changes intro- duced by Locke in the second edition of the *Essay* (1694). In the first edition of the *Essay* (1690) desire is only briefly referred to in II. xx. 6. In the second edition Locke adds to II. xx. 6 some remarks about desire similar to those in the present entry, and in the chapter 'Of Power' (II. xxi. 28–66) he substitutes a full discussion of desire as the true cause of willing for the theory expressed by him in that place in the first edition that the will is ultimately determined by 'the greater good in view'. In a sense, therefore, the present entry anticipates

---

[1] Printed by R. I. Aaron and J. Gibb, *An Early Draft of Locke's Essay*, &c., 1936, pp. 80–81.   [2] *Essay*, II. xx. 3.

[3] Power, considered by Locke at the end of the present entry as one of the simple ideas, is discussed by him in the *Essay* in a lengthy chapter (II. xxi) *following* that on the passions; however, it is briefly introduced as one of the simple ideas in a chapter preceding that on the passions, i.e. in II. vii. 8.   [4] II. xx. 18.

Locke's final views on this question in the second and subsequent editions of the *Essay*.

(*d*) *Power.* Next to desire Locke analyses the idea of power (pp. 343–7), discussed by him at length in the *Essay* of 1690 (II. xxi), but only briefly and inadequately treated by him in the two drafts of the *Essay* of 1671. In connexion with his discussion of it in the present entry Locke introduces for the first time his criticism of the Cartesian doctrine that the mind is essentially thinking.[1]

It is for the several reasons here given that the entry printed below is important.

(p. 325) In *voluptas* and *dolor*, pleasure and pain, I mean principally that of the mind, there are two roots out of which all passions spring and a centre on which they all turn. Where they are removed, the passions would all cease, having nothing left to wind them up or set them going. To know our passions, then, and to have right ideas of them, we ought to consider pleasure and pain and the things that produce them in us, and how they operate and move us.[2]

God has so[3] framed the constitutions of our minds and bodies (p. 326) that several things are apt to produce in both of them pleasure and pain, delight and trouble, by ways that we know not, but for ends suitable to His goodness and wisdom.[4] Thus the smell of roses and the tasting of wine, light and liberty, the possession of power and the acquisition of knowledge please most men, and there are some things whose very being and existence delights others, as children and grandchildren. So that where anything offers itself to the understanding as capable to produce pleasure, there it constantly and immediately produces love,[5] which seems to be nothing but the consideration or having in the mind the idea of some thing that is able in some way of application to produce delight or pleasure in us. It is true there accompanies this thought as well as all other passions a particular motion of the blood and spirits, but that being such as is not always observed nor a necessary ingredient of the idea (p. 327) of any passion, it is not necessary here, where we are only seeking the ideas of the passions, to inquire into it.[6] To love, then, is nothing but to have in our mind the idea of some thing which we consider as capable to produce satisfaction

---

[1] Cf. *Essay*, II. i. 9 ff.   [2] Cf. ibid. xx. 3.   [3] *so* added by Ed.
[4] Cf. *Essay*, II. vii. 2–6; also Locke's fourth essay on natural law, ff. 56 and 59.
[5] Locke's discussion of love in the *Essay* consists only of eight lines (II. xx. 4).
[6] Instead of *it*, Locke uses a sign meaning *them*.

or delight in us, for when a man says he loves roses, wine, or knowledge, what does he mean else but that the smells of roses, the taste of
wine, and knowledge delight him or produce pleasure in him, and
so of all other things? Indeed, because man considers that that particular
thing that delights him cannot be had without the preservation of
several others that are annexed to it or go to the producing of it, he is
said to love them when he wishes and endeavours to preserve them.
Thus men are said to love the trees that produce the fruit they are
delighted with, and thus they often love their friends with whose good
offices or conversation they are delighted, endeavouring (p. 328) and
wishing their good, thereby to preserve to themselves those things
they have pleasure in; which though we call love of their friends is
not truly love of their persons but a care to preserve with their persons
and friendship those good things which they do love and which they
cannot have without them. For we often see that, when the good
offices cease, love to the person often dies and sometimes turns into
hatred, which does not so in our love to our children, because nature
for wise ends of her own has made us so that we are delighted with
the very being of our children. Some wise minds are of a nobler constitution, having pleasure in the very being and the happiness of their
friends, and some yet of a more excellent make are[1] delighted with the
existence and happiness of all good men, some with that of all mankind
(p. 331)[2] in general, and this last may be said properly to love. Others
with their *amor concupiscentiae* are only provident, so that in this and,
I believe, in all other instances love will be found to take its rise and
extent only from objects of pleasure and to be nothing else but having
in our minds the idea of some thing that is so suited to our particular
make and temper as to be fit to produce pleasure in us. This gives us
the reason why love, the principal and first of[3] all passions, is the most
untractable of all the rest and to be represented as blind. Desire and
hope, though their proper and ultimate objects be the same with that
of love, yet they may be prevailed on by reason and consideration to
fix upon painful and troublesome things when they may be a means
to another end; but talk, reason, and consider as much as you will,
love is not moved till you propose some thing that in itself is delightful.
Many have desired to take off a limb and in some cases have desired
and (p. 332)[4] hoped for pains, as in childbirth, but I think nobody was

---

[1] *are* omitted in manuscript.   [2] pp. 329–30 are left blank in the manuscript.
[3] *of* omitted in manuscript.
[4] At the bottom of p. 331 Locke wrote *France* (in shorthand), *1676*.

ever in love with them. Love fixes only upon an end and never embraces any object purely as serviceable to some other purpose, nor could it be otherwise, since it is a sympathy of the soul and is nothing but the union of the mind with the idea of something that has a secret faculty to delight it, and whenever such an idea is in the mind and considered there as such, then it is that we properly exercise the passion of love.

Hatred[1] is placed directly opposite to love, and so there needs not much ado to find that it is nothing but the presence of an idea in the mind considered as naturally disposed to disease and vex us and has the same effect that love has,[2] for when that that troubles us cannot be separated from the thing it is in, hatred often carries us to desire and endeavour the destruction of the thing, as love for the same reason carries us to desire and endeavour its preservation. But this passion of hatred usually carries us farther and (p. 333) with more violence than that of love, because the sense of evil or pain works more upon us than that of good or pleasure; we bear the absence of a great pleasure more easily than the presence of a little pain. Ἀναισθησία is not in the middle between pleasure and pain; insensibility that is not perpetual is reckoned on the better side: sleep, that always robs us of the sense of our enjoyments, is never complained of, but when it gives a cessation from any of our pains we take it for a pleasure.

The pleasure and pain[3] I spoke so much of here is principally that of the mind, for impressions made on the body, if they reach not the mind, produce neither pain nor pleasure. As the mind is delighted or disturbed, so have we pain or pleasure. Whatever motions may be produced in the body from some degree of heat that causes pleasure by its application to one hand moderately cold and[4] causes great pain being applied at the same time to the other (p. 334) hand very much chilled with snow, and at the same time a sudden occasion of great joy or sorrow supervening, neither of them is felt. That pleasure or pain coming from the body is quite lost and perishes as soon as the mind ceases to be affected by them or to take notice of them.

This pleasure and pain, *dolor* and *voluptas animi*, distinguished by several degrees and other circumstances, i.e. made into several complex ideas, come to have several names; some, whereby to show these two simple ideas a little more clearly, it cannot be amiss to mention.[5] For

---

[1] Locke's discussion of hatred in the *Essay* (II. xx. 5) is brief and different from that here.
[2] *has* omitted in manuscript.   [3] Cf. *Essay*, II. vii. 2–4, xx. 1–2.   [4] *and* added by Ed.
[5] Of the modes of pleasure and pain mentioned here only 'joy' and 'sorrow' are discussed by Locke in the *Essay* (II. xx. 7 ; 8).

instance, a pain of the mind, when it arises from the long continuance of anything, is called weariness; when from some small cause,[1] whereof the mind is very sensible, vexation; when from a thing that is past, sorrow; when from the loss of a friend, grief; when from a violent pain of the body, torment; when it hinders discourse and conversation, (p. 335) melancholy; when accompanied with a great feebleness, anxiety; when very violent, anguish; when it is the utmost we can conceive without any mixture of comfort, misery. There are several other differences of this idea that is disagreeable to the mind and more names to distinguish it than there are of the pleasures, because we are more sensible of, and in this world more accustomed to, pain than to pleasure. On the other side, this pleasure of the mind, when it arises from light causes, especially in conversation, is called mirth; when from the presence of agreeable sensible objects, delight; when from the consideration of some great and solid good, joy; when from[2] some precedent sorrow which it removes, comfort; and when perfect and free from all trouble, happiness. So that happiness and misery[3] seem to me wholly to consist in this pleasure and pain (p. 336) of the mind, of which every little trouble or satisfaction is a degree; and the completion of either is when the mind to the highest degree and utmost capacity is filled and possessed by the ideas of either kind.

Thus we see from the simple ideas of pain and pleasure which we find in our minds, when extended and enlarged, we get the ideas of happiness and misery, for whatsoever makes any part of our happiness or misery, that which produces in us any pleasure or pain, that is so far properly and in its own nature good, and whatsoever serves anyway to procure any thing of happiness to us that is also good, though the first is that which is called *bonum jucundum*, which ought not to be understood only in reference to the body, but, as we have used the name pleasure, as belonging principally to the mind. And under the latter (p. 337) are comprehended two other sorts of good which are called *utile* and *honestum*, which, were they not ordained by God to procure the *jucundum* and be a means to help us to happiness, at least in some degrees of it, I do not see how they would be reckoned good at all. What good were there more in diamonds than pebbles, if they cannot procure us more of those things that are pleasant and agreeable

---

[1] The manuscript has *case*.   [2] *from* omitted in manuscript.
[3] 'Happiness' and 'misery' are fully discussed by Locke in his *Essay* chapter 'Of Power' (ii. xxi. 42 ff.).

than pebbles will? What makes temperance a good and gluttony an evil but that the one serves to procure us health and ease in this world and happiness in the other, when gluttony does quite the contrary? And repentance and sorrow for some would have but very little good in it, if it were not a means and way to our happiness.

If it were not beside our present purpose, we might here observe that we have no clear and distinct ideas of pleasure but such as we have felt in ourselves.[1] The imagination of fuller and greater is but by way of similitude and resemblance (p. 338) to those we have experimented, and so are confused and obscure, not being able clearly to conceive the pleasure which unknown objects can produce in us (the pleasure that is in the tasting of pine apple or in having children to those that are not experimented being very hard to be fancied); and how much more inconceivable are the pleasures of spiritual objects (which certainly as more proportioned to the nature of the mind are more capable to touch and move it with lovely and ravishing delights) to us who,[2] being immersed in the body and beset with material objects, when they are continually importuning us, have very little sense or perception of spiritual things, which are as it were at a distance and affect us but seldom; and therefore it is that I believe that our idea of happiness, such as the blessed enjoy and such as we are capable of, is very imperfect in this world; yet such as it is leaves us inexcusable and under the brand and condemnation of the greatest folly, if we use (p. 339) not our greatest care and endeavours to obtain it. But this *in transitu*.

To return to our ideas of the passions. The mind finding in itself the ideas of several objects which, if enjoyed, would produce pleasure, i.e. the ideas of the several things it loves, contemplating the satisfaction which would arise to itself in the actual enjoyment or application of some one of those things it loves and the possibility or feasibleness of the present enjoyment, or doing something toward the procuring the enjoyment, of that good, observes in itself some uneasiness or trouble or displeasure till it be done, and this is that we call desire,[3] so that desire seems to me to be a pain the mind is in till some good, whether *jucundum* or *utile*, which it judges possible and seasonable, be obtained.

[1] Cf. here *Essay*, II. xx. I (fin.). [2] *who* substituted by Ed. for *when*.

[3] In the first edition of the *Essay* of 1690 desire is only briefly referred to in II. xx. 6. In the second edition of 1694, however, Locke adds to II. xx. 6 some remarks about desire similar to those in the following passages, and at the same time he omits sections 28–38 in the chapter 'Of Power' (II. xxi) and in their place introduces thirty-five others (sections 28–62), containing a full discussion of desire.

To have the clearer idea of this passion, it cannot be amiss to consider that desire is of far less extent than love, for love, being but the looking (p. 340) on any thing as delightful or capable to produce pleasure in us, embraces at once whatever appears to be so, whether near or remote, attainable or not. But desire, terminating in enjoyment, is moved with nothing farther than as it is capable of present enjoyment or may present a means towards it.

Desire also, which, as I have said, is nothing but a pain the mind suffers in the absence of some good, is increased and varied by divers considerations; for instance, when it is in pursuit of a positive good, the first consideration that sets it on work or at least quickens it is the possibility, for we have little desire for what we once conceive impossible. It is true, men sometimes wish for roses in winter and that their daughters were sons, which is no more but saying or thinking that such things, if they were possible, might please them, but when they consider them as impossible, not having them leaves but little trouble upon their mind, and so little desire. But in the desire of the removal of some present evil it (p. 341) is quite otherwise, for there, the evil causing a constant pain, there is a constant desire to be eased of it, whether it be considered as possible or no. Whereby we might see how much desire consists in pain.

If possibility excite our desire, easiness of attainment is certainly a farther incentive to it, which we very much judge of by the season wherein such things used to be had and the enjoyments of others of the same good. Thus men, that wish but for health and strength to their children when infants, desire obedience and docility in them in their youth, and skill or knowledge and preferment when they are grown up.

Another thing that governs and regulates our desire is the greatness or smallness of the good, which is not estimated barely as it is in itself or as it has naturally a fitness to produce pleasure in us or is a fit means in itself to procure it, but as it is consistent with other enjoyments that we have. Love, indeed, extends itself universally to (p. 342) all that has the appearance of being able to do us good, i.e. produce pleasure in us, because it lies barely in the contemplation and so may extend itself to things incompatible and inconsistent: it being as easy to have the ideas of the pleasures of company and conversation and play with those of retirement and study and contemplation, and consequently to love them both at once, as it is to have at once the ideas of white and black, which never yet exist and not together in the same subject. But desire employing itself only about the actual enjoyment of some good which

consists in actual existence and application, which bears not with contrarieties, it very much is regulated by the agreement or contrariety it is conceived to have with other good things we either enjoy or desire.

(p. 343) The simple ideas we have from the mind are thinking, power, pleasure, and pain. Of thinking we have spoken already,[1] and to understand what the idea of power[2] is and how we come by it, it will be convenient to consider action a little, which is always a product of power. There seems, then, to me to be but two sorts of actions in the world, viz. that which belongs and is peculiar to matter or body and that is motion, and thought which is proper only to the soul. Motion though it be a property of body, yet body in itself is indifferent to it, so that it can indifferently be in motion or in rest but cannot move itself, and, on the other side, though thinking be a property of the soul, yet the soul is indifferent to think or not to think.[3] This, I say, I imagine, speaking of the soul and finite spirits, that, thinking being their action, it is not necessary to conceive that they would be always in action, i.e. think, any more than that a body would be always (p. 344) in motion. But be that as it will, this is certain, that the inherent inseparable property of the soul is a power to act, i.e. a power to produce some motions in the body and some thoughts in the mind. Thus a man finds that he can rise out of a seat where he sat still and walk, and so produce a motion that is not before, and can also at pleasure, being in France, think of England or Italy, of respiration, playing at cards, the sun, Julius Caesar, anger, &c., and so produce in his mind thoughts that are not there before; and so by this means and this experience within itself the mind comes by the idea of power. I grant the mind, in a waking man, is never without thought, but whether sleep without dreaming be not an affection of mind as well as body may be thought worth an inquiry by one who considers that it is

---

[1] Cf. Locke's longhand entry in his Journal for 13 July 1676 (ed. Aaron, pp. 80–81). In that entry the 'four simple ideas we have from the mind' are given as 'perception' (or 'thinking'), 'willing', 'pleasure', and 'pain'. In the passage above Locke adds 'power' and omits 'willing'; he mentions both, however, together with the three other ideas, in the concluding sentence of the present entry. The reference to 'L.1, c. 3', written by Locke along the margin next to the passage above, occurs also in the margin of the longhand entry for 13 July 1676 (ed. Aaron, p. 80). In the *Essay* of 1690 the reference would be to Bk. 11, ch. iii ('Of simple Ideas of Sense'), because what was the opening Book of the *Essay* in 1676, as also of Draft A, became Bk. 11 of the *Essay* of 1690.

[2] Locke's discussion of 'power' in the *Essay* is in the chapter 'Of Power' (11. xxi. 1 ff.).

[3] Here and farther on (p. 344) Locke anticipates his criticism of Descartes in the *Essay*, 11. i. 9 ff. on the question of the mind's essence. Descartes held that the mind is always thinking and that thinking is its essence. The issue is not raised in the two drafts of the *Essay* of 1671.

hard to imagine that the soul should think and not be conscious of it, and that it will be difficult to give a reason why the soul out of the body cannot be in a state without perceiving any ideas and wholly insensible of any pleasure or pain (p. 347),[1] as well as in the body. But to put by this speculation and that other whether the primary and inseparable affection of spirit be not power as that of matter is extension, I say one of the simple ideas that a man gets from the observation of what passes within himself is that of power, which when it exerts itself in consequence of any thought is called the will;[2] which happens not always, for the several notions in our sleep and the first thoughts we have when we wake, being without choice or deliberation and not consequent to any precedent thought, cannot be ascribed to the will or be counted voluntary. By these steps and by such observations of its own internal operations it is that the mind comes to have the ideas of pain, pleasure, thinking, power, and will (*memo.*, all this about these ideas should come in before the discourse of the passions).[3]

VI

FAITH AND REASON

MS. Locke f. 1, pp. 412–32: Journal entries for each day between 23 and 28 August 1676, and for 1 September 1676.

Marginal key-words in longhand, which are not reproduced here, indicate the beginning of each topic in Locke's discussion. First he deals with toleration and peace, then he gives a long account of the relations between faith and reason, which includes digressions on ignorance and transubstantiation, and in conclusion he discusses knowledge. The entries are edited here under the title 'Faith and Reason', for this is their central theme. The paragraphing is Locke's.

(*a*) *Toleration*. Locke's plea for toleration in this entry (pp. 412–14) is of interest for the lively illustrations by which it is supported. His main points are established by way of answers to objections put in the

---

[1] pp. 345–6 are left blank in the manuscript.

[2] For a full discussion of 'will' in the *Essay* see II. xxi. 5 ff.

[3] The simple ideas referred to, except 'will', are discussed, or at least mentioned, by Locke in the *Essay* of 1690 'before the discourse of the passions', which is ch. xx of Bk. II. His discussion of 'will' and, for the most part, of 'power' is in the following chapter, i.e. ch. xxi of Bk. II. The *memo.*, in effect, concerns only the ideas of 'pleasure' and 'pain', for these, as Locke says (II. xx. 3), 'are the hinges on which our passions turn'.

mouth of an imaginary interlocutor. There are no parallels with any
of Locke's other writings on toleration, though in spirit and style the
entry anticipates some of Locke's central arguments in *A Letter concerning Toleration* of 1689,[1] and in a lesser degree his exhortation to
peace in a paragraph of the *Essay*.[2] A short passage (pp. 414–15) concerning the difference between religion and civil government, and the
magistrate's sole duty to secure the peace, leads to a discussion of faith
and reason.

(*b*) *Faith and Reason.* Locke's ideas on this theme in the present
entries (pp. 415 ff.) are the earliest version of his thoughts on the
relations between faith and reason in the *Essay* of 1690, Book IV,
chapter xviii.[3] The entries can thus be regarded as an early draft of
the *Essay* in this field of inquiry. Many passages in the Journal entries
resemble passages in the *Essay* chapter to the point of exact correspondence.

It is difficult to point with any precision to the sources of Locke's
views on faith and reason. The great apologetic controversy in the
seventeenth century was opened by Grotius in his treatise *De Veritate
Religionis Christianae* (1622). Culverwel's *Discourse of the Light of
Nature* (1652) belongs to an early stage of this controversy, and from
him Locke may have derived his view that while revelation itself is
independent of reason, faith is throughout consistent with it and rests
on it. A further stimulus to Locke's thought on the question may have
been the persistent inquiries of his friend Robert Boyle into the nature
of 'things above reason' and 'things not against reason'. Boyle's *Reconcilableness of Reason and Religion* was published in 1675, a year before
the present entry was written.

(*c*) *Ignorance.* The Journal entries on faith and reason include a
brief digression on ignorance (pp. 417–18). This anticipates remarks
by Locke in the chapter 'Of Reason' in the *Essay* (iv. xvii. 9–13); it
has little connexion with his main arguments concerning ignorance in
the chapter 'Of the Extent of Human Knowledge' (iv. iii).

(*d*) *Transubstantiation.* Another digression is on the doctrine of
transubstantiation (pp. 421–4). Brief references to this doctrine occur
in Draft A, par. 42,[4] and in the *Essay* of 1690, Book IV,[5] but these
have no analogy to the development of Locke's argument in the

[1] Cf., for example, pp. 157 ff. (ed. by J. Gough, 1946).   [2] iv. xvi. 4.
[3] On p. 415 there is a book and chapter reference to the *Essay* (i.e. 'L.   c.   '), but no
numbers are given.   [4] Edited by R. I. Aaron and J. Gibb, 1936, p. 64.
[5] Chs. xviii. 5; xx. 10.

present entry. There is a parallel, however, between a passage in the *Essay* chapter 'Of Enthusiasm',[1] added by Locke in the fourth edition of 1700, and a passage in the Journal entry (pp. 423–4), where mention is made of the miraculous change of Moses' rod into a serpent.

(*e*) *Knowledge.* In conclusion Locke adds a few general remarks on knowledge (pp. 430–2), which are not unlike those in the *Essay*, IV. xvii. 24. An appeal to the light of nature, under whose guidance men come to know of God and their moral duties, ends the philosophical shorthand entries in Locke's Journal for 1676.

(p. 412) *23rd August 1676*: Penal laws, made about matters of religion in a country where there is already a diversity of opinions, can hardly avoid that common injustice which is condemned in all laws whatsoever, viz. in retrospect. It would be thought a hard case, if by a law, now made, all would have to be fined that should wear French hats for the future, and those also who had worn them at any time in the year past. It is the same case to forbid a man to be a Quaker, Anabaptist, Presbyterian, for it is as easy for me not to have had on the hat yesterday, which I then wore, as it is in many cases not to have the same opinions, the same thought, in my head as I had yesterday—both being impossible. The great dispute in all this diversity of opinions is where the truth is. But let us suppose at present that it is wholly and certainly on the State's side, though it will be pretty hard to suppose it so in England, in France, Sweden, and Denmark at the same time; and yet in all these places they have an equal power (p. 413) to make laws about religion. But let us suppose yet that all dissenters are in error, are out of their wits, *esto*; but your law found them in this delirium, and will you make a law that will hang all that are beside themselves?—[2]But we fear their rage and violence.—If you fear them only because they are capable of a raging fit, you may as well fear all other men, who are liable to the same distemper. If you fear it because you treat them ill, and that produces some symptom of it, you ought to change your method, and not punish them for what you fear because you go the way to produce it. If a distemper itself has a tendency to rage, it must be watched and fit remedies applied. If they are perfect innocents, only a little crazed, why cannot they be let alone, since, though perhaps their brains are a little out of order, their hands work well enough?—But they will infect others.—If those others are in-

[1] iv. xix. 15.
[2] I put dashes to indicate the objections of an imaginary interlocutor.

fected but by their own consent, and that to cure[1] another disease that they think they have, why should they be hindered (p. 414) any more than a man is that might make an issue to cure palsy, or might willingly have haemorrhoids to prevent an apoplexy?—But then all people will run into this error.—This supposes either that it is true and so prevails, or that the teachers of truth are very negligent and let it, and that they are to blame; or that people are more inclined to error than truth: if so, then, error being manifold, they will be as distant one from another as from you, and so no fear of their uniting, unless you force them by making yourself an enemy to all by ill-treatment.

To settle the peace of places where there are different opinions in religion, two things are to be perfectly distinguished: religion and government,[2] and their two sorts of officers, magistrates and ministers, and their provinces, to be kept well distinct (the not doing whereof was perhaps a great cause of distraction); a magistrate only (p. 415) to look at the peace and security of a city, ministers only concerned[3] with the saving of the soul, and if they were forbidden meddling with making or executing laws in their preaching, we should be perhaps much more quiet.

24th August 1676: In matters of religion it would be well, if anyone would tell how far we are to be guided by reason, and how far by faith.[4] The want of this is one of the causes that keep up in the world so many different opinions, for every sect, as far as reason will help them, makes use of it gladly, and where it fails them, they cry out that it is matter of faith and above reason. And I do not see how they can ever be convinced by any who makes use of the same plea, without setting down a strict boundary between faith and reason, which ought to be the first point established (p. 416) in all disputes of religion.

(p. 417) *25th August 1676*: Q. Whether our ignorance comes from anything but the want, imperfection, or confusion of ideas?[5] For our reason seems not to fail us but in the second case. (1) The fallacy of words in a long train of consequences, and this is our fault, not the fault of our reason; (2) the imperfection of our ideas, and there we are involved in difficulties and contradictions. Thus, not having a perfect idea of the least extension of matter, nor of infinity, we are at a loss

---

[1] Meaning perhaps 'that they may cure'.
[2] Cf. Locke's paper 'On the Difference between Civil and Ecclesiastical Power', of 1673-4, printed in Lord King's *Life and Letters of John Locke* (ed. 1858), pp. 300 ff.
[3] *concerned* added by Ed.
[4] For this passage and the following see *Essay*, IV. xviii. 1-2.
[5] For the following passage see ibid. xvii. 9-13.

Faith and Reason

about the divisibility of matter; but having perfect as well as clear and distinct ideas of number, our reason makes no mistakes or meets with no contradiction in numbers. Thus we, having but imperfect ideas of the first motions of our own wills or minds, and much imperfecter yet of the operations of God, run into great difficulties about 'free will', which reason cannot resolve. This perhaps may give us the measure where to appeal to faith and quit reason, (p. 418) which is only where, for want of clear and perfect ideas, we find ourselves involved in inextricable difficulties and contradictions of our notions, and nowhere else decided. I say of such doubts faith and revelation take the place, as they do also in the discovery of truths which reason, acting upon our natural ideas, cannot reach; for if we had but such a clear and perfect idea of the operations of God as to know whether that power would make a 'free agent', wherein, I think, lies the bottom of the question about predestination and free will, the dispute about it would quickly be determined by human reason, and faith would have little to do in the case. For[1] in a proposition, built upon clear and perfect ideas, we need not the assistance of faith as absolutely necessary to gain our assent and introduce them into our minds; because through[2] knowledge I have settled them there already, or am able to do it; which is the greatest assurance we can possibly have of anything, unless it be where God immediately reveals it to us: and there, too, our assurance can be no greater than our knowledge (p. 419) is that it *is* a revelation from God. And in propositions that are contrary to our clear and perfect ideas, faith will in vain endeavour to establish them or move our assent. For faith can never convince us of anything that contradicts our knowledge. Because, though faith be founded on the testimony of God (which cannot lie), yet we cannot have an assurance of the truth of it greater than our own knowledge. Since the whole strength of that certainty depends upon our knowledge that God revealed it, which, in this case, where revelation is pretended to contradict our knowledge or reason, will always have this objection hanging to it, that we cannot tell how to conceive that to come from God, the bountiful Author of our being, which, if believed for true, must overturn all our principles and foundations of knowledge, render all our faculties useless, and wholly destroy the most excellent part of His workmanship, our understanding, and put a man in a condition wherein he will have less light, less conduct than the beasts that perish. Indeed,

---

[1] For what follows see *Essay*, IV. xviii. 5.
[2] *Through* or *by* should be added here.

276

in matters above our reason, which what they are I have said, we ought not only to admit, but we stand in need of, revelation, and there faith is to (p. 420) govern us wholly. But[1] this takes not away the landmarks of knowledge; this shakes not the foundations of reason, but leaves us the full use of our faculties. And[2] if the distinct provinces of faith and reason are not to be set out by these boundaries, I believe, in matters of religion, that there will be no use, no room, for reason at all; and those extravagant opinions and ceremonies that are to be found in the several religions of the world will not deserve to be blamed. For to[3] this crying up of faith in opposition to reason, we may, I think, in good measure ascribe those absurdities that fill almost all the religions which possess and divide mankind. For men having been principled with an opinion that they must not consult reason in the things of God, which were above or contrary to it, have let loose their fancies and natural superstitions, and have been by them led into so strange opinions, and extravagant (p. 421) practices in religion, that a considerate man cannot but stand amazed at their follies, and judge them so far from being acceptable to God that he cannot avoid thinking them ridiculous and offensive to sober men. So that, in effect, in that wherein we should show ourselves most to be rational creatures, that which most properly should distinguish us from beasts, we appear most irrational, and more senseless than beasts themselves. *Credo, quia impossibile est* might, in a good man, pass for a mark of zeal, but would prove the very last rule for men to choose their opinions by.

26th August 1676: It cannot be amiss here to apply this our rule of determining the bounds of faith and reason to one main point, which is guarded by the Church of Rome, which is very dexterous in this matter, from the examination of reason, by being decreed a matter of faith; and that question of 'transubstantiation',[4] which, being founded upon an interpretation of revealed truth, we are to examine: whether we are to use our reason, which leads us to a figurative sense very plain and easy, and as intelligible as calling the paschal (p. 422) lamb the body of the Passover,[5] or else by faith take the words in a literal sense, inconsistent with all the principles of our knowledge, all the evidence of sense, and which, if granted, leaves us no foundation of knowledge, certainty, or faith at all. Faith comes unto our assistance where the light of reason fails, but where we have knowledge there faith

---

[1] For this passage see *Essay*, iv. xviii. 10.
[2] For the following sentences see ibid. 11.
[3] *to* added by Ed.
[4] Cf. *Essay*, iv. xviii. 5; xx. 10.
[5] Exod. xii.

Faith and Reason

interposes not, nor indeed can, to contradict it. There needed no faith to persuade beholders that it was fire that the three children[1] were put into; they knew it, they saw it, there was no need to believe; faith would not have given them so great an assurance. The thing to be believed was a proper object of[2] faith and not of sense, a mental proposition, viz. that the God of the three children was the true God. So in the matter of transubstantiation: the question is not a matter of faith but of philosophy. It is a thing we exercise our senses and know-ledge on[3] and not our faith, and so clear that there is not room to doubt. For the reality (p. 423) and essence of bread being in respect of us nothing but a collection of several simple ideas, which makes us know it, distinguish it from flesh, and call it bread, it is as impossible for a man, where he finds that complex idea, to know it to be flesh or receive it for such, as it is to believe himself a loaf; for it is as easy for him to believe that, under that complex idea or that collection of accidents he finds in him of man, there is the substance or essence of bread, as to believe that under the complex idea of bread there is the substance of flesh, though perhaps by custom and the terrible name of heresy men[4] may be frightened from regarding their own ideas, have their thoughts confounded and, taking names for things, believe it flesh, because they used to call it so, and give a wrong name to it. Whereas, if they deal plainly and sincerely with themselves, I say it is as impossible not to know that the Host in consecration is bread, having all the accidents of bread, as it is impossible not to know that Moses' rod is not a serpent,[5] when (p. 424) it had the accidents of a rod, and is not a rod, when it had the accidents of a serpent; and if one could not know that, I dare boldly say a man can know nothing, nor God work a miracle to convince him of anything that indeed was a real transubstantiation and like the other of God's miracles; which always, by addressing themselves to the senses (the surest foundation, it seems, we should have of certainty, for God always made use of it to convince us), confirmed some doctrines of faith, but never, begin-ning at the other end, made use of invisible miracles to destroy the testimony of our senses, overturn all our knowledge, and confound (*27th August 1676*) all measures of faith and reason, which seem to me to stand thus:

1. There is the knowledge of names, and of things as ranged under them: thus we know a man from a horse. Names of things being

---

[1] Dan. iii.   [2] *of* omitted in manuscript.   [3] *on* added by Ed.
[4] *men* added by Ed.   [5] Exod. iv. 2–3. Cf. *Essay*, iv. xix. 15.

perfectly voluntary, we do, or may, know what ideas (for we signify nothing else) we signify by certain names. (p. 425) Wherein I shall be bold to say we never regard nor include a particular substance, which we neither do, nor can, know, but only particular ideas, which we do know. So when with others we call one thing wheat and others bread, we neither regard, nor mark, anything but sensible qualities, without considering whether the same substance be in them both or no. And if a man should believe never so much that the substance of wine was in vinegar (for till he knows what the substance of wine is he cannot know it), he most certainly knows that he called it amiss, if he called it wine, knowing that the name of wine belonged unto such a complex idea, to such sensible qualities, whatever the substance it was united to. So that about the defined names and distinctions for things they belong to, faith cannot be a judge at all, because we ordinarily do, and, where we do not, may certainly, know them and perhaps nothing surer. Whether the Host, then, be the same thing really before and after consecration, we can only (p. 426) know by our senses; whether it be to be called by the same name or no, it is men that agree on it, and we may know that too, as soon as they define their name, and I wish they would those of bread and flesh, which are the foundation of this controversy.

2. As we name things, so we also know and distinguish them by the ideas we have of them, which of a corporeal thing are all sensible.

3. By our senses also we know the nature of a fact which comes within their reach.

4. Reasonings also and deductions upon clear and perfect ideas are parts of our knowledge, and in all this we interpose not a judgement of faith, nor ever appeal to it. We do not believe that a man is there and talks with us, when we see and hear him, but we know it; and there needs no faith to assure us that two and two are four, or that the three angles of a triangle are equal to two right ones, if we will make a demonstration. But since our senses reach but a few of the matters of fact that pass, when our senses fail, faith grounded upon the testimony of another comes unto our information; and so likewise, since many of our ideas are obscure and imperfect, which yet for want of a better we are forced to reason upon and so arrive (p. 427) at propositions involved in inexplicable difficulties, which though natural reason has discovered, it cannot resolve, nor determine the understanding to either side, nor by a clear light discover on which side truth lies, since on both sides he finds something that carries a contradiction to some of the ideas and

notions he proceeds on, as whether that be an angle which is[1] less than the tangent, and therefore, though he cannot come to a certain knowledge in this, yet he may by faith take to either side, i.e. he may believe one to be true before the other, as it best agrees with his ideas.

There are yet other propositions, which, though they bear no contrariety to other ideas nor notions, yet are such as, proceeding upon them, we should never come to discover, for reason as well as sense failing us in the discovery of many truths necessary for us to know, God supplied both the one and the other defect in things necessary to our salvation, and this I take properly to be the objects and the matter of divine faith, where it has properly to do and nowhere else. Thus it is a matter of faith to all that did not see it, for to them (p. 428) that did see it it was no matter of faith, that Jesus Christ died at Jerusalem. But it is a matter of faith to all and of divine revelation, that He died to save sinners, which proposition or truth that[2] reason tracing its own ideas, i.e. acting upon its own natural principles, would never arrive at, and in this chiefly, I think, lies the nature of divine revelation and of divine faith, which we are neither to expect nor introduce in every occasion; (*28th August 1676*) and though besides this God has by the mouth of His prophets, and our Saviour by Himself and by the Apostles, declared other both historical and moral truths, to help our weak faculties that proceed but slowly in the discovery of truth, and cleared up many propositions necessary for us to know, and which men were not utterly incapable of before, which thereby become of divine authority, yet I may confidently say there is not one of them that bears any contrariety, or gives the lie to, our senses (p. 429) or our reason. He that helps me to see or to see clearer what I did either not see before or but dimly, or gives me notice of some thing my eyes might never discover, does me a kindness I can make profit of, but he that would have me assent to what is contrary to what I see desires what is altogether unreasonable and impossible. What is thus true of our eyes is so also of our reason and natural knowledge, for no authority nor testimony can come to me with a greater certainty and assurance than a thing that I see and know already.

Thus it seems to me that God has plainly set out the boundaries of our several faculties, and showed us by which we are to conduct our

---

[1] *which is* added by Ed. to make the sentence grammatically complete. However, Locke expresses himself in such terms as to make it difficult to know exactly what he wants to convey by this example. It may be that he has in mind the concept that there can be no angle less than that made by the direction of a curve at a point and the tangent to the curve at that point. [2] *that* seems superfluous.

lives, viz. by our senses in the cognizance of sensible objects, by reason in the deductions and discourses from perfect and clear ideas, and by faith in matters that the senses nor reason will not reach to, and though reason often helps our senses, and faith our reason, yet neither the one nor the other ever invalidates the authority, or destroys the evidence, of the inferior and subordinate faculty.

(p. 430) *1st September 1676*: Men, by the common light of reason that is in them, know that God is the most excellent of all beings, and therefore deserves most to be honoured and beloved, because He is good to all His (p. 431) creatures and all the good we receive comes from Him. By the same light of nature we know also that we ought to do good to other men, because it is good for ourselves so to do. Men are capable of it, it is the only tribute we can pay to God for all the good we receive from Him, and it cannot but be acceptable to God, being done for His sake, and to men whom we cannot but know that He has the same kindness for as for us. They, then, that consider that they ought to love God and be charitable to men, and do to that purpose seek to know more of Him and His mysteries, that they may better perform their duty of love to Him and charity to their neighbours, shall no doubt find all that God requires of them to know, and shall run into no damnable errors, but will find God and His truth. The same cannot be said of those who begin at the other end, who, giving way to their lusts, and taking their swing in the prosecution of their own desires, making themselves their own god and their own end, will not hearken to any of the truths of natural or revealed religion, till they can have all objections answered, all scruples removed, and will, if there (p. 432) remains but a little doubt in the whole system, reject the whole, because some one part has some difficulty. It is not, I say, likely that these men should find truth, because both they seek it unreasonably, i.e. otherwise than rational men and they themselves too do in other cases, and also they seek it not for that end for which God designed it, which is not as an improvement of our parts and speculations, but of our love of Him and charity to our neighbour, and that increase of our knowledge should make our lives better.

Notes to pages 112, 113

NOTE A, *p.* 112.

Here follows a passage from f. 13, l. 23, to f. 15, l. 19, which Locke deleted, though he had previously corrected faults in it. He deleted it probably because it contains views concerning the general consent of men that run counter to those expressed in his fifth essay. The passage reads: cum dantur aliqua morum principia quae agnoscit totum genus humanum et unanimi consensu amplectuntur qui ubique sunt homines, quod fieri non poterat nisi esset a natura. Quamvis enim nonnulla sint de quibus inter se dissentirent[1] homines, stabiles tamen fixique apud omnes sunt (f. 14) virtutum termini; quod si hae leges essent positivae et ab hominibus pro libitu sancitae sine aliqua praevia sui aut notione aut obligatione, non tam similes sui ubique essent nec tam inter se consentirent; alia apud Indos alia apud Romanos esset virtus, cum nihil sit in quo magis discrepant, in quo magis in diversum a se invicem abeunt homines quam civitatum leges et morum positiva instituta. Hoc inde etiam manifestum est quod doctrina de virtutibus intra scientiae limites comprehendi possit, sic enim *quae ex constituto veniunt a naturalibus recte separantur: nam naturalia, cum semper eadem sint, facile possint in artem colligi: illa autem quae ex instituto veniunt, cum et mutantur saepe et alibi alia sunt, extra artem posita sunt;*[2] ex quibus recte concluditur dari legem a natura. Neque enim vana res est et nullius prorsus momenti communis hominum consensus qui aliunde deduci non potest nisi a communi aliquo omnibus hominibus principio cujus fons sit ipsa natura. Nam ubi multi diversis temporibus et locis idem pro certo affirmant, id ad causam universalem referri debet quae alia esse non potest quam dictamen ipsius rationis et communis natura, cum nihil aliud esse potest quod omnium mentes iisdem principiis imbuere et in eandem sententiam cogere (f. 15) potest; ex eo enim hominum inter se conspirantium universali consensu colligi potest non solum quid liceat homini agere, cum ea quae contra naturam sunt non videntur homines facturi, sed etiam quid oportet, cum plurimos, non utilitate ducti nec voluptatis alicujus suasu pellecti, id facere et faciendum praedicare videmus cujus nulla alia reperiri potest causa quam obsequium illud quod se legi naturae praestare debere sentiunt; quod etiam factum omnes laudant, qua in re calculo suo hanc esse legem comprobant, cum id laudant quod dum non faciunt ipsi potius deridendum videretur: cum sine lege hac aliis prodesse ita ut tibi noceas (quod in servanda fide saepe accidit) non tam probi esset quam stulti.

---

[1] Doubtful reading; perhaps, previous to Locke's incomplete correction, *dissentire videretur*, or *dissentire videntur*.

[2] This is a quotation from Grotius, *De Jure Belli ac Pacis*, proleg., par. 30.

NOTE B, *p.* 113.

The deleted passage reads in translation: 'For there are some moral principles which the whole of mankind recognizes and which all men in the world accept unanimously; but this could not happen if the law were not a natural one. Though there are indeed some principles about which men disagree among themselves, nevertheless the definitions of virtues are fixed and invariable among them all. But if these laws were positive and arbitrarily laid down by men without any concept or obligation antecedent to such laws, they would not be everywhere so similar to one another, nor would there be so much agreement among them: virtue would be one thing among the Indians, another among the Romans, for in nothing do men differ and diverge from one another more than in their civil laws and their positive regulations of manners and customs. This argument is also demonstrated by the fact that the theory of virtues can be comprised within the limits of a science, for it is by this that 'whatever depends on convention is rightly distinguished from things natural; for things concerning nature, being always the same, can readily be gathered into a science, while those which are the outcome of convention form no part of science, because they often change and are different in different places.' Hence it is rightly concluded that there is a law laid down by nature. Nor,

in fact, is the general consent of men a matter without meaning and of no importance at all; for this general consent cannot be derived from any other source than some principle which is common to all men and of which nature itself is the source.[1] Surely, when many men in different times and places affirm one and the same thing as a certain truth, this thing must be related to a universal cause which can be nothing else but a dictate of reason itself and a common nature. For there cannot be anything else which is capable of instilling into the minds of all the same principles and forcing them to think alike. Indeed, from this general consent of men in agreement with one another conclusions can be drawn not only as to what action man may do, since men do not seem likely to do what is against nature, but also as to what they ought to do, since we see that most men when not urged by expediency or enticed by the attraction of some pleasure, both do, and declare that they must do, that for which the only reason is the obedience which they feel they ought to pay to the law of nature. And further-more such an action, when performed, they all applaud, so that by their own reckoning they affirm that this law exists; for they applaud an act which would seem rather to be a fit object of ridicule, so long as they are not doing it themselves; for, without such a law, it would be the mark not so much of a virtuous as of a foolish man to do good to others and so harm himself (and this thing often happens in keeping faith).'

---

[1] Here and in the next sentence Locke seems to be borrowing from Hooker's *Laws of Ecclesiastical Polity*, bk. i, ch. 8, par. 3. (Keble's ed. of Hooker's *Works*, 1865, i. 227, and n. 80.)

INDEX OF NAMES

(All references to the text of the Essays are to the English translation.)

Index of Names

287

INDEX OF SUBJECTS

Index of Subjects

Law—*cont.*

56, 183, 189; Divine, 28 f., 32 ff., 40, 67 f., 71, 75 ff., 181, 187 f.; divisions, 28, 67, 68; and human nature, 40, 50, 52, 54, 56–57; intellectualist theory of, 40, 43, 51, 55 n. 1, 56, 58; of nations, 39, 48, 161 n. 4, 163; penal, 274; positive, 113, 119, 131, 133, 187 f., 199, 282; of *Reputation or Fashion*, 63 n. 6, 67 f., 75, 78, 129; requisites of, 49–50, 68 n. 5, 70, 78, 86, 111, 113, 151 ff., 173, 187 f.; retrospective, 274; Roman, 35; Thomistic definition of, 67; voluntarist theory of, 40, 43, 51 f., 55 n. 1, 56 ff., 67, 113, 183 n. 1.

Law-giver, 27, 40, 49, 57, 62, 68 n. 5, 70, 75, 78, 133, 151, 155, 173, 183, 187 f.

Law of nature: abolished, 139, 189, 199, 201 f., 215; ambiguity of, 44 and n. 1, 59–60; analysis of, 43 ff., 49, 59–60; appeal to, 25–27, 30, 62, 68, 77; arguments for, 36 f., 41, 45, 54, 68 n. 6, 74 f. 83, 86, 113 ff., 158 n. 3, 161 n. 3, 201, 282–3; basic idea of, in Locke, 13, 21, 26, 29 f., 34, 60, 62, 70, 77, 80, 82; basis of, 53, 199, 205 ff.; binding force of, 50 ff., 54, 56 f., 59–60, 74 n. 7, 84 ff., 133, 181 ff., 187 f., 191 ff., 205 f.; Cicero's definition of, 35, 110 n. 2, 193 n. 1, 197 n. 1, 199 n. 1, 200 n. 1; and the demonstrability of ethics, 54–56, 74–75; dictates of, 34, 41, 50, 53, 70, 127 f., 139 f., 159, 163, 173, 189, 191 ff., 205; disputations about, 12, 20, 61, 83, 85, 218, 237 n. 3; and God, 50 ff., 173, 187 f., 201; and the Gospel, 82 ff.; and hedonism, 71 ff.; and Hobbes, 53, 161 n. 4; and human nature, 40, 50 ff., 56–57, 62, 83, 111, 193, 199 f., 283; and immortality of soul, 173; innate, 117, 131, 133; knowledge of, 41 f., 45, 48 ff., 57, 59, 61 f., 64 f., 68 nn. 5 and 6, 113 f., 123 ff., 143, 147 ff., 158 n. 3, 161 ff., 177 f., 187 f.; 199; and Law of nations, 39, 48, 161 n. 4, 163; and moral rectitude, 72, 77, 129, 141, 282 f.; and the Mosaic Law, 82 ff.; and natural right, 27 n. 1, 111; not innate, 41, 65, 86, 123 ff., 137 ff.; objections against, 10, 13, 64, 76–77, 86, 113 f.,

201 f., 205; obscure, 139; and property, 81, 195, 201, 207, 211, 213; and reason, 44 ff., 52, 80, 84, 111, 125, 149, 199; and self-interest, 53, 205 ff.; and self-preservation, 53, 157 f., 181; and social contract, 34; and society, 34, 49, 81, 119, 157 f., 189, 201, 213; and state of nature, 80, 81; theories of, 35 ff., 43 ff., 57 n. 2; Towerson on, 82 ff.; and utility, 35, 48, 121, 163, 181, 205 ff.; validity of, 54 ff., 59, 84, 199 ff.; and virtues and vices, 167; and will, 40, 51, 56 f., 80, 111, 113, 187 f., 199. *See* Law, Divine.

Legislation, retrospective, 274.

Lex, see Law; Law of nature.

Liability, see *Debitum.*

Liberty, 25–29, 43, 58 n. 6, 119, 121, 123, 193, 195, 199, 205 f.

Licitum, 68.

Light of nature (or reason), 25 n. 4, 26, 28, 33, 40, 41, 49, 57, 61, 64, 73, 75, 85, 111, 113, 115, 123 ff., 137, 147 ff., 167, 187 f., 199, 274, 277, 281.

Linguistic difficulties, 73 ff., 275 ff., 279 f.

Love, 264, 265 ff., 270.

Man: his duties, 54, 127, 135, 157 f., 193 ff., 199, 207, 213, 274, 281, 283; 'fallen', 139 and n. 2; God and existence of, 48 f., 109, 153 f., 157, 187; rational nature of, 35 f., 40, 44 ff., 50 ff., 53, 54 ff., 59, 87, 113, 133 f., 157, 199 ff.; social nature of, 39, 53 and n. 7, 157.

Mathematics, 41, 44, 54–56, 58, 59, 60, 74, 75, 133 f., 149, 280 n. 1.

Matter, 275 f.

Maxims, 63, 66, 149 n. 2.

Melancholy, 268.

Mind, 265 ff.; *see* Soul.

Miracle, 109, 278.

Mirth, 268.

Misery, 268 and n. 3.

Morality, 'eternal and immutable', 55 n. 1, 57; *see* Ethics.

Motion, 151, 258, 265, 267, 271.

Mutatio materiae, 203 n. 3.

Names, 278 f.; *see* Words.

Naturalism (ethical), 50, 52, 58.

290

Index of Subjects

Nature: ambiguity of, 44 n. 1; human, teleological interpretation of, 49–50, 117, 151 f., 157; live according to, 111, 139, 141, 191; promises derived from, 119; uniform, 139, 282. *See* Law of nature; Light of nature; Man; State of nature.

Necessity, logical, 55–56, 59–60, 199 ff.

Neoplatonism, 42, 55 n. 1, 58.

Nominalists, 43, 51.

Nonconformity, 17, 25, 69, 274 f.; *see* Calvinism; Presbyterians; Puritanism; Sects.

Number, 65, 133, 276.

Obedience, 27–28, 32, 34, 43, 50 f., 57, 60, 68 n. 5, 71, 119, 129, 183 ff., 193 ff., 203 and n. 2, 215, 283.

Obligation, 27–30, 32 and n. 5, 33 f., 40, 50 ff., 55 ff., 60, 66, 68 n. 5, 70, 73, 80 f., 83 f., 87, 119, 177, 181 ff., 191 ff., 205 ff., 213; absolute, 195, 197; conditional, 195, 197; formal, 40, 50, 52, 113, 185; moral, 40, 50 f., 53, 87; natural, 40, 50 ff., 57, 181. See *Debitum*.

Officium Civile, 67.

Opinion, 17, 47, 129 f., 165, 167 ff., 177, 274 ff.

Orthography, 255.

Pain, 71 ff., 79, 155, 246, 263–72.

Papists, *see* Roman Catholics.

Parents, 171, 187, 195, 197, 203, 213.

Passions, 246, 263–72.

Peace, 272 f., 275.

Perception, 264, 271 n. 1; *see* Sense-perception.

Persians, 177.

Philosophy, 221 f., 239 f., 278.

Phonetics, 255.

Piety, 171.

Piracy, 51, 169, 185, 189.

Platonists, Cambridge, 39, 42, 43, 53, 55 n. 1, 56 n. 1, 58, 86, 190 n. 1.

Pleasure, 71 ff., 79, 155, 246, 263–72.

Polygamy, 171.

Polytheism, 175, 261.

Pope, the, 177.

Possibility, 270.

Power: absolute, 27, 30, 81, 119, 183; civil, *see* Civil Magistrate; creative, 153; directive and coercive, 27, 183,

189; idea of, 246, 264 and n. 3, 265, 271 f.

Predestination, 276.

Prejudice, 63.

Presbyterians, 23 n. 5, 31, 42.

Presuppositions: of knowledge, 125, 149 f.; of law, *see* Law, requisites of.

Principium, 149 n. 3.

Principles: innate, *see* Ideas; practical (moral), 41, 46 f., 60 f., 64 f., 72, 143, 145; self-evident, 41, 54 f., 64, 145 n. 2, 165 n. 1; speculative, 41, 46 f., 64, 145, 165 and n. 1, 179. *See* Contradiction.

Probability, 63, 79.

Promise, 80–81, 119, 129, 213, 215.

Pronunciation, 255–7.

Property, 81, 163, 195, 201, 207, 211, 213.

Propositions, 276, 278 ff.; *see* Statements.

Punishment, 28, 32, 51, 62, 68 n. 5, 70, 71, 73, 76, 78, 87, 119, 173, 181, 183 f., 215, 274.

Puritanism, 17, 25, 30, 33, 34, 36; *see* Calvinism; Nonconformity; Presbyterians; Sects.

Quakerism, 10, 13, 16–17, 79; *see* Dissenters; Nonconformity; Puritanism; Sects.

Qualities, 151 and n. 1, 279.

Realists, 51.

Reason, 25, 28, 40 f., 44 ff., 49, 52 f., 56, 59, 61, 63, 80, 111, 115, 125, 129 f., 147 ff., 199, 279; ambiguity of, 44 ff.; dictate of, 37, 45, 51 ff., 56, 111, 115, 125 f., 199, 283; and faith, 79, 272–81; and Puritanism, 17; 'right reason', 45, 51, 53, 56 n. 1, 111, 125, 137, 149; and the senses, 41, 48 ff., 64, 68 n. 5, 125 f., 133 f., 147 ff., 278 ff. *See* Light of nature.

Reasoning, 35, 44, 45–46, 49, 54, 59, 63, 125, 131, 133 f., 147 ff., 279 f.

Recoinage of 1695–6, 4.

Rectitude, 67, 71, 72, 73, 77, 139 f., 165, 167 f., 213 f.; *see* Right, moral.

Reformers, 43, 51.

Relations, 258–9; moral, 62, 66, 77–78; *see* Conformity.

291

Index of Subjects

Religion, 22 ff., 34, 61, 65, 167, 201, 248, 260 ff., 273 ff., 281; natural, 3, 73, 281.
Restoration of 1660, 10, 30.
Revelation, 28, 40, 46, 50, 61, 62, 66, 123, 134 n. 1., 167, 187, 273, 276 ff., 280 f.
Right: of contract, 51, 81, 185; of creation, 50, 183, 185; of donation, 50 f., 81, 185, 189; of legislation, 187; moral, 40, 57 f., 71, 75, 77, 80 f., 129, 185, 205 f., 213 f.; natural, 27, 40, 50, 57, 81, 111, 183, 185 f., 189, 203; of ownership, 213.
Righteousness, *see* Rectitude.
Rights, 3, 15, 25, 26, 27, 29, 81, 205 f., 213.
Roman Catholics, 21, 134 n. 1, 175 and n. 4, 260 ff., 277 ff.
Romans, 48, 169, 175, 197, 282.
Rosicrucians, 3.
Rules (moral), *see* Conformity; Good (moral).

Scholasticism, 27 n. 3, 36, 37, 51, 149 n. 2, 193, 203 n. 3.
Sciences, 151, 282; division of, 69, 70.
Scripture, 17, 25, 26, 30, 73, 82–83, 261 f.
Sects, 17, 79, 275; *see* Calvinism; Dissenters; Nonconformity; Puritanism; Quakerism.
Self-interest, 53, 205 ff.
Self-preservation, 53, 65, 84, 157 f., 173, 181.
Sense-perception, 41, 46, 48–49, 50, 59, 62, 63, 64, 65, 123 ff., 131 ff., 147 ff., 278 ff.
Sign, 279.
Sin, 63, 67, 68; *see* Fall.
Social instinct, 53 and n. 7, 157 f.
Society, 28, 34, 49, 53, 54, 73 n. 2, 81, 119, 129, 157, 159 n. 1, 201, 213.
Socinianism, 22 n. 1.
Sorrow, 267 n. 5, 268.
Soul, 271 f.; immortal, 3, 173, 252.
Space, 65, 258–9.
Spartans, 169, 175.
Spelling, 246, 254–7.
Spirits, 63, 125.
State of nature, 44 n. 1, 80, 81, 163.
Statements, identical, 63, 165 n. 1; moral, 44, 55 f., 137; *see* Types.

Stoics, 109, 111, 223.
Substance, 65, 278 f.
Suicide, 173.
Suttee, 173.
Syllogism, 125.

Tabula rasa, 137, 149 n. 1.
Teleological interpretation, 49–50, 109, 117, 133, 151 f., 157.
Testimony, 63, 79, 279 f.
Thinking, simple idea of, 264, 271 f.
Thomism, 36, 38, 67.
Time, 65, 258–9.
Toleration, 3, 21–22, 26, 27, 29, 30, 272–3, 274–5.
Torment, 268.
Tradition, 41, 46–47, 62–63, 79, 86, 123, 127 ff., 134 n. 1.
Transubstantiation, 272, 273–4, 277 ff.
Travellers, 141, 155, 175.
Triangle, 54, 55, 58, 74 n. 7, 199, 279.
Trust, *see* Belief.
Truth, 44, 47, 54, 59, 64, 123, 129, 149, 165 n. 1, 177, 201, 274 f., 279 f.
Types of statement, 44–46, 59.
Tyrant, 51, 81, 189.

Understanding, the, 61, 64 and n. 1, 66, 137, 276.
Uneasiness, 269.
Universality, 44.
Utility, 35, 38, 48, 121, 129, 181, 205 ff.

Vexation, 268.
Vice, 63, 68, 75, 77, 109, 119, 121, 165, 167 f.
Virtue, 58, 63, 67, 75, 77, 109, 119, 121, 141, 167 f., 169, 181, 207 f., 213, 282.
Virtus, 67.
Vitium, 67.
Vituperium, 67.
Voluntarist theory of law, *see* Law.
Voluptas, 265, 267.
Vox populi vox Dei, 41, 42, 160.

War, 53, 80, 163, 213.
Weariness, 268.
Will, 29, 49, 56 ff., 62, 68 n. 5., 70 ff., 111, 119, 137, 151, 175, 183, 185, 264, 271 n. 1, 272 and n. 3; free, 276; God's, 27 f., 39 f., 50 ff., 56 ff., 70, 71 and n. 1, 80, 86, 157, 183 ff., 201 f.
Words, 65, 73 ff., 275 f.; *see* Names.

292

B   **Locke, John, 1632-1704**
1255 Essays on the law of nature
.L49 and associated writings
2002

DATE DUE
